Canadian Society
A MACRO ANALYSIS
Fifth Edition

Harry H. Hiller
University of Calgary

PEARSON

Prentice
Hall

Toronto

Library and Archives Canada Cataloguing in Publication

Hiller, Harry H., 1942–
    Canadian society : a macro analysis / Harry H. Hiller. –5th ed.

Includes bibliographic references and index.
ISBN 0-13-196941-2

Nationalism—Canada—Textbooks. 2. National characteristics, Canadian—Textbooks.
3. Multiculturalism—Canada—Textbooks. 4. Regionalism—Canada—Textbooks. I. Title.

FC97.H55 2006   971   C2005-901041-X

ISBN 0-13-196941-2

Vice-President, Editorial Director: Michael J. Young
Acquisitions Editor: Patty Riediger
Executive Marketing Manager: Judith Allen
Associate Editor: Jon Maxfield
Production Editor: Charlotte Morrison-Reed
Copy Editor: Reena Kreindler
Proofreader: Anne Holloway
Production Coordinator: Janis Raisen
Manufacturing Coordinator: Susan Johnson
Composition: Carolyn E. Sebestyen
Art Director: Julia Hall
Cover Design: Miguel Acevedo
Cover Image: Masterfile Royalty Free

Statistics Canada information is used with the permission of the Minister of Industry, as Minister
responsible for Statistics Canada. Information on the availability of the wide range of data from
Statistics Canada can be obtained from Statistics Canada's Regional Offices, its World Wide Web
site at http://www.statcan.ca and its toll-free access number 1-800-263-1136.

  2 3 4 5   10 09 08 07 06

Printed and bound in the United States of America.

With Gratitude
To My Family
"always there"

and

To Kendall S. McCaig
"project assistant extraordinaire"

Contents

Chapter Three: The Issue of Inequality   87

Chapter Six: The Question of Uniqueness   230

Preface

In some ways, the subject of this book may appear old-fashioned. Globalization has reduced the nation-state to rubble. Decisions made by supra-national organizations like the World Bank, trading blocks, or transnational corporations; the free flow of ideas and information through telecommunications and the Internet; and the mobility and migration of peoples may have made the study of national societies obsolete. Political states are being pressured by these external factors, as well as by internal demands from sub-state units for more autonomy. Sovereignty and defended borders sometimes seem to represent archaic ideas. So why study a national society such as Canada's?

There is no evidence that the world will not continue to be organized into political states. Increasing interconnectedness may be posited, but the national state still remains the basic location for the democratic politics out of which institutions are created and established to organize human life among people who share a territory. It is important to study Canadian society because the Canadian political state continues to exist as the mechanism organizing the lives of people sharing the geographic territory called *Canada*. The important thing to remember is that societies are not fixed or immutable but constantly changing in response to the pressures and conflicts they face. Accordingly, we must not expect the study of Canadian society to be the study of some enduring monolithic entity intent on the preservation of tradition and the maintenance of tranquility and harmony. Rather, it must be understood as the study of a *negotiated entity* in continual transformation as its constituent populations struggle over their collective life together.

The approach taken in this analysis could be called constructionist—not in the postmodern sense according to which there are no historical facts and everything is contingent,[1] but in the sense that the realities that a resident of this society encounters are the result of on-going human activity.[2] This means that as children we might begin by appropriating or internalizing the substance and structure of this society as though it had always existed and could be taken for granted, but would soon learn that it is *people* who propose, debate, and create new structures in response to changing conditions. Therefore, it is very useful to understand how and why Canadian society is contingent, fluctuating, and always in process, i.e., continually being constructed and reconstructed. It is the purpose of this book to provide some sense of the forces contributing to this ongoing societal change.

This perspective is consistent with the work of Michael Mann, who argues that it would be a mistake to conclude that the new forces of globalization spell the death of the nation-state.[3] Instead, he notes, emphasis should be placed on how the nation-state is *changing*. The mistake is in seeing the nation-state as either hegemonic or obsolete; on the contrary, the analytical focus should be placed on transformation.

One of these transformations is away from classic nationalism's old notion that the ideal towards which political states must strive is the establishment of a single and homogeneous national identity. In the contemporary era, there has been a shift towards both plural and shifting national identities, which David McCrone refers to as "the new nationalism" or "neo-nationalism." Not surprisingly, this transformation is plagued with problems and debates; McCrone, however, argues that our goal should not be to recover the past but to "debate with the past about who we are now and who we want to become."[4]

It is in this spirit that this book has been written and should be read. The objective of the book is to provide the reader with a sense of the transformations which Canadian society is facing and to sketch the forces producing them, as well as to provide a sense of the debates surrounding these issues and the options available in eventual outcomes. Such a goal may be overly ambitious, but five objectives can be listed. First, I wanted to provide an overview of Canadian society that would be useful to a beginning analyst, but to do so with some depth and comprehensiveness. Often we understand a society primarily in terms of some small segment but do not see the whole, and this book attempts to place issues in their macro context. Second, I wanted to bring a wide range of scattered literature together to provide an integrated portrait and to do so in a "state of the art" review. Third, while there may be too many footnotes and references for a general overview, these have been provided in order that the book may serve as a reasonable reference-work for those interested in further reading and reflection. The provision of these references in earlier editions of this book has proven valuable to both undergraduate and graduate students, as well as to the general public and others looking for relevant references. In the light of this, I have continued this tradition. Fourth, I have highlighted key concepts in my discussions in order to point out prominent themes and to accentuate "buzzwords" that may help in the recollection of important processes. Fifth, I have tried to present the material in such a way as to convey the liveliness of debate and controversy in addition to the more substantive content. The boxed inserts, the "Real People" segments, and the "Research Clips" found throughout the text are meant to contribute to that objective. The quotation at the beginning of each chapter is taken from some classic work on Canadian society in order to give the reader a sense of the history or tradition of the themes discussed in that chapter. A section in each chapter called "Differing Perspectives" attempts to show how theory can be applied to the chapter topic, with different resulting points of view.

Readers often look for a point of view in the material they are reading, and I have enjoyed hearing about readers' attempts to give this work a theoretical label. Strangely enough, they often try to do so after having read only one chapter. In attempting to provide a reasonably comprehensive overview of Canadian society, I have deliberately tried not to limit myself to one theoretical perspective, and the section in each chapter called "Differing Perspectives" reflects my attempt to make that clear. My goal has been to present a balanced treatment of a variety of issues from a variety of viewpoints. The reader will have to determine to what extent I have succeeded in reaching the goals and objectives stated here.

Each chapter attempts to understand Canadian society in terms of what I call *questions* and *issues* about the realities of a national society. This book is structured around four questions and three issues, presented here as the most critical themes in a macro understanding of Canadian society. The four macro questions which begin and end the book are *The Question of Society* (To what extent does the population of Canada form a society?), *The Question of Autonomy* (To what extent is Canadian society an independent societal unit?), *The Question of Uniqueness* (Are the problems of Canadian society unusual?), and *The Question of Identity* (Why is Canadian society so complex and fragmented?). The middle chapters (Three, Four, and Five) develop the *issues* of *inequality*, *regionalism*, and *ethnicity* as a way of providing the contextual information for understanding the questions framed by Chapters One and Two at the outset and Six and Seven at the end.

The use of the term *Canadian society* makes this book's orientation clear: As the author is a sociologist, the focus of the book is on the people who reside in the political unit of Canada and on their relationships. One of the unique elements of the book continues to be its comparative focus (Chapter Six). I am acutely aware that this book is read by Canadians who frequently think that theirs is the only society with certain kinds of problems, as well as by persons outside Canada who need some international benchmarks to put things in perspective. Chapter Six provides the mechanisms to help determine the unique contours of Canadian society more clearly.

There are plenty of reasons for either a pessimistic view of national societies in general or for the revisionist view that Canadian society has not only changed already but that the changes of the future will be even more substantial—and perhaps even painful for those who thought they knew what Canadian society was or should be like. The need to accommodate a multiplicity of interest groups within the country, as well as the inexorable pull of global forces without, is bound to produce a very different society in the future. But the process is already unfolding before our eyes—even when we are not fully conscious of its ramifications. This is what makes the study of Canadian society so fascinating and so exciting, and why this book was written—to help the reader understand the issues and processes of change more clearly.

I would especially like to welcome to this book readers located around the world. It has come to my attention that in other countries there is indeed interest in learning about Canadian society—another reflection, perhaps, of globalization. It is my hope that international readers who have learned about this book through embassies, consulates, high commissions, and university libraries may find herein the tools to better understand this complex but fascinating society.

NOTES

1 For an excellent critique of this form of constructionism, see Ian Hacking, *The Social Construction of What?* (Cambridge: Harvard University Press, 1999).

2 See Peter Berger and Thomas Luckmann, *The Social Construction of Reality* (Garden City: Doubleday, 1966); and Rogers Brubaker, *Nationalism Reframed: Nationhood and the National Question in the New Europe* (Cambridge: Cambridge University Press, 1996).

3 Michael Mann, "Nation-States in Europe and Other Continents: Diversifying, Developing, Not Dying," *Daedalus* 122, 3 (1993): 115–140; and "Has Globalization Ended the Rise of the Nation-State?" *Review of International Political Economy* 4 (1997).

4 David McCrone, *The Sociology of Nationalism* (London: Routledge, 1998), 138.

Acknowledgments

This book is at least partially the product of over thirty years of teaching courses on Canadian society; therefore, one of my primary acknowledgments must be to the hundreds of students who have taken the journey with me to uncover and explore the vicissitudes of this intriguing society. Their questions and comments have helped to shape my thinking and have provoked me to explain things as clearly as possible.

I am also grateful to colleagues who have been supportive and/or encouraging in one way or another. These include Rick Ponting, Bob Stebbins, Simon Langlois, Leslie Laszlo, Jim Frideres, Cora Voyageur, Linda Di Luzio, Rebecca Chan Allen, Mark Dickerson, Gretchen MacMillan, Bohdan Harasymiw, and Don Barry. I am also grateful for the support and assistance of the staff in the Academic Data Centre, especially Laurie Schretlen and Sharon Neary, who are always willing to help. The good humour, splendid co-operation and team spirit of the staff in the Department of Sociology have been invaluable, and I particularly want to thank Tom Huang, Vivian Hansen, Lynda Costello, Diane Field and Jordan Bell. The editorial assistance of Patty Riediger, Jon Maxfield, Allegra Robinson, and Charlotte Morrison-Reed, at Pearson Education, plus freelance editors Reena Kreindler and Anne Holloway, played a key role in expediting production of the manuscript. I am grateful to the following reviewers for their thoughtful comments and suggestions: David Nock, Lakehead University; Dr. Meg Luxton, York University; Janice Noel, University of New Brunswick; Kwame Boadu, University of Alberta; and Victor Ujimoto, University of Guelph.

I never thought that my first feeble attempt at understanding Canadian society, with the publication in 1976 of *Canadian Society: A Sociological Analysis* by Prentice-Hall, would lead to a new book with the current modified title now being published in its fifth edition. What has made this edition possible more than anything else is the research support of Kendall McCaig. Kendall knows this book from the inside out; I first met her as a student in my Canadian Society course, and her mastery of its content amazed me. In that sense, the content of this book has been student-tested once again. Furthermore, Kendall's knowledge of the Statistics Canada database became highly proficient. Her work with me on a number of research projects has provided her with background skills which facilitated the preparation of data for this book. It is seldom that anyone encounters the assistance of someone who is so thorough, so knowledgeable, so dependable, and still so much fun. To be honest, Kendall made doing this edition a genuine pleasure, and I am deeply grateful to her.

Harry H. Hiller

Introduction

WHAT IS A MACRO ANALYSIS?

A macro analysis is the study of social phenomena in terms of society-wide aggregates. Whereas micro analysis focuses on the individual, macro analysis takes an entire society as its focus. For our purposes, the boundaries for our unit of analysis are the geopolitical borders of the country of Canada.

Early social scientists (e.g., Durkheim, Weber, Marx, Spencer) preferred the macro approach because they were interested in the broad scope of change which had occurred over time in societies and civilizations. Later social scientists believed that the essence of human action occurred in face-to-face interpersonal micro situations. Recently, there has been a renewed interest in the macro approach to global patterns of social relations.

Social scientists refer to society as though it were a meaningful unit of analysis. Yet the careful application of scientific method requires that studies first be conducted on specifically defined components of a society at the micro level. This leaves us with a series of fragmented conclusions about different aspects of a society, which, when merged, can help us see the society at a general level. Macro analysis attempts to build a broader portrait of a society so that its form and nature may become clearer.

Macro analysis involves more than working from the particular to the universal. It requires that special attention be given to the structural features of a society that provide the framework or context around which its everyday life takes shape. These structural features include class structure, region, the state and other institutions, and structured relationships with other societies. In other words, macro analysis implies a societal analysis which should enable us to return the flow of analysis from the universal to the particular. Once we understand a society at the macro level, we can develop a clearer understanding of its micro level and of the dialectic or exchange that takes place between the two.

As long as political states serve as a basic unit of world order, it is both useful and imperative to study societies as politico-national entities. Furthermore, if we remain aware of the fact that these national societies are not simple and homogeneous but complex and diverse, we can look for the emergent properties of a society that provide it with form and character. Macro analysis should complement the numerous micro studies available on particular aspects of society and should also stimulate the desire for a thorough knowledge of a society's constituent features. Indeed, the macro approach is necessary both within Canada and elsewhere if we are to understand the broader dimensions of any society.

There are *three dominant perspectives* for understanding a society. The first is known as *structural functionalism*. It understands a society as an ongoing social system of structures or parts, each of which has a function or role in providing stability and continuity over time in spite of disruptions and change. The second perspective, known as the *conflict perspective*, understands a society as being composed of competing social groups that are in repeated confrontation with each other as a result of differences in power or social position. Even when conflict is not overt but submerged, it is still possible to analyze a society in terms of groups that have positions of dominance in relation to other less powerful, even powerless, groups. So whereas structural functionalism attempts to ascertain how a society seeks to sustain its equilibrium over time, the conflict model understands society more in terms of change and of attempts by social groups to retain power, exert power, or overcome their powerlessness. The third perspective is known as *symbolic interactionism* and begins with the individual rather than with society-at-large or social groups. Its focus is on how an individual creates meaning and how these meanings are shared with others.

STRUCTURAL FUNCTIONALIST PERSPECTIVE

Structural functionalism attempts to determine how a society holds together as an entity. This perspective is known as *functionalism* because its object is to determine how the structural feature under analysis contributes to the integration of the society. For example, broadcasting can be assessed in terms of how it contributes to national unity (or disunity). Do Canadian radio stations give priority to recordings by Canadian artists, thus promoting the development of Canadian culture, or does the American music industry dominate and negatively impact Canadians' understanding of their own culture? Is hockey really Canada's national sport, bringing Canadians together, or—because there are more National Hockey League teams in the United States than in Canada—does hockey contribute to North American continental integration? How then does hockey or sport function to strengthen or weaken Canadian society? What function does immigration have in supplying needed labour for the society and how might it also function to create disharmony? What is the role of regionalism in creating sectionalism rather than societal unity? All of these questions focus on the function an aspect of society has in developing or hindering cohesion or integration within the society.

One of the problems of structural functionalism is that it assumes that all societies seek stability. While at one level this may be true, most societies exist in considerable tension, and various forms of internal conflict may challenge both the form and the structure of a society. This equilibrium model of society is often thought to be conservative because it does not pay enough attention to the dynamics of change.

CONFLICT PERSPECTIVE

The second perspective tends to see society less as a system striving to maintain equilibrium than as the site of a struggle between conflicting groups. It is known as the *conflict perspective* because its focus is on which groups have power within a society, which groups possess less power, and how the use of that power determines what the society is like. Terms such as *dominance* and *subordination*, *centre* and *periphery*, and *privilege* and *poverty* all express different relationships of hierarchy and inequality between people within a society. For example, the fact that in Canadian society persons of British descent have historically had more power than persons of French descent led to the creation of a set of institutions expressing a British heritage and the dominance of the English language. But as numerous changes in recent years have transformed this relationship from one of dominance–subordination to one of greater equality, power struggles have erupted among both language groups about whose definition of Canadian society will prevail. Therefore it is useful to analyze, for example, whose conception of language (bilingualism, French unilingualism, English unilingualism) will dominate in Canada and how different conceptions will be expressed in different segments of the society.

The functional perspective usually begins with the assumption that all societies require at least a minimal amount of unity, and that such social processes are *natural*. The conflict perspective focuses on the more seamy underside of society, exposing the tensions and struggles between opposing groups; it visualizes existing inequalities as *created* through the use of power. Thus, while functionalism interprets regionalism as evidence of the natural diversity and character of a society, the conflict perspective views regionalism as being created by the struggle for control and dominance among different social groups within geographic units of the society. For a conflict theorist, issues of power explain how societies are shaped.

In more recent years, the emphasis in conflict analysis has broadened from conflict between groups within a society to conflict between societies. Because a society is part of a complex global relationship, a *world systems approach* considers it important to show how inequalities in power between national societies also help to explain a society's character.

SYMBOLIC INTERACTIONIST PERSPECTIVE

The third general perspective works from the individual to the large group in order to understand how individuals and groups relate to and understand each other. *Symbolic interactionism* focuses on how personal identity is related to the wider society and how personal identities emerge from and contribute to the societal identity. How does the individual relate to the symbols of a society and how does the individual contribute to those symbols? What is the meaning of being "Canadian," and how do different people understand the meaning of being Canadian in different ways? At the macro level, the symbolic interactionist approach looks at how individuals project their identity to the collectivity or receive their identity from the wider group. The key point, however, is that society is fluid and constantly being socially constructed and reconstructed or negotiated through the actions of individuals. Whereas functionalism and conflict theory focus on the structural nature of society, symbolic interactionism notes that what is important is the meaning or different meanings which individuals or groups give to human activity. Symbolic interactionism, then, stresses the more subjective aspect of society by focusing on the individual's relationship to society.

Perhaps the classic symbolic-interactionist macro question is "Who am I?" in terms of how I, the individual, understand myself in relation to the wider group. Who I am is shaped by my relationship to my family (one important group); it is also related to the community where I live (another important group). But how important is who I am in relation to my province or my country? How do I learn about this identity, and how do I relate my personal identity to a bigger collectivity of people linked to the nation-state that makes us Canadian? What does it mean to "be Canadian," and what meanings and symbols of being Canadian are important to each person? Some people might associate being Canadian with a particular *symbol*, the maple leaf, while others who live in places in Canada where maple trees are not common might *interpret* the maple leaf as a symbol of Central Canadian dominance. Some people think of Canada as a British-type society and interpret policy in terms of that assumption. Others might think of Canadian society as a bilingual or French–English dual-identity type society and interpret policy from that perspective. Still others might think of Canadian society as essentially multicultural and view new immigrants as just as legitimately Canadian as other, more entrenched groups. What is the process whereby individuals acquire the vision of Canadian society which they embrace? This vision, whatever it may be, has a huge impact on the interpretations we give to reality because our interpretations are so intimately related to our personal identities and relationships to the broader collectivity. How do you understand what it means to be part of Canadian society and what words (words are symbols) do you use to express your identification with the society?

Symbolic interactionism focuses on how, in the context of everyday living, differences in meaning emerge whereby people attempt to make sense of their own lives and of the social group to which they belong. A maple leaf means one thing to some Canadians and a fleur-de-lys has a different meaning to others. Whether the national anthem is sung in its English or bilingual version has extremely important symbolic significance to different people, reflecting personal identities. Similarly, terms like "distinct society" or "self-government" are important code words of identity that are positive to some but threatening to others. How do they acquire these meanings? How are these meanings related to personal identity? And what are their societal consequences?

Symbolic interactionism helps us to focus on the social construction of the world view of individual Canadians. Understanding an individual's viewpoint or consciousness is known as understanding his or her *voice*. When we try to understand the viewpoint or voice of a particular group, we try to understand how they experience reality or how they define a situation. We become aware that the voices of some groups are heard more clearly than others and we need to understand why. How do the dominant symbols of a society reflect the voices of particular groups and leave others out? For example, in some parts of Canada, francophones may feel that they have no voice because they have no input into the symbol system, which is English. On the other hand, anglophones in Quebec may feel that they have no voice in the changing symbol-system in that province. Aboriginal people are another group who feel that their meanings of social reality are not understood, nor their cultural symbols accepted within the broader society. A symbolic interactionist perspective begins with the individual and the collectivities with which s/he associates and then moves to the macro level; for this reason, it makes a different contribution to a macro analysis than that obtained through functionalism or conflict theory.

Each of these perspectives has an elaborate theoretical tradition and different nuances of interpretation, but such distinctions are not the focus of this book. However, the various theories referenced within the book, such as feminist theory, world systems theory, or postmodernist theory, can be placed within the framework of these three base theories. Strands from each of the three perspectives will be drawn on at various points within the text. Chapters One and Seven, for example, deal with questions more typical of functionalism. Chapters Two to Four explore more of the conflict perspective. Symbolic interactionist questions are touched on in Chapters Five and Seven and in several other places as well. Moreover, each chapter has a boxed section called "Differing Perspectives" which attempts to show how these theories can be applied to that chapter's theme. By studying these theoretical perspectives, the reader will have a better sense of how the realities of Canadian society can be interpreted in different ways, and why this society must be viewed as dynamic rather than static. While this book tends to accentuate conflict-laden issues, all three perspectives illuminate our macro analysis of Canadian society.

chapter one

The Question of Society

Canada is not the only society which has been created by large numbers of human beings moving into vacant areas, but it is unlikely that any other society has resembled a huge demographic railway station.

—John Porter, a Carleton University sociologist,
in his ground-breaking study *The Vertical
Mosaic* (1965), 33

What is it about Canadian society that is so intriguing? Is it the dilemmas and problems of a society created by wide open spaces? Is it the fact that Canada, despite some longevity, is still a relatively young society? Is it the search for common ground among a far-flung, diverse, and changing population? Is it the sense of belonging together that persists in spite of crises that threaten to tear the society apart?

It may seem ironic indeed that even though the Canadian state is over 130 years old, the precise nature of Canadian society and its existence as an entity is still in question. In fact, the stormy years after the centennial birthday in 1967 suggested more than ever that the concept of a Canadian society could not be taken for granted. While Quebec was contemplating what degree of distance from the rest of Canadian society was most appropriate, the Symons Report was concluding that Canadians knew little about their own society, and a Federal Task Force on Canadian Unity was scouring the country for clues about ways to create a more integrated and cohesive society. More recently, the failure of the Meech Lake Accord and the Charlottetown Agreement with their "distinct Quebec society" ideas, as well as the anxieties produced by two Quebec referendums (and now the threat of a third), have continued to highlight the fragility of national unity. What kind of society is this that has been problematic for so long?

The use of the term "Canadian society" implies that our society can be differentiated from other societies and that it has some measure of internal coherence. Yet there seems to be evidence to suggest that the internal coherence of Canadian society has been continually in question. Repeated waves of immigration and emigration, British and American influences, French–English differences, a relatively sparse but clustered population in a vast territory, and uneven economic development are only some of the factors that have contributed to fragmentation rather than societal unity.

It is, therefore, by no means certain that there really is such a thing as a Canadian society. Does the strength of the various small-scale sub-societies in Canada preclude any meaningful discussion about Canadian society as a whole? Do differences in the resident population overwhelm whatever may be held in common?

Canada exists as a nation by dint of the *British North America Act*, a political and legislative decree passed by the British parliament in 1867. As this document created an independent national unit, we are compelled to raise sociological questions regarding the nature and character of its people and their interaction within its geographic and political borders. But does merely living within these boundaries create a society? If so, why have Canadians been so preoccupied with the lack of national unity and the need for greater understanding? What is it about the people living within the political entity called Canada that contributes to a weak sense of society?

Certainly there are many things about Canada's population that make it unique among other national populations. Within Canada's national boundaries are various regional, ethnic, occupational, economic, and environmental distinctions which all contribute to what is known as the *national character*.[1] But in what way can we speak of the population within Canada's borders as a society?

Historically, it has been customary to describe Canada not as one society but as two: French-Canadian and English-Canadian. Seen from this perspective, the differences between the two societies were so striking that the idea of a "single society" seemed almost meaningless. Using multicultural or regional categories, we might conclude that Canadian society is nothing but an amalgam of numerous sub-societies that make up the whole in the manner of a jigsaw puzzle. Let us assume, however, that national political boundaries force the population within these borders to interact and to be cognizant of each other at least in some minimal way, if only because they share a common territory and political system. Thus, we use the term "Canadian society" to refer to the total population contained within the politico-national unit.[2]

DESCRIBING A HUMAN SOCIETY

Having raised the question of whether or not it is appropriate to use the term "society" to describe Canada's population, we must specify the basic characteristics of a society and then determine the degree to which Canadian society exhibits those characteristics. From a sociological point of view, a human society must possess the following characteristics: *locality, organization, durability,* and *self-identification.*

Locality

A society requires that its members share a common environment or locality. A common territory encourages and facilitates interaction that binds together the many smaller groups within the area. Thus, living together in a common environment creates the potential for the formation of a society.

Assessment It is true that Canadians share a common territory, but perhaps the predominant characteristics of that territory are its enormous size and relatively sparse and unevenly distributed population (see Figure 1.1). The larger the territory, the more we may expect regions and sub-regions to be significant. As we will see later in this chapter and in Chapter Four, each region has its own characteristic economy and population base (in terms of occupation, ethnic background, and length of residence in Canada), as well as its own aspirations for growth and development. Clearly, geographic features such as mountains, climate, arability of the soil, and distance also affect the way the territory is inhabited, enhance the divisive nature of regionalism, and create problems for the development of a sense of society.[3]

Various forms of mass communication and transportation have reduced some of the effects of a vast territory, but others are much more difficult to overcome. For example, many Canadians have little understanding of life in regions of the country they have never visited and for which they have perhaps constructed negative or unrealistic stereotypes. There is also a tendency to view fellow Canadians living in other regions as competitors rather than compatriots; each region tends to become fiercely protective of its own lifestyle and economic development. In sum, the problem of locality has meant that merely living within the geographic boundaries of Canada has not automatically knit residents into a common pattern of interaction from which a sense of society could easily develop.

Organization

For a society to survive, it must have an internal organization that draws its members together in mutually benefical interaction. An internal web of interrelationships must be present that creates interdependencies. Some persons (e.g., politicians) are given special roles in order to protect the society and to establish guidelines that will foster interaction both within the national unit and with other units. Government agencies in areas such as transportation, broadcasting, and commerce regulate these activities in the national interest, presumably in such a manner as to draw all members of the society together.

Assessment In Canada, the various levels of government, together with large corporations and community institutions, give organization and structure to the society. For example, everywhere you go in Canada, you will find local branches of national chartered banks, political parties, and federal agencies; these enhance our ability to recognize a locale as part of "our" society. Furthermore, members of a society learn to depend on each other for goods and services. Atlantic Canada, for instance, possesses fishing stock and fishing technology lacking in other parts of the country, while Saskatchewan specializes in grains, and Ontario possesses large pools of capital for investment. From this perspective, a society organizes itself so that interdependencies develop.

The federal government has historically used its powers to protect and expand a national societal organization in order to reaffirm the boundaries of the society. This was particularly necessary because the distribution of the Canadian population along the southern extremities of its territory tended to encourage interaction in a north–south direction (i.e., across the US border) rather than in an east–west direction (across Canada); expertise, products, and knowledge were more easily exchanged with adjacent neighbours to the south than with fellow Canadians thousands of kilometres away. In consequence, the federal government constructed regulatory agencies and mechanisms, such as tariffs and

FIGURE 1.1   The Canadian Ecumene

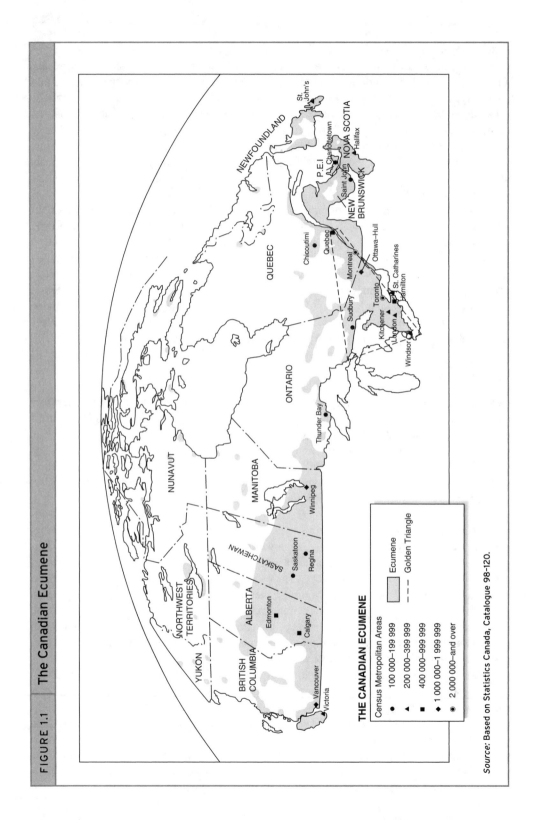

Source: Based on Statistics Canada, Catalogue 98-120.

immigration rules, in order to establish and reinforce the organizational structure of Canadian society and promote greater intrasocietal interaction. Tariffs force consumers to turn to Canadian industries, and immigration laws monitor and control movement across national borders.

While some might argue that such policies somewhat artificially create a sense of society, their removal (through free-trade agreements, for example) may threaten the boundaries which help to maintain that sense. Many feel that without incentives or regulations to ensure greater intrasocietal interaction, the viability of Canadian society may be at risk. In any case, with or without government controls, we are repeatedly reminded of the fragility of our society.

Durability

A society requires that interactive organization be relatively permanent and durable. When generations of families have inhabited an area and interacted more or less continuously over a long period of time, a heritage of common behavioural patterns and national societal coherence is likely to develop.

Assessment Canada is a relatively young country that has experienced considerable growth in its short history. In other words, the Canadian society in existence at the time of Confederation in 1867 was very different from the Canadian society we know today, and certainly had a much smaller population. In 1867 the population of Canada was largely confined to southern Ontario, southern Quebec, and the Atlantic provinces. Since that time, not only has the population density of this territory increased dramatically, but population has moved north as well as west. Much of this growth has been attributable to the large numbers of immigrants who have arrived from various countries in different time periods or *waves*. Between 1991 and 2001, 1.8 million people (6% of Canada's total population as of 2001) immigrated to Canada, and the percentage of foreign-born (18.4%) reached its highest level since 1931. The English–French balance that characterized Canada's population in the early days of the society has now been altered by the influx of persons from other ethnic traditions. Emigration has also resulted in considerable population turnover.[4]

Durability, then, has been thwarted by the changing nature of the population, which has hindered the emergence of societal traditions and a greater national societal consciousness. Furthermore, only during the last three or four decades has our educational system (particularly anglophone schools) developed materials designed to give Canadian youth a better understanding of their society and its heritage. Durability requires not only a stable population but the development of common reference points through which greater societal interaction can be facilitated.

Self-Identity

Finally, a society must be aware of itself as a unique and independent entity. Participants in one society must differentiate themselves from participants in another by an awareness of their society and a sense of belonging to it.

Within the international social world, members of Canadian society must be able to locate themselves by adopting the societal identity "Canadian." Customs, symbols, folk heroes, and important landmarks contribute to an awareness of societal identity. For example, public display of the maple leaf assists Canadians in differentiating their society from other societies and helps them to establish their own national identity.

Assessment A collective Canadian identity has been slow to develop within the society. One of the most significant retarding factors has been the presence of two distinct societies within the polity. For reasons which are discussed in Chapter Five, French

The Need to "Know Ourselves"

In the 1970s, it was generally felt that Canadians were rather ignorant of their own country and society. One of the major issues at that time was whether Canadian educational institutions were providing students with adequate knowledge of the elements of their own society, or whether they were too dependent on material emanating from other societies, such as England and the United States. Thomas H.B. Symons, former president of Trent University, conducted hearings across the country, the end result of which was a document entitled *To Know Ourselves*, published in 1975.

Instead of linking the need for Canadian Studies to patriotism, the Commission on Canadian Studies adopted a rationale based on the need for self-understanding as reflected in Plato's dictum "Know Thyself." Self-knowledge was understood to be a basic societal need; the Commission deemed an "awareness factor" or "sensitivity" to the Canadian context or perspective to be crucial to that quest for self-knowledge.

The Report confirmed the suspicions of many that Canadian Studies were being neglected in fields as diverse as art history, literature, economics, folklore, sociology, and the performing arts. It also determined that more government and private-donor support was needed for Canadian archives development and audio-visual resources, and even for the promotion of Canadian Studies abroad.

The Report argued that universities should be concerned not only with the generation of knowledge but with service to the communities that support them. Since young people were interested in learning more about Canada, educational institutions should become actively involved in fostering this goal. It was also felt that new emphasis should be placed upon research into Canada's unique environmental, social, and other problems, and that assumptions and methodologies should be critically investigated before being borrowed from other countries. Persons training for the professions (e.g., architecture, business) should also be assisted in relating their craft more directly to the needs and uniqueness of their own society.

Source: To Know Ourselves: The Report of the Commission on Canadian Studies, Vols. I and II. Ottawa: Association of Universities and Colleges of Canada, 1975. Volume III was published in 1984. An abridged version of the Symons Report, published in 1978 by the Book and Periodical Development Council, is available. Reviews of the Report appeared in periodicals of many disciplines in the period immediately following its appearance. Six reviews (one by a sociologist) expressing a range of sentiments are contained in the *Journal of Canadian Studies*, 11 (1976) and 12 (1977). Also see "What Did Symons Say? A Retrospective Look at the Commission on Canadian Studies," *Canadian Issues* 2 (1977): 1.

Canada has always had a well-developed conception of itself as a society, in contrast to English Canada's more diffuse sense of its societal identity. In addition, Québécois have been apprehensive about English-Canadian intentions regarding an emerging national society, which francophones fear may destroy Quebec society. For this reason, even the reformulated identity of Canada as a bilingual state has produced considerable controversy and dissension.

In addition to the "dual society," the so-called "hyphenated-Canadian" (e.g., Italian-Canadian, German-Canadian) identity has persisted. Members of Canadian society are frequently identified in terms of their society of origin. While these social groupings of hyphenated Canadians are celebrated by some as having given Canada its unique collective identity, others lament such pluralism as reducing the society's ability to establish a single self-identity which all its members can recognize and participate in.

Perhaps in no national population are the characteristics of locality, organization, durability, and self-identification combined in such a way as to constitute the "ideal type" of society. It is clear, though, that Canada has particular problems in overcoming her spatial challenges, developing the web of social organization that binds her members together, creating durable patterns of interaction among a permanent population, and fostering a sense of identification with the socio-political unit. Many of the reasons for this fact will be developed in this chapter and throughout the book; as well, we will explore why a sense of society is problematic and cannot be taken for granted.

THE PROBLEM OF SOCIETY WITHIN POLITICAL UNITS

Traditional societies were easy to identify because people lived in virtual isolation from other collectivities; thus, the boundaries and distinctive social patterns of a society were clearly discernible and the network of interrelationships could be simply traced. This conception of society changed as populations expanded and as wars and economic relations between societies resulted in an intermingling of peoples. The advent of industrialization and the breakdown of the feudal world prompted early sociologists (e.g., Durkheim, Spencer, Weber) to think deeply about the nature of society and its growing complexity.[5] The breakdown of the traditional simple society provided opportunities to examine how different peoples could be joined within a single political entity.[6]

A *state* is a political organization or structure with the power to govern. The emergence of the state as a primary institution with sovereignty over other institutions was a significant development in human history. The state as a complex of institutions, comprising government, the judiciary, and civil-service bureaucracies (e.g., public corporations and regulatory commissions), creates, enforces, and interprets rules which attempt to control the behaviour of large numbers of people.

As the state expanded its sphere of influence, it increasingly gathered under its governing umbrella societies which differed in various ways (ethnic, racial, class, regional, linguistic, or religious) from the dominant group controlling the state. In its attempt to be all-encompassing, the state embraced numerous sub-societies to form what we would now call a *pluralist society* (i.e., a society consisting of many meaningful sub-units). Submission to the authority of the state was frequently at odds with personal commitment to these sub-units, some of which had links beyond the political boundaries of the country. The state was thus an instrument of human power which frequently welded people into political units irrespective of their own sense of society.

The characteristics of a society (delineated earlier) produce among its members the feeling that they belong together. This group consciousness is heavily dependent on the concept of *nation*. The word *nation* stems from the Latin word *nasci*, meaning "to be born," and originally meant a group of people born in the same place.[7] Similarity of birthplace (the objective dimension) provides the basis for fellow feeling (the subjective dimension) arising out of shared origins, traditions, and institutions.[8] The concept of nation is related to ethnicity because of the ethnic commonality of background and sense of belonging together. For this reason we can speak of the francophone community in Quebec as a nation and legitimately refer to the existence of a Quebec society.

Native peoples have also developed an awareness of being part of the Canadian state yet being different as Aboriginals. The designation *First Nations* (note the plural) does not only suggest prior occupation of the Canadian territory but also implies cultural differences producing nationhood.[9] Different languages and cultural practices are found among different groups of Aboriginal peoples; accordingly, reference is made to the Sarcee Nation, the Iroquois Nation, the Dene Nation (in the North), etc.

The point is that there may be many nation groups residing in the same political jurisdiction. A polity composed of only one ethnic group is considered mono-ethnic. Some countries, however, such as Switzerland and Nigeria, may contain more than one nation due to the existence of two or more ethnic identities. Nation groups can also be participants in more than one state (e.g., the French in Belgium, France, and Switzerland). When polities contain more than one ethnic nationality, they may attempt to create a new single nationality based on the political entity. In the medieval world, a multiplicity of languages and cultural traditions was common and was not incompatible with allegiance to the lord or king.[10] Only in the contemporary world has the political unit, as defined by its jurisdictional boundaries and globally identifiable name, been inclined to demand a single allegiance, insisting on an identity between nation and state. This demand may ignite a desire for secession and lead to the emergence of regionally based nationalist movements that may challenge the political unit. A *pluralist society* is one in which several national/ethnic groups reside within a polity (although one group may dominate). In pluralist societies, people are held together by a mutual commitment to abide by the regulations of the state even though the emotional dynamic of togetherness is lacking. Nevertheless, changes and adaptations over several generations may result in a growing sense of national identity as a single society. As this occurs, it becomes increasingly possible to speak of a national society as delimited by the political entity.

In sum, a state is the jurisdictional apparatus that organizes people within a political unit. If there is more than one ethnic or national group within a polity, there may be difficulty in determining who controls the state. This explains why Canada has been described as "two nations warring within one bosom" and clarifies why the idea of a single national society is problematic.

Some countries are held together more by regulation than by the desire for integration.[11] According to the dominant anglophone model of Canadian society, whatever regulation was initially needed to make the society viable would eventually be replaced by popular desire for greater integration. From the francophone perspective, on the other hand, any loss of ethnic identity in favour of a pan-Canadian identity has been seen as undesirable. Clearly, the weakness of Canadian nationalism is rooted in the weak existence of a unitary Canadian society.

It may be that whatever sense of society exists at the federal level in Canada is based on an acknowledgement by both anglophones and francophones of the state's authority to

The Sense of "Nation"hood in Quebec

the fleur-de-lys—the national flag
the Maple Leaf—the Canadian flag
Quebec City—the national capital
Ottawa—the Canadian capital
MNA (Member of the National Assembly)—elected member of Quebec legislature
MP (Member of Parliament)—elected member of Canadian parliament

serve as final arbiter of grievances and of its role in maximizing mutual well-being.[12] It has been argued that Canada is a nationless state and can more legitimately be considered a *state nation* than a nation-state because it is the *state* that strives to create a sense both of society and of nationhood.[13] In this sense we are an *invented community*: We constantly work at "willing" ourselves into existence as a community and developing a "Canadian" sense of society. This process will be the focus of Chapter Seven.

REGION AS A UNIT OF SOCIETY

The question of whether people who live within the boundaries of Canada form a society might first be examined by using region as the unit of analysis. Region, as a smaller unit of analysis than the state, is potentially more reflective of local peoples, their histories, and their cultures. While it may be difficult to identify a society at the level of the nation-state, it may be easier to observe society in the context of region. At the very least, by contrasting various regions we should be able to determine the extent to which the society of the nation-state is fragmented.

Regionalism is a recurrent theme in Canadian society. Geographers are most likely to draw our attention to regions as places affected by physiographic, climatic, or topographical factors which are related to where and how people live;[14] they may also characterize a regional society as one structured around *growth poles* (i.e., central places which provide employment and opportunity).[15] Geographically, a region is an area of land which is in some way physically distinct from other regions. Mountains, prairies, woodlands, and coastal regions, along with their respective supporting economies, can be distinguished and boundaries established. But, as geographers are aware, space is not neutral and humans transform physical space into *lived space* to which they attribute specific meanings.[16]

With some exceptions, sociologists have traditionally left the "region" variable to geographers.[17] Perhaps the most troublesome aspect of the concept is that it is difficult to locate a region's social boundaries. Regions seldom contain homogeneous social groupings, and differences within a region may be more significant than superficial similarities. To discover that the average income of a region's population is low in comparison to that of other regions may be less important than to know that there are significant disparities in income *within* the same region. In sum, for sociological purposes, region may be too imprecise a division to serve as a unit of analysis.

Yet there remains a lingering conviction that region is an important variable in understanding society. While it may be difficult to determine what aspects all residents of a region may have in common, it is clear that a combination of cultural and physical characteristics do make one area distinctive, in some measure, from another. The sociologist looks for whichever characteristics of the population (e.g., ethnicity, occupation, income) seem to be held in common and contrasts them with those found in other regions. The sociologist might also look for attitudes and opinions endemic to one area and compare them with those prevalent in others. This approach suggests that a region can be considered as having a *psycho-social dimension* that essentially transforms the concept of region from geographic space into social space.[18] Sociologists look for *objective indicators* of region in the characteristics of the population and for *subjective indicators* in residents' attitudes, identities, and feelings.[19] In most instances, however, the identification of a region as a social construct is still largely dependent on geographic boundaries.

Differences in population characteristics or attitudes do not necessarily create regionalism.[20] It is only when these differences are specifically recognized as a differentiating feature that they may produce, reinforce, or sustain regionalism. In other words, *regionalism* has a *political dimension* that involves a consciousness of kind, a collective identity, and a defence of territorial interests.[21] It involves the politicization of regional concerns and the articulation of regional commitments. What has made region a critical factor in understanding Canadian society is not just that regional differences exist, but that the evaluation of these differences has led to an articulation of regional interests, which in turn has spawned heightened regionalism.[22] An understanding of how regionalism is created will be examined in greater detail in Chapter Four.

Before the dynamic relationship between regions can be discussed, it is important to determine the extent to which the populations of Canada's regions differ. The nature of the commitment to region (i.e., regionalism) can be understood more clearly if we develop an understanding of such differences. This exercise will also yield a comprehensive picture of the components of Canadian society.

We are still left with the problem of determining what constitutes a region. The six traditional regional units in Canada are the Atlantic provinces, Quebec, Ontario, the Prairie provinces, British Columbia, and the Territories. Other than the Atlantic and Prairie regions and the Territories, the other regional units coincide with established provinces—which may or may not be an adequate means of determining regionalism. There are problems with assuming that, for example, Northern and Southern Ontario are essentially the same and should be deemed one region—or that the prairie provinces constitute a single region, when in truth Alberta has developed so differently. What does lend some credence to the "province as region" argument is that provinces possess the political apparatus to create a collective regional identity based on socio-political interaction within that unit. So while we cannot be totally satisfied with the equation of region with province, it is possible to use provincial units as the context in which regional differences in Canada can be identified. Provinces can be clustered as long as we acknowledge that regional boundaries are more difficult to determine than simple provincial boundaries.[23]

It is possible, then, to begin with the assumption that the experiences, interests, and attitudes of Canadians will vary with the territory in which they reside. While it may be possible to identify regional differences in population and environmental factors, the ultimate question is whether these factors produce regional societies. Is there a Maritime or a

Prairie society with unique and distinctive characteristics? And if these regional societies do exist, are they eclipsed by sub-regional societies at a local or community level?

Clearly there is a hierarchy of human relationships, from the simple small-scale community to the complex large-scale society. We can expect the smallest, most intimate relationship to be more important than the more distant and anonymous relationship. Thus society, region, sub-region, and community are ranged along a continuum from "lowest commitment" to "highest commitment." For that reason, we should not expect region to be a primary unit of group identity; that kind of collective consciousness is more likely to emerge when *region* is politically transformed into *regionalism*.[24] For our purposes, it is only important to determine whether regional differences might serve as the basis for regional societies.

The branch of sociology that deals with the statistical study of human population is known as *demography*.[25] In a country of enormous size, it is important to look for possible demographic differences between regions within that political entity. Regions, then, are important not because of some assumed homogeneity *within* the region but because of differences *between* regions. Regional demographic differences fall under four main headings: *population distribution, population composition, population change,* and *internal population shifts*.

Population Distribution

Perhaps the most basic fact about the Canadian population is that it is unevenly dispersed. While the country is vast (9 922 330 square kilometres), approximately 89% of its territory is devoid of permanent settlement on account of inhospitable climate and terrain[26]; in other words, much of the land is uninhabited.

The term used to describe settled areas is *ecumene*, literally meaning "inhabited space." Traditionally, settlement took place on land supportive of agriculture. These same locations, however, have also been preferred by urban dwellers. In consequence, the 8% of the land surface available for farming also contains the largest urban populations. Figure 1.1 (page 4) depicts the Canadian ecumene. In general, the ecumene consists of land adjacent to the American border, extending farther to the north in the Western provinces than elsewhere (80% of all farmland is located in the three Prairie provinces).[27] Canada's largest cities are also located in the southern extremity of the country, with its three largest less than one hour's travelling time from the US border. In fact, 72% of Canada's total population live within 150 kilometres of the Canada–US border. It is easy to see why north–south interaction across the border has frequently been less difficult than east–west relationships within Canada.

Canada's ecumene is virtually divided in two by the Canadian Shield, which separates east from west in Ontario. Furthermore, some segments of the ecumene are more densely populated than others. Figure 1.2 reveals that 62% of Canada's population of 31 629 677 (2003) live in the provinces of Ontario and Quebec—although Ontario, with 38.8% of the population, has become much more dominant than Quebec (23.6%)—16.8% are located in the three Prairie provinces (with more than one half in Alberta), 7.5% can be found in the Atlantic provinces, and 13.1% reside in British Columbia. The three territories combined do not contain even 1% of the country's population. Clearly, while provinces and territories are important political units in Canadian society, they carry differential weight—from Ontario's 11 million people to Prince Edward Island's 135 000.

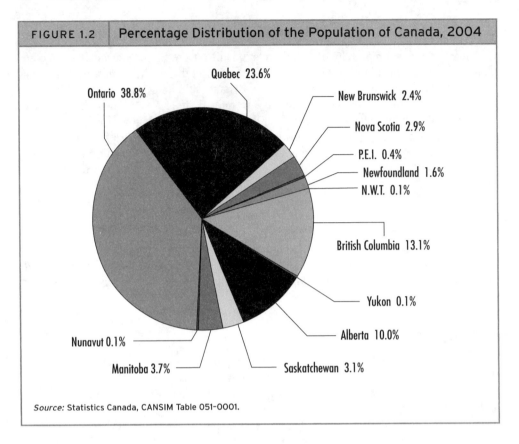

FIGURE 1.2 | **Percentage Distribution of the Population of Canada, 2004**

Quebec 23.6%

Ontario 38.8%

New Brunswick 2.4%

Nova Scotia 2.9%

P.E.I. 0.4%

Newfoundland 1.6%

N.W.T. 0.1%

British Columbia 13.1%

Yukon 0.1%

Alberta 10.0%

Saskatchewan 3.1%

Manitoba 3.7%

Nunavut 0.1%

Source: Statistics Canada, CANSIM Table 051-0001.

From a historical perspective (Figure 1.3), it is significant that the Atlantic provinces have experienced a continuous erosion of their proportion of the population—from 16.6% in 1901 to 7.4% in 1998. British Columbia, on the other hand, has experienced incremental growth, from 3.3% in 1901 to 13.1% in 1998. Quebec has also experienced an erosion of its earlier population strength, the result of a declining birth rate, an exodus of anglophones, and the fact that this province has been a less popular destination for international immigration than Ontario. While there was large-scale settlement of the Prairie provinces during the first few decades of the twentieth century, many of those immigrants later left their farms in response to the mechanization of agriculture and increasing urbanization. Therefore, the Prairie provinces' 22.3% proportionate share of the population in 1921 was eroded in subsequent years; in recent years, further erosion has been curtailed, thanks primarily to growth in Alberta. Canada's general tendency towards industrialization and urbanization has particularly benefited Ontario, where more than one in every three Canadians resides. In contrast to Quebec, where the percentage distribution of the population has been continuously eroding since 1941, Ontario's proportion of the population has been increasing, with consequences which will be outlined later.

Figure 1.4 illustrates how one-sided the redistribution of the population actually is. While all provinces displayed an increase in total population between 1951 and 2001, some grew much more than others, with the result that all provinces except Ontario, British Columbia, and Alberta reduced their proportionate share of the Canadian population.

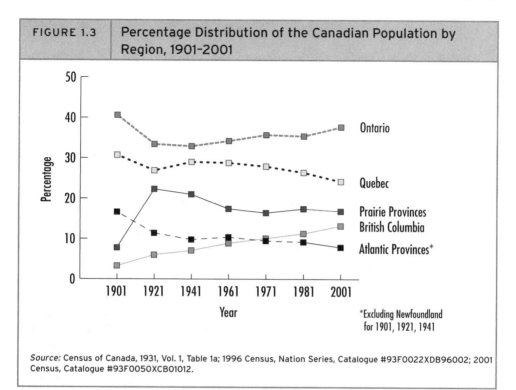

FIGURE 1.3   **Percentage Distribution of the Canadian Population by Region, 1901–2001**

Source: Census of Canada, 1931, Vol. 1, Table 1a; 1996 Census, Nation Series, Catalogue #93F0022XDB96002; 2001 Census, Catalogue #93F0050XCB01012.

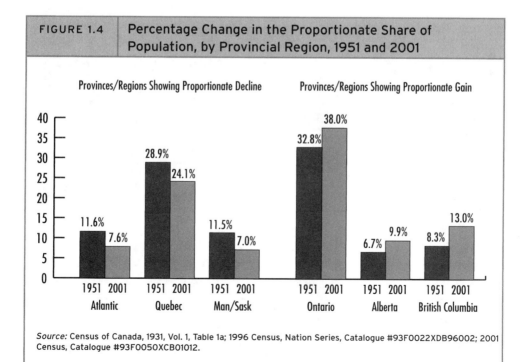

FIGURE 1.4   **Percentage Change in the Proportionate Share of Population, by Provincial Region, 1951 and 2001**

Source: Census of Canada, 1931, Vol. 1, Table 1a; 1996 Census, Nation Series, Catalogue #93F0022XDB96002; 2001 Census, Catalogue #93F0050XCB01012.

Differences in the distribution of the population can also be illustrated another way. Table 1.1 demonstrates that size of land surface varies considerably among Canada's provinces/territories, from the smallest (Prince Edward Island) to the largest (Nunavut). The land area of the Atlantic provinces is particularly small but density is high. These provinces are considerably different from other provinces, whose individual constituent area is larger than that of many of the world's countries. Prince Edward Island is the only province completely occupied, and therefore has the highest population density. The large segments of unoccupied land in most other provinces (in which a significant proportion of the land surface is in the north but most of the population is in the south) means that population densities are unusually low.

The differences between urban and rural population distribution are also quite revealing. Rural populations can be *farm* (primarily engaged in agriculture) or *non-farm* (rural but not dependent on agriculture as a source of income). Figure 1.5 indicates that although 20.4% of Canada's population can be considered rural, only 2.5% are engaged in agriculture. The highest proportion of the population engaged in agriculture is found in the Prairie provinces (followed by Prince Edward Island); even there, mechanization has meant that fewer people are needed to farm the land. A very interesting component of the rural population is the non-farm population, which, at 17.9%, is much larger than the farm population. The proportionately largest group of rural non-farm residents is found in the Atlantic provinces, where almost half of the provincial population live in small villages, many organized around fishing. The preference for rural non-farm residence is also a phenomenon of urban growth and the desire for living space. As Figure 1.5 shows, 60% or more of the populations of the Atlantic provinces and Saskatchewan reside in rural areas small

TABLE 1.1	Population Distribution and Land Area, by Province, 2003		
	Population	Land Area (sq. km in thousands)	Density (in thousands)
Newfoundland	519 570	371	1.4
Prince Edward Island	137 781	6	24.2
Nova Scotia	936 025	53	17.7
New Brunswick	750 594	71	10.5
Quebec	7 487 169	1 358	5.5
Ontario	12 238 300	908	13.5
Manitoba	1 162 776	552	2.1
Saskatchewan	994 843	587	1.7
Alberta	3 153 723	640	4.9
British Columbia	4 146 580	926	4.5
Yukon	31 060	475	0.1
Northwest Territories	41 872	1 141	0.0
Nunavut	29 384	1 925	0.0

Source: Statistics Canada, 2001 Census, Catalogue No. 93F0051XIE and CANSIM Table 051-0001.

REAL PEOPLE 1.1	Demographic Shifts: Exporting People from Saskatchewan

Rider Pride Nationwide "Every Game Is a Home Game"

He is a big burly guy. He is a football player in the Canadian Football League. He plays for the Saskatchewan Roughriders. People in Saskatchewan bleed green and white. They love those green Riders. The Roughriders play in Regina, which is the smallest city in the CFL.

"The thing I like the most about playing for Saskatchewan is that the people in this province love football. Even if people don't get out to the game, you can drive down the street of any small town on game day and everybody is listening to the game or watching it on TV. But what is even better, most teams talk about how when they play at home, they like that best because they have the home fans cheering for them. But not with Saskatchewan. Even

when we go on the road, we have fans everywhere and they are always cheering for us. So many Saskatchewan people have moved elsewhere and left the province that it seems like every game is a home game. When we play in Calgary, it sometimes seems that there are more people cheering for us than the Stampeders. And when we played the Grey Cup in Toronto, it seemed like all the former Saskatchewan people in all of Ontario were there cheering. Same thing in Edmonton and Vancouver. Rider Pride Nationwide!"

Questions to Consider

Which regions are losing population and which regions are gaining? Why is this happening? Is this good or bad for the regions involved, and what are the implications for Canadian society?

towns or cities of fewer than 100 000 people; in fact, in most of these provinces, the majority of the population live either in rural locations or in small towns of fewer than 25 000. In contrast, the majority of the populations of the remaining five provinces live in cities of more than 100 000 inhabitants.

In general, the Atlantic provinces and Saskatchewan are predominantly rural and small-town in nature whereas the other provinces are more urban (in spite of a large rural component in some Western provinces). The highest level of urbanization, however, can be found in central Canada in what is known as the *Golden Triangle*: The industrial heartland of Canada, north of the American border and south of a line extending from Quebec City to Sault Ste. Marie, is home to about 60% of the Canadian population.

Demographic analysis of Canada's population reveals that people are unevenly distributed throughout the country. We may also draw the following demographic conclusions:

1. Most of the population lives adjacent to the American border and in growing cities built on land suitable for agriculture.

2. History, climate, and industry have favoured the population growth and demographic dominance of Ontario and Quebec, particularly as represented by these provinces' southern high-density settlements.

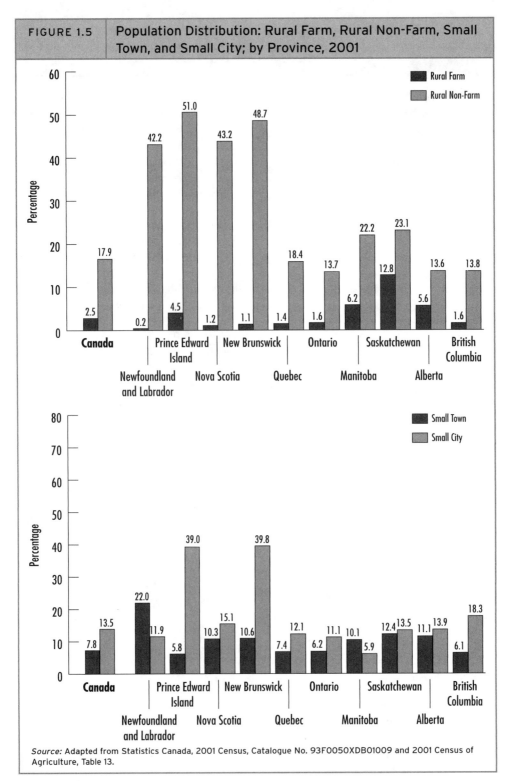

FIGURE 1.5	Population Distribution: Rural Farm, Rural Non-Farm, Small Town, and Small City; by Province, 2001

Source: Adapted from Statistics Canada, 2001 Census, Catalogue No. 93F0050XDB01009 and 2001 Census of Agriculture, Table 13.

3. The smallest provinces have the highest population densities but also have larger rural non-farm populations.

4. Very few Canadians are agriculturalists and most are big-city residents. The larger the provincial population, the greater the likelihood that it will be concentrated in big cities. Conversely, the smaller the provincial population, the more likely it is to be rural (though not necessarily agricultural).

5. In terms of its proportionate share of the population, Ontario continues to become larger and less rivalled by Quebec than it once was. British Columbia and Alberta have become the new growth provinces in the West.

Population Composition

The uneven distribution of Canada's population contributes to regional differences, which are further compounded by other factors. Three such population characteristics are *ethnicity, language,* and *religion*.

Canadian society is typically characterized as an ethnic mosaic. What is less frequently noted is that this mosaic varies with territoriality; that is, the diverse ethnic groups are rather unevenly dispersed throughout the nation. One of the fundamental reasons that regional cultures exist in Canada is that the ethnic composition of the population varies considerably from locale to locale

Table 1.2 reveals something of the ethnic heterogeneity of Canadian society. Up to and including 1981, the Canada Census allowed for the identification of only a single ethnic origin. Since that time, the census has allowed respondents to indicate multiple origins (e.g., "Mother is French and Father is German"), increasing the accuracy of the responses but also making it more difficult to make a simple statement about the ethnic origins of the Canadian population. Table 1.2 presents a location index which measures the extent to which various ethnic origins are represented within each province and allows for some comparison between provinces.

People of United Kingdom origin (i.e., English, Scottish, Irish, and Welsh) and people of French ethnic origin are the two largest groups in Canada. While German is the next most common European origin, a variety of other European origins are represented as well. Since the table combines people with single and multiple origins, it is important to note that the longer ago respondents immigrated, the more likely they were to report multiple ethnic origins. For example, a high proportion of persons from northern, western, and eastern Europe reported multiple origins; on the other hand, a low proportion of persons of more recent immigration, such as Koreans or Chinese, reported multiple origins.

Persons of English, Scottish, and Irish origin are considerably overrepresented in the Atlantic provinces, while persons of French descent are strongly represented in Quebec and New Brunswick. Other Europeans—especially those of German, Dutch, Polish, Norwegian and Ukrainian descent—are weakly represented in Atlantic Canada but much more strongly represented in western Canada. South Asians and Chinese are strongly represented in Ontario and British Columbia but weakly represented in many other provinces. Aboriginals are particularly strongly represented in Manitoba, Saskatchewan, and the Territories. Generally speaking, eastern Canada is more British whereas western Canada is more ethnically diverse—with the exception of Quebec and New Brunswick, which are more French. The French component of the population is weakest in the West and North,

TABLE 1.2 Location Index by Ethnic Origin for Each Province/Territory 2001

	Canadian/ Canadien	English	Irish	Scottish	French	Aboriginal	Caribbean	Dutch	German	Polish	Ukrainian	Italian	Jewish	South Asian	Chinese
Canada	39.4	20.2	12.9	14.0	15.8	4.5	1.7	3.1	9.3	2.8	3.6	4.3	1.2	3.2	3.7
Newfoundland	53.4	39.4	19.7	6.0	5.5	5.5	0.1	0.3	1.2	0.1	0.1	0.2	0.1	0.2	0.2
Prince Edward Island	45.0	28.7	27.9	38.0	21.3	2.0	0.2	3.1	4.0	0.5	0.2	0.5	0.1	0.1	0.2
Nova Scotia	47.4	28.1	19.9	29.3	16.7	3.7	0.3	3.9	10.0	1.0	0.7	1.3	0.4	0.4	0.4
New Brunswick	57.8	23.0	18.9	17.7	26.9	4.0	0.1	1.9	3.8	0.3	0.3	0.8	0.2	0.2	0.3
Quebec	68.7	3.1	4.1	2.2	29.6	2.2	1.5	0.3	1.2	0.7	0.3	3.5	1.2	0.9	0.9
Ontario	29.7	24.0	15.6	16.3	10.9	2.7	3.1	3.9	8.6	3.4	2.6	6.9	1.7	5.3	4.6
Manitoba	22.9	22.1	13.0	17.7	12.6	14.5	0.8	4.7	18.2	6.7	14.3	1.7	1.4	1.3	1.3
Saskatchewan	25.0	24.5	14.5	17.9	11.4	14.0	0.2	3.4	28.6	5.3	12.6	0.8	0.2	0.4	1.0
Alberta	27.7	25.6	15.7	18.9	11.3	6.8	0.6	5.1	19.6	4.7	9.7	2.3	0.5	2.5	3.7
British Columbia	24.3	29.6	14.5	19.4	8.6	5.6	0.4	4.7	12.9	2.8	4.6	3.3	0.8	5.4	9.7
Yukon	26.8	27.1	19.1	21.9	13.4	24.5	0.4	3.6	14.3	2.0	5.3	1.8	0.4	0.7	1.0
Northwest Territories	19.6	16.6	12.0	14.0	10.4	51.1	0.3	2.0	8.1	1.8	3.4	1.1	0.1	0.5	0.8
Nunavut	4.4	6.9	3.6	5.5	3.0	85.7	0.2	0.4	1.5	0.4	0.5	0.4	0.0	0.1	0.2

Note: A location index measures the extent to which a particular ethnic origin is represented within an entity. It includes people who claim that origin as their only ethnic origin, as well as those who claim that origin along with other ethnic origins. Therefore, it counts some people twice or more and weights those of mixed origin the same as those of single origin. The purpose of the location index is to provide some sense of comparison between provinces. Read the columns downwards and compare the index for each province with the index for Canada. A number higher than the index for Canada suggests a greater representation of that ethnic origin in that province, whereas a number lower than the index suggests a lower representation of that ethnic group. For example, Ukrainians are overrepresented in Manitoba and Saskatchewan but underrepresented in Nova Scotia and Quebec.

Source: Calculated by dividing total responses (single and multiple) for each ethnic group in each province. Adapted from Statistics Canada 2001 Census, Catalogue No. 97F0010XCB01001.

Is "Canadian" an "Ethnic Origin"?

The census defines *ethnic origin* as the ethnic or cultural group(s) to which an individual's ancestors belonged. Ethnic origin does not refer to place of birth or citizenship; it is a self-reported declaration of ethnic heritage. The concept of ethnic origin is very fluid and often depends on an individual's understanding of his/her own family history and on the effect of intermarriage on that sense of ethnic identity. How people respond is also affected by the options offered in the census. If, for example, it is assumed that all Canadians must have a foreign ethnic origin, the census would list other countries as options. If, however, "Canadian" is accepted as an ethnicity—which it was for the first time in 1991 but only on a write-in basis—things change dramatically. Because 3% of respondents in that year did choose the option of writing "Canadian," Statistics Canada decided to provide "Canadian" at the top of its list of options in 1996; the result was that 19% of respondents declared themselves single-origin Canadians. This number increased to 23% in 2001.

The most important result of the decision to allow "Canadian" as an option was a decline in the number of persons reporting French, English, Irish, or Scottish ethnic origin. The other effect was that an additional number of persons listed "Canadian" as one of multiple origins. Using this definition, an additional 16% identified one of their ethnic origins as "Canadian," producing a net total of 39% who selected "Canadian" as at least part of their ethnic origin. Fifty-five percent of these persons had parents who were born in Canada. Not surprisingly, having parents born outside Canada was the best predictor of claiming a non-Canadian ethnic origin.

The question is, is "Canadian" a true measure of ethnic origin or is it just the easiest response, especially for those who are Canadian citizens?

Source: Statistics Canada, *The Daily*, February 21, 2003, "Canada's Ethnocultural Portrait: The Changing Mosaic." See also Rhoda Howard-Hassman, "Canadian as an Ethnic Category: Implications for Multiculturalism and National Unity." *Canadian Public Policy* 35(4):523-35.

and, among the provinces, is weakest of all in Newfoundland and British Columbia. The Atlantic provinces show much less ethnic diversity than western provinces, which received heavy German and eastern-European immigration to rural areas. Whereas Quebec was formerly essentially French and Ontario was in contrast predominantly British, Ontario has now become much more multi-ethnic, particularly in its cities. Other significant minorities, though smaller in size than those listed in Table 1.2, include people of Greek, Portuguese, Spanish, and Yugoslavian descent, and are primarily found in the large metropolitan cities of Ontario, British Columbia, and Alberta. Toronto, for example, has the largest Polish, Greek, Portuguese, Jewish, and Filipino communities in Canada.

These regional variations can largely be explained in terms of differences in settlement patterns. The Atlantic region was first settled by British and French colonists, who also created what became known as Upper and Lower Canada through settlement along the St.

Lawrence and in the Great Lakes region. By the late nineteenth century, significant settlements had also been established in the Red River area of Manitoba and on the West Coast in Victoria and Vancouver. In the early twentieth century, massive immigration from other European countries was required to populate the western plains. It was this and subsequent waves of immigration (including the recent immigration from Asia) that altered the dominantly bi-ethnic composition of the Canadian population and which have resulted in greater ethnic diversity. Even more significantly, different locations in Canada possess considerably different mixes of these ethnic backgrounds in their populations.

If ethnicity is an important indicator of differences between people, then clearly the regions of Canada are very different from each other. Multiculturalism has a totally different meaning in the West than in Quebec or the Atlantic provinces. Eastern Europeans, for example, make up almost one fifth of the population of Manitoba, but they are virtually absent in New Brunswick. On the other hand, New Brunswick has a strong French minority (about one third of the population), whereas British Columbia has a small proportion of this ethnic group. Being French in Quebec has a totally different meaning than being of French descent in other provinces—particularly those farther away from Quebec. The large Aboriginal population in the Northwest Territories makes that region considerably different as well, and the large Asian population found primarily in the largest metropolitan cities distinguishes regions with large metropolitan populations from regions with only small urban populations. The "old" immigration into the agricultural west at the beginning of the twentieth century is certainly different from the "new" immigration into the largest urban centres. Not only is there a rural/urban difference, but European origins have been replaced with third-world origins. It is these ethnic differences which lead to significantly different regional cultures and which make a sense of society at the national level difficult to achieve.

In some ways, using ethnic origin as an indicator of the importance of ethnicity may exaggerate the role of ethnicity, because in most cases immigrants eventually adapt to the dominant culture, as the high response-rate to the designation "Canadian" indicates. The data in Table 1.2 do not tell us whether the respondent was a first-, third-, or fifth-generation immigrant, and later generations may cling to their ethnic origin only with nostalgia. For this reason, ethnic descent may not be nearly as important as current ethnic identity.

One indicator of the salience of ethnicity might be the language people choose to use (Figure 1.6). If the focus is on the language first learned in childhood (known as the *mother tongue*), it becomes clear that while English is the mother tongue of the majority (59.1%) of Canadians, only 7.9% of Quebecers claim English as their mother tongue. The other regions to significantly depart from the norm of 80%–90% English mother tongue are New Brunswick, where the English–French mother-tongue ratio is 2:1; Quebec, where French is the mother tongue for 82% of the population; and Nunavut, where Native languages are the mother tongues of 72% of the population. The other exceptions are more recent: Ontario and British Columbia have a growing population of *allophones* (i.e., speakers of neither of the two official languages). The highest percentages of English mother tongue are found in the Atlantic provinces (where there was little post-war immigration), with the exception of New Brunswick, which possesses a significant francophone population. The multi-ethnic character of the West is demonstrated by the significance in that region of languages other than French or English. But it is in British Columbia and Ontario that "Other" mother tongues are most rapidly growing in significance. At the national level, allophones now account for 18% of the population, up from 16.6% in 1996. As a result, the proportion of anglophones has declined slightly to 59.1%, and of francophones to 22.9%.

FIGURE 1.6	Language First Learned in Childhood (Mother Tongue) and Language Most Often Spoken at Home (Home Language) in Canada's Provinces and Territories by Percentage of Population, 2001

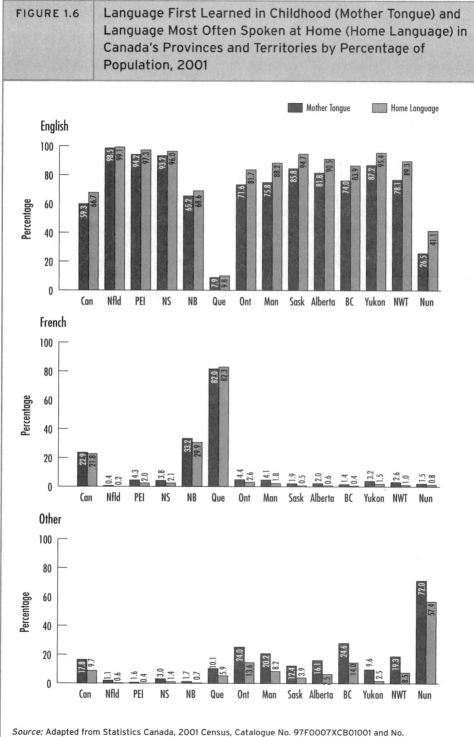

Source: Adapted from Statistics Canada, 2001 Census, Catalogue No. 97F0007XCB01001 and No. 97F0007XCB01003.

But it is not enough to know what language was learned in childhood. It is also important to know whether that language is still spoken at home. In order to see to what extent language shifts have occurred from childhood to current usage, it is useful to compare mother tongue with *home language*. In all provinces, the percentage using English as a home language is greater than the percentage claiming English as mother tongue—even in Quebec. In all provinces except Quebec, the percentage using French as a home language is lower than the percentage claiming French as mother tongue. Also in all provinces, the percentage speaking languages other than English or French at home is lower than the percentage claiming another language as mother tongue. The lesson is clear: English has gained importance as the language of everyday usage largely as the result of the loss of usage of "Other" languages. While 17.8% claim a mother tongue other than English or French, only 9.7% still use that language at home. Persons who claim French as their mother tongue also experienced erosion in home-language usage as well, though at the national level the drop is much smaller, from 22.9% to 21.8%. The one notable exception is Quebec, where the proportions of the population whose mother tongue is French and who use French as their home language are almost identical. In fact, slightly more use French as a home language than claim French as a mother tongue, indicating that francophone policies in Quebec are working. Areas where English is not the overwhelmingly dominant home language in usage, then, are Quebec and Nunavut. But it should not be forgotten that languages other than the two official ones are used in about 14% of the homes of Ontario and British Columbia, with somewhat lower figures in the western provinces. Very few persons use one of the non-official languages at home in Atlantic Canada. Insofar as a language spoken at home indicates ethnic identity, it is clear that there are significant differences between various regions of Canada.

According to official government policy, Canada is a bilingual country. We will have the opportunity to discuss the meaning of this policy in Chapter Five, but Figure 1.7 indicates that only about one in six Canadians considers him/herself French–English bilingual. This number, however, has grown over the last 30 years, from 13.5% in 1971 to 17.7% in 2001. In fact, all provinces have seen some growth in their bilingual population over that time. The highest rate of French–English bilingualism is found in Quebec (40.8%) and New Brunswick (34.2%). The lowest rates of bilingualism are found in Newfoundland (4.1%) and Saskatchewan (5.1%); in most of the other provinces, about 10% (or less) of the population are bilingual. In English-speaking regions, people are most likely to speak English only, with only a small minority able to use both official languages. In contrast, in areas where French is spoken (Quebec and New Brunswick), people are much more likely to be French–English bilingual. In Quebec in 2001, for example, although 82.3% of the population used French as their home language, 40.8% of the population spoke both English and French—up from 35.4% in 1991. Thus, the likelihood of being able to converse in both official languages is much greater in francophone regions than in those that are predominantly anglophone. The fact that French remains the dominant language in Quebec will, however, continue to distinguish that region from the rest of Canadian society.

Ottawa's increasingly bilingual nature contributes to the level of bilingualism in Ontario, and historic French communities in Nova Scotia and Manitoba contribute to higher levels of bilingualism in those provinces (although the rate still remains only about 10%). But the generally low level of French–English bilingualism that prevails from Ontario westward is countered by a much higher rate of bilingualism involving a non-official language. Thus, for example, only 9.3% of the population of Manitoba are French–English bilingual, but

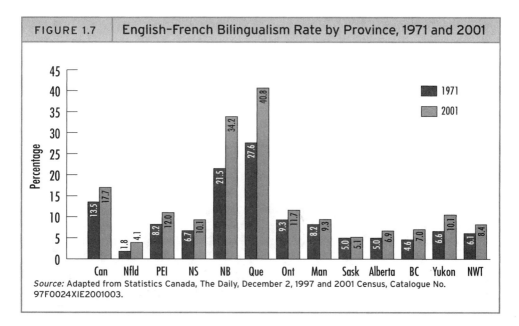

FIGURE 1.7 | English–French Bilingualism Rate by Province, 1971 and 2001

Source: Adapted from Statistics Canada, The Daily, December 2, 1997 and 2001 Census, Catalogue No. 97F0024XIE2001003.

20.2% are able to use a non-official language. In British Columbia, 7% are French–English bilingual, but almost 25% can use a non-official language. In sum, there is considerable variation from region to region in the languages spoken and in the population's ability to speak both rather than only one of Canada's official languages.

Another important aspect of regional differentiation is religious affiliation (Figure 1.8). Just as there is a relationship between ethnicity and language, there is also a relationship between ethnicity and religion. Census data on religion obviously are not indicative of commitment or participation, but they do give us some indication of religious preference. In this data we find further evidence of regional differences. For example, while 83.2% of the Quebec population are Roman Catholic, only 17.2% of the population of British Columbia claim that affiliation. Similarly, while 19.5% of Saskatchewan's population identify as United Church members, less than 1% of Quebec's are affiliated with that church. The largest single religious body in Canada is the Catholic Church (43%); in locations where there are many people of French descent (e.g., New Brunswick), the percentage of Catholics is considerably higher. Generally, the farther west from Quebec one goes in Canada, the lower the percentage of Catholics in the population. However, the sizeable number of Catholics found in certain other parts of Canada is usually tied to ethnic heritage (e.g., German Catholics in Saskatchewan). Provinces which have received large numbers of recent immigrants are more likely to have a higher proportion of persons who embrace a non-Christian religion or who claim no religion at all (British Columbia and Alberta stand out particularly in that regard). Evidence of European immigration is reflected in the significant Lutheran presence in the West, and early immigration from the United Kingdom is revealed in the comparative strength of Protestant groups, such as Baptists, Presbyterians, and Anglicans, in the Atlantic provinces.

Variations in ethnicity, language, and religion among Canada's population give us further evidence of regional differences in the composition of the society. Again, differences within regions may be as important as differences between regions, and we should not

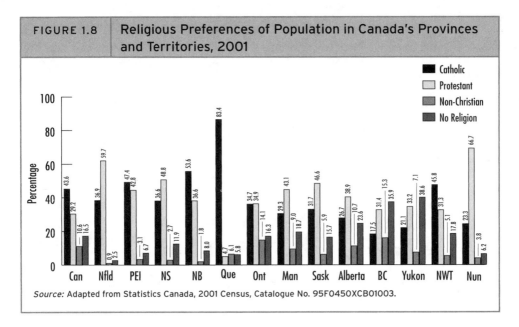

FIGURE 1.8 **Religious Preferences of Population in Canada's Provinces and Territories, 2001**

Source: Adapted from Statistics Canada, 2001 Census, Catalogue No. 95F0450XCB01003.

conclude that regions represent a homogeneous set. It is clear, however, that different demographic patterns within the society contribute to regional patterns that distinguish parts of the society from each other. The characteristics of the populations of Newfoundland, Quebec, and British Columbia, for example, are truly different on these dimensions, illustrating that regional character involves much more than the mere fact of separation by enormous distances. These variations can be summarized as follows:

1. Ethnicity, language, and religion exhibit a close regional correlation. A British heritage, Protestantism, and the English language are, respectively, the most common ethnic origin, religion, and language in the Atlantic provinces, Ontario, and the West; a French heritage, Catholicism, and the French language are most likely to be found in Quebec and the adjacent border region of northern New Brunswick. Thus, Quebec and northern New Brunswick are significantly different from the rest of Canada on these dimensions.

2. Earlier-settled and more rural areas, such as those in Atlantic Canada, tend to be more ethnically homogeneous than more recently settled rural areas in the West, which are more ethnically and religiously heterogeneous. In general, the area west of Quebec is much more heterogeneous on all three dimensions than the area east of Quebec.

3. Native persons are found primarily in the West and the North, where many maintain the use of their own languages. They are likely to be affiliated with either the Catholic or Anglican church.

4. Asians, Africans, Italians, those who speak neither English nor French, and non-Christians are more likely to be found in provinces with large metropolitan areas.

5. Bilingualism is more likely in areas where French is spoken than in areas where English is the primary language. Persons whose mother tongue is other than English or French increasingly use English as the language of home, except in Quebec and to a lesser extent the Northwest Territories.

Population Change

Population Turnover Our discussion so far has noted that ethnic diversity is a significant characteristic of the Canadian population. What is less well known is that the influx of people into the society (*immigration*) which has brought about this phenomenon has historically combined with an out-migration of people (*emigration*). It has been estimated that even though eight million people immigrated to Canada between 1851 and 1961, more than six million emigrated or left the country during that same period.[28]

Figure 1.9 illustrates how closely emigration has shadowed immigration through much of Canada's history. A large number of the emigrants were former immigrants who used Canada as a stop-off point for later migration to the United States in what is known as a *stepping stone migration*. These and other Canadians emigrated to the United States to take advantage of employment opportunities, particularly before industrialization increased in Canada. Quebecers in particular migrated to the New England states, where they found work while still remaining reasonably close to home.[29] However, at about the same time that migration to the United States became much more difficult as a result of the tightening of American immigration laws in the 1970s, the United States became a less attractive destination because of the urban problems it experienced in the 1960s and other quality-of-life issues. A prosperous Canadian economy has also reduced the out-migration of immigrants, considerably widening the gap between immigration and emigration in recent years. However, such factors as government cutbacks in such areas as health care, significant decline in the value of the Canadian (relative to the American) dollar, etc., do provoke a flow of emigration to the United States.

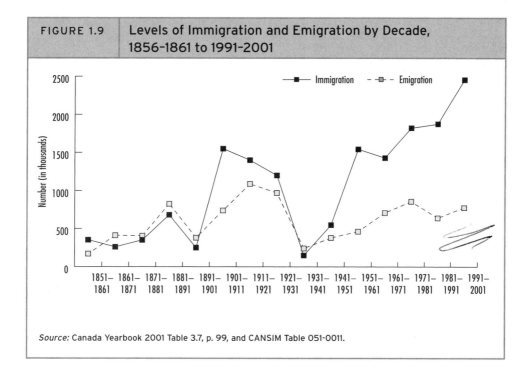

| FIGURE 1.9 | Levels of Immigration and Emigration by Decade, 1856-1861 to 1991-2001 |

Source: Canada Yearbook 2001 Table 3.7, p. 99, and CANSIM Table 051-0011.

Understanding Emigration from Canada

Between 1851 and 1991, 7.9 million people left Canada permanently, while 12.5 million immigrated to this country; thus, the net migration flow has been positive. It was primarily in the time period prior to 1900 that the net migration flow was negative. From 1851 to 1901, 2.2 million persons left Canada and 1.9 million entered. The decade with the largest number of persons emigrating was 1911–1921, when 1.1 million left. Up to the end of World War II, emigration from Canada was largely tied to lack of employment and economic opportunities, particularly in comparison to the United States. After World War II, immigration became a much stronger counterbalance to emigration—although emigration continues to be a factor in Canadian society.

Persons emigrating from Canada may or may not be Canadian citizens. However, of those holding Canadian citizenship who live abroad, 84% live in the United States and only 6% in the United Kingdom. Canadians are the third largest foreign-born group in the United States, and about one half have become naturalized US citizens. Since the Second World War, about 30% of all emigrants from Canada to the United States were not Canadian-born. Although recent data have not been collected, the 1970 US census revealed that 2.2 million persons in the United States had at least one parent born in Canada—meaning that many persons in the United States were eligible for Canadian citizenship.

Source: Craig McKie, "A History of Emigration from Canada." Adapted from *Canadian Social Trends* 35 (Winter 1994): 26-29. Statistics Canada Catalogue 11-008E.

It is also noteworthy that the source countries of immigration have changed over time. If we examine Table 1.3, we notice that at one time, Canada's largest categories of foreign-born originated in European countries; more recently, however, new source countries have superseded Europe. European countries provided most of their migrants to Canada before 1980—with the exception of Eastern Europe, which has provided more recent immigration. On the other hand, immigration from Central/South America, Africa, and Asia has been particularly strong since 1981. In fact, over half of Canada's Asian immigrants and 80% of its Central/South American immigrants arrived during the ten-year period from 1991 to 2001. It becomes evident as a result of this review not only that immigration has repeatedly injected new populations into Canada but also that each wave of immigration has brought people from different countries—a fact which has contributed to considerable societal diversity and continual change.

Immigration also has its regional components. Ontario is home to over one half (55.6%) of all Canada's immigrants or foreign-born, with British Columbia (18.5%), Quebec (13%), and Alberta (8%) far behind (Figure 1.10). Clearly this distribution gives Ontario a multicultural character quite unlike that of the other provinces, especially in light of the fact that it has the country's largest population. Forty-four percent of Toronto's population are immigrants, and more than one quarter of Ontario's population are foreign-born (Figure 1.11), which fact indicates that the processes of absorption and adaptation continue

TABLE 1.3 | Percentage of 2001 Population Born Outside Canada, by Source Countries/Regions and Proportion Immigrating in Selected Time Periods

Time Period of Immigration to Canada (%)

Country of Birth	% of All Foreign-born in 2001	Before 1961	1961–1970	1971–1980	1981–1990	1991–2001	Examples
OLD Source Countries/Regions							
United States	4.4	14.7	19.7	26.4	17.6	21.6	
Western Europe	7.8	50.8	16.9	10.7	9.3	12.3	Germany, France
Eastern Europe	8.7	28.7	7.8	6.4	22.2	34.9	Poland, Russia
Northern Europe	12.4	37.1	25.9	20.2	9.8	7.0	Norway, UK
Southern Europe	13.1	29.1	32.5	17.6	7.8	13.1	Italy, Spain
NEW Source Countries/Regions							
Central/South America	5.6	3.7	9.8	35.4	72.1	79.1	Mexico, Brazil
Caribbean and Bermuda	5.4	2.4	14.5	31.1	23.4	28.6	Haiti, Jamaica
Africa	5.2	1.6	8.4	19.3	21.1	49.5	Nigeria, Ghana
Western Asia & Middle East	5.2	1.6	4.7	10.4	26.6	56.8	Turkey, Israel, Jordan
Eastern Asia	13.4	2.5	5.0	13.4	21.2	57.9	China, Japan, Korea, Vietnam, Phillipines
Southeast Asia	8.6	0.5	3.0	22.9	34.0	39.6	Singapore
Southern Asia	9.2	0.8	5.3	15.3	20.1	58.6	India, Pakistan
Oceania	0.9	6.3	16.8	26.5	20.1	30.3	Australia, New Zealand

Source: Adapted from Statistics Canada, 2001 Census Catalogue No. 97F0009XCB01002.

| FIGURE 1.10 | Percentage Distribution of National Immigrant Population, 2001 |

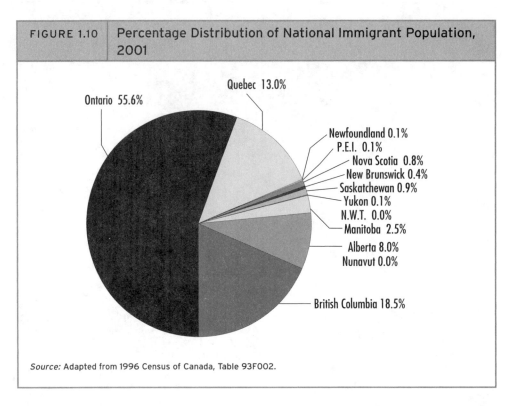

Ontario 55.6%

Quebec 13.0%

Newfoundland 0.1%
P.E.I. 0.1%
Nova Scotia 0.8%
New Brunswick 0.4%
Saskatchewan 0.9%
Yukon 0.1%
N.W.T. 0.0%
Manitoba 2.5%

Alberta 8.0%
Nunavut 0.0%

British Columbia 18.5%

Source: Adapted from 1996 Census of Canada, Table 93F002.

| FIGURE 1.11 | Percentage of the Provincial Population Born Outside Canada, 2001. |

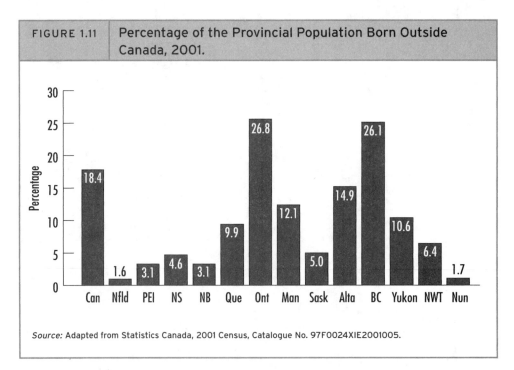

Source: Adapted from Statistics Canada, 2001 Census, Catalogue No. 97F0024XIE2001005.

at a high level in that province. While British Columbia has almost the same percentage of foreign-born (26.1%) as Ontario, the smallest proportions of immigrant populations are found in the Atlantic provinces, Saskatchewan, and two of the Territories. The regions with the largest numbers of foreign-born are those containing the metropolitan cities, specifically Ontario and British Columbia. Nationally, however, one in six persons (18.4%) is born outside Canada. Fully 95% of all immigrants in 2001 resided in four provinces: Ontario, Quebec, British Columbia, and Alberta.

Unlike earlier waves of immigrants, the majority of the immigrants who have arrived in Canada since the 1970s are members of visible minority groups.[30] The Employment Equity Act defines persons who are non-Caucasian in race or non-white in colour and who are not Aboriginal peoples as *visible minorities*. The four million persons in this group make up 13.4% of the Canadian population, with Ontario containing over half (54%) of that number, while 21% live in British Columbia, 12.5% in Quebec, and 8% in Alberta. Much of this transformation is due to the fact that in the 1990s three quarters of all immigrants to Canada were members of a visible minority. Of all the provinces, British Columbia has the highest proportion of visible-minority residents (22%, up from 14% in 1991). Ontario's share was 14% in 1991 but increased to 19% in 2001. Almost all visible-minority members live in big cities, with Toronto and Vancouver the most popular destinations. Toronto is home to 43% of Canada's visible minorities; members of these groups make up 37% of the population of that city. Eighteen percent of Canada's visible-minority members reside in Vancouver, making up 37% of its population. The figures for other large Canadian cities are 17% for Calgary, 15% for Edmonton, 14% for Ottawa-Hull, and 12% for Winnipeg. Whereas Chinese and South Asians are the largest visible minorities in Toronto and Vancouver, Blacks are the largest visible minority in Montreal. Over two thirds of visible minorities are foreign-born, although persons of Japanese descent are more likely to be Canadian-born.

It is not surprising that some regions of the society are growing through immigration more than others, but what is more significant is that some regions have a rather stable population with relatively few immigrants while others have a substantial foreign-born component, indicating considerable flux and change. The largest Canadian cities have been particularly attractive to new immigrants from visible-minority groups, producing a very different cultural milieu from that found in regions that have not experienced this kind of immigration.

Source of Growth The movement of populations into a country or region (*immigration*) minus the movement of population out of a country or region (*emigration*) produces a rate of *net migration*. It has already been established that Canada's level of net migration has been reduced by the fact that immigration has been somewhat counterbalanced by emigration. What then has been the primary source of Canada's significant population growth?

Natural increase is determined by subtracting the total number of deaths in an area from the total number of births in that same area. The data reveal that high fertility levels have been the primary source of population growth. Canada has completed the *demographic transition* from high growth rates attributable to high fertility levels. The theory behind the concept of demographic transition is that growth initially accelerates when improved medical care and improved nutrition cause mortality rates to decline. When this occurs, fertility rates usually also drop and natural increase becomes less important as a source of growth. The transition occurs when the period of high fertility and low mortality produce a high rate of natural increase. The traditionally high fertility rates in Quebec have reversed in recent years and the fertility rate in Canada has dropped. It is now assumed that Canada has completed the demographic transition as both fertility rates and mortality rates have dropped.[31]

Table 1.4 shows that natural increase has been a much more important source of growth in Canada than net migration. However, even here there are regional variations. Quebec, which has had a rather low level of migration, has depended heavily on natural increase (see, for example, 1931–1971) to maintain the francophone share of the total Canadian population. The emphasis placed on high birth rates in Quebec has been referred to as the "revenge of the cradle"—a way of restoring the provinces's original high francophone–anglophone ratio, which had supposedly been disturbed by immigrants who were assimilating anglophone culture.

Several provinces (particularly Prince Edward Island, New Brunswick, Manitoba, and Saskatchewan) have been perennially lost population through net migration, but these losses have been offset by population gains through significant levels of natural increase. Ontario has gained population through high rates of both net migration and natural increase—as has Alberta, except during the 1980s when the oil boom collapsed, producing a reverse migration out of the province. British Columbia is of special interest because for much of its history it has had both positive net migration and strong rates of natural increase; however, as compared to that of other provinces, its net migration always substantially exceeds natural increase as a source of growth. Internal migration will be discussed further in the next section, but we should recognize that net migration produced a total population gain of only 2.4 million in the first one hundred years of Canada's existence, whereas growth due to natural increase was a dynamic 14.5 million.[32] Even provinces with negative or low net-migration levels have enjoyed population increases thanks to high fertility.

Aging High levels of population turnover, coupled with high fertility rates, have meant that Canada's population has traditionally been rather youthful (Table 1.5). The drop in the percentage of those under 15 years of age in 1941 is a consequence of the Depression, and the higher levels in 1961 are the result of the post-war baby boom. The lower levels in 1981 and 2001 indicate completion of the demographic transition and lower fertility rates. The implications of lower fertility become clear when we consider that the proportion of the population in each age cohort over 35 was higher in 2001 than it was in 1921. For example, follow the line across the page for the 65–74 age group and note how the group steadily expands in size. In general, the proportion of the population over the age of 35 is increasing, particularly at both ends: The under-25 population is shrinking while the over-65 population is growing—a classic expression of population aging. While 4.7% of the Canadian population was over 65 years of age in 1921, that number had jumped to 12.8% in 2001.

In 2001, the median age of the Canadian population was the highest ever at 37.6 years, an increase of over 11 years from 1971, when it was 26.2.[33] This is a substantial jump in only 30 years, and the median age will continue to rise. Nova Scotia and Quebec have the oldest populations (median age 38.8 years) and Alberta has the youngest (35 years).

A more graphic way of displaying population aging is shown in Figure 1.12 in what is known as a *population pyramid*. The population pyramid gives a snapshot of the Canadian population in 2001 by year of birth. Notice the big bulge of persons aged 35 to 55 (representing the post-war baby boom), after which there is a drop in fertility and a baby-boom

TABLE 1.4   Rates of Natural Increase and Net Migration by Province, 1931-1941 to 1991-2001

Provinces	1931-1941 Nat. Incr.	1931-1941 Net Migr.	1941-1951 Nat. Incr.	1941-1951 Net Migr.	1951-1961 Nat. Incr.	1951-1961 Net Migr.	1961-1971 Nat. Incr.	1961-1971 Net Migr.	1971-1981 Nat. Incr.	1971-1981 Net Migr.	1981-1991 Nat. Incr.	1981-1991 Net Migr.	1991-2001 Nat. Incr.	1991-2001 Net Migr.
Newfoundland	-	-	-	-	265	-29	222	-90	148	-65	90	-30	30	-98
Prince Edward Island	105	-28	121	-86	157	-96	127	-62	78	15	73	1	37	25
Nova Scotia	109	10	177	-72	183	-46	127	-59	73	-1	64	1	29	6
New Brunswick	132	-18	184	-64	196	-49	144	-85	93	0	70	-7	32	-13
Quebec	139	8	194	2	222	36	132	4	79	-13	71	-88	43	16
Ontario	72	27	117	76	180	123	124	86	77	36	78	146	56	82
Manitoba	94	-53	116	-54	171	-	125	-55	85	-47	83	-37	53	-18
Saskatchewan	126	-155	107	-181	186	-80	137	-136	88	-44	100	-63	48	-42
Alberta	132	-47	139	26	236	109	162	38	113	202	136	-53	82	80
British Columbia	46	118	114	236	172	160	101	190	72	155	78	135	48	129

Note: Rates are per 1000 average population for the decade.

Source: Compiled and computed from Statistics Canada, 1986 Catalogue No. 91-0001, Vols. 1 to 15, no.1; Catalogue No. 96-304E, p.98; 91-209E, Table A.1 and Table 1.B; 1997 Catalogue No. 91-209-XPE, Summary Table, pp. 14-15 and Table 34; Catalogue No. 91-213, Table 1.1, and Catalogue 93-301 and 93-304, Table 1; Catalogue 91-213, 2003, Tables 1.3-1.14.

TABLE 1.5	Percentage Distribution of the Population by Five-Year Age Groups at Selected Intervals, 1921–2001				
Age Group	**1921**	**1941**	**1961**	**1981**	**2001**
0–4	12.0	9.1	12.4	7.3	5.6
5–9	12.0	9.1	11.4	7.3	6.5
10–14	10.4	9.6	10.2	7.9	6.7
15–24	17.3	18.7	14.3	19.1	13.2
25–34	15.3	15.7	13.6	17.3	13.1
35–44	13.2	12.5	13.1	12.2	16.8
45–54	9.1	10.7	10.3	10.3	14.5
55–64	5.9	7.9	7.1	8.9	9.4
65–74	3.3	4.6	4.9	6.1	7.0
75–84	1.2	1.8	2.3	2.8	4.4
85+	0.2	0.3	0.4	0.8	1.4

Source: Compiled and computed from 1991 Census of Canada, Catalogue 93-310, Table1, and 2001 Census of Canada, Catalogue No. 95F0300XCB01003.

echo. Notice also how the Depression and World War I contributed to a decline in births, and that at older ages, widowed women are a larger group than same-aged males. What is also striking is the decline in the number of children under ten years of age.

The primary contributor to demographic aging is a decline in the birth rate.[34] The replacement rate is approximately 2.1 births per woman, but the fertility rate has now shrunk to 1.5 from a post-war high of 3.9 in 1959. The decision of contemporary couples to have fewer children or to forego parenthood altogether has created some concern; the fertility rate, now at sub-replacement levels, has declined "from baby-boom to baby-bust." Declining fertility is of special concern to certain ethnic groups, such as the Québécois and Native peoples. But low fertility is also of concern to the population at large because it suggests that immigration will be increasingly important in stabilizing the population or in producing growth (particularly since it is persons of child-bearing age who are most likely to immigrate).

What then are the consequences of population aging? Earlier we considered the problematic aspects of immigration and emigration for the development of a durable society. Societal aging does have certain benefits in that it helps a country to develop a sense of permanence. But a too-rapid aging of the population can result in an increased economic burden on the society and a shortage of manpower to meet the economy's basic needs. If immigration again becomes the solution, and if that new wave of immigration is from new source-countries, Canadian society could undergo more of the dramatic changes which are already underway. An increased influx of third-world immigrants into Canada (assuming that residents of other industrialized countries are content to stay where they are) and the concentration of these immigrants in particular regions could create new bases for intrasocietal conflict.

FIGURE 1.12 | Age Pyramid of the Canadian Population, 2003

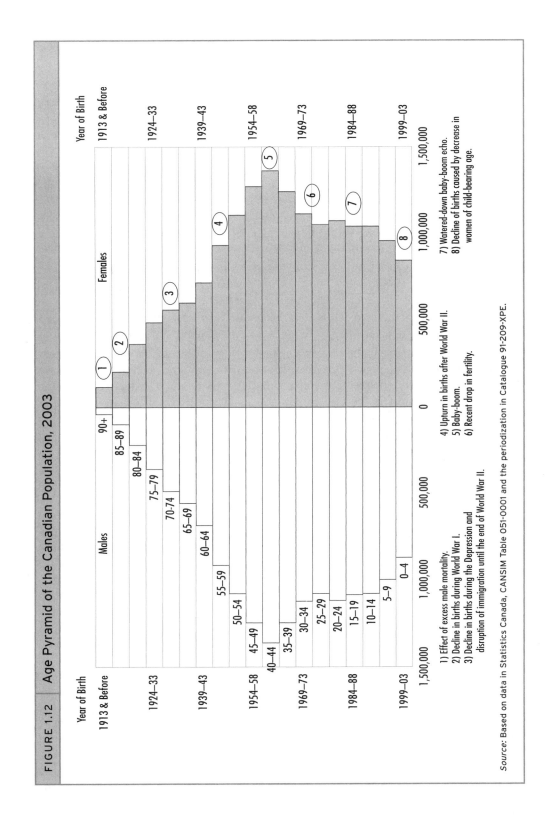

Source: Based on data in Statistics Canada, CANSIM Table 051-0001 and the periodization in Catalogue 91-209-XPE.

Population change has meant that Canadian society has been rather unstable for much of its existence. The reasons for this instability can be summarized as follows:

1. Both immigration and emigration have been at very high levels, resulting in significant population turnover. Furthermore, different waves of immigration have had different sources and this has increased ethnic diversity. During the twentieth century, regions west of Quebec experienced considerably more growth through immigration than regions east of Quebec.

2. The significant shift in sources of immigration from the old source countries of the United Kingdom and Europe to the new source countries of Asia, South America, and Africa has meant the introduction of new cultural elements into Canadian society. This is particularly the case for Canada's largest cities, to which visible minorities have flocked, contributing to a very different sense of Canadian society than that found in locations that have not experienced this immigration.

3. While a high rate of natural increase through the demographic transition has contributed to solid population growth in all regions, natural increase has been a more important source of growth in Quebec and the Atlantic provinces. A recent decline in the rate of natural increase below replacement levels suggests that any significant population growth in Canada may require a more active immigration policy.

4. The aging of the population has important consequences for Canadian society. Although on the one hand it suggests a sense of durability, on the other it implies shrinking fertility, with serious implications for the future. The fact that there are regional differences in the median age also implies an internal redistribution of the population.

Internal Population Shifts

The distribution and composition of the Canadian population have not been static over time; there has been a rearrangement of population within Canada's borders. Through a voluntary form of migration known as *population drift*, individuals have chosen to relocate in more suitable surroundings. Migration might be prompted by a "push," such as the presence of a surplus population in relation to labour demands, or by the "pull" of better opportunities elsewhere. An analysis of these "push" and "pull" factors helps us to understand why population rearrangement takes place.

Many persons might decide to relocate because their current location is unsuitable as a place to earn a living, carry on a career, or just live. It also follows that immigrants who do not know the country well may try several locations before settling down permanently. Shifts in employment demands, the policy of employer-instigated transfers, and the long-term trend towards urbanization have also been important factors in internal migration. Table 1.6 shows that the provinces with the greatest population stability (as measured by the proportion of current residents who were born there) are Newfoundland (95%) and Quebec (96%). A surprisingly high percentage of the residents of Prince Edward Island, Nova Scotia, and New Brunswick were born elsewhere in Canada; this is likely a consequence of the fact that many young people leave these provinces temporarily while young and return later with small children. Alberta and British Columbia stand out in that only two thirds of their Canadian-born residents were born in those provinces; the table's second column, which shows that these provinces have the highest percentages of residents

TABLE 1.6	Among Canadian-born, Percentage Born in Province of Residence, Precentage Born in Another Province, and Number Born in Another Province, 2001		
	% Born in Province of Residence	**% Born in Another Province**	**# Born in Another Province**
Newfoundland	95.0	5.0	25 015
Prince Edward Island	80.8	19.2	24 735
Nova Scotia	82.5	17.5	149 365
New Brunswick	85.3	14.7	102 215
Quebec	96.0	4.0	254 220
Ontario	87.8	12.2	998 325
Manitoba	84.8	15.2	146 660
Saskatchewan	86.2	13.8	125 585
Alberta	67.3	32.7	811 640
British Columbia	66.1	33.9	956 955

Source: Statistics Canada, 2001 Census, Catalogue no. 95F0357XCB01004.

born in another province, suggests that they are major recipients of internal migration. These two provinces are joined by Ontario in each having almost a million residents who were born in another province; the proportionate impact, however, is much greater in the two western provinces.

Table 1.7 follows the effects of interprovincial migration over a 30-year period from 1972 to 2002. During that time period, over 10 million Canadians moved interprovincially. Here we see that Ontario benefited the most from this migration (having received 25.7% of it), but Alberta (21%) and British Columbia (19.6%) were right behind. This time period reflects the two booms in Alberta's growth through internal migration (1975–1982 and 1996–2002), which moved that province ahead of British Columbia as a preferred destination for Canadians. While interprovincial migration is quite common (compare columns 1 and 3 of Table 1.7, which reveal the high incidence of both in-migration and out-migration), the Table also shows that most other provinces lost more people than they gained through internal migration. In short, the internal rearrangement of the population is an ongoing phenomenon within the society as a whole, but some regions grow through this exchange more than others.

In most instances, population shifts have been a response to urbanization. The initial movement was rural-to-urban within regions; in later years, it became urban-to-urban between regions. In 1871 only 19.6% of the population was considered urban, whereas by 2001, 80% was urban (defined as living in a centre having a minimum population of 1000). Furthermore, almost 60% of Canada's population now lives in Census Metropolitan Areas (CMAs), which are cities with populations of more than 100 000; most of these people (46% of all Canadians) live in cities with a population greater than 500 000. These statistics indicate the magnitude of the rural–urban shift.

TABLE 1.7	Interprovincial In- and Out-Migration for Each Province, 1972-2002		
Province	**In-Migration**	**% of all Migrants**	**Net Migration**
Newfoundland	274 339	2.7	-108 827
Prince Edward Island	101 496	1.0	5 604
Nova Scotia	585 524	5.8	-2 939
New Brunswick	439 671	4.4	-10 401
Quebec	808 562	8.1	-480 312
Ontario	2 573 022	25.7	125 964
Manitoba	587 844	5.9	-158 295
Saskatchewan	584 629	5.8	-180 358
Alberta	2 107 330	21.0	346 760
British Columbia	1 965 558	19.6	480 759

Source: Computed from Statistics Canada, CANSIM Table 051-0012.

Migration to Alberta: A Modern-Day Gold Rush?

From 1996 to 2001, Alberta had the highest growth rate of any province; most of this growth resulted from internal migration. This was the second time that Alberta had experienced a rapid growth rate from interprovincial migration. The first wave occurred from 1975 to 1982 and was even stronger than the second (although it will long be remembered as the boom that became a bust as the result of the National Energy Policy and declining oil prices). In fact, throughout the 1980s, more people left Alberta than moved into the province. The second wave, however, looks to be much more enduring as well as gentler.

Alberta's economy is bolstered by a strong energy industry in oil and gas, but it appears that more may be involved in its appeal. For example, Alberta has a strong free-enterprise tradition that is sometimes at odds with that of other provinces where governments operate more from the left. This makes Alberta attractive to people and businesses looking for that kind of environment. Alberta's two major cities are also attractive to those looking to move from the mega-cities where real estate and housing prices are high. In addition, there are signs that these cities are more attractive to internal migrants than Toronto and Vancouver, which have recently been magnets for international migration. Some come to Alberta expecting the streets to be "paved with gold" as the result of the boom in black gold (oil), but not everyone finds it that way at all. What will be the long-term effect of this growth for Canada?

RESEARCH CLIP 1.1	**Migration and the Transformation of Quebec**

Interprovincial migration flows are changing the nature of Quebec. The ongoing confrontation between Quebec and the rest of Canada has had a clear demographic impact upon Quebec's population profile since the mid-1970s. French-speakers residing in Quebec tended to remain in Quebec while the English left, and when migration into Quebec occurred, it was more likely to be French-speakers rather than the non-French who moved there. Migration has thus led to increasing segregation of the two linguistic groups.

More recently, the out-migration flow from Quebec has declined considerably, but so has the in-migration rate. Overall, however, migration flows into Quebec are relatively small; overall, the province loses population through migration. People with the highest levels of education are the most likely to leave Quebec; they are also the most likely to move to the province. But since the net migration flow is negative, Quebec incurs a net loss of the most highly educated. Persons with the lowest skill-levels are also among those leaving, but people with low skills are not among those entering the province. French-speaking migrants returning home account for most of the in-migration. Approximately two thirds of all migrants from Quebec go to Ontario.

Migration means that the linguistic duality of Canada is also leading to a territorial duality. In spite of federal policies of bilingualism, migration has made Quebec increasingly more French.

Source: K. Bruce Newbold, "The Ghettoization of Quebec: Interprovincial Migration and Its Demographic Effects," *Canadian Studies in Population* 23, 1 (1996): 1–21.

The relationship between urbanization and industrialization meant that population would be attracted to those locations where employment opportunities were greatest. Thus developed the *Windsor–Quebec City urban axis*, which contains the majority of the national population, most of the manufacturing employment in the country, and boasts an average income greater than that of the rest of the nation.[35] Within this axis are the largest metropolitan cities of Toronto and Montreal and their satellite regions. Building from their initial (historical) advantage, their natural (resource-based) advantage, and their central location in relation to national markets, they serve as natural magnets in population redistribution. Yet the data show that Toronto, having surpassed Montreal in size, is increasingly dominating all of Canada.

The most recent trend in urban-related migration has been *counter-urbanization*— movement away from the urban core and towards the satellite regions of urban areas. The growth of non-metropolitan areas began in the 1970s, as people, moving in the opposite direction to the one taken in previous decades, flowed from metropolitan to non-metropolitan areas in what has been dubbed *non-metropolitan turnaround.* [36] With the continued growth of major cities in Canada, this type of internal migration can be expected to continue.

The Four Urban Regions of Canada

About 15.3 million people or 51% of the Canadian population live in four urban regions:

1. In Ontario, the extended "Golden Horseshoe" from Oshawa to Niagara, including Toronto, Hamilton, and Kitchener, is home to 22% of the nation's people;

2. The Montreal region contains 12% of Canada's population;

3. British Columbia's Lower Mainland and southern Vancouver Island contribute 9% of the national total;

4. The Calgary–Edmonton urban corridor is Canada's new urban hub, accounting for 7% of the national population.

Source: Statistics Canada Catalogue 96F0030XIE010012001.

Table 1.8 indicates that there is considerable regional variation in the percentage of the population living in Census Metropolitan Areas. Only 17% of the population of New Brunswick lives in such metropolitan areas, whereas 76% of Ontarians reside in them. Furthermore, some provinces (e.g., Nova Scotia), have only one such city, whereas Ontario has eleven and Quebec five. Saskatchewan has only small cities, while the neighbouring Prairie province of Manitoba has one big city that accounts for about 60% of the entire provincial population. Some provinces have no cities whose population exceeds 500 000, while in those that do have cities of this magnitude the majority of the provincial population tends to be concentrated therein. Toronto (4.7 million) and Montreal (3.4 million) are unsurpassed in size among Canadian CMAs, with Vancouver a distant third (2 million). Edmonton and Calgary have experienced stunning growth since the 1960s and are now pushing towards a million in population. Thus, not only are there enormous variations in urbanization but there is a continuing tendency for the bigger cities to become even bigger. In each of the four provinces with the largest populations (Ontario, Quebec, British Columbia, and Alberta), over 50% of the provincial population lives in cities of more than half a million people.

Internal population movement changes the character of the society, creates regional resentments, fosters further population imbalances, and is symptomatic of underlying inequities within the society. Further, a comparison between regions with large metropolitan concentrations and regions of weak urban development suggests that the nature and substance of life varies considerably within the national society.

Internal population shifts can be summarized as follows:

1. Some regions of Canada have been more likely than others to attract internal migrants; these regions have also been more likely to retain locally born persons. Ontario and British Columbia are the strongest examples of such regions. Obviously, in provinces with comparatively few interprovincial migrants (e.g., Quebec and Newfoundland), a higher proportion of the population is likely to have been locally born.

2. Population movements within Canada have been in the direction of large metropolitan areas. Toronto in particular has assumed a dominant position in the national landscape.

TABLE 1.8	Percentage of Provincial Population in Census Metropolitan Areas of over 100 000, 2001			
		CMA Population	% Provincial Population	% Provincial Population in CMAs over 500 000
Newfoundland	St.John's	172 918	33.7	
Nova Scotia	Halifax	359 183	39.6	
New Brunswick	Saint John	122 678	16.8	
Quebec*	Montreal	3 426 350		
	Quebec City	682 757		
	Chicoutimi-Jonquiére	154 938		
	Sherbrooke	153 811		
	Trois-Riviéres	137 507		
	Total	4 555 363	62.9	56.8
Ontario	Toronto	4 682 897		
	Ottawa–Hull*	1 063 664		
	Hamilton	662 401		
	London	432 451		
	Kitchener	414 284		
	St. Catharines-Niagara	377 009		
	Windsor	307 877		
	Oshawa	296 298		
	Sudbury	155 601		
	Kingston	146 838		
	Thunder Bay	121 986		
	Total	8 661 306	75.9	56.2
Manitoba	Winnipeg	671 274	60.0	
Saskatchewan	Saskatoon	225 927		
	Regina	192 800		
	Total	418 727	42.8	
Alberta	Calgary	951 395		
	Edmonton	937 845		
	Total	1 889 240	63.5	63.5
British Columbia	Vancouver	1 986 965		
	Victoria	311 902		
	Abbotsford	147 370		
	Total	2 446 237	62.6	50.8

*While Hull is in the province of Quebec, Ottawa-Hull is identified as the national capital region, with the largest part in Ontario.

Source: Adapted from Statistics Canada, 2001 Census, Catalogue No. 93F0051X1E.

3. Regions experiencing positive net-migration flows are more likely to have larger and more numerous cities. Regions experiencing negative migration flows have smaller and fewer cities.

4. The dominance of the Windsor–Quebec City urban axis remains unchallenged, but some new growth has occurred in the Alberta urban corridor and in southwestern British Columbia.

ASSESSING THE SOCIETY WITHIN CANADA'S BORDERS

A sense of society does not just happen; it requires time, structure, opportunity for interaction, and a growing collective consciousness. We can now summarize the factors that affect our perceptions of a Canadian society in evolution.

The Demographic Factor

Canadian society has experienced a large measure of population change. A number of demographic factors have impeded the development of a feeling of "belonging together" within Canadian society; these include population turnover through emigration and immigration, the fact that immigration has occurred in numerous waves of different ethnic composition, variation in the degree of assimilation of immigrants, and regional differences in population characteristics. Furthermore, it could be argued that policy adaptations to these demographic differences, such as bilingualism or multiculturalism, may be politically useful but reassert old loyalties and old traditions at the expense of distinctively Canadian loyalties and traditions.

The Regional Factor

The national society within the state is further divided by the fact that the continuous demographic changes noted above have a compelling regional context. The uneven distribution and redistribution of population groups, the early settlement of some areas and the recent settlement of others, the differences in ethnic backgrounds and language usage, and the differential in population gains and losses have produced imbalances and numerous grounds for conflict within the societal unit.

Perhaps the most critical demographic feature promoting the regionalization of Canadian society is the uneven distribution of the population, whereby Ontario and Quebec contain the majority of the country's population. As noted, this fact has certain concomitants, such as the regional concentration of political, economic, and industrial power. Regions at a distance from central Canada often feel a sense of powerlessness which may coagulate into some form of regional hostility. The second important demographic factor is the ethnic/linguistic uniqueness of Quebec in relation to the rest of Canada. As Quebec is a centrally located, heavily populated province, a form of regionalization exists at the core of the country. We have also seen how sheer distance helps to promote regional feelings, as regional cultures develop from the experiences of sharing a territory.

There is ongoing debate as to whether regional identities or regional feelings are more important than national feelings. Much is often made of Westerners or Atlantic residents constituting a region, and certainly Quebec is generally assumed to be a region. Even

Ontario, as the national heartland, has its own sense of regional leadership which it projects to other regions. Such discussions often overstate the unity existing in these entities, for as we will see, Quebec is home to Canadian nationalists as well as to Québécois nationalists. What is more, Newfoundland is somewhat different from other Atlantic provinces, and British Columbia somewhat different from the other Western provinces. As Canadians become more aware of each other through interaction within the national context, they also become more aware of how their regional political and economic cultures are both similar and different. Newfoundlanders, for example, have long been known for their intense regional feeling and loyalty, which even carry over when they migrate to other parts of Canada for employment purposes (with the desire to eventually return).[37] This sense of regional pride and loyalty is not surprising, particularly as they encounter other regions on the national stage, with different cultures and agendas. The evidence as to whether regional identities are more important than national identities is mixed; these identities may be catalyzed by issues and political events. Most studies suggest that about three quarters of the Canadian population identify primarily with Canada rather than with their region; Ontario shows the highest tendency to do so, while Quebec—followed by Atlantic Canada—is least likely.[38] In other words, regional demographic differences do not necessarily efface national attachments.

But more recently, a new concept, *glocalism*, has been proposed to account for the weakening of national identities and national states and the converse strengthening of local identities.[39] "Thinking globally but acting locally" is more than a contemporary expression; it is increasingly becoming a reality as Canadians participate more and more in international cultures. The clear tension between local, national, and global levels of identification, which are dynamic rather than static, is an issue which we will explore in more detail in Chapter Six.

The Normative Evaluation Factor

How do we interpret and evaluate the evidence provided in this chapter? In some ways, our analysis has presented regional differences and regional identities as a societal problem. From this perspective, one might conclude that regional differences ought to be eradicated and society-wide homogeneity and equality ought to be the goal. In other words, the evidence could lead us to evaluate regional diversity and population differences as problematic. But, from another perspective, it is possible to conclude that it is precisely this regional variability that gives Canadian society its unique character. From the first perspective, regional differences are viewed more negatively; from the second, they are viewed more positively and almost cherished. The point is that opinions about how to evaluate these characteristics may vary because of our differing opinions about *what Canadian society should be like*—our ideas about the norms to which Canadians should subscribe (i.e., what is normative). It is for this reason that our interpretation and evaluation of the facts are open to such debate. The "Differing Perspectives" box on the next page gives some indication of how the evidence can be differently interpreted from various theoretical points of view—but ultimately, the approach you take in evaluating the data depends on your perspective.

Another way to look at this issue is to point out that federal policies designed in the best interests of Canada may have different or even opposite effects on regional units.[40] Several examples illustrate this point. Early federal policy may have encouraged

Differing Perspectives

Structural Functionalism

The structural functionalist perspective visualizes Canadian society as a giant complex organism whose many structures work together to give it its unique character and to sustain the whole social system. The movement of people from one region to another, for example, illustrates the self-regulating or self-correcting function of the society, whereby unemployed people seek economic opportunity in another region. Similarly, the unique spatial distribution of the population may create certain difficulties, but, over time, institutional adjustments and accommodations will occur in order to maintain the viability and equilibrium of the society. In other words, the regional differences discussed in this chapter are not big problems, for the society will make adjustments to preserve itself.

Conflict

The conflict perspective emphasizes the tension inherent in Canadian society, particularly as the result of inequalities. There are vast differences and disparities between regions, and the huge variations in population size mean that regions vary greatly in political power. Some regions gain population at the expense of other regions, causing regional inequities to grow. Even international migrants to Canada tend to settle in the same few locations, thereby changing the character of these loca-tions while disadvantaging areas experiencing little growth. Furthermore, ethnic and language differences make people aware of what divides them rather than what unites them as Canadians. Thus, in so many ways, the Canadian population is in constant overt or submerged conflict, and these internal differences have persisted rather than waned over time.

Symbolic Interactionism

The symbolic interactionist perspective notes that when people interact through sharing a territory (e.g., nation, province, sub-region), they develop a particular understanding about themselves, which is reflected in their unique cultural attributes (e.g., symbols, language forms) and which sets them apart from other national societies. In a vast country, regional identities based on common experiences may be particularly strong and may produce collective definitions of situations that differ from those held by members of other regions. Furthermore, immigrants bring with them old loyalties and identities that compete with their new identities as Canadians. Language differences (particularly between English and French) help to promote linguistic identities which divide the Canadian population between two very different cultural worldviews. The differences pointed out in this chapter are not so much irresolvable problems but realities that just need to be understood.

immigration to populate the land and stimulate the economy. But to francophones, particularly in Quebec, this policy was seen as altering the bi-ethnic balance of Canada, because an immigrant population would eventually embrace English culture, thereby threatening the francophone community's identity and power as a "founding partner" in Confederation. So, in order to obviate such an outcome, Quebec's response in recent years has been to make it more difficult for immigrants to that province to become anglophones. Another example might be that what is in the best interests of the oil-producing regions (e.g., higher incomes, employment) may not be in the best interests of the oil-consuming regions (e.g., higher costs). Furthermore, the industrial strength of one region may come at the expense of another because federal policy made in the "national interest" has negative effects on their region. It is for this reason that regional differences are not always just benign facts but are charged with emotion. Clearly, meeting the needs of such a diverse national society means addressing repeated challenges from regions whose best interests frequently conflict.

Bell, noting that regions may be so different that their objectives may be in competition or opposition, has labelled this phenomenon *conflictual regionalism*.[41] But he has also posited the existence of *co-operative regionalism*—a basic commitment to the federal state and participation in its structures (e.g., law, Parliament). Thus, although regional disparities may seem to hinder the viability of the nation-state, allowances are made to accommodate the regions' diverse needs because regional differences play a significant role in giving Canadian society its unique form and character. In other words, while to those concerned with creating a unitary sense of society regionalism has divisive aspects, it is those very aspects which make the society what it is.

In addition, some persons may favour a decentralized federal system with strong regional identities, while others may prefer a strong pan-Canadian society (nation-state) in which Canadian national identity dominates over regional loyalties. Indeed, there is evidence to suggest that commitments to region and country may not be mutually exclusive and that it is possible to maintain both allegiances at the same time.[42] We will return to region in the context of national identity in Chapter Seven, but at this point we should recognize that the significance of region depends on a subjective assessment of what kind of society Canada should be.

CONCLUSION

Regional differences and regional disparities are not unique to Canada and are probably characteristic of all federal states. Yet in Canada, factors such as geographic size, population imbalances, ethnic commitments, and differences in economic development enhance the role that region plays in retarding the emergence of a more unitary national society. In reality, it is unreasonable to expect that in a national society all people should be the same and have the same level of commitment to the federal system. We have already seen how this is impossible given a constantly changing population. But this fact does suggest that a sense of society cannot be taken for granted and must be constantly renegotiated. National-unity strategies are constantly being proposed and evaluated.[43]

The point is that people who share a territory and a political system do strive for some sense of societal unity. Amidst population flux and diversity, there is indeed at least a core segment of the population who have made their home in Canada for generations and who view themselves as ethnically "Canadian." Public expressions of regionalism may vary, but a commitment to the federal state continues. It is from this basic commitment that a "Canadian" society struggles to continue as a meaningful reality.

FURTHER EXPLORATION

1. Do you think that people in your region identify more with your region or with the nation? What events seem to alter the diversity of opinions on this issue?

2. What do you think is *the* most important reason that residents of Canada form a weak sense of society? Analyze why that reason is important and suggest policies which might overcome this weakness.

3. Watch your local newspaper for concrete examples of regionalizing events and perspectives as well as nationally integrating ones. Which kind dominates the news?

4. Ask a hyphenated Canadian (e.g., Ukrainian-Canadian, Japanese-Canadian) which identity is most important to him or her. Has that identity changed over time?

SELECTED READINGS

Beaujot, Roderic and Don Kerr. *Population Change in Canada.* 2nd ed. Toronto: Oxford University Press, 2004.

Cheal, David, ed. *Aging and Demographic Change in Canadian Context.* Toronto: University of Toronto Press, 2002.

McVey, Wayne W., and Warren E. Kalbach. *Canadian Population.* Scarborough: Nelson, 1995.

Statistics Canada. *Canadian Social Trends,* quarterly publication of demographic trends by Statistics Canada.

Statistics Canada. *Report on the Demographic Situation in Canada.* Annual publication.

ENDNOTES

1 Don Martindale, "The Sociology of National Character," *The Annals of the American Academy of Political and Social Science* 379 (1967): 30–35.

2 For a discussion of the potential of using the political or national entity as a unit of analysis in understanding human populations as societies, see T.B. Bottomore, *Sociology: A Guide to Problems and Literature*, rev. ed. (London: Allen and Unwin, 1971), 116.

3 See David V.J. Bell, *The Roots of Disunity*, rev. ed. (Toronto: Oxford University Press, 1992). See also A. Breton and R. Breton, *Why Disunity? An Analysis of Linguistic and Regional Cleavages in Canada* (Montreal: Institute for Research on Public Policy: 1980).

4 See Raymond Breton, Jill Armstrong, Les Kennedy, *The Social Impact of Changes in Population Size and Composition: Reactions to Patterns of Immigration* (Ottawa: Manpower and Immigration, 1974).

5 For example, see Emile Durkheim, *The Rules of Sociological Method* (New York: Free Press, 1950), chap. 4.

6 S.M. Lipset, *Political Man* (Garden City: Doubleday, 1960), 2–4.

7 Dankwart Rustow, "Nation," *International Encyclopedia of the Social Sciences*, vol. 11, 7–14.

8 Daniel Chirot, *Social Change in the Twentieth Century* (New York: Harcourt Brace Jovanovich, 1977), 11.

9 Lilianne E. Krosenbrink-Gelissen, "First Nations, Canadians and Their Quest for Identity: An Anthropological Perspective on the Compatibility of Nationhood Concepts," in André Lapierre, Patricia Smart, and Pierre Savard, eds., *Language, Culture and Values in Canada at the Dawn of the*

21st Century (Ottawa: Carleton University Press and International Council for Canadian Studies, 1996), 329–45.

10 E.J. Hobsbawm, *Nations and Nationalism Since 1780* (Cambridge: Cambridge University Press, 1990).

11 Ali Mazrui, "Pluralism and National Integration," in Leo Kuper and M.G. Smith, eds., *Pluralism in Africa* (Berkeley: University of California Press, 1969), 345.

12 For a discussion of this type of argument, see Donald Smiley, *Canada in Question: Federalism in the Seventies*, 2nd ed. (Toronto: McGraw-Hill Ryerson, 1976), 218.

13 Richard Gwyn, *Nationalism Without Walls* (Toronto: McClelland and Stewart, 1995).

14 L. McCann and Angus M. Gunn, *Heartland and Hinterland: A Regional Geography of Canada,* 3rd ed. (Scarborough: Prentice Hall, 1998).

15 See N.H. Lithwick and Gilles Paquet, "Urban Growth and Regional Contagion," *Urban Studies: A Canadian Perspective* (Toronto: Methuen, 1968), 18–39.

16 E. Carter, J. Donald, and J. Squires, eds., *Space and Place: Theories of Identity and Location* (London: Lawrence and Wishart, 1993).

17 The University of North Carolina is best known for its work on the sociology of regionalism in the 1920s to 1940s. In particular, read the work of Howard Odum, Katherine Jocher, and Rupert Vance. More recently, see the work of John Shelton Reid, particularly *One South: An Ethnic Approach to Regional Culture* (Baton Rouge: Louisiana State University Press, 1983).

18 Raymond Breton, "Regionalism in Canada," in David M. Cameron, ed., *Regionalism and Supra-nationalism* (Montreal: Institute for Research on Public Policy, 1981), 58.

19 The subjective-objective distinction is made by Ralph Matthews in *The Creation of Regional Dependency* (Toronto: University of Toronto Press, 1983), 18.

20 Matthews also argues that regionalism may be present even "when there does not appear to be much in the way of objective difference." See "Regional Differences in Canada: Social Versus Economic Interpretations," in Dennis Forcese and Stephen Richer, eds., *Social Issues: Sociological Views of Canada* (Scarborough: Prentice Hall, 1982), 86.

21 For one discussion of the political aspects of region, see Mildred A. Schwartz, *Politics and Territory: The Sociology of Regional Persistence in Canada* (Montreal: McGill-Queen's University Press, 1975), 5.

22 The comparative conception of disparities between regions is developed in Paul Phillips, *Regional Disparities* (Toronto: James Lorimer, 1982); and *Living Together: A Study of Regional Disparities* (Economic Council of Canada, 1977).

23 For a discussion of some of the issues associated with regionalism in Canada, see Mason Wade, ed., *Regionalism in the Canadian Community*, 1867–1967 (Toronto: University of Toronto Press, 1969); and B.Y. Card, ed., *Perspectives on Regions and Regionalism* (Edmonton: University of Alberta Press, 1969); R.J. Brym, ed., *Regionalism in Canada* (Toronto: Irwin, 1986); and Janine Brodie, *The Political Economy of Canadian Regionalism* (Toronto: Harcourt Brace Jovanovich, 1990).

24 Alan Cairns has argued that instead of being based on societies, the provincial governments mould their social environments to help create societies. "The Governments and Societies of Canadian Federalism," *Canadian Journal of Political Science* 10 (1977): 695–725.

25 For a good review of the history of demography in Canada, see Sylvia T. Wargon, "Demography in Canada: Looking Backward, Looking Forward," *Canadian Studies in Population* 25, 2 (1998):199–228.

26 *Canada Yearbook* 1980–8, 1; and Rick Mitchell, *Canada's Population from Ocean to Ocean,* 1986 Census of Canada, Catalogue 98–120, 16.

27 *Canada Yearbook* 1999, 51.

28 Leroy Stone, *Migration in Canada: Regional Aspects* (Ottawa: Statistics Canada, 1969), 22–26.

29 Cf. Yolande Lavoie, *L'Émigration des Canadiens aux États-Unis avant 1930* (Montreal: Presse de l'université de Montréal, 1972).

30 Statistics Canada, Catalogue #97F0024XIE2001006.

31 Wayne W. McVey and Warren E. Kalbach, *Canadian Population* (Toronto: Nelson, 1995), 31–37. It is now accepted that variations in the birth rate are not related solely to industrialization, and that other variables, such as wars or depressions, may intervene. In other words, the demographic transition theory is more complex than described here. See also Rod Beaujot and Kevin McQuillan, "The Social Effects of Demographic Change: Canada 1851–1981," *Journal of Canadian Studies,* 21 (1986): 57–69.

32 T.R. Weir, "Population Changes in Canada, 1867–1967," *Canadian Geographer* 2 (1967): 198.

33 Statistics Canada, Catalogue #96F0030XIE2001002.

34 Statistics Canada, The Daily, April 19, 2004. See also A. Romaniuc, *Fertility in Canada: From Baby Boom to Baby Bust*, Statistics Canada Catalogue 91-524E; Leroy Stone and Hubert Frenken, *Canada's Seniors,* Catalogue 98–121; and Susan McDaniel, *Canada's Aging Population* (Toronto: Butterworths, 1986); Blossom T. Wigdor and David K. Foot, *The Over-Forty Society: Issues for Canada's Aging Population* (Toronto: James Lorimer, 1988); *A Portrait of Seniors in Canada,* 2nd ed., Statistics Canada, 1997; and Ellen M. Gee and Gloria Gutman, eds., *The Overselling of Population Aging* (Toronto: Oxford University Press, 2000).

35 Maurice Yeates, "The Windsor–Quebec City Urban Axis," in Robert M. Irving, ed., *Readings in Canadian Geography*, 3rd ed. (Toronto: Holt, Rinehart and Winston, 1978), 68–72. See also his *Main Street: Windsor to Quebec City* (Toronto: Macmillan, 1975).

36 Statistics Canada, *Canadians on the Move,* Catalogue 96-309E, 47.

37 Robert D. Hiscott, "Recent Migration from Ontario to Atlantic Canada: A Comparison of Returning and Non-Returning Migrants," *Canadian Review of Sociology and Anthropology* 24 (1987): 586–99.

38 There are a variety of studies on this topic. An example of an older one is Jon H. Pammett, "Public Orientation to Regions and Provinces," in David J. Bellamy, Jon H. Pammett, and Donald C. Rowat, eds., *The Provincial Political Systems: Comparative Essays* (Toronto: Methuen, 1976), 86–99. An example of a newer one is Roger Gibbins and Sonia Arrison, *Western Visions: Perspectives on the West in Canada* (Peterborough: Broadview, 1995), 59–65.

39 Carey Hill and Roger Gibbins, "Glocalism and the New Electronic Technologies: Calgary in the Global Environment," unpublished paper, 1998.

40 For a good discussion of the issues and remedies attempted, see Garth Stevenson, *Unfulfilled Union: Canadian Federalism and National Unity*, rev. ed. (Toronto: Gage, 1982).

41 David Bell, *The Roots of Disunity: A Study of Canadian Political Culture,* rev. ed. (Toronto: Oxford University Press, 1992), 140–52.

42 David J. Elkins examined data that indicated that Canadians may have multiple loyalties, and that (except in the case of a separatist group in Quebec) loyalties to the nation-state need not necessarily erase regional attachments or vice versa. "The Sense of Place," in David J. Elkins and Richard Simeon, eds., *Small Worlds: Provinces and Parties in Canadian Political Life* (Toronto: Methuen, 1980), 21–24.

43 Kenneth McRoberts, *Misconceiving Canada: The Struggle for National Unity* (Toronto: Oxford, 1997).

WEBLINKS

www.iom.ch

The International Organization for Migration acts with its partners in the international community to assist in meeting the operational challenges of migration, to advance understanding of migration issues, to encourage social and economic development through migration, and to uphold the human dignity and well-being of migrants.

chapter two

The Question of Autonomy

Canada has ceased to be a nation, but its formal political existence will not end quickly. Our social and economic blending into the empire will continue apace, but political union will probably be delayed.

—George Grant, a social philosopher, in his widely read *Lament for a Nation* (1965), 86

It is often said that it is impossible to understand Canadian society without recognizing that it is in many ways a product of European and American influences. The fact that older and more dominant societies have played and continue to play a formative role in the society's development gives rise to a number of questions. One of the big questions is how a society can remain open to foreign influences and at the same develop more independently. Despite the recent trend towards global interdependence, questions remain about how a young and less powerful society can more independently establish and control its own traditions and institutions. This chapter will describe the nature, evolution, and implications of external influences upon Canadian society, for they provide a context for understanding the conflicts and cross-pressures existing in the society today.

COLONIALISM AS A HISTORICAL PROCESS

Historically, Canada has always lived in the shadow of more powerful societies. These societies derived their power and international stature from their industrial, economic, technological, and military strengths, which they used to pursue expansionist objectives around the globe. Canadian society actually emerged as a direct outcome of the power and influence of European societies, which supplied the people, goods, and capital needed for what they saw as a frontier society. The early Anglo-Saxon inhabitants felt that Canadian society was in some way an extension of their own, dominant society; as a result, they believed that Canadian Native peoples should be pushed aside so that the society of the "new world" could be established. *Colonialism* is the process whereby an imperial state maintains and extends its powers over a subordinate territory. The expansion of the British and French powers beyond their own national borders and around the world enabled both those societies to participate in the molding of Canadian society. By initiating settlements in what is now Canada, they were able to establish and propagate their national influences in a foreign land. After France lost control of Canada to Britain, British influence became ascendant in Canada.

The paternalistic relationship between the countries of origin and Canada was thus established early on. It was later perpetuated by Canada's refusal to join the American colonies in their rebellion against England; in rejecting autonomy in favour of preserving her colonial ties, Canada maintained an intricate set of economic, political, and cultural dependencies.

The first shift in Canada's colonial orientation was from France to Britain. Following World War II, however, the decline of the British Empire and the emergence of the United States as a world power prompted another shift in colonial status. Even though Canada had become an independent political entity with loose ties to the British Commonwealth, the cultural and economic strength of its neighbour to the south (the United States) drew Canada into a new form of colonialism. But where the earlier form of colonialism had been direct and formal, the new colonialism was less so, though not necessarily any less powerful. The term *imperialism* is frequently used to describe this form of domination, in which the more powerful state uses whatever means necessary to extend its control beyond its borders in order to ensure its pre-eminent position. So, while colonialism implies political control, imperialism implies more subtle forms of influence and control (e.g., foreign corporations, resource control, fiscal indebtedness). The extent to which nations react to and participate in such control varies over time and is dependent on other global events. The analytical approach that views national societies in the context of global power differentials is known as *world systems theory*.[1] Basic to this theory is the idea that capitalism developed a world system of economic power, consisting of core societies, peripheral societies, and semi-peripheral societies. Core societies are highly industrialized and invest in societies weaker than themselves. Peripheral and semi-peripheral societies seek to emulate core societies through the adoption of economic, technological, and political systems and processes. Despite this imitation, peripheral societies remain subordinate to the core economic powers, which possess the capital needed for development. Because core societies need the markets, resources, and labour of the weaker societies, they tend to assume an expansionist posture. France, England, and Germany were core societies at the beginning of the twentieth century but were eventually superseded by the United States (among capitalist countries) and the USSR (among socialist ones). Canada is considered to be semi-peripheral because although it has an advanced infrastructure, it has fallen under the economic and cultural influence of one core society, the United States, and is subject to economic influence by other industrialized core societies (e.g., Germany, Japan). The world systems approach thus ties developments within Canadian society into an international framework.

From a sociological point of view, the significance of a subordinate position within the global system is that non-core societies are on the receiving end of a continuous transferring process known as *diffusion*. Diffusion is the transmission of economic forms, knowledge, traditions, or technology from one society to another. The originating society shares elements of its culture with the receiving one, resulting in increasing similarity between the two societies. Institutional and organizational linkages (e.g., unions, business franchises, professional associations, social clubs) serve as cultural pipelines from one society to another. Theoretically, diffusion is not a one-way process; through interaction with each other, societies share cultural traits to produce a *homogenization* of culture. But because of the greater strength of the core society in all aspects of its culture—economic, political, or recreational—the flow of influence tends to be unidirectional in a phenomenon known as *penetration*. The core society absorbs from the peripheral society what it prefers and what it needs, but influence predominantly flows in one direction. Because the core society possesses capital, technology, and information which other societies need, its dominant position is maintained.

The Staples Thesis

Harold Innis, writing before world systems theory was proposed, pointed out that Canadian society was founded upon staple industries established for export to empire societies.[2] Whether what they offered was cod fishing, trapping, lumbering, mining, or agriculture, Canadian hinterlands were developed for exploitation by external markets. From this perspective, Canadian society may be viewed as a series of resource-based communities centring around extractive processes and primary industries. Innis pointed out that the societal development that occurred along the St. Lawrence River and in Atlantic seaports was based upon trading in staples, such as fur or grain, that could be shipped to European metropoles. A protégé of Innis, S.D. Clark, has described the instability and boom-and-bust economies that were typical of these staple-based communities.[3] But Innis also showed how this Canada–Europe trade axis was later supplemented by a Canada–US axis as American industry and technology created new demand for Canadian staples. Innis felt that it was impossible to understand Canadian development without viewing its rich resources as commodities in demand by more industrialized nations. Recent years have seen a renewed interest in the staples thesis because Canada, although considered an industrial nation, possesses a truncated industrial base which is still highly dependent on natural resources. In contrast to the resources described by Innis, the new resources include minerals (e.g., nickel, potash), hydroelectric power, and of course oil and gas. Rex Lucas identified 636 single-industry communities in Canada.[4] Most of these communities are small (fewer than 8 000 people) and resource-based (e.g., mining, pulp-and-paper, smelting); often up to 75% of the labour force works in a single industry. The dependence of many Canadians on resource-based employment means that the staples thesis is an important way of understanding the society and its dependence on external forces.

There are two important aspects to a resource-based economy. First, much of the impetus, capital, and technology for resource exploitation come from core nations (particularly the United States at present, but also countries like Japan), resulting in a high degree of foreign ownership. Second, resource-based economies are highly vulnerable to market demand. When market demand increases, boom conditions prevail; when market conditions are poor, the result is poverty, unemployment, and displacement of population.[5] Thus a society heavily dependent on the extraction of resources for export will require a large blue-collar workforce and will lack the employment diversification necessary to achieve full industrial performance. In sum, when Canada exports raw materials to meet the industrial needs of other countries, it is exporting labour-intensive industrial jobs and is said to be caught in a *staples trap*. Core nations, such as Japan, the United States, and Germany, require natural resources to maintain their industrial base, and Canada needs those markets to maintain its productivity—even though this productivity is dependent on non-renewable resources. So while Canada reaps benefits by exporting its resources, it loses the benefits that could accrue were those resources to be used in Canadian industries

The autonomy issue goes beyond economic penetration or dependence; it involves politics, education, entertainment, and other aspects of culture. While many Canadians eagerly emulate core societies, others feel that such emulation is destructive of the society's own independence. Persons who oppose and seek to reduce foreign influences that threaten Canadian independence are called *nationalists*. *Continentalists*, on the other hand, minimize the importance of independence; they feel that because Canada shares the North American continent with the United States, it only makes sense that the two countries be closely integrated. Moreover, the many residents of Canada with ethnic or business ties outside North America have an even broader international scope. In its attitude towards autonomy, Canada usually vacillates between the positions of the nationalists and the continentalists, particularly in the matter of free trade.

FOCI OF THE AUTONOMY ISSUE

The Canadian dilemma is to determine how much foreign influence is acceptable. No society can be totally independent of other societies, but when is foreign influence harmful and when is it to be welcomed? Who is to decide when foreign influence is in a society's best

---

The Effect of Staples on Local Communities

It is possible to analyze the impact of resource extraction on local areas (and even entire societies) by distinguishing between *forward linkages* and *backward linkages*.

If, after a staple is harvested, it generates new jobs and economic benefits in the local area through value-added activity, then the staple is said to create forward linkages. If, after harvesting, the resource is shipped out of the area (or even the country) in its raw form and transformed into a finished product elsewhere, then the jobs generated by that staple accrue elsewhere.

Backward linkages refer to the production of machinery and supplies needed by the staple industry in the extraction process. If these items are shipped in from elsewhere ready for use, without benefit to the local area through the stimulation of employment and technology, then the staples create no backward linkages for the region.

Staple industries generate notoriously few forward or backward linkages for local or regional communities—sometimes even for the country as a whole—because they create little new employment or diversification. That is why staple industries produce hinterland effects.

Note: For an application of these principles, see Patricia Marchak, *Green Gold: The Forest Industry in British Columbia* (Vancouver: University of British Columbia Press, 1983).

interests? In what sectors of a society is foreign influence a more critical issue than in other sectors?

A *shadow society* is one whose independence and uniqueness is overshadowed by alien influences. In the late 1960s and early 1970s, concerted efforts were made to minimize that shadow. Most of these efforts focused on three issues: foreign ownership, the importation of skilled labour, and cultural penetration. While concern about these matters has abated somewhat, they continue to engage public debate at various points in time.

Foreign Ownership

Foreign ownership is not unique to Canadian society. However, the proportion of foreign ownership in Canada has traditionally been substantially higher than in other industrialized nations. Whether the issue has been the need for venture capital in order to exploit Canadian staple products to meet other countries' industrial demands or the opening of foreign corporations' Canadian subsidiaries (e.g., in manufacturing), foreign ownership has remained a matter of continuing significance.

There are two main ways in which foreign investment takes place in Canada: portfolio investment and direct investment. In *portfolio investment,* foreign money enters the country in the form of a repayable loan or a bond, which promises a fixed return but does not allow the investor direct control over the operation in which the investment is made. In

---

REAL PEOPLE 2	Hockey in the Heat: A New Canadian Export

Fort Worth, Texas—Reflections of a Southern Rink Rat

"When people here think about Canada, they think about two things: natural resources and hockey. We know all about oil and gas and minerals, and now we also know about hockey. They are all things you export, right?

It's 84 degrees Fahrenheit (about 27 degrees Celsius) and humid. The Fort Worth Brahmas are in the playoffs of the Western Professional Hockey League—a league consisting mostly of Texas cities. Almost all of the players are from Canada. But then so is the game. As they say, the only ice people know about here is the ice that keeps your drinks cold.

Hockey—a little bit of Canada in Texas. On the wall of the arena is a huge American flag. Right next to it hangs a small Canadian flag, less than one tenth the size of the American one. Nobody here knows what 'icing the puck' means. What's a power play? Nobody knows—yet.

Fort Worth was always known as 'Cowtown' because of its historic stockyards. Now the downtown is promoted as 'Wowtown,' with its 20-block Sundance Square of entertainment, restaurants, shopping, theatre, and galleries. Hockey has no cultural meaning in the American South. Now it is packaged as entertainment. When you talk about sports, people here live for football. So I just tell them hockey is like football on skates—lots of body contact and a fast pace. The Canadians that come down here sure put on a great show!"

direct investment, on the other hand, foreign money enters the country through a share-holder's ownership or acquisition of control. A shareholder can acquire minority or majority ownership either by acquiring a controlling interest or by wholly owning a subsidiary. Thus, through direct investment, foreign owners can come to possess decision-making power over a substantial proportion of the Canadian economy.

Prior to World War I, three quarters of the foreign investment in Canada was British. Much of this investment was of the portfolio type, although it has been pointed out that there was also a significant degree of direct investment.[6] By World War II and during the period immediately afterwards, most investment was American—primarily direct investment through the establishment of American subsidiaries in Canada. Capital also enters Canada as portfolio investments, particularly in the form of loans to help finance government deficits.[7] The periodic pilgrimages of provincial premiers to the New York money markets attest to this fact. But as we will see later, direct investment has expanded considerably in recent years.

Generally speaking, while portfolio investment may result in a distressing drain of money in the form of interest paid to investors outside the country, it is usually viewed as preferable to direct investment because ownership and control are retained within the country. Direct investment, on the other hand, represents a more palpable foreign presence. When all corporations operating in Canada are considered, the foreign component of all assets accounts for 22% to 30% of all operating revenue. About 14.9% of the total assets of Canada's financial/insurance corporations and 28% of the assets of the non-financial corporations are foreign-owned. Foreign control of Canadian non-financial corporations reached its peak at 37% of all assets in 1971, then declined to 23.4% by 1985 as a result of government and private acquisitions (primarily in mining and petroleum).[8] For example, the creation of federally owned Petro-Canada in 1975 led to the purchase of American-owned Atlantic Richfield and Pacific Petroleum and Belgian-owned Petrofina. The BC Resources Investment Corporation bought American-owned coal producer Kaiser Resources, and Canadian Pacific bought Dominion Bridge and Algoma Steel from German owners. Government policy throughout the '70s was to closely monitor foreign investment.

However, in recent years foreign ownership of both financial and non-financial corporations, as measured by assets, has once again been increasing (to 28% in 2002 [See Figure 2.1]), though not nearly to the levels of 1971. Some notable examples of acquisitions by US corporations include Amoco's purchase of floundering Dome Petroleum in the late '80s, Wal-Mart's purchase of all Canadian Woolco stores in the '90s, and just before the turn of the century, Weyerhaeuser's purchase of long-standing Canadian firm MacMillan Bloedel (itself having US interests) to form one of the world's largest integrated forest-products companies. Free-trade agreements produced a flurry of acquisitions and mergers. Changes in suppliers and differences in labour costs also produced industry rationalizations. The degree of foreign investment is probably underestimated in these statistics, as it is also possible for foreign corporations to be minority investors.[9] The fact that many Canadian corporations are listed on the New York Stock Exchange enhances the likelihood of foreign investment.

One way to measure foreign control is by determining the nationality of assets and profits. Figure 2.1 shows that foreign control is highest in the manufacturing sector, oil and gas extraction, and coal mining, and lowest in construction, utilities, agriculture, the arts and entertainment, and education and health care. Since about 22% of the assets of all industries are foreign-owned but 30% of all profits are distributed to foreign owners, foreign-owned industries garner more than their share of the profits.[10] The United States owns about 62%

of Canada's foreign-controlled assets and 67% of her foreign-controlled operating revenue, while Great Britain, Germany, and France combined own about 22%; this means that corporations from other countries control only the remaining 11%. It has been argued that American corporations operating in Canada are more profitable because they are equity- rather than debt-financed and are concentrated in industrial sectors where profit is highest (for example, profits are lower in utilities than they are in manufacturing).[11] Thus, the significance of foreign control has to do not only with the proportion of assets controlled but also with the nationality of the foreign owner and with the sector of concentration.

How has this high level of foreign ownership come about? Some, stressing Canada's hinterland status (as a supplier of staples to external metropolitan industrial centres) and focusing on the implicit power differential inherent in that status, have inferred that Canada had no choice. However, it has been argued that Canadian capitalists mediated the entry of foreign capital into Canada at times when domestic capital was either unwilling to risk venture capital on Canadian industrial companies or acquiesced to the superior technology of foreign corporations.[12] The result was that Canadian commercial capital pursued those industries in which profits were safest and, in eschewing riskier ventures, left a vacuum to be filled by foreign investors.

Gordon Laxer has noted that all arguments about foreign ownership usually end up with what he calls a "Canada-as-victim" perspective.[13] The emphasis on a staple-driven economy always lays stress on external pressures, Canadian vulnerability, and above all the absence of a strong export market for industrial products. Laxer points out that Canada did have a high ratio of exported manufactured goods in the late nineteenth century, especially in textiles and clothing, agricultural implements, and steel products. He notes that in the period prior to World War I a regression began to take place because of the tendency of

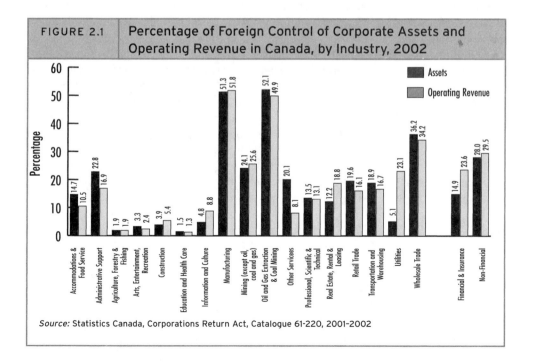

FIGURE 2.1 **Percentage of Foreign Control of Corporate Assets and Operating Revenue in Canada, by Industry, 2002**

Source: Statistics Canada, Corporations Return Act, Catalogue 61-220, 2001-2002

Canadian manufacturers, seeking to license technology from American firms, to enter into agreements that gave them rights only to the Canadian market. This trend ultimately led to American buyouts, with stringent restrictions against subsidiaries' competing with the parent company in the international marketplace.

Laxer notes that the reason that Canada did not benefit from the military industries of wartime was not merely the commercial banking sector's unwillingness to support industry, but Canada's decision to remain under British military tutelage. Furthermore, the decision to build expensive railroads increased foreign indebtedness (especially British portfolio investment). But more importantly, the politics of French–English sectionalism led conservative English-speaking business interests to accentuate British dependencies rather than take strategic action to become more independent—with the result that the liberalizing effects of Canadian popular-democratic movements (particularly among farmers) were minimized. The primary contribution of Laxer's important work on the factors responsible for foreign ownership has been to shift focus from external factors to dynamics and actions internal to the country. Other explanations of how and why foreign capital entered Canada will be discussed later in the chapter. The shift in emphasis from the role of foreign capital to that of indigenous capital will also be discussed in Chapter Three.

Among the reasons why foreign ownership is problematic is that large payments, in the form of dividends, interest, franchise fees, management and consulting fees, and research costs, are made annually to non-residents by corporations operating in Canada. The export of capital each year as payment to foreign owners affects exchange rates and removes capital from the country in which those monies were generated. So while foreign capital may initially have been needed to stimulate Canada's economic development, the export of made-in-Canada profits does not help the economy. Others point out that the problem of foreign ownership is exacerbated by the fact that the retention of profits in this country to enlarge equity ultimately means that profits made in Canada are used to increase the size of the foreign-controlled operation; in other words, retained earnings are used to increase the foreign presence.

During the late 1960s and early 1970s, a number of studies, including the Gray Report and the Task Force on the Structure of Canadian Industry, were commissioned to examine the issue of foreign ownership.[14] An organization called "The Committee for an Independent Canada" was established by persons interested in promoting economic repatriation and economic nationalism.[15] In the early '70s, the federal government established the Foreign Investment Review Agency (FIRA) to review and approve sales and transfers of corporations involving foreign capital. The Committee for an Independent Canada disbanded in 1981, and in 1985 FIRA was reorganized to be less restrictive and renamed "Investment Canada." As a government agency, Investment Canada represented the new federal approach of welcoming foreign investment while still reviewing the impact of larger investments on Canadian society. The free-trade era has led to a muting of much of the public concern over foreign ownership—in fact, as we will see, Canadian companies are themselves now investing in other countries—yet the issue has by no means been forgotten. It continues to surface in formal and informal ways, helping keep concern about societal autonomy alive.

Importation of Skilled Labour

For much of Canada's history, the country has experienced both a *labour drain* and a *brain drain*. The industrialization of the New England states created strong employment demands in that area's textile and manufacturing industries and led many Canadians to emigrate to the United States. Other urban opportunities that arose elsewhere in the United States (prior to the growth of industrial opportunities in Canada) contributed to the ongoing population drain. Furthermore, many of Canada's best students received their education at prestigious institutions in Britain, France, and (particularly) the United States, and frequently remained in those countries when faced with a lack of opportunity in Canada. Even those educated here, if offered work in those core countries, took advantage of the more varied occupational possibilities. The same process of temporary or permanent emigration has occurred in athletics, entertainment, the sciences, medicine, and various forms of entrepreneurship. Attracted by new challenges in the United States, even such prominent Canadians as the economist John Kenneth Galbraith, American Broadcasting Corporation's news anchorman Peter Jennings, and entertainer Celine Dion have left the country to advance their careers.

The 1960s were a time of enormous change in Canadian society. Post-war industrial expansion reached its apex, universities grew rapidly, and student enrollment increased dramatically. New opportunities abounded and out-migration dropped significantly. In fact, the lack of adequate manpower in Canada resulted in a government policy of liberal immigration designed to attract skilled migrants into the country. University faculty, medical doctors, scientists, accountants, etc., willingly migrated to Canada, not only from the war-ravaged countries of Europe but also (owing to stresses created by the war in Vietnam and urban social tensions) from the United States.[16] Throughout the rest of that decade and part of the next, Canada's manpower needs were met to a significant degree by an influx of immigrants that some have nicknamed the *brain swamp* and *labour swamp*.

However, just as the foreign-ownership issue heightened awareness of foreign-capital intrusion, it also raised the question of whether to continue the policy of importing foreign labour. Young Canadian university graduates, facing unattractive emigration prospects and expressing a preference to find employment in Canada, pressured the government to be much more restrictive in its immigration policies.[17] Immigration rules were tightened considerably during the 1970s and tightened still further in the early 1980s as the recession increased unemployment. Technically, immigration regulations now require employers to extensively advertise available positions to Canadians first, but a variety of mechanisms exist to bring skilled/professional labour into the country. Furthermore, persons applying to immigrate to Canada are usually given priority if they possess needed skills. A recent OECD study has pointed out that the United States is not the only magnet in the brain trade: Canada also is a net importer of human capital, particularly of highly skilled professionals in information technology—a siphoning-off of talent which harms other less-developed countries.[18] It is interesting that Canadians feel most threatened when immigrants are perceived as taking the jobs to which they aspire. If an immigrant takes a labouring job, such as working on the kill floor of a packing plant or doing janitorial work, not much of an issue is made of it. Yet employers' desire to fill specialized personnel needs by importing leading people with special talents or simply new people with new ideas has sometimes sparked controversy over whether Canadians are being bypassed for available positions. Corporations, professional sports teams, arts groups, religious organizations, and the scientific community constantly struggle with issues related to the availability of Canadian talent, their own organizational goals, and foreign expertise that they might like to acquire. Thus, although on the one hand it is thought that Canadian society should be self-sufficient in supplying its own manpower, public debate is often intense when others, in view of globalizing pressures, argue for a less restrictive policy.

Cultural Penetration

At the root of the question of who should be given employment priority within the society lies a fundamental concern about defending national culture. The concept of *cultural penetration* suggests that more dominant core societies flood Canadian society with foreign influence against the national will and in the face of little apparent defence. While there is a real sense in which this is true, the one-way diffusion process is, ironically, also welcomed. For example, Canadians enjoy American movies and American entertainers and consider access to American television programming almost a right. Any restriction of access to such "foreign" aspects of popular culture would clearly be resisted.[19] This ambivalence creates paradoxical situations, as exemplified by the attempts of the Canadian Radio-television and Telecommunications Commission (CRTC) to increase opportunities for "Canadian" artists and production while at the same time increasing the accessibility of cable networks that bring American television into Canada.[20]

Clearly the proximity of the United States means that American cultural influences will be strong. The real issue appears to be not so much whether these foreign cultural elements should be allowed into Canada but whether their presence inhibits the emergence of an indigenous Canadian culture.[21] Perhaps the most well-known instance of this debate erupted in the magazine industry (about 50% of the magazines sold in Canada are pro-

---

Canadian Content and Canadian Culture

In Canada, almost all of the sound-recording, television, and film industries with high-volume sales are foreign-owned. Smaller Canadian companies do produce recordings, but with smaller sales.

Foreign programming accounts for about two thirds of all television programming watched by Canadians. This percentage would be even higher if francophones were removed from the calculation, as foreign programming is more likely to be in English and francophones are more likely to watch French programs. In fact, only 4% of comedy programming, 7% of dramas, and 10% of variety and game shows watched by anglophones are Canadian. However, news and sports programs are more likely to be Canadian—about two thirds for anglophones, but a much higher 77% (sports) and 97% (news) for francophones.

In order to encourage more Canadian content, federal regulations were established in 1971 that supported this aspect of Canadian culture. At least 30% of all music aired by Canadian AM stations must either be composed, written, or performed by a Canadian, or be performed live or wholly recorded in Canada. Such content must be played between the hours of 6:00 a.m. and 7:00 p.m., Monday through Friday. On television, Canadian content must fill at least 60% of the overall schedule. While many Canadians have access to American stations, the ultimate goal of these regulations was to ensure that Canadian stations would offer distinctively Canadian programming.

Source: Jeffrey Frank and Michel Durand, "Canadian Content in the Cultural Marketplace," *Canadian Social Trends* Vol. 2 (Toronto: Thompson Educational Publishing, 1994), 297-300.

duced in the United States) over what is known as *split-run editions* (See "Canadian" Magazines and Globalization: Split-Run Editions below). This issue first surfaced in 1976, when Parliament passed Bill C-58, taking away the financial advantages of American-based *Time* magazine, which was printing a split-run Canadian edition, and giving those advantages to the Canadian newsmagazine *Maclean's*. Specifically, this Bill made it no longer possible for Canadian advertisers to deduct the costs of advertising in *Time*; this measure in effect channelled those advertising dollars to the Canadian magazine, helping it become a viable operation. Some critics hurled the epithet "dictatorship" at the government and claimed loss of freedom; the government, however, responded that *Time* was certainly still available for purchase in Canada in its American edition, but that it was important that Canadians should have the opportunity to see themselves and others through their own eyes rather than through those of reporters and editors representing other societies with different agendas.[22]

Government policies have also been devised to encourage other aspects of Canadian culture. The CRTC has the power to approve all foreign-based channels (recently, for example, it approved the Fox News network) and ensures that Canadian sports (TSN) are available on television rather than only US sports (ESPN). Government policy also requires that symphony orchestras receiving federal grants (usually crucial for their fiscal survival) play a certain proportion of Canadian music and use Canadian artists in order to retain their funding. While some complain that Canadian composers do not even remotely compare with Beethoven or Bach ("so why must we listen to Canadian music?"), others argue that unless Canadians give their own composers a chance, creative talent will be stifled within the society and Canadian culture will never develop.

Perhaps even more threatening to Canadian culture are digital satellite service (which will give Canadians access to a huge number of foreign radio and television stations) and the information highway, which have given rise to renewed concerns about the protection of Canadian culture. In all of these instances, foreign ownership and Canadian content are recurring issues brought before the Canadian government and its agencies for action.

"Canadian" Magazines and Globalization: Split-Run Editions

Are "Canadian" magazines an aspect of *culture*, i.e., an element of a way of life that should be protected? Or are such magazines a cultural *commodity*, i.e., an aspect of trade? How you answer this question reflects how you feel about split-run editions of foreign magazines.

American magazines are published essentially for the American market. Their news stories are selected and edited with the American market in mind. Their advertisers are largely American companies, and advertisements are pitched to American readers. Their editorial policies reflect American issues and perspectives. Their revenues and expenses are predicated on their domestic sales.

A split-run edition provides a magazine with the opportunity to add a small amount of Canadian news while otherwise retaining most of the American content, and then to sell the magazine as a Canadian edition. Expanded readership in Canada allows the magazine to obtain more revenues because of expanded sales to American advertisers who do business in the Canadian market. The Canadian edition may also be attractive to Canadian advertisers, who may be offered lower advertising rates because the major costs of production have already been covered in the American edition. At little additional cost, the American magazine thus gains entry into the Canadian market, reaping increased profits through additional sales and advertising.

From a Canadian point of view, split-run editions pose three problems. One is the fact that Canadian magazines lose advertising revenue which would otherwise accrue to them; a related fact is that because the basic costs of Canadian magazines (unlike split-run editions) are not covered, their advertising rates must remain high, which makes them uncompetitive for the advertising dollar. The second problem is that Canadians reading split-run editions obtain their news through an American lens, which may not focus on issues and persons specifically relevant to Canadians. The third problem is that split-run editions reduce jobs (editorial, advertising, production) in the Canadian publishing industry.

Among the most high profile split-run American magazines in Canada are *Time*, *Newsweek*, and *Sports Illustrated*.

In response to American complaints, the Geneva-based World Trade Organization ruled in 1997 that Canada's policy contravened international trade agreements (the General Agreement on Tariffs and Trade—GATT) that prohibit discrimination in the trade of goods. The argument was that split-run editions were not a cultural issue, and that Bill C-58 was in reality protection for powerful publishing interests in Canada (e.g., Rogers Communications, which publishes *Maclean's* and *Chatelaine*). Canadian representatives countered by pointing out that it was also powerful publishing interests in the United States (e.g., Time-Warner, Hearst) that were behind the opposition. In 1999 Canada proposed Bill C-55, which again attacked split-run editions; the Americans responded by threatening trade sanctions in lumber, steel, and textiles. After negotiation with the American government, the government decided to allow split-run editions to carry only up to 18% Canadian advertising per issue; this decision, however, was also attacked, so the government used postal subsidies as a way of giving preferential treatment to Canadian magazines.

While the battle to defend Canadian culture appeared valiant, international trade agreements prevailed, apparently because these magazines were deemed commodities. But more recently, state control has also become problematic: Developments in information technology have made the transmission of magazine content via satellite and phone lines so rapid and so hidden that it easily bypasses any regulations.

Further Reading: Sarah Armstrong, "Magazines, Cultural Policy and Globalization: The Forced Retreat of the State?" *Canadian Public Policy* 26, 3 (2000): 369-85.

These are but a few examples of a counteroffensive that has become a trademark of Canadian society: government intervention, even in the field of the arts and popular culture, to strengthen Canadian culture in the face of foreign influence. This intervention, which has varied among different federal governments, generally focuses on increasing Canadian content. Whether what is at stake is the labour component in the manufacture of an automobile or the number of songs by Canadian artists played on a radio station, *Canadian content* refers to the proportion of Canadian participation in an activity. Even though government guidelines or regulations involve a degree of "forced choice" which is obviously controversial, intervention designed to promote a significant Canadian cultural presence has a long history of public acceptance.

It is true that Canadian culture has traditionally been thought to be too weak and poorly organized to withstand the power of American cultural industries. Attempts to change this perpetual condition have focused on internal measures to improve cultural productivity. These internal measures, however, are largely a response to the external cultural influences of other societies (particularly the United States) which are viewed as threatening to societal autonomy.[23]

FACTORS CONSTRAINING SELF-DETERMINATION

The historical causes of Canadian society's dependency can be located in the country's strong linkages with core societies. As a young and expanding society possessing few indigenous traditions, Canadian society, while striving to forge its own independence, has endured repeated struggles against rather formidable odds. In spite of trying to be the centre of its own universe, Canadian society has been continually pulled like a satellite into the gravitational orbit of more dominant societies. Rocher noted that such satellite status makes a society peripheral, unbalanced, and inhibited.[24] Decisions made elsewhere and over which it has little control impinge on the society. Efforts to exert control are at best only partially effective, and the feeling persists that the satellite society is inferior to the real centres of power and influence. While the way the world is organized is changing due to internationalizing forces, Canadians have repeatedly struggled with a sense of being subordinate or dependent as the result of being on the margins of power. Why is this so? Five factors contributing to this dependency will be discussed.

1. The Era of the American Empire

It has already been suggested that in its relationship with core societies, Canada started out with old-style colonialism in its ties to France and Britain and has proceeded to neocolonialism in its ties with the United States. What all three of these core countries have in common is that they have each been a dominant global force during a certain period. The concept of *empire* suggests groups of nations, people, states, or territories united under the direction of a dominant power.[25] Throughout history, groups of states have occasionally been united under the influence of a more dominant state, through direct administrative and military subordination, or through loose allegiances and mercantile ties, or both. The Roman Empire, for example, tied a vast territory together through a common language, technological leadership, military strength, mercantile coordination, and rule of the seas. Similarly, the French settlement around the St. Lawrence River was part of an expansion of military influence and mercantile strength that saw France establish colonial ties all over the new world. Colonials taught indigenous peoples their language and drew their marketable products into the empire economy.

The British also experienced an era of empire expansion during which they extended their influence far beyond their small island territory. With a strong naval and mercantile fleet, they "ruled the waves" and the territories beyond. The decline of the British Empire has been followed by the rise of the American empire, whose military, industrial, and technological strength have made it a dominant global power and brought much of the world under its direct or indirect influence. In many ways, American dominance has only increased with the end of the Cold War, so that in spite of other moderating forces, the whole world has become America's empire.

From a conceptual point of view, all empires have a core society that establishes and sustains directions of influence. The language of the core society becomes the major vehicle of communication among all societies within the empire. The core society dispatches its members to teach societies under its influence the technologies and skills needed to improve their productivity. It attracts promising leaders from other societies to be trained in its schools and absorb its culture. Through its technology and industry, it establishes interdependencies with these other societies, which provide markets, desired resources, or products. Its marketing apparatus fosters the widespread distribution of its goods and its culture.

While some would argue that the American empire has begun to go into eclipse or that it is being replaced by huge trading blocs such as the European Community,[26] there is no doubt that the United States is a core society. It has absorbed the best technologies developed elsewhere and promises prestige and handsome financial rewards to scientists, entertainers,

---

"McDonaldization"

There is a new way to describe the global impact of Americanization and it is known as *McDonaldization*. Springing from the fast-food industry, which got its start in the United States, McDonaldization is different from "cocacolonization" in that it refers not just to the exportation of products but to the United States' role in creating, producing, and exporting new means of consumption.

McDonaldization stands for a rationalization process that emphasizes efficiency, predictability, calculability, control, and homogeneity at any outlet. Bright colours and seats are designed to keep traffic moving. It saturates first the American market and then seeks to expand globally. On an annual basis, McDonald's is now opening more outlets internationally than in the United States.

McDonaldization focuses on the globe as the unit of analysis. It exports American eating styles, making minor adaptations to fit the local culture. For example, in Norway a grilled salmon sandwich, called a *McLak*, appears on the menu. In Uruguay, a burger with a poached egg is called a *McHuevo*. In the Philippines, tomato sauce with frankfurter bits make *McSpaghetti*. Nevertheless, the base menu is always the same and is standardized. Other retailers and food companies are seeking to follow the same model.

Source: George Ritzer, *The McDonaldization Thesis* (Thousand Oaks: Sage, 1998), Chapter 7.

athletes, and other leaders in their fields who participate in that society. Decisions made in the United States, as a centre of capital control, automatically affect other societies. Promising students from abroad are attracted to American educational institutions; these students return to their own societies as decision makers, frequently taking American culture back with them. The distribution network is effective and elaborate, and American manufactured products have been made available in many countries—a process known as *cocacolonization*.[27] American influence currently prevails throughout much of the world and is particularly strong in Canada because of the geographic proximity of the two countries.

It is important to stress the current position of the United States as a dominant *world* power lest it be assumed that the pervasiveness of American influence is a uniquely Canadian concern. American cultural influence—through books, films, magazines, television, and entertainers—is intertwined with American capital and American technological and military influence. American presidential elections or American space launches are as newsworthy in Sweden and Germany as they are in Canada. While the current influence of the United States is virtually a universal factor, there are clear signs that the empire is changing or breaking down under new forces of globalization. Yet despite this shift, Canadian society, for a variety of reasons, continues to exhibit markedly weak resistance to American economic and cultural penetration.

2. Continentalism

The presence of a global power (e.g., the United States) at one's border must be considered a factor of special importance. It is natural for bordering nations to establish both formal and informal patterns of interaction over common interests. Californians love Banff in the summer while Ontarians love Florida in the winter. Wheat farmers in Kansas and Saskatchewan share common technologies and work styles. Religious groups interact across the border, sometimes with common organizations.[28] Leisure organizations, such as Shriners, Masons, and even barbershop singing groups, cross the border. Americans and Canadians both drive the same brands of cars. Fast-food franchises are similar and sports leagues cross the border. There are many other examples of the ongoing integration of the two major societies on the North American continent.[29]

And yet the relationship is frequently lopsided. Canadians are often appalled at American ignorance of Canada, and the two countries' perceptions of each other are sometimes filled with inaccurate stereotypes. Canadian society is affected by political and economic policies established in Washington, where decision makers either do not understand or dismiss Canadian concerns. For example, the decision to allow interest rates to rise in the United States forces interest rates to rise even higher in Canada because of Canadian dependence on US money markets. A metaphor which has frequently been used to describe the relationship between the two countries is "the mouse and the elephant": The mouse (Canada) exists independently of the elephant (the United States), but must be ever alert to the elephant's movements because virtually every twitch affects it. Another metaphor is "life with uncle" (alluding to the nickname for the United States, "Uncle Sam"), which suggests the United States' paternalistic relationship to Canada.[30]

The increasing economic interaction between the two countries (free trade will be discussed later in this chapter); the sharing of a common language (except French); the participation of both countries in common sports leagues, such as baseball and hockey; and the sharing of common defence interests (e.g., NORAD) are just some of the factors that

---

RESEARCH CLIP 2.1	**American War Resistance and Canadian Sovereignty**

The Iraq War brought out an interesting dilemma related to the ramifications of the fact that Canada and the United States have different policies. This is not a new problem; at the time of the American War of Independence, many British Empire Loyalists left the United States and moved to Canada. Should American war resisters be allowed or encouraged to relocate to Canada?

The Vietnam War in the late 1960s produced the greatest flood of politically motivated American migrants to Canada since the Loyalists. Between 1965 and 1973, approximately 50 000 young Americans moved to Canada in opposition to the war and to the draft which made military service compulsory. Some were "draft dodgers" (escaping before they were to be drafted), some were military deserters, and others were fleeing other aspects of US policy. Women were just as likely to flee to Canada as men. During that time period, it was possible to apply for landed-immigrant status either at the border or once in Canada.

One of the big questions was, What should Canadian government policy be about admitting people who had broken the law in the United States? Were these people truly exiles or refugees?

Canada ultimately resolved the dilemma by shifting the way such resisters were defined: from irresponsible and undesirable lawbreakers to people of conscience. This solution was made possible by framing the issue as a matter of national sovereignty: Canadian decisions should be made independent of American law and Canada had a right to a different foreign policy. At the same time, the issue was touchy because Canada risked offending the United States.

Source: John Hagan, *Northern Passage: American Vietnam War Resisters in Canada* (Cambridge: Harvard University Press, 2001).

---

contribute to greater continentalism and the blurring of societal boundaries (or at least to the increased exposure of Canadians to things American). Many Canadians prefer American television shows and are totally unaware of the nationality of the shows they are watching. Exposure to American sitcoms leads to an almost unconscious blending of Canadian ideas and values with American ones, making the two difficult to differentiate. Even Canadian newspapers, on a daily basis, feature both hard news and human-interest stories about the United States. Thus American cultural influence is far more subtle than economic and political influence.

One of the most overlooked aspects of continental integration is the Canadian investment of capital in the United States—a reversal of the usual pattern of American investment in Canada. Jorge Niosi discovered that Canada, somewhat surprisingly, has been a capital-exporting country for many years.[31] On a per capita basis, Canadians invest almost as much outside their country as Americans do. Such companies as Alcan Aluminum, Bata Shoes, Cominco, Nortel Networks, Polysar, and Seagram are major international players. Niosi discovered that over the years the significant thing about Canadian investment has been that it has had little Canadian technological content, as demonstrated by the fact that the percentage of patents registered in Canada to local residents was one of the lowest in the world. In other words, Canadian investors used technology developed elsewhere to a greater degree than expected and therefore did not own the technology they used. Thus, historically (with only some exceptions), Canadian foreign investment did not represent the application of Canadian technology in other countries but largely represented the application and management of American technology. However, there are strong indications that this pattern is changing, as Canadian innovations in such areas as telecommunications and software are penetrating the US market.

Because of limitations in the size of the Canadian economy and the desire for corporate growth, Canadian subsidiaries in the US have recently become quite active in such cities as Minneapolis and Denver, and in growth areas in the American South.[32] For example, Montreal-based Nortel Networks expanded into the United States because it already controlled 70% of the Canadian market and was looking for new productivity gains. Canadian investments in US property and real-estate developments, such as shopping centres and office towers, have also been significant. While such investments are sizeable, they are certainly not of the proportional magnitude of American capital flow into Canada. Nevertheless, these examples illustrate another aspect of continental integration which, as a consequence of free-trade thinking, is increasing significantly.

Airport Pre-clearance: American Jurisdiction in Canada

One of the most intriguing peculiarities of Canadian–American relations is the fact that in seven Canadian international airports, American Customs and Immigration officials are based and act almost as if they were on US soil. *Pre-clearance* refers to the performance in Canada of clearance duties normally conducted at the American border. Hundreds of American officials reside in Canada to help process the thousands of travellers proceeding to the United States by air.

Pre-clearance is performed as a convenience to air travellers, permitting them to enter the United States directly at the time of departure, thereby avoiding clearance at the American destination. This is particularly important for passengers making connections in the United States. For example, a flight from Toronto to Houston may require a stop or a change of planes in Dallas.

Pre-clearance obviates any delays at a stopover point and speeds up connections, which is beneficial to American carriers in particular. Pre-clearance is also useful when Customs and Immigration officers are not stationed at smaller destinations.

Major Canadian airports with transborder routes must reserve a significant amount of space for the operations of American authorities. In a strange way, then, US laws are administered in Canada, though any criminal matters must be dealt with by Canadian authorities. US Customs and Immigration halls in Canadian airports are adorned with US murals and pictures, and passengers are welcomed by the US Department of Homeland Security. This phenomenon is probably unique in the world, but is another illustration of the special relationship between Canada and the United States.

Although continentalism is in many ways inevitable, it repeatedly raises the question of autonomy for a society unsure of its independence. Particularly in earlier stages of Canadian development, government has frequently intervened to facilitate east–west interaction within Canada (rather than the continentalism-promoting north–south interaction). For example, the Canadian Broadcasting Corporation (CBC) was established by the government with an explicit mandate to foster greater national understanding and knowledge of matters of general societal interest. The establishment of railroads (CNR/Via Rail) and airlines (Air Canada) also reflected a government mandate to facilitate communication within the society. Taking a *key sector approach* to the issue of foreign control, government has always sponsored communication links as an important mechanism of societal interaction. One of the most interesting recent examples of this function was the role the CBC played in 2004 in creating national interest and debate about who was "The Greatest Canadian."

Disagreement often rages, however, about the role the federal government should play in sustaining national unity. In recent years, for example, reduced public subsidies to the Canadian Broadcasting Corporation (among other enterprises) threaten this historic Canadian institution; what is more, the belief that Crown corporations should be turned over to the private sector has led to the sale of Air Canada. Indeed, the general shift to privatization, and the abrogation of government responsibility in these areas of historical national key-sector concern, have eroded the countervailing influence that had always been considered necessary to thwart continentalist pressures. Thus, in spite of growing maturity as a society, Canada continues to face major questions raised by the integrating dynamic of continentalism.

3. The Multinational/Transnational Corporation

The third factor accentuating the issue of autonomy for Canadian society has been the activity of huge multinational corporations. Committed to profit and to their own expansion, these corporations cross national boundaries and make decisions that affect the economies and standard of living in whichever countries they operate. Multinationals, along with their conglomerates, holding companies, and subsidiaries, effectively challenge the nation-state as the type of social organization most characteristic of the post-industrial world. Their capital growth, reflected in increased assets and profits, promotes their growth in power, which they can express by providing employment and handsome benefits as a reward for loyalty. The primary advantage of this form of organization is that the parent company's home office can manipulate its resources from country to country in order to maximize its net gain. Although the state may attempt to establish rules whereby it can control the multinational's operation in that country, the fact that multinationals can transfer their resources to other, more cooperative countries considerably reduces the control of the state.[33] Thus, for our purposes, the significant fact about multinational corporations is that they are *transnational*; i.e., they operate within national boundaries but follow an ethic in which profit transcends national concerns.

What are some of the ways a multinational corporation can exercise its unique flexibility? It can move its capital or use its borrowing power to establish new ventures in locations of its choosing. It can use the profits generated in one country to subsidize an operation in another country. It can move its own pool of skilled labour or management to new locations. It can bargain with governments competing against each other for the establishment or expansion of new operations. More specifically, through the use of subsidiaries, the parent company can use its massive resources to reduce or destroy competition by underpricing other domestic operations or by purchasing the products of subsidiaries below market value while domestic competitors must purchase the product at market cost.[34] Because the multinational is transnational, it can create a book loss in one country in order to reduce taxes there and shift funds and profits to a more favourable location. Thus, the desire of political units to retain or acquire the capital and technology of the corporation and the ensuing employment benefits for its citizens can lead to the state's general acquiescence to corporate demands and needs. Some view these corporations as the newest form of imperialism, while others see them as the most practical solution to world order because of the present plurality of many small interdependent nation-states.[35] The power of multinational corporations threatens the autonomy and control of national societies. It is not surprising, given the strength of the American economic empire, that many of these multinational corporations have been American, whether operating in Canada or elsewhere in the world. Yet multinationals based in other countries are both active and growing, as money is moved to take advantage of new opportunities and as corporate strategies change.[36] But whether the corporation is Japanese, German, or American, only the nationality is different, not the principles by which multinational corporations operate.

What problems do the multinational corporations raise for Canadian society? One problem is the tendency towards *truncation*, which occurs because a subsidiary seldom performs all the major functions which a major corporation requires for its operation. For example, scientific research, commonly referred to as *R & D* (research and development), and marketing are operations that are vital to the existence of the subsidiary but that are often centralized in one country by the parent firm. While the branch plant may provide employment for residents of Canada, truncation contributes to the technology and professionalization gaps by reducing the demand for such trained personnel in Canada. For example, a multinational American-based tire company might decide that it only needs one research site and decide to locate it in the United States, closer to its head office. Truncation may be tolerated in the early stages of a subsidiary's development, but once it becomes established, it perpetuates restricted professional-employment growth in Canada.

Another problem with the multinational corporation is that the government of the country in which the home office is located may attempt to put controls on the corporation's operations regardless of where it operates. This control is known as *extraterritoriality*.[37] While an internationally operating corporation may have no single national allegiance, its operation may be bound by the home country's regulations, which can interfere with the interests of the subsidiary country. For example, the United States has had a law called the *Trading with the Enemy Act*, which prohibited American companies or their subsidiaries from doing business with countries identified as enemies of the United States. Cuba was such a country for many years, and the Act was invoked in order to block the sale of Canadian-made locomotives to Cuba (the Montreal firm manufacturing the locomotives was owned by a majority shareholder corporation in New Jersey). While the sale eventually went through, this instance illustrates how jobs and general industrial expansion can be thwarted by an extension of the laws of foreign countries. More recently, when a Canadian company called Bow Valley Energy signed an agreement with the government of Iran to build oil wells in the Persian Gulf, the United States referred to their Iran–Libya Sanctions Act, which called for trade sanctions against any country that invested in Iran's petroleum sector.

A third problem with multinationals is that Canadian subsidiaries may be prevented from increasing their productivity if they are prohibited from seeking export markets. In this practice, known as *export blocking*, the parent firm may not allow the subsidiary to compete for foreign contracts because either the parent firm or another of its subsidiaries does not want competition in a market that it also wants to enter. Given the fact that increased exports mean more jobs in Canada, lost exports mean lost jobs.

The federal government has sought to counter the slipperiness of multinationals not only by creating rules and regulations but also by establishing incentives. One such incentive is a *Canadian content component* in certain contracts (i.e., "we will buy your product if a certain proportion of the labour you use is Canadian or if you use materials produced in this country"). A second type of incentive is an *interest subsidy,* given to purchasers of Canadian products. The sale of 825 subway cars made by Montreal's Bombardier company to New York City was successful largely because the Canadian government offered financing to New York at interest rates well below the prevailing prime rate. A related method is to require any major Canadian project receiving federal financial support to maintain a certain level of Canadian-made materials and/or labour. This is known as *industrial offsets,* because it gives specialized contracts to foreign companies with the proviso that the company turn other aspects of its business into Canadian production. Ironically, the sale of subway cars to New York was subject to a US "Buy American" law which resulted in Bombardier establishing a subsidiary in Vermont.

One other possible method of exerting some control over multinationals is a *unitary tax* that minimizes the advantages of the bookkeeping shifts practised by multinationals. The government determines what percentage of a company's business is conducted in its territory, then taxes the company based on that percentage of the parent-company's worldwide profits. In all of these methods, the goal is to mitigate, in the national interest, the adverse effects of the practices of multinational corporations.

A fourth problem multinationals present to a society is that they often move their personnel between countries in response to the requirements of the corporate structure. Transfers in and out of various countries accord with the corporate mentality of loyalty and devotion to the corporation. In her research, Levitt found that some Canadians employed by multinationals have been promoted through the ranks to managerial positions in subsidiaries around the world.[38] House, on the other hand, found that petroleum multinationals have tried to "Canadianize" their subsidiaries' management in this country as much as possible.[39] The point is that persons working for multinationals are likely to be good corporate employees who have no objections to the nature of their corporate structure as long as they are treated well. Thus, large corporations that operate transnationally establish their own set of loyalties which may or may not be in tune with national concerns and societal goals.[40]

A final problem that multinationals present to national societies is their tendency to contribute to the *homogenization of culture.* The Gray Report speaks of the subsidiary as a "continuous transmission belt" of culture in general.[41] Examining the new values, beliefs, and other influences that have emerged in the city of Galt, Ontario, Perry discovered a "subculture of subsidiaries."[42] The duplication of products and commercials (especially advertising jingles), for example, contributes to cultural similarity. One explanation of this phenomenon will be offered in the next section.

4. Relatively Small Population

The impact of continentalism and international corporatism is at least partially related to the fact that Canada has a population which is only one tenth the size of that of the United

States and which is dispersed throughout a vast territory. This fact has produced a collective feeling of comparative weakness in the face of the large-scale capital, bigger organizations, and greater diversity and specialization of the society to our south. These feelings have left many groups open to the support to be gained by linkage with American organizations, and also make foreign penetration that much easier.

At the economic level, the relatively small Canadian population means a small domestic market, in which economies of scale sometimes cannot be practised. Until 1879, when the federal government approved the establishment of a protective tariff, small Canadian industrial operations struggled to compete with American industries importing into Canada.[43] Regrettably, the establishment of a protective tariff did little to stimulate Canadian investment in the manufacturing sector. Canadian capitalists were reluctant to invest in relatively inefficient Canadian industries, favouring investment in the finance, transportation, and utility sectors of the economy. This left the door open for foreign capital to establish manufacturing branch plants in Canada, which brought with them their proven product lines, technology, and experience. The protective tariff ensured that foreign corporations would have to service their Canadian market through Canadian plants, turning out product lines identical to those in the United States in what is known as the *miniature replica effect*.

Operating on a smaller scale because of the smaller domestic market and insulated from competition because of the tariff walls, Canadian branch plants' production costs were higher than those of their American parents. However, the tariff gave Canadian producers an additional margin (the tariff charge) by which their product's price could be increased and yet still be competitive. Canadians, therefore, were likely to pay more for products identical to those produced in the United States; moreover, because of these

Signs That Tell a Story

"United States Dollar Accounts Available. Now banking in the USA and Canada is as accessible as your favourite desk chair"
—*sign in the window of a bank*

"Celebrate Canada Week, February 10–17"
—*ad in a Florida newspaper*

"This advertisement is directed to Canadian citizens and permanent residents only"
—*employment notice in the bulletin of a professional association*

"The Royal Visit . . . Get Your Souvenir Pictorial Book Today"
—*sign in a bookshop*

"Here is a great buy this week. Canada No. 1 California tomatoes $1.52 a kilogram."
—*radio station ad*

"US cash now available at this banking machine. Chinese language option also available."
—*sign at a banking machine in Canada*

higher prices, surplus products could not enter the world market. But what the branch plants provided was employment for Canadians in the industrial sector, which, as we have seen, became foreign-owned with the agreement of indigenous capital.[44] In this context, Clement has referred to Canada as "a mature branch plant society."

The availability of similar products in both Canada and the United States helps to support cultural homogeneity. Smaller-scale Canadian operations in the economic sector (or in social organizations or leisure activities) frequently look to larger enterprises in the United States for cooperation in their mutual concerns. The emulation or modification of American procedures is frequently practised in many sectors of society, and formal or informal ties are maintained. More than that, the branch-plant organizational structure produces a branch-plant mentality, in which initiative, ambition, and creativity are suppressed in deference to the dominant society.[45] While there is no doubt that these "branch-plant" effects remain significant within Canadian society, it is also true that their impact has been transformed in more recent years by the forces of globalization, especially free trade. More and more, instead of branch plants and the miniature replica effect, Canadian companies are producing a limited range of product lines for the whole continent in a process known as *continental rationalization*.[46] Of course, the corollary of this development is that other products may not be manufactured in Canada at all anymore, leaving the Canadian market to be serviced from the United States or elsewhere. The end result is still dependence on foreign capital.

5. Globalization

There are many forces at work promoting global integration. At the economic level, there are free-trade or trading blocs, mobile international capital and multinational corporations, and global marketing of products and culture. At the communications level, there are computers, the World Wide Web, faxes, and all kinds of new technologies which eliminate the problems of distance which formerly represented enormous barriers between societies. *Globalization* means increased access to all parts of the world for whatever purposes. But globalization also means the creation of new international bodies and regulators (e.g., World Trade Organization, European Union, NAFTA) beyond the nation-state to foster such intersocietal interaction. Globalization suggests that nation-states are increasingly facing a transfer of powers and loss of control, and is the other side of the glocalism or glocalization thesis presented in Chapter One.[47] The earlier discussion pointed out that regional or local identities and collective action are a response to weakened political states; here it is argued that this weakening of states is the result of the transfer of powers to supra-national structures, which threatens the traditional control of the nation-state.

A strong case can be made that the future of nation-states may be at risk, or at least that their role may undergo a significant transformation. *Glocalization* suggests that the international economy allows local communities to become much more assertive because, as a result of now being directly linked to the world economy, they no longer need the old national political structures to ensure their economic well-being. Quebec, for example, has already argued that whatever form of independence they may seek would always be in association with the global economy and that they have no intention of isolating themselves from their economic partners. As we will see, other places, such as Scotland and Wales, are experiencing the same process.

RESEARCH CLIP 2.2	**Forestry as a Staple Product: Globalization and Industry Restructuring**

Northern countries (including Canada) still produce most of the world's lumber, pulp, and paper but cannot meet the global demand. Therefore countries in the southern hemisphere (e.g., Brazil) have been subjected to rapid deforestation through industrial logging; they have also provided locations for forest plantations because their climate supports more rapid tree growth and labour costs are lower.

But automation has played a key role in restructuring the industry, reducing employment and threatening the existence of many logging and mill communities, such as those in peripheral resource regions of the British Columbia interior. Whereas, in the past, the forest industry had been highly labour-intensive, its dependence on expensive machinery has made it more capital-intensive—which means that large integrated multinational companies have taken it over. The interesting global effect is that the northern hemisphere has become the supplier of both capital and technology to the southern hemisphere forestry industry, which serves as a hinterland and exports wood chips with weak employment multipliers. As a consequence of the dual impact of timber-reserve depletion and an automated industry, the capacity of sawmills and pulp mills has far exceeded the availability of raw materials, both in Canada and in other parts of the world.

Japan has played a particularly important role in globalizing the forest industry due to its own small forest reserves and its need for lumber for housing, paper, and wood products. In northern Alberta and northern Quebec, for example, Japanese companies like Daishowa and Al-Pac (a conglomerate of three Japanese companies) have become more dominant actors, replacing American companies to a significant degree. Other Asian countries, such as Korea and Taiwan, are also competing for pulp and paper in the same global market. Thus, an old and historic staples product in Canada is experiencing both industry- and globalization-related changes, especially in comparison to the industry's post-war boom (ending in the early '80s), which provided employment for many Canadians.

Source: Based on M. Patricia Marchak, *Logging the Globe* (Montreal: McGill-Queen's University Press, 1995).

The evidence of how internationalization or globalization is transforming our lives is rather overwhelming.[48] For example, access to information, whether for investment purposes or education (including courses for credit), is now available on the Internet from anywhere in the world. Of specific interest in Canadian society is the fact that in 1981, all provinces were trading more with each other than with the rest of the world.[49] By the mid-1990s, however, only Prince Edward Island was exporting more to the rest of Canada than to the rest of the world, and some provinces' exports to the rest of the world were more than double their exports to Canadian places. Imports have shown a similar pattern, indicating that within-Canada trade has been declining in importance compared to external trade. But it is also apparent that various regions are more internationalized in certain directions than in others (e.g., British Columbia to the Pacific Rim, Ontario to the United States) and therefore develop different international alliances. The increasing international role played by levels of government lower than the federal is known as *intermesticity*.[50]

The Impact of New Media Technologies

The role of the Canadian Radio-television and Telecommunications Commission (CRTC) is to regulate all forms of communications in Canada in the public interest and "to sustain the characteristics which make Canadians and Canada unique." For example, private television licences must achieve a yearly Canadian-content level of 60% per broadcast day to include programming about local and national events and issues. Not only is this approach supposed to help Canadians understand each other better, but it also benefits Canadian film and video industries and provides employment for writers, actors, dancers, musicians, and other artists in Canada.

However, there is a new form of media—the Internet and the World Wide Web—that uses digital technologies and combines text, graphics, data, audio, and various video images and seems to be impervious to traditional forms of regulation. Anyone can place a product or program on the Internet and gain immediate access to a global audience. The Internet appears to be outside the control of traditional national interests because of its borderless distribution.

Forty percent of all households are expected to have access to the Internet by 2001, and already 42% of connected households spend over 20 hours per month online, with 61% connecting at least seven times per week through personal computers or television sets. What would happen if large conglomerates like Disney or MGM were to distribute their video products directly through the Internet, thereby bypassing Canadian broadcasting intermediaries? Would this threaten Canadian television stations by taking away both their audiences and their revenue source?

The CRTC investigated this new medium and concluded that for now it is complementary rather than a substitute for traditional media. Massive improvements in technology would also have to occur before the Internet could replace traditional media, but the CRTC acknowledged that the Internet does have advantages in being more interactive, unscheduled, and low-cost than traditional media, which are one-way and high-cost in spite of their mass appeal. They also noted the existence of a strong Canadian presence on the Internet. Canadian websites represent about 5% of all websites, and the use of search engines helps users to identify Canadian sites.

However, the Internet clearly demonstrates how changing technologies may make it more difficult to ensure that Canadian content remains a major factor in the lives of national residents in the future.

Source: Report on the New Media, Canadian Radio-television and Telecommunications Commission, 1999.

Globalization is a phenomenon unlike any we have experienced before. It means that national societies like Canada are no longer tied to only a few international partners with whom they have historic relations; instead, new partnerships and relationships can be established all over the globe for different purposes. As noted above, it also means that different segments of Canadian society may establish these ties with very diverse parts of the world. Furthermore, it moves Canadian society away from the old dependency relationships and makes possible the establishment of new relationships with new partners or provides the dynamic to restructure old relationships. Thus the impact on Canadians of the four factors we have just discussed may have been significantly altered by the new experience of globalization, which encourages Canadians to interact with the new world in a more assertive fashion.

Nothing better exemplifies this new era than the way in which free trade is breaking down old barriers—a process the end result of which is still unknown. Our discussion of globalization will continue in the next section with specific reference to the role that free trade plays in this reorganization of macrosocietal issues. However, let it be said here that contemporary globalization is at root the worldwide expansion of capitalist forces that seek to break down national barriers to corporate investment and facilitate corporate business strategies. Although globalization is clearly more complex, free trade as a phenomenon reflects this primary objective, which happens to have social and cultural consequences.

FREE TRADE: A CASE STUDY IN SOCIETAL AUTONOMY

Background: Globalization as a New Phenomenon

The 1990s began with a series of startling events on the world stage that made us aware that intersocietal relations were changing. For Canadians, perhaps the most compelling development was the end of *bipolarity*, i.e., the end of the Cold War, during which the Soviet Union and the United States stood as matched superpowers and the rest of the world was defined in terms of its alignment with one or the other political axis. There is no better evidence of the end of the Cold War than a comparison of the "space race" of the 1960s, with its competition between the Soviet Union and the United States to land the first person on the moon, with the 1995 launch of a joint Russian–American space expedition. The collapse of the Berlin Wall in 1989 and the disintegration of the Soviet Union in 1991 were stunning developments that also contributed to the end of American hegemony in the West. Whereas Germany and Japan had been propped up by the United States in the post–World War II era as a strategic counterbalance to the Soviet bloc, these two nations (in particular) had become so economically strong by the 1980s that in important respects they rivalled the United States. Furthermore, the growth of the European Community and the openness of China suggested that a new world order was developing.

Another aspect of the process of globalization which has had an impact on Canada is *deindustralization*.[51] Capitalism has moved into a new phase in which capital is highly mobile and is more readily transferred around the globe in order to maximize profits. In the previous pattern, known as *Fordism*, manufacturing took place on the domestic front and foreign countries were viewed as markets for our goods. Now, capital and industry have been transferred to less-developed countries, where cheaper labour is available. This has led to the deindustrialization of formerly industrial countries, such as Canada, turning them into service economies. But it has also meant that the Third World is now more intimately linked into the global economy. Check the labels of the clothes you wear and products you buy to verify the extent of this process of deindustrialization. Even when assembly has taken place in Canada, there has usually been contracting-out of parts for "just-in-time supply" in order to minimize inventories and costs in what is known as *vertical disintegration*. In other words, the old patterns of industrial development have been significantly restructured in a manner that is bringing the world together in a new way.

Featherstone refers to this new level of persistent international cultural interaction and exchange as the *global ecumene*.[52] Advances in communication, particularly through computers and faxes, make global interaction virtually instantaneous. Vast pools of capital can be transferred with the push of a button and the media can simultaneously tell us about it, even with pictures, regardless of where it happens. In this context, national governments are rendered virtually helpless to control their own destinies, and national societies become more clearly part of a global network. Globalization has thus taken on a new meaning, because it has eroded national boundaries through the internationalization of the production and distribution of goods and services. [53]

Robertson has pointed out that globalization is a natural extension of the welding-together of people-groups into nation-states and the subsequent building of international linkages (a kind of "international society") through such means as the Olympic movement, the United Nations, civil-rights movements, and ecological concerns.[54] But at the same time that these processes contribute to the making of "the-world-as-a-whole," there also exist particularizing tendencies to accentuate the local, as reflected in the rise of polyethnicity within national societies. Thus *localism* (territorially bounded cultures) both coexists and is in conflict with *cosmopolitanism* (transnational and global cultural networks), with considerable overlapping and intermingling.[55] From this perspective, globalization is not so much about uniformity or homogeneity as it is about diversity, but a diversity not limited to demarcated territories.

At the core of globalization stands a world view that has come to be described as neo-liberalism. *Neo-liberalism* advocates economic freedom and free markets with minimal state interference as the primary means to obtain the public good. The key operative word is *deregulation* of markets, trade, labour, or social policies in order to foster global competitiveness. This emphasis minimizes notions of national sovereignty and threatens to contradict much of the discussion of this chapter; indeed, it could be incompatible with a unique and distinct sense of Canadian society. If the economic and cultural nationalism of Canada in the 1960s and 1970s came from the ideological left, then the contemporary triumph of the ideological right with its free-market policies could overwhelm concerns about societal autonomy.[56] It will be interesting to observe how the forces of cosmopolitanism and localism affect the pendulum of change in the future.

Canada and Globalization

As the 1990s demonstrated remarkable annual increases in worldwide capital flows, *Foreign direct investment (FDI)* became a significant driving force in globalization.[57] This aspect of the process of globalization has blurred the distinction between "domestic" and "foreign" companies, as mergers and acquisitions (as well as majority and minority shares) make ownerships very complex. Global outflows of capital have increased at an unprecedented rate since 1985. The most significant development of the past decade has been the transformation of the United States from the dominant source country of worldwide direct investment to a major host country of foreign direct investment.[58] Japan, on the other hand, has experienced a dramatic increase in its share of foreign direct investment as a source country but not as a host country.

In 1997, inward FDI to Canada and outward capital flows were about the same for the first time (until that time, inward FDI had always been higher [Figure 2.2]). Inward FDI doubled in the three years from 1997 to1999 and was said to account for 1.3 million jobs, half of all exports, and three quarters of all manufacturing exports.[59] In 1987, 66% of inward FDI came from the United States, but that share has been declining with increases from the European Union (but not the United Kingdom) and Asian countries. It is argued that formerly the primary goal of inward capital flows was to access the Canadian market, but now, as a result of free trade, they are seen as a means to access the North American market. It is also argued that FDI contributes to technology transfer, as was the case when Ericsson of Sweden brought their technology to Montreal and set up a plant hiring 800 Canadian engineers. Such cases certainly change the old concept of what subsidiaries do in Canada. In one case, a French vaccine manufacturer established an operation in Toronto, giving it—by explicit corporate strategy—a specific project which would not be carried out anywhere else in their system. FDI is said to change the way the entire corporate community thinks and to give it an outward orientation rather than one of just serving the Canadian market.

Figure 2.2 shows how inward flows of capital (FDI) have increased since 1983. It also shows that Canadian companies are not just the recipient of inward capital flows but also participate in outflows of capital, known as *Canadian direct investment abroad (CDIA)*. In fact, by 1997, outflows exceeded inflows for the first time, reaching $430 billion by 2002

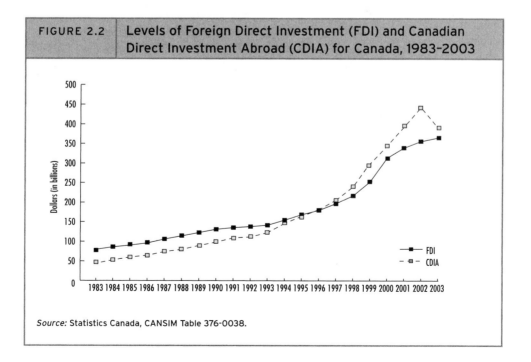

FIGURE 2.2 | **Levels of Foreign Direct Investment (FDI) and Canadian Direct Investment Abroad (CDIA) for Canada, 1983–2003**

Source: Statistics Canada, CANSIM Table 376-0038.

(only trailing off in 2003 because of the revalued dollar). The United States continues as the destination of the majority of the investment abroad but its share is declining, and the share of the European countries, Japan, and Mexico is increasing, as is that of numerous other countries in the world.

Whereas foreign investment in Canada was a major issue in the early 1970s, now it is quite clear that Canadian corporations are just as active in other countries and that Canadian investment abroad is even stronger than inward investment. Examples of corporations investing abroad include Seagrams (operating in 33 countries), Moore Corporation (operating in 28 countries), and Nortel Networks (operating in 33 countries).[60] But also included are all major Canadian banks, previously considered "pillars" of the Canadian economy, which now have subsidiaries in Europe, Asia Pacific, and Latin America. This evidence demonstrates most clearly the globalization of capital, which is no longer just inbound to Canada but also outbound from Canada. Certainly the traditional dependencies and linkages to the United Kingdom and the United States have been considerably modified and globalized. Canada is clearly part of the global economy, in which national sovereignty has become a questionable concept. Similar patterns of increased FDI and CDIA can be found among other countries with active investment economies.

Free Trade: Context and Controversy

The collapse of the Soviet Union and the Soviet bloc, coupled with the rise of the European Community, Japan, and China, have clearly altered the position of the United States in the world. One of the key aspects of this global realignment has been the emergence of regional trading blocs, which remove protectionist barriers among linked countries in the name of economic growth. In response to the transformations occurring in the non-communist world—and specifically the emerging strength of the European Community as a trading bloc—the United States sought to cement its relationship with its continental partners, particularly Canada and Mexico. Canada, on the other hand, was aware that the United States was its largest trading partner (and vice versa) and that Canadian industries might be healthier if they had guaranteed access to American markets. *Free trade*, then, represents a special case of globalization in which countries form trading blocs to enhance economic interchanges in the face of increasing competition and to enhance access to each other's markets. Because free trade, for Canada, has meant lowering historic barriers against the United States, it raises once again the issues of societal autonomy and the influence of Canada's age-old friend and American nemesis.

The matter of free trade with the United States is not new.[61] What is new is that after twice being explicitly rejected (in 1891 and 1911), and considered several times since and turned aside, free trade with the United States become law in 1989 as Bill C-130. Free trade was the major issue in the 1988 federal election won by the Mulroney Conservative government. At least partly because of its alliance with business interests (such as domestic manufacturers), the Conservative party, previously always the champion of Canadian protectionism, reversed course and became the champion of free trade. Why did free did trade become acceptable? Some of the reasons can be listed briefly.

One of the key factors in the decision to embrace free trade was that the 1985 Report of the Macdonald Royal Commission lent considerable weight and credibility to the idea of free trade. The global realities of European and Asian trading blocs made it apparent that in the absence of international trade agreements, Canada's access to foreign markets could be reduced. Of greatest concern was the growing mood of protectionism in the United States which ostensibly threatened Canada's trade relationship with its largest trading partner. If the international trading climate was changing, then indeed Canada needed a new trade policy in order to ensure a growing rather than a declining economy. The fact that unemployment was high in the 1980s as a result of the recession only made the promise of jobs more compelling. Hence the Macdonald Royal Commission recommended that adjustments be made to Canadian policies to make them more adaptive to new international conditions and give them a more market-driven and competitive character.[62]

Based on the assumption that Canadian industries were inefficient as a consequence of protectionism, it was argued that a free trade-driven "growing" economy would result from greater access to the larger US market. Some Canadian businesses were already obtaining access to the American market by setting up subsidiaries in the US to service that market. The argument was that the new jobs created as a result of an expanded market should be created in Canada. It was also argued that the sectoral trade agreement in automotives (known as the Auto Pact) had already created significant prosperity in Ontario and Quebec, and other regions wanted to experience similar benefits.

From a different perspective, free trade could be considered the natural next step in an economy that already had a substantial foreign presence.[63] But the support of the Canadian business community—and in particular the Canadian Manufacturers' Association, which had always advocated protectionism—was a significant reversal for many who now wanted to be more competitive and have "preferred access" to American markets.[64] The Business Council on National Issues (BCNI), which included the executives of the most important corporations in Canada, was also a key advocate of free trade.

Whatever the reasons (and they are far more complex than sketched here) free trade did become acceptable to the business community, which in turn made considerable efforts to convince the general public.[65] The anti-free trade forces were represented by the Pro-Canada Network and a coalition of interest groups (e.g., labour, environment, some women's groups), while the Canadian Alliance for Trade and Job Opportunities represented business as pro-free trade.

Why was free trade so controversial?[66] In the first place, there was no guarantee that a bilateral agreement would create more jobs in Canada. In fact, one fear was that companies would decide to move out of Canada to places like the American Deep South or Mexico, where pools of cheap labour were available, and service the Canadian market from there. Opponents of free trade argued that since in some American states the minimum wage was low and employers were not required to contribute to any benefits packages (e.g., medicare), Canadian firms would be more competitive if they relocated. Even if they did not relocate out of the country, they would likely bargain for a "level playing field," demanding that Canada withdraw its distinct social programs in order to allow Canadian firms to be competitive with firms in the United States. The net result, argued the critics, could be fewer jobs in Canada—particularly if US subsidiaries in Canada, losing the incentive of tariff protection, closed their plants.

A second fear was that free trade might make it difficult for the Canadian state to use policy instruments (e.g., financial aid, procurement practices, subsidies, and local content rules) to accomplish certain national objectives without reprisal. For example, equalization grants to poorer regions and agricultural subsidies had been accepted aspects of Canadian life. If your trading partner perceives these as unfair subsidies, a countervailing duty could be imposed on the product when it enters their country, putting your product at a competitive disadvantage. Would the Canadian government then lose its sovereignty to deal with aspects of its own society as it sees fit? Would the government still be able to subsidize a company to establish a plant in an economically depressed region of Canada without fear of being charged with unfair competition? Could it continue to subsidize seasonal industries, such as fishing and lumbering, without running the risk of being accused by the importing country's government of violating the free trade agreement? Thus, the concerns about free trade included the loss (rather than gain) of jobs, the threat to social programs, and the lack of government policy control.

Third, free trade was controversial because of its socio-cultural implications. Would the removal of barriers between Canada and the United States mean the free exchange of labour and culture? Would it eventually mean, for example, that job opportunities in Canada could no longer be reserved for Canadians in the first instance? Presumably Canadians would have access to US employment opportunities as well, which potentially would bring about more intermingling of people in both countries. Would this mean that various elements of American popular culture (e.g., magazines, films, and books) would have free entry to Canada, overwhelming the fledgling Canadian cultural industry, which would no longer be protected? In other words, is it possible that free trade would ultimately mean the erasure of the border between the US and Canada? From this perspective, free trade was perceived as much more than an economic agreement; it raised questions about the independence, sovereignty, and distinctiveness of Canadian society in relation to the United States. How much economic integration is possible without the loss of cultural and policy independence?

An Evaluation

Free trade puts the emphasis on harmonization rather than sovereignty. *Sovereignty* refers to the capacity of a nation-state to control its own destiny; *harmonization* emphasizes the creation of similar rules, policies, and regulations between nation-states. Free trade, then, establishes policies whereby nation-states may encounter each other with as few discrepancies as possible—at least in matters of commerce and public policy. In this context, it becomes clear why free trade is a vital issue in societal autonomy. The problem is that it is difficult to ascertain whether harmonization and sovereignty are mutually compatible or whether, in the long run, they are in radical opposition to each other.

In 1994, the Canada–US free-trade zone was extended to Mexico in what is known as the *North American Free Trade Agreement (NAFTA)*. It was claimed that NAFTA countries comprised the largest free-trade zone in the world, with 360 million people compared to the 325 million of the European Community. Mexico had been a highly regulated socialist state, which, with its low-wage economy, had perhaps the most to gain from NAFTA. The benefits for Canada were not considered to be substantial; free trade with Mexico did provide some new opportunities for Canadian industries, while at the same time Mexico's cheap labour seemed a threat. But the inexorable forces of internationalism have gone beyond continentalism towards *hemispherism:* Discussions have been underway with Latin American nations to form a future *Free Trade Agreement of the Americas (FTAA)*. Thus the three forces of *continentalism*, *hemispherism*, and *globalism* represent a striking alternative to the isolationist–protectionist outlook that dominated Canadian thinking for so long, and this change surely must have socio-cultural consequences.[67]

Currency Harmonization

Will the US dollar replace the loonie? Should there be a common currency between Canada and the United States?

The Canadian government says there is no way it would consider the elimination of a separate Canadian currency in what is called *policy dollarization*. However, *market dollarization* already exists; this is the use by Canadians of the US dollar—whether by a private citizen holding a US-dollar account in a Canadian bank or a corporation reporting its financial results in US dollars.

Some see differences in the exchange rate as giving Canadian companies a market advantage and a cost advantage because Canadian goods become cheaper in the US market, and argue that therefore policy dollarization would be a bad thing. Others say that US dollars have become a worldwide standard, so any company doing international business needs to find a common benchmark. Some sports teams (including the National Hockey League) and multinational corporations operating in Canada pay their employees in US dollars. If increasingly Canadian organizations have some of their expenses in US dollars and some of their revenue in Canadian dollars with a different value, how much longer can currency harmonization be resisted?

Would monetary union with the United States (or with both the United States and Mexico, in what is called a North American Monetary Union) mean that economic policy would really be made in the United States? Would it provide more economic stability? What about the issue of national sovereignty?

See Eric Helleiner, "Toward a North American Common Currency," in Wallace Clement and Leah Vosko, *Changing Canada: Political Economy as Transformation* (Montreal: McGill-Queen's University Press, 2003), 265-86.

It is difficult to assess the impact of these free-trade initiatives on Canadian society because there are so many complicating factors, such as a fluctuating exchange rate.[68] On the positive side, new jobs have been created and trade with the United States has grown greatly, including both exports to and imports from that country. The two countries have become much closer economic partners. On the negative side is the fact that jobs have also been lost as the result of free trade (or of the consolidation or restructuring that accompanies it), and it is difficult at this point to determine the net effect on balance in employment. For example, manufacturing jobs may have been lost but knowledge-industry jobs may have been created. One study of small Ontario communities that thought themselves fortunate to have a significant employer highlighted the huge effect of lost jobs on worker displacement.[69] A Canada Packers plant in Elora was bought by a British multinational company and closed, and a Westinghouse Electric plant in Mount Forest was closed and its equipment moved to the southern United States. Gains and losses were typical of this rationalization, with uneven effects.

What is indisputable is that free trade submerges Canada in a trading bloc with the more powerful United States and renews continentalist pressures. Free trade has meant that

Canada's economic dependence on the United States has grown. This fact can be interpreted both positively and negatively. Some see this trend as inevitable anyway, given what is happening in the global economy, and feel therefore that this linkage should be celebrated. Others view it as a huge step in the direction of Canada's losing its sovereignty altogether as it is drawn into the orbit of the United States, whose superior economic strength prevents Canada from being a true equal in the partnership. For example, Canadian businesses are putting increasing pressure on the Canadian government to lower tax rates in order to ensure that they remain competitive with American businesses. This could mean the erosion of the tax base necessary to support the social safety net (including medicare), which has been a characteristic part of Canadian society, representing a deliberate attempt to make it "a kinder and gentler society" than the American.[70] We have already seen how Canada's concern to protect its cultural industries by excluding them from free trade agreements became problematic when the United States defined these industries as businesses rather than culture.

Thus the success of free trade is clearly mixed; moreover, its evaluation depends on one's perspective and point of view. It is also complicated by factors, such as the role played by the exchange-rate gap and the roles played by the European Union or the recession in Asia in contributing to restructuring. What is clear is that the Canada–US border is no longer the same economic barrier that it once was, and there will be increasing pressures to make it even more permeable, if not to remove it in significant ways.[71] The implications of greater economic union—whether or not it leads to greater political integration—bring us back to the quotation from George Grant (written in 1965) that appears on the first page of this chapter.

FOREIGN INFLUENCE RECONSIDERED

The extent to which foreign influence is problematic for Canadian society is open to much debate. While nationalist arguments occasionally provoke widespread support, the majority of Canadians have accepted the standard and quality of living that have come with at least partial continental integration. Those who felt most disadvantaged by the old order (e.g., persons living outside the industrial heartland) were the most likely to support continentalism.[72] On the other hand, those clamouring most strongly for economic and cultural nationalism seemed to be those with the most to gain from protectionism (e.g., the middle and working classes). It is more than coincidental that the widest public concern for societal autonomy came during the 1960s and 1970s, when a large wave of young university-educated persons were entering the workforce and wanted employment protected in Canada. It appears that many of the current wave of new university graduates have a different view of the opening of borders, perceiving it as leading to an enlargement of opportunities. In fact, a 1999 study showed that most Canadians were optimistic about the consequences of globalization—a significant change of attitude from the beginning of the 1990s. While Canada is still considerably dependent on the export of raw materials, most young Canadians think of Canada as more of a high-technology economy with a major role to play on the world stage.[73]

Yet support for integration that fosters economic growth is not necessarily the same as support for complete integration, though it may be a slippery slope from one to the other. We have seen in this chapter that at the level of popular culture, for example, Americanization may be an overwhelming force. Yet there may be other factors that act to

Differing Perspectives

Structural Functionalism

The structural functionalist perspective understands Canadian society as part of a complex international system in which different countries play different roles in the world economy. Because Canada possessed raw materials needed by empire economies, Canadian development needs to be understood as a natural result of the expansion of more dominant societies. Over time this role has changed somewhat, yet Canada remains part of a huge global exchange system in which we must constantly search for new niches. There is little point in worrying about independence, because independence is not possible in the contemporary world. What is necessary is to develop the society's own assets (e.g., skills, creative technologies, cultural icons), so that Canada's contribution to the global system is obvious and important. In short, in a global economy, each society has its own role, and it is up to its residents to enhance that role through deliberate effort.

Conflict

The conflict perspective points out that the international economy is essentially one of unequal relationships. Some societies are more dominant than others because they are able to subordinate other societies, not only through economic power but also through military, cultural, and ideological power. But it is economic power, and especially the role of the capitalist class in seeking to maximize its profits, that establishes a global dynamic. While Canada has never seen itself as a world power, Canadians depend on societies with lower labour costs to provide many of the things that are part of their daily lives; thus, as an intermediate society, Canadians feel exploited at the same time as they participate in the exploitation of weaker societies. In terms of Canada's attempt to sustain its own sovereignty, the globalization of the economy only draws Canada into American dependency more tightly, and the Americanization of Canada will continue unless deliberate efforts at resistance occur.

Symbolic Interactionism

The symbolic interactionist perspective focuses not so much on economic relations between societies but on how societies develop their own cultural attributes within the world. How do cultural distinctions develop and how do societies share their culture? The unique history of each society in interaction with other societies not only helps to explain where elements of culture have originated but also forces us to look for ways in which local peoples modify what they have received, making it their own through a process of sifting and exchange. What is interesting is how Canadian society has indeed developed its own institutions, heroes, and dialects or colloquialisms (e.g., *toque, eh*?) in spite of globalizing pressures. So while there are many instances of foreign symbols operating in Canada, there are also many ways in which these symbols have been Canadianized.

sustain an indigenous Canadian culture; in other words, while we may embrace many elements of American culture, we still modify and reformulate at least some of what we do absorb in a manner which is peculiarly Canadian.[74] However, an empirical study of the values of Canadians, Americans, and Mexicans concluded that along with free trade (the economic aspect of integration), a convergence of values has also taken place (for example, in how citizens view government); these findings suggest that political boundaries have become less important and that a fundamental value-shift is occurring towards a post-materialist culture.[75]

Even in regard to economic issues, some have argued that criticizing foreign capital does not get at the root of the matter, because corporations—whether Canadian or foreign—do not make decisions on the basis of the national good but rather on the basis of profit.[76] Others declare that the repatriation of the economy has been made into a false panacea.[77] Still others insist that integration theory is wrong to assert that interaction will inevitably lead to the breakdown of national attributes and the creation of a single polity; they claim that when two units interact with uneven capacity, a self-regulator in the smaller nation may inhibit the integrative process.[78] In fact, what we see in Canadian–American relations is just such a partial integration. One analyst has described Canadian–American relations as a *disparate dyad,* because Canada's goal, despite the inequality, has been to modify the nature of the relationship rather than terminate it, as termination would be unrealistic.[79] Thus, it could be argued that in continually seeking to control the nature of that relationship, Canadian society is expressing its autonomy.

Canada's objective struggle to maintain the precarious balance between integration and independence has had its subjective effects. The *cumulative impact hypothesis* suggests that the years of debate and controversy, as well as of the realities engendered by Canada's dependent position, have produced a feeling of societal *inferiority*.[80] This reveals itself in Canada's *mixed emotions* of envy and admiration towards the more dominant societies which serve as its models, as well as in the hostility and antagonism expressed in the struggle against subordination.

It is impossible to understand Canadian society without knowing of this perpetual search for autonomy. In fact, S.D. Clark has argued that historically, in struggling to discover itself, the society attempted to discover *what it is not* by distinguishing itself from American society.[81] This resulted in a *paranoiac* form of *nationalism* based on a sense of persecution and powerlessness, which sometimes had little positive content or led to the seeking of protection in Britain as mother country. Ironically, globalization has now brought with it the twin themes of deregulation and privatization—both of which minimize the role of the state, which had played a key role in providing protection from at least some external forces. In this context, the meaning of sovereignty is thus in transition, as Canadians, on the horns of the integration–independence dilemma, are left to seek new methods of sustaining their society. Canada's recurring attempts to take control of its own destiny represent the more *positive* side of society-building, which will be discussed in Chapter Seven.

FURTHER EXPLORATION

1. Some people think that one way out of Canada's continentalism dilemma is to support economic continentalism alongside cultural nationalism. Assess the merits and problems of this position. Is this possible through free trade?

2. What staples are characteristic of your province? How do those staples tie your province into the world system?

3. Take a position on the foreign-ownership question. Defend your position with whatever examples you can find and anticipate criticisms from people who hold other positions on the issue.

4. What do you think the impact of free trade has been? Watch for illustrations in your newspaper and bring them to class for discussion.

SELECTED READINGS

Brodie, Janine, and Linda Trimble, eds. *Reinventing Canada: Politics of the 21st Century*. Toronto: Prentice Hall, 2003.

Clarkson, Stephen. *Uncle Sam and Us: Globalization, Neoconservativism, and the Canadian State*. Toronto: University of Toronto Press, 2002.

Flaherty, David H., and Frank E. Manning, eds. *The Beaver Bites Back? American Popular Culture in Canada*. Montreal: McGill-Queen's University Press, 1993.

Teeple, Gary. *Globalization and the Decline of Social Reform: Into the Twentieth Century*. Toronto: Garamond Press, 2000.

ENDNOTES

1 Gordon Laxer has argued that Canada had more independence by the beginning of World War II, when the influences of Britain and the United States were more balanced. But that balance was lost by the end of the war, when the United States became a pre-eminent world power, and especially when the Cold War drew sharp battle lines between East and West. See Gordon Laxer, "Constitutional Crises and Continentalism: Twin Threats to Canada's Continued Existence," *Canadian Journal of Sociology* 17, 2 (1992): 218.

2 See Immanuel Wallerstein, *The Modern World System* (New York: Academic Press, 1976) and Daniel Chirot, *Social Change in the Twentieth Century* (New York: Harcourt Brace Jovanovich, 1977) for discussions of world systems theory. For its adaptation to Canada, see Lorna R. Marsden and Edward B. Harvey, *Fragile Federation: Social Change in Canada* (Toronto: McGraw-Hill Ryerson, 1979).

3 H.A. Innis, *The Fur Trade in Canada* (Toronto: University of Toronto Press, 1930); *The Cod Fisheries* (Toronto: University of Toronto Press, 1940); *Problems of Staple Production in Canada* (Toronto: Ryerson Press, 1933).

4 S.D. Clark, *The Social Development of Canada* (Toronto: University of Toronto Press, 1942).

5 Rex Lucas, *Minetown, Milltown, Railtown: Life in Canadian Communities of a Single Industry* (Toronto: University of Toronto Press, 1971). For a further discussion of some of the problems produced by big industry for human populations in small towns, see Roy T. Bowles, ed., *Little Communities and Big Industries: Studies in the Social Impact of Canadian Resource Extraction* (Toronto: Butterworths, 1982).

6 For illustrations of these problems in the mining industry, see Wallace Clement, *Hardrock Mining: Industrial Relations and Technological Change at Inco* (Toronto: McClelland and Stewart, 1980).

7 Donald G. Paterson, *British Direct Investment in Canada, 1890–1914* (Toronto: University of Toronto Press, 1983).

8 Richard Starks, *Industry in Decline* (Toronto: James Lorimer, 1978), 71.

9 *Corporations and Labour Unions Act* Report for 1986, Part I "Corporations," Statistics Canada Catalogue #61-210, 21.

10 Note that a corporation is not reported as foreign unless it is at least 50% foreign-owned. Edward Grabb, "Who Owns Canada? Concentration of Ownership and the Distribution of Economic Assets, 1975–1985," *Journal of Canadian Studies* 25 (1992): 72–93.

11 Statistics Canada Catalogue No. 61-220-XIE, 2001–2002.

12 See also Daniel M. Shapiro, *Foreign and Domestic Firms in Canada* (Toronto: Butterworths, 1980), 74, regarding the profitability of American firms.

13 This argument can be found in a number of places, e.g., Patricia Marchak, *In Whose Interests: An Essay on Multinational Corporations in a Canadian Context* (Toronto: McClelland and Stewart, 1979), 101; Wallace Clement, *Continental Corporate Power* (Toronto: McClelland and Stewart, 1977), 79; and R.J. Richardson, "Merchants Against Industry: An Empirical Study of the Canadian Debate," *Canadian Journal of Sociology* 7 (1982): 279–95, who argues that merchant capital and industrial capital merged.

14 Gordon Laxer, "Foreign Ownership and Myths About Canadian Development," *Canadian Review of Sociology and Anthropology* 22 (1985): 311–45; and his *Open for Business: The Roots of Foreign Ownership in Canada* (Toronto: Oxford University Press, 1989).

15 M.H. Watkins, *Foreign Ownership and the Structure of Canadian Industry, Report of the Task Force on the Structure of Canadian Industry* (Ottawa: Privy Council, 1968); Gray Report, *Foreign Direct Investment in Canada* (Ottawa: Information Canada, 1972). See also A.E. Safarian, *Foreign Ownership of Canadian Industry* (Toronto: McGraw-Hill, 1966); a good introductory discussion in Malcolm Levine and Christine Sylvester, *Foreign Ownership* (Toronto: General Publishing, 1972); and a good retrospective discussion in Michael Bliss, "American Investment," in Norman Hillmer, ed., *Partners Nevertheless: Canadian–American Relations in the Twentieth Century* (Toronto: Copp Clark Pitman, 1989), 259–70.

16 Abraham Rotstein and Gary Lax, *Independence: The Canadian Challenge* (Toronto: Committee for an Independent Canada, 1972); and *Getting It Back: A Program for Canadian Independence* (Toronto: Clarke Irwin, 1974).

17 See Erick Jackson, ed., *The Great Canadian Debate: Foreign Ownership* (Toronto: McClelland and Stewart, 1975).

18 As manpower importation relates to universities, see Robin Matthews and James Steele, *The Struggle for Canadian Universities* (Toronto: New Press, 1969); as it relates to other areas, see Ian Lumsden, ed., *Close the 49th Parallel: The Americanization of Canada* (Toronto: University of Toronto Press, 1970).

19 Mario Cervantes and Dominique Guellec, *The Brain Drain: Old Myths and New Realities,* OECD, 2002.

20 John Meisel speaks of a masses–elite dichotomy on this issue, with better-educated high-income groups more interested in indigenous cultural products. "Escaping Extinction: Cultural Defence of an Undefended Border," in D.H. Flaherty and W.R. McKercher, eds., *Southern Exposure: Canadian Perspectives on the United States* (Toronto: McGraw-Hill Ryerson, 1986), 155–56.

21 For a good review of the issues in American influences on Canadian broadcasting policy, see Bruce Feldthusen, "Awakening from the National Broadcasting Dream: Rethinking Television Regulation for National Cultural Goals," in David H. Flaherty and Frank E. Manning, eds., *The Beaver Bites Back? American Popular Culture in Canada* (Montreal: McGill-Queen's University Press, 1993), 42–74.

22 For a good review of all of Canada's cultural industries, from newspapers to film to music, see Michael Dorland, ed., *The Cultural Industries of Canada: Problems, Policies, and Prospects* (Toronto: Lorimer, 1996).

23 *Reader's Digest* was initially also a target of Bill C-58, but was exempted on the grounds that it was not news-oriented. For a discussion of some of the issues in this debate, see Isaiah Litvak and Christopher Maule, *Cultural Sovereignty: The* Time *and* Reader's Digest *Case in Canada* (New York, Praeger, 1974); and M. Patricia Hindley, Gail M. Martin, and Jean McNulty, *The Tangled Net: Basic Issues in Canadian Communications* (Vancouver: J.J. Douglas, 1977), chap. 2. For a more recent discussion of cultural industries (especially film, broadcasting, and publishing) in the pre- and post-NAFTA eras, see Peter Karl Kresl, "The Political Economy of Canada's Cultural Policy," in André Lapierre, Patricia Smart, and Pierre Savard, eds., *Language, Culture and Values in Canada at the Dawn of the 21st Century* (Ottawa: Carleton University Press, International Council for Canadian Studies, 1996), 223–45.

24 For a good review of the issues, see Janice L. Murray, ed., *Canadian Cultural Nationalism* (New York: New York University Press, 1977); and S.M. Crean, *Who's Afraid of Canadian Culture?* (Don Mills, ON: General Publishing, 1976).

25 Guy Rocher, *A General Introduction to Sociology* (Toronto: Macmillan, 1972), 513–14.

26 The concept of empire developed here has been influenced by the work of George Grant, who has applied it to Canada's relationship with the United States. See his *Technology and Empire: Perspectives on North America* (Toronto: House of Anansi, 1969); and *Lament for a Nation* (Toronto: McClelland and Stewart, 1965), 8. See also John Hutcheson, *Dominance and Dependency* (Toronto: McClelland and Stewart, 1978), chap. 3; and Michael W. Doyle, *Empires* (Ithaca, NY: Cornell University Press, 1986).

27 For example, see Joel Kurtzman, *The Decline and Crash of the American Economy* (New York: W.W. Norton, 1988); Pearl M. Kramer, *The US Economy in Crisis* (New York: Praeger, 1988); and Bertrand Bellon and Jorge Niosi, *The Decline of the American Economy* (Toronto: Black Rose, 1988), and "Whither the American Empire: Expansion or Contraction?" *Annals of the American Academy of Political and Social Science* 500, Special Issue (1988).

28 Kari Levitt, *Silent Surrender: The Multi-National Corporation in Canada* (Toronto: Macmillan, 1971), 112.

29 See Harry H. Hiller, "Continentalism and the Third Force in Religion," *Canadian Journal of Sociology* 3 (1978): 183–207.

30 Norman Hillmer, ed., *Partners Nevertheless: Canadian–American Relations in the Twentieth Century* (Toronto: Copp Clark Pitman, 1989); and R. Lecker, ed., *Borderlands: Essays in Canadian–American Relations* (Toronto: ECW Press, 1991).

31 John W. Holmes, *Life with Uncle: The Canadian–American Relationship* (Toronto: University of Toronto Press, 1981).

32 Jorge Niosi, *Canadian Multinationals* (Toronto: Between the Lines, 1985).

33 Susan Goldenberg, *Men of Property: The Canadian Developers Who Are Buying America* (Toronto: Personal Library, 1981); Steven Globerman, *Canadian-Based Multinationals* (Calgary: University of Calgary Press, 1994); and Wendy Evans, Henry Lane, and Shawna O'Grady, *Border Crossings: Doing Business in the United States* (Scarborough: Prentice Hall, 1992). At one point in the early 1980s, Oxford Development Group of Edmonton controlled about 40% of the downtown office space in Minneapolis (*Calgary Herald*, 28 Aug. 1981).

34 For a discussion of these points, see George Modelski, ed., *Multinational Corporations and World Order* (Beverly Hills: Sage, 1972), 20–24.

35 Patricia Marchak, *In Whose Interests*, 102. See also her second edition of *Ideological Perspectives on Canada* (Toronto: McGraw-Hill Ryerson, 1981), particularly Chapter 8, which expresses her pessimism about the role of multinational corporations.

36 C.S. Burchill, "The Multi-National Corporation: An Unsolved Problem in International Relations," *Queen's Quarterly* 77 (1970): 3–18.

37 For a study of a Japanese-transplant auto-assembly plant in Ingersoll, Ontario, see James Rinehart, Christopher Huxley, and David Robertson, *Just Another Car Factory? Lean Production and Its Dissidents* (Ithaca, NY: ILR Press, 1997).

38 A.A. Fatouros, "Multi-National Enterprises and Extraterritoriality," *Journal of Contemporary Business* 1 (1972): 36.

39 Kari Levitt, *Silent Surrender*, 108.

40 J.D. House, "The Social Organization of Multi-National Corporations: Canadian Subsidiaries in the Oil Industry," *Canadian Review of Sociology and Anthropology* 14 (1977): 1–14.

41 For an interesting study of seven multinational corporations in Canada, see I.A. Litvak, C.J. Maule, and R.D. Robinson, *Dual Loyalty: Canadian–US Business Arrangements*. For a reverse study of Canadian multinational corporations, see I.A. Litvak and C.J. Maule, *The Canadian Multinationals* (Toronto: Butterworths, 1981). See also Ahmed Idris-Soven and Mary K. Vaughan, eds., *The World as a Company Town* (The Hague: Mouton, 1978).

42 *Foreign Direct Investment in Canada*, chap. 12.

43 Robert L. Perry, *Galt, USA.: The American Presence in a Canadian City* (Toronto: Maclean-Hunter, 1971), 36.

44 J.H. Dales, *The Protective Tariff in Canada's Development* (Toronto: University of Toronto Press, 1966), particularly Chapter 6.

45 This is essentially the argument of Wallace Clement, most clearly presented in his *Class, Power, and Property: Essays on Canadian Society* (Toronto: Methuen, 1983), chap. 3.

46 See Rex Lucas, *Minetown, Milltown, Railtown*, 338.

47 Wallace Clement and Glen Williams, "Resources and Manufacturing in Canada's Political Economy," in Wallace Clement, ed., *Understanding Canada: Building on the New Canadian Political Economy* (Montreal: McGill-Queen's University Press, 1997), 56.

48 Thomas J. Courchene, "CHASTE and Chastened: Canada's New Social Contract," in Raymond B. Blake, Penny E. Bryden, J. Frank Strain, eds., *The Welfare State in Canada: Past, Present, and Future* (Toronto: Irwin, 1997), 11–13.

49 Gary Teeple, *Globalization and the Decline of Social Reform: Into the Twentieth Century* (Toronto: Garamond, 2000); and Ted Schrecker, ed., *Surviving Globalism: The Social and Environmental Challenge* (New York: St. Martins, 1997).

50 Thomas J. Courchene, "CHASTE and Chastened: Canada's New Social Contract," 11–13.

51 Earl H. Fry, "Regional Economic Development Strategies in Canada and the United States: Linkages Between Subnational, National and Global Settings," *International Journal of Canadian Studies* 16 (1997): 69–91.

52 Ricardo Grinspun and Maxwell A. Cameron, *The Political Economy of North American Free Trade* (Montreal: McGill-Queen's University Press, 1993).

53 Mike Featherstone, ed., *Global Culture: Nationalism, Globalization, and Modernity* (Newbury Park, CA: Sage, 1990), 6.

54 Two excellent references on the process of globalization are M. Albrow and E. King, eds., *Globalization, Knowledge, and Society* (London: Sage, 1990); and Roland Robertson, *Globalization: Social Theory and Global Culture* (Newbury Park, CA: Sage, 1992).

55 Roland Robertson, "Mapping the Global Condition: Globalization as the Central Concept," in Mike Featherstone, ed., *Global Culture: Nationalism, Globalization and Modernity*, 24–28.

56 Ulf Hannerz, "Cosmopolitans and Locals in World Culture," in Mike Featherstone, ed., *Global Culture: Nationalism, Globalization, and Modernity*, 237–51.

57 The notion that neo-conservatism as an ideology is incompatible with the continued existence of Canada and that the damage already done is difficult to reverse is proposed by Stephen McBride and John Shields, *Dismantling a Nation: Canada and the New World Order* (Halifax: Fernwood, 1993).

58 *World Investment Report 1998.*

59 Industry Canada, *Economic Integration in North America: Trends in Foreign Direct Investment, 1994* (Ottawa: Minister of Supply and Services, 1995), Charts 2 and 3.

60 From a speech given by John Manley, "Who Benefits From Foreign Investment?" Industry Canada 1999. See also "Consultation Paper on WTO/FTAA Investment," Department of Foreign Affairs and International Trade, 1999.

61 For a history of free trade as a societal issue, see J.L. Granatstein, "Free Trade Between Canada and the United States: The Issue That Will Not Go Away," in Dennis Stairs and Gilbert R. Winham, *The Politics of Canada's Economic Relationship with the United States* (Toronto: University of Toronto Press, 1985), 11–54

62 William K. Carroll, "Does Disorganized Capitalism Disorganize Corporate Networks? *Canadian Journal of Sociology* 27, 3 (2002): 339–71.

63 One of the key elements of the Commission's recommendations was the reduction of government ownership or federal subsidies, which had been used for many years to sustain national sovereignty in various ways. For an abridged version of the report of the Royal Commission, see Rod McQueen, *Leap of Faith* (Toronto: Gowan, 1985). See also a special issue of *Canadian Public Policy*, XII Supplement, February 1986 for a series of reviews of the final Report. Many of the critiques of free trade also assess the Report.

64 R. Jack Richardson, "Free Trade: Why Did It Happen?" *Canadian Review of Sociology and Anthropology* 29 (1992): 316.

65 C. Bruce Doern and Brian W. Tomlin, *Faith and Fear: The Free Trade Story* (Toronto: Stoddart, 1991), 46–49, 103–110.

66 William G. Watson, "Canada–US Free Trade: Why Now?" *Canadian Public Policy* 13 (1987): 337–49.

67 For good overviews of what was at issue at the time of the free trade negotiations, see C.D. McLachlan, A. Apuzzo, and W.A. Kerr, "The Canada–US Free Trade Agreement: A Canadian Perspective," *Journal of World Trade* (1988): 9–33; Robert M. Campbell and Leslie M. Pal, *The Real World of Canadian Politics* (Peterborough: Broadview, 1989), 315–68 (which also includes an abridged summary of the agreement); Gordon Ritchie, *Wrestling with the Elephant: The Inside Story of the Canada–US Free Trade Negotiations* (Toronto: Macfarlane, Walter and Ross, 1997); and Michael Hart, *Decision at Midnight: Inside the Canada–US Free Trade Negotiations* (Vancouver: UBC Press, 1994).

68 These concepts are discussed in Alan K. Henrikson, "The US 'North American' Trade Concept: Continentalist, Hemispherist, or Globalist?" in Donald Barry, ed., *Toward a North American Community? Canada, the United States, and Mexico* (Boulder: Westview, 1995), 155–84.

69 There are many attempts to assess free trade and its consequences. In addition to sources cited in this chapter, other references that take a variety of perspectives include Steven Globerman and Michael Walker, *Assessing NAFTA: A Trinational Analysis* (Vancouver: Fraser Institute, 1993); A. R. Riggs and Tom Velk, eds., *Beyond NAFTA: An Economic, Political, and Sociological Perspective* (Vancouver: Fraser Institute, 1993); Nora Lustig, Barry P. Bosworth, and Robert Z. Lawrence, eds., *North American Free Trade: Assessing the Impact* (Washington, D.C.: The Brookings Institute, 1992); Ann Weston, Ada Piazze-McMahon, and Ed Dosman, *Free Trade with a Human Face? The Social Dimensions of CUFTA and NAFTA* (Ottawa: North–South Institute, 1992); Andrew Jackson, *Impacts of the Free Trade Agreement (FTA) and the North America Free Trade Agreement (NAFTA) on Canadian Labour Markets and Labour and Social Standards* (Ottawa: Canadian Labour Congress, 1997); and Mel Watkins, ed., *Alternatives to the Free Trade Agreement* (Ottawa: Canadian Centre for Policy Alternatives, 1988).

70   Anthony Winson and Belinda Leach, *Contingent Work, Disrupted Lives* (Toronto: University of Toronto Press, 2002).

71   For a discussion of this issue in a global perspective, see Gary Teeple, *Globalization and the Decline of Social Reform* (Toronto: Garamond, 1995).

72   See, for example, Lawrence Martin, "Continental Union," *Annals of the American Academy of Political and Social Science* 538 (1995): 143–50.

73   In an earlier study, Carl Cuneo found that underprivileged groups (e.g., those with low education or low family income, older people, and residents of Atlantic Canada) were most likely to support continentalism, because they presumed they had nothing to gain by retaining the old order. "The Social Basis of Political Continentalism in Canada," *Canadian Review of Sociology and Anthropology* 13 (1976): 55–70.

74   The study was done by Ekos Research Associates and was reported in the *Calgary Herald*, July 10, 1999.

75   The thesis that Canadian culture has been Americanized while at the same time American hegemony has been resisted through Canada's reconstitution or recontextualization of American culture rather than passive acceptance of it is the theme of David H. Flaherty and Frank E. Manning, eds., *The Beaver Bites Back? American Popular Culture in Canada.*

76   Ronald Inglehart, Neil Nevitte, and Miguel Basanez, *The North American Trajectory: Cultural, Economic, and Political Ties Among the United States, Canada, and Mexico* (New York: Aldine De Gruyter, 1996).

77   See Jorge Niosi, *Canadian Capitalism: A Study of Power in the Canadian Business Establishment* (Toronto: James Lorimer, 1981); and Gary Teeple, ed., *Capitalism and the National Question in Canada* (Toronto: University of Toronto Press, 1972).

78   John G. Craig, "What Is a Good Corporate Citizen?" *Canadian Review of Sociology and Anthropology* 1 (1979): 181–96.

79   Denis Stairs, "North American Continentalism: Perspectives and Policies in Canada," in David M. Cameron, ed., *Regionalism and Supranationalism* (Montreal: Institute for Research on Public Policy, 1981), 95.

80   Naomi Black, "Absorptive Systems Are Impossible: The Canadian–American Relationship as a Disparate Dyad," in Andrew Axline et al., *Continental Community: Independence and Integration in North America* (Toronto: McClelland and Stewart, 1974), 92–108.

81   Rocher uses the terms *marginality* and *ambivalence* to describe the relationship and feelings of the colonized for the colonizers. See *A General Introduction to Sociology*, chap. 14.

82   "Canada and Her Great Neighbor," *Canadian Review of Sociology and Anthropology* 1 (1964): 197. Glen Frankfurter has argued that English-speaking Canadians created an imaginary ideal Britain to which they could be loyal, as a means of distinguishing themselves from the United States, in *Baneful Domination* (Toronto: Longmans, 1971).

WEBLINKS

www.dfait-maeci.gc.ca/nafta-alena/over-e.asp

An overview of the North American Free Trade Agreement (NAFTA), provided by Canada's Department of Foreign Affairs and International Trade.

www.macleans.ca

Maclean's is Canada's premiere weekly newsmagazine.

chapter three

The Issue of Inequality

Many Canadians are reluctant to admit that their country has a class structure ... But this does not dismiss the other evidence of the class division of the population which exists in terms of inequality of wealth, opportunity and social recognition. These barriers are not the horizontal ones of geographical regions or distinctive ethnic cultures but the vertical ones of a socio-economic hierarchy.

–Leonard C. Marsh, one of Canada's first social researchers,
in his classic study *Canadians In and Out of Work* (1940), 403

Now that we have some sense of the crucial role that external factors play in shaping Canadian society, we can turn our attention to how people are sorted out within it. One of the most important ways of doing that is to focus on the differences that exist within the population in terms of power and access to resources. That people share a territory does not mean that there is equality, nor that goods are randomly distributed. Rather, some persons have advantages that others do not—a fact that produces both visible and less visible (but just as real) evidence of the existence of a hierarchical society. Virtually every society has a system of *ranking* its members. We are most accustomed to thinking of such ranking in terms of personal characteristics (e.g., income, ownership, education, personal abilities). But ranking is also related to group characteristics (e.g., gender, ethnicity, race) whereby some groups gain dominance or control over other groups by dint of particular qualities. Dominant groups obviously have the ability to define what is important, how things are done, and who obtains the largest rewards. The study of the structure and consequences of the ranking patterns that exist in a society is known as *social stratification* (or *class*) *analysis*.

There is no modern society in which all people are equal; some people are just more equal than others. Yet the notion of human equality is deeply embedded in the ideology of Western democracies.[1] The Preamble to the United States Constitution, for example, states that all men are created equal (note that women are not explicitly mentioned), yet

87

the long history of the subordination of Blacks indicates that equality does not exist in that society. While many people like to think that the gap between rich and poor is narrower in Canada, inequality still exists along a variety of dimensions. There is a rich legacy of research on inequality in Canadian society. The purpose of this chapter is to outline the basis for this inequality and to indicate how inequality contributes to the dynamics of life within the society.

INDICATORS OF INEQUALITY

The most visible indicator of inequality in everyday life is income or wealth. You have probably established a connection between income, education, and occupation. We frequently see people with little or no education in low-paying occupations; conversely, we see people with considerable education in high-paying positions. The relationship between income, education, and occupation is not always so clear—a real-estate agent with a high income may not have a high level of education. Generally speaking, however, the three dimensions of income, education, and occupation are good objective indicators of where one might be placed in a society's ranking system. What evidence is there that a differential of these qualities exists?

Income

Because income is directly related to purchasing power—which in turn determines standard of living and lifestyle—a person's income level is an important index of social stratification. By dividing the total population into five equal parts, or *quintiles,* Figure 3.1 shows how income is unequally distributed within the population. If total income were distributed equally, each quintile's share would be 20%; as the data show, however, the lower the quintile, the lower its share of aggregate income. For example, the quintile with the lowest earnings earns only 2.3% of the aggregate income, while the quintile with the highest income earns 49.3%—more than double its share. But there is also evidence that the middle quintile is slipping (from 18.3% in 1951 to 15.4% in 2002), while the highest quintile is gaining (from 42.8% in 1951 to 49.3% in 2002); this suggests that inequality is growing.

Figure 3.2 shows that the sources of income of persons in different income deciles vary. Persons in the lowest decile receive most of their income (62%) from *transfer payments,* such as old age assistance, family subsidies, unemployment insurance, and other forms of government assistance. The largest groups in this category are female single-parent families, elderly persons, and families in which the husband does not work. In contrast, those in the highest decile receive most of their income from employment (80%). Husband-and-wife families in which both spouses work make up a majority of this decile, although it should be noted that such dual-income families are also making up a greater part of other income deciles as well.

The picture which emerges, then, is that of a population with a wide range of incomes. Underemployed and unemployed persons, the elderly, and lone-parent families have the lowest incomes, while dual-income, highly professional, and well-educated salary-earners have the most substantial incomes.

Education

In an industrial society, differences in the levels and types of education obtained by its members are a significant factor in stratification. Because industrialization demands a

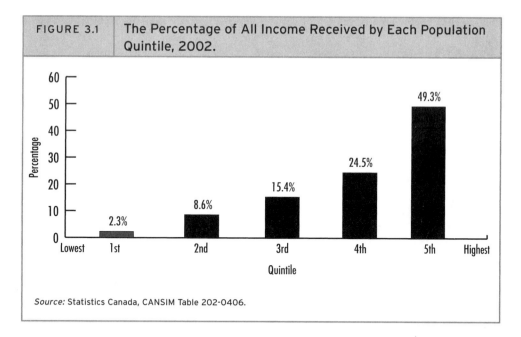

FIGURE 3.1 | The Percentage of All Income Received by Each Population Quintile, 2002.

Source: Statistics Canada, CANSIM Table 202-0406.

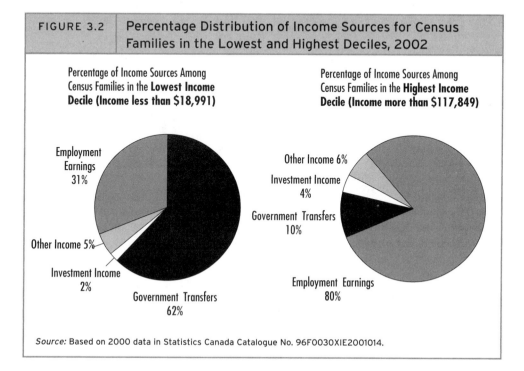

FIGURE 3.2 | Percentage Distribution of Income Sources for Census Families in the Lowest and Highest Deciles, 2002

Percentage of Income Sources Among Census Families in the **Lowest Income Decile (Income less than $18,991)**

Employment Earnings 31%

Other Income 5%

Investment Income 2%

Government Transfers 62%

Percentage of Income Sources Among Census Families in the **Highest Income Decile (Income more than $117,849)**

Other Income 6%

Investment Income 4%

Government Transfers 10%

Employment Earnings 80%

Source: Based on 2000 data in Statistics Canada Catalogue No. 96F0030XIE2001014.

high level of specialized training and job expertise, education is thought to be the key to success in the system. A better education is perceived as leading to a better occupation, which should generate higher income. Access to education and actual attainment, then, become the basis for further ranking within the society.

Table 3.1 shows that there is indeed a wide range of levels of educational attainment within the Canadian population and that these levels have changed significantly over time. In 2001, among persons aged 25 and over (i.e., those likely to have completed their formal schooling), 34.3% held university degrees and 17% had less than a Grade 9 education. The most striking evidence for the change in levels of educational attainment over the years

TABLE 3.1	Population 25 Years or Older and Highest Level of Education Attained, Canada, 2001			
	Highest Level of Schooling Attained (%)			
	Less than Grade 9	Grades 9–13	Some Post-secondary	University Degree
Total Population				
1951	54.9	42.9	-	2.3
1976	32.0	36.8	23.7	7.6
2001	17.0	31.6	17.0	34.3
By Gender, 2001				
Males	16.4	31.6	16.6	35.4
Females	17.6	31.6	17.5	33.3
By Province, 2001				
Canada	17.0	31.6	17.0	34.3
Newfoundland	27.6	41.2	11.2	20.0
Prince Edward Island	19.5	40.5	15.1	25.0
Nova Scotia	16.0	39.7	14.3	30.0
New Brunswick	25.0	36.1	14.3	24.6
Quebec	27.2	27.2	13.5	32.1
Ontario	13.9	30.2	17.5	38.4
Manitoba	16.3	39.2	17.5	27.0
Saskatchewan	16.4	42.0	17.3	24.3
Alberta	9.9	35.9	20.2	34.0
British Columbia	10.6	31.8	21.4	36.2
Yukon	8.4	28.0	24.6	39.0
Northwest Territories	22.6	26.2	20.7	30.6
Nunavut	41.3	19.7	23.1	15.9

Source: Adapted from Statistics Canada, 2001 Census, Catalogue No. 97F0017XCB01001.

(shown in the top part of the table) is the comparison with 1951, when over half (54.9%) of the population had less than a Grade 9 education (a proportion that had shrunk to 17% in 2001). In that same year, only a small minority had a university education (2.3%), while the overwhelming majority had less than a high-school education. Comparisons of 1951, 1976, and 2001 make it clear that there has been a massive upgrading of educational levels within the general population. We will return to the meaning of this important shift later. At this point, however it is important to note that significant differences in educational attainment constitute an important basis for hierarchical differentiation. Gender and provincial differences in education will also be discussed later.

Table 3.2 indicates that higher education is indeed linked to higher income. Each category includes many who are not in the labour force or who may only be in the labour force part-time, but the evidence is clear: The higher the education, the higher the income. Those with university degrees earn about two and a half times the amount earned by the poorest-educated category.

Occupation

Occupation is also an important dimension of inequality because it provides clues to a whole series of facts about an individual. We know that some occupations require particular kinds of credentials while others do not, and we know that remuneration and lifestyle vary from one occupation to another.

Table 3.3 shows the correlation between selected occupations and both education and income. In almost every category, persons with less than a high-school education earn less than those with university degrees, certificates, or diplomas. The major exception is athletes; among this group, those with less than a high-school education have higher incomes. Again, average income does not give a sense of the wide range of incomes in a category, and we can only guess that the income difference between NHL athletes and aspiring Olympic athletes, for example, must be huge. Senior managers with a university degree make double what a poorly educated person makes; even people in sales do better if they are better educated. However, the lower the skill-level required in an occupation, the less difference education-level makes to income. It is clear from this table that education and income are correlated and contribute to a hierarchical occupational ranking.

TABLE 3.2	Average Income for All Individuals, by Education and Sex, Canada, 2001		
Education Level	All Individuals	Males	Females
Less than high-school diploma	$19 604	$24 272	$14 973
High-school diploma and some post-secondary	25 043	30 885	19 880
Trades certificate or diploma	31 898	37 711	21 650
College certificate or diploma	32 573	41 404	26 435
University certificate, diploma, or degree	48 655	60 822	36 716

Source: Adapted from Statistics Canada, 2001 Census, Catalogue No. 97F0020XCB01001.

TABLE 3.3	Average Employment Income for Those with Less than High-School Education and Those with University Degrees, by Selected Occupation, 2001

	Average Employment Income	
	Less than high-school diploma	University certificate, diploma, or degree
Senior managers	$67 589	$ 121 911
Managers in retail trade, food and hospitality services	29 358	41 015
Securities agents, investment dealers and traders	68 646	104 848
Secretaries	22 744	25 459
Clerical occupations	21 273	26 361
Physicists and astronomers	0	63 838
Health occupations	21 011	62 140
Physicians, dentists, and veterinarians	0	114 919
Judges	0	142 401
Athletes	112 713	35 924
Sales and service occupations	13 329	29 169
Dry cleaning and laundry supervisors	21 783	0
Retail salespersons and salesclerks	13 931	23 416
Police officers and firefighters	46 717	56 721
Truck drivers	34 142	32 121
Trades helpers and labourers	19 866	20 578
Farmers and farm managers	19 654	23 507
Labourers in processing, manufacturing, and utilites	20 864	20 211

Source: Statistics Canada, 2001 Census, Catalogue No. 97F0019XCB01050.

Table 3.4 shows that earnings differ greatly among various occupations. Note that even within fields such as health care there is a clear hierarchy among the various roles (e.g., physicians and dentists earn more than nurses and dental assistants), just as there is between managers and clerical workers in the business field. While this table also reveals an important gender difference (which we will explore later), the income differences between occupations are indisputable.

INTERPRETING INEQUALITY

Now that we have established that socio-economic inequality exists in Canadian society, we need to interpret it. While many theories propose to explain inequality, there are two

TABLE 3.4	Number of Earners and Average Earnings in Selected Occupations, by Sex, 2001			
	Number of Earners		Average Earnings	
	Male	Female	Male	Female
Senior Management	126 770	37 660	$114 519	$69 933
Bookkeepers	4 990	42 530	36 202	29 232
Secretaries	4 095	198 910	40 460	30 086
Clerical	239 505	587 710	35 914	30 632
Family Physicians	15 260	6 775	133 789	96 958
Registered Nurses	9 400	116 735	49 536	46 142
Dentists	6 715	2 000	129 104	82 254
Dental Assistants	205	11 270	32 676	27 846
Judges	1 380	445	146 008	131 663
Lawyers	32 630	14 660	114 894	77 451
Social Workers	7 225	23 255	45 346	41 227
Elementary-school Teachers	32 185	128 600	50 901	46 732
Cashiers	8 830	49 945	22 925	19 391
Trades / Labourers	134 430	14 315	34 426	26 359

Source: Adapted from Statistics Canada, 2001 Census, Catalogue No. 97F0012XCB01049.

core explanations: the functional and the conflict.[2] The *functional approach* suggests that a stratified society is not only natural but inevitable given the differential rewards and opportunities found within the society. The key notion here is that individuals attain the class position they deserve; in other words, individual merit or achievement generates differences in salaries or status. Inequality is viewed as functional for a society in that it serves to motivate individuals to strive to achieve more. Critics of the functionalist view suggest that inequality is not so much natural as it is traditional or even hereditary. Merit or achievement is always conditioned by where you start out; if you are born into a home with an unemployed father, live in low-cost housing, and are surrounded by family and friends who have a pessimistic view of the world, how can you be faulted if you have little ambition or feel that the odds against which you struggle are too formidable? Compare such a person to one who has parents who are both professionals, who own property, and who inculcate values of optimism and ambition. Do the two persons have an equal chance of attaining the position they deserve? What about people who have not earned their substantial rewards and yet have inherited large sums of money? Are janitors paid less than professional athletes because they are really less important to the functioning of a society? In sum, the functional view more or less justifies the inequality that already exists by ignoring other factors that affect an individual's ability to respond to opportunities in the society.

RESEARCH CLIP 3.1	The Relationship between Education and Earnings

Hunter and Lieper studied the issue of *credentialism*—the use of credentials (certification, degrees) to determine job-eligibility and earnings. They found that people with more years of schooling and with certification do indeed earn more money than those without. But they also found that it was not the education or the certification per se that produced the earnings effect, but the position that required them. In other words, the primary impact of educational attainment was to make an individual eligible to be considered for higher-paying positions; thus it was the position (rather than the certificate per se) that was the primary determinant of higher earnings.

Source: Alfred A. Hunter and Jean McKenzie Lieper, "On Formal Education, Skills, and Earnings: The Role of Educational Certificates in Earnings Determination," *Canadian Journal of Sociology* 18 (1993): 21-42.

While the functional approach places great emphasis on the individual, the *conflict approach* places its emphasis on the shared nature of inequality. Class consciousness arises when people become aware that they share a certain vital condition—namely, ownership or non-ownership of private property or of the means of production. The class of owners is the *bourgeoisie*; the non-owners are the *proletariat*. Members of a society grow increasingly aware of to which of the two classes they belong. Even when conflict theorists acknowledge the existence of an interstitial middle class, they see its members— even if employed as experts or credentialled managers—as, essentially, wage labourers. A society's dominant ideas and beliefs can be viewed as ideologies which sustain the class structure of inequality. Whether or not the labouring class eventually challenges and overthrows the capitalist class, repeated struggles by groups resisting capitalist domination can be expected.

Critics of the conflict view of inequality suggest that, just as the functionalist approach appears to be a rationale for inequality, so the conflict view appears to be a rationale for social change. The antagonism between these two opposing groups or classes (as the original advocate of this perspective, Karl Marx, had envisioned it) has been weakened by the fragmentation of the non-owners of the means of production into sub-groups (or *class fractions*), which lack unity and which may be in opposition to each other. There are also differences between owners who hire large pools of workers and small owners who hire no workers. The complexity of inequality, some argue, cannot be reduced to simple class divisions, especially when large numbers of people enjoy a reasonable standard of living. It might also be argued that in a society where individualism prevails, many people resist adopting a perspective that requires class action or a group view of class condition.

The functionalist view explains inequality on the basis of differences in *individual* abilities and tasks. The conflict view explains inequality in terms of *group* differences in power and capital accumulation and of the conflict which develops when groups struggle to preserve or rearrange their relationships.

Differing Perspectives

Structural Functionalism

The structural functional perspective accepts that inequality is present in all societies, the result of differences in individual abilities to achieve and compete. Individuals endowed with superior ability may have advantages over other, less fortunately endowed individuals; the result may be a mosaic-type society with hierarchical dimensions. However, in Canadian society, stratification is not necessarily permanent and fixed; individuals can and do take advantage of opportunities to change their class position. Movement in the class structure, known as *social mobility*, is what is important. All societies require people at a variety of class positions, from low- to high-status, in order to fulfill all societally needed functions. Inequality in Canadian society is thus seen as natural and inevitable.

Conflict

The conflict perspective understands Canadian society in terms of groups in which power and ultimate authority are unequally distributed. The concentration of power in the hands of the privileged few (known as the *elites*) engenders resistance on the part of others who lack power and desire it. In a capitalist society, persons with economic power are handsomely rewarded, and structure the society in such a way as to retain and justify their power and maximize their profits. Groups are constantly forming to chal-lenge the distribution of power. Societal change is best understood in terms of how people organize themselves to challenge the hegemony of dominant groups. In addition to social class, other bases for dominance may be region, gender, ethnicity, and race. Power thus produces countermovements that attempt to rearrange the distribution of power.

Symbolic Interactionism

As seen from the symbolic interactionist perspective, inequality leads to different ways of understanding and communicating reality. Symbols of wealth and prestige can be contrasted with symbols and lifestyles of poverty. Being poor, disadvantaged, or marginalized must be understood in terms of a social world in which there are few choices for those with few resources; the social world of those with more resources is characterized by different cultural assumptions, norms, and values. In fact, each social class (as well as each segmented group) has its own cultural symbols and world view, which help to sustain differences within the society. Inequality leads to the development of different behaviours and expectations; this means that people will feel most comfortable with people from their own group. From this perspective, it is not so much that inequality is good or bad, natural or created, as that it produces different social worlds which must be analyzed and understood.

Class Analysis

When the focus is on differences in individual attributes, "social class" becomes a loose statistical category of persons with similar characteristics (e.g., similar incomes). Higher income presumably means higher social-class position, and arbitrary distinctions can be made between, for example, upper middle class and middle class. When the focus shifts to the opposing interests of capital and labour and the basic split between them, the concept of social class identifies social groups formed on the basis of their relationship to the means of production.[3] It is not how much income or education you have that matters but where you fit into a society structured by corporate capital.

It is important to discuss the concept of social class in this latter sense, because much of the critical analysis of Canadian society has been informed by it. Instead of merely being compared on the dimension of income level, people in the labour force can be classified according to their status as employers or employees. One such analysis pointed out that 2.7% of the labour force were employers, constituting the capitalist class (though many of these persons ran small businesses whose incomes represented only a small proportion of the total income of that class), 6.4% were self-employed, and 90% were employed in either the private or public sector.[4] Once the basic distinction has been made between employees and employers, the employee category can be further broken down into managers and technocrats, supervisors, semi-autonomous workers, and workers.

Another analysis (with a similar conclusion) identifies two primary instruments of power: the ability to command the means of production and the ability to command the labour power of others.[5] The capitalist/executive class, which possesses both instruments of power, makes up 6.2% of the population. On the other hand, the working class, which has neither instrument of power, makes up 57.6%. The old middle class (11.3%) may have some capital/property but little labour power, whereas the new middle class (24.9%) have no control over the means of production but some control over labour through bureaucratic power. In any case, power ultimately lies with a few.

According to this kind of analysis, the capitalist class is very small and interlocked through its corporate power. This analysis also shows that workers are by far the largest group in the labour force. The existence of an intermediate group between capital and labour is acknowledged, though it is most typically identified as a class fraction within the subordinate class.

Over the last 20 years, the predominant class-based interpretive model for understanding Canadian society has been *political economy*.[6] Developed from the conflict model, political economy looks first at how people earn their living (the economic dimension), then explores the conflicting social relations that develop out of this process (the political). Some people accumulate capital (the capitalist class), others work for wages (labourers), while still others are self-employed (the *petite bourgeoisie*). Political economy maintains that those who possess capital hold the ultimate power and that the exercise of this power, unless challenged, will automatically be exploitative of workers. Studies in political economy can be either liberal or Marxist. What they all have in common is a focus on how power is used or experienced in a stratified society.

The focus in the political-economy paradigm is on property rights and capital accumulation, which have social consequences since economic control produces social power. Capital concentration can be viewed in a national context but it also has international implications, affecting other societies. Political economy looks at class interests to find the economic basis of public and private decision-making. Canadian political-economy theory is usually rooted in the staples thesis of Harold Innis; it has been influenced by the elite studies of Porter and Clement, by numerous studies on region, gender, and ethnic conflict, and by various forms of dependency analysis.

Does the evidence of inequality cited here support the functional or the conflict perspective? The answer depends upon whether people who share similar characteristics (on the aforementioned ranking dimensions) are merely a statistical category or whether they actually possess a group consciousness. If we view categories of income or education as artificial constructs, then the people who fall within particular categories need not be seen as anything more than a statistical aggregation of individuals. On the other hand, if members of various groups do indeed share economic interests and a similar world view (in contrast to other groups with different interests and world views), then repeated conflicts are likely to occur between diverse groups seeking to preserve or rearrange the structure of power. In Canadian society, notions of group or class interest are repeatedly challenged by individualistic ideals of reward based upon merit and achievement. However, from a macro perspective, the analysis of Canadian society is greatly enriched by examining how

The New Political Economy

Political economy emphasizes how a society is organized for the production of goods and services and points out how these arrangements reflect the realities and consequences of social inequality. By questioning the dominant ideas about economy and polity and pointing out their contradictions and tensions, political economy demonstrates that inequality is a statement about power relations within a society. One of its key notions is that the capitalist class seeks to mobilize the power and authority of the state for its own interests.

Political economy is keenly interested in societal change—understood as challenge or resistance to the established order—over time. For example, labour may challenge the capitalist class, as in the well-known Winnipeg General Strike of 1919, or protesters may challenge global economic hegemony at world economic summits or conferences. More recently, political economy has shown how globalization and deregulation have strengthened the capitalist class but weakened the power of workers, resulting in greater inequality in society.

What makes the new political economy "new" is that it does not claim to be value-free but is motivated by values of economic and social justice. Currently, political economy challenges the assumption that neo-liberalism is a natural and inevitable trend. Its goal is to understand how the economy structures social processes, in order to discover how to facilitate interventions or transformations.

Further Reading: Wallace Clement and Leah Vosko, eds., *Changing Canada: Political Economy as Transformation* (Montreal: McGill-Queen's University Press, 2003); Wallace Clement, ed., *Understanding Canada: Building on the New Canadian Political Economy* (Montreal: McGill-Queen's University Press, 1997); and Wallace Clement and Glen Williams, eds., *The New Canadian Political Economy* (Montreal: McGill-Queen's University Press, 1989).

dominant ideas and structures are sustained and how groups emerge to challenge or resist dominant forms considered unfair or oppressive.[7]

It is important that the differences between these two conceptions of inequality be grasped at the outset, since each perspective applies its own interpretive schema and proposes its own solutions. We will use both perspectives in our continuing analysis of inequality because they represent opposing streams of thought within our society.

OTHER DIMENSIONS OF INEQUALITY

Thus far, we have discussed inequality as a socio-economic phenomenon, without considering cross-cutting variables. However, three other dimensions of inequality in Canadian society have received considerable attention. They are ethnicity, region, and gender.

Ethnic Inequality

Perhaps the earliest form of inequality acknowledged in Canadian society was ethnic inequality. Beginning with French–English relations and continuing through later phases of immigration, ethnic groups have had different positions in the status hierarchy. Ethnic descent or ethnic origin, then, may be an important dimension of inequality.

In 1965, John Porter, a sociologist at Carleton University, published *The Vertical Mosaic*, which has become a Canadian classic. The underlying theme of the book was that ethnicity was intimately related to the stratification structure in Canada. The cultural mosaic of Canada was not random, argued Porter; some ethnic groups possessed a more favourable position in the society than others. Porter tied this ethnic hierarchy to the early settlement of the country and particularly to French–English relations. When the British and French first settled in Canada, their tendency was to re-create the stratified societies of their homelands. After the British defeated the French, the two cultures existed side by side, each with its own individual structure of social organization; the British, however, held the dominant position. Nevertheless, Quebec's social structure remained relatively intact, with doctors, lawyers, and the clergy having the highest social standing in a largely agrarian community. British farmers also retained their rural social structure. The major hierarchical differences were in the areas of commerce, trade, and administration, in which persons of British descent held overwhelming control.

With the onset of industrialization and the shift away from an agricultural economy, the entrenched English-Canadian upper class became the industrial leaders, not only in English Canada but also in Quebec. The situation was exacerbated by the fact that the Quebec educational system, which emphasized classical studies, was not designed to prepare its students for technological occupations. As a result, the British were considerably overrepresented at the professional, administrative, and financial levels of the Quebec labour force, whereas the French were overrepresented in the agricultural, primary, and unskilled occupations of that province. When the French moved to urban areas, they formed a convenient working class (or "oppressed majority") under English-Canadian control.[8] The implications of this kind of class subordination will be discussed in Chapter Five, but at this point it should be noted that virtually from the beginning, ethnicity and class position combined in such a way that the social status of persons of French descent was lower than that of the English. Dofny and Rioux speak of this convergence of class consciousness and ethnic identity as "ethnic class" or *eth-class*.[9] This focus on ethnic differences may have ignored class differences among English Canadians, but it did sensitize Canadians to the fact that ethnicity was an important component of the stratification of Canadian society.

The addition of other ethnic groups to the society through immigration contributed to greater complexity in ethnic stratification patterns. It is important to note that federal government policy determines which ethnic groups are preferred as immigrants, and a change in admittance qualifications can significantly affect the nature of ethnic representation.[10] The government, then, determines which ethnic groups will be allowed in on the basis of what work they are likely to do. For example, the Eastern Europeans who entered the country in the 1920s were largely rural peasants and were encouraged to settle remote western farmlands (e.g., the Ukrainians in northern Saskatchewan), whereas the wave of Asian immigration in the 1990s comprised many skilled and professional persons destined for urban centres. The term used to refer to the class position at which immigrants enter a society is *entrance status*.

The key contribution of Porter's *The Vertical Mosaic* was the idea that while Canadian society could be likened to a changing kaleidoscope of ethnic groups, there was a vertical or hierarchical dimension to this patterning. Not only was there asymmetry between the English and French; other ethnic groups as well had distinct locations in the hierarchy, related not only to their entrance status but also to their ability to respond to their new environment.

Recent research has suggested that the ethnic component of stratification is now eroding.[11] It is possible that ethnicity may have been more relevant at an earlier point in the society's history or that it now it may primarily be an issue for the foreign-born. With some exceptions (which we will note), ethnic status may be increasingly irrelevant among those born in Canada, regardless of ethnic origin. The evidence is that ethnic stratification has become greatly attenuated among persons of European ancestry.[12] One study even found that when other variables were controlled for, Canadians of French ancestry earned significantly more than Canadians of British ancestry at all educational levels.[13] When French–English differences do exist, they may be accounted for by generational factors more relevant to the older generation. Moreover, the language first spoken at home is no longer a predictor of educational attainment in Canada.[14] Thus, being born abroad may be the most important variable in ethnicity's significance in inequality.

But such a conclusion may be far too simple. We know that some immigrants born abroad have greater advantages than others in Canadian society. After reviewing the literature and completing their own analysis of the data, Lautard and Guppy argued that although there has been a decline in the significance of ethnicity as measured by occupational differences, that decline has not totally erased ethnic origin as a factor.[15] The ethnic division of labour has been reduced by about 50% and is now less prominent than the gendered division of labour. This, of course, is not to deny that some groups have distinctive occupational concentrations (e.g., people of British and Jewish ethnicity in managerial/professional fields, Asians in personal services or professional occupations).[16] But in general, the *"new" vertical mosaic* is understood more in racial than in ethnic terms, as Aboriginal people (who are Canadian-born) and visible minorities (who may or may not be) encounter definite barriers in the stratification system.

When we measure educational attainment, we find that the dominance of persons of British descent has clearly waned; there is also some evidence that the children of immigrants are particularly keen to use education to change the class position of their family of origin. Furthermore, recent immigration policies giving priority to persons with professional skills have produced a more educated immigrant stream. But the question is whether similar education generates similar incomes or whether occupational position is liable to ethnicity-related penalties.[17] There are two conclusions here: One is that immigrants educated abroad receive lower returns (in terms of occupational status and earnings) on their educational investment than the native-born;[18] the second is that immigrants who belong to visible minorities earn less, on average, than other immigrants with similar levels of education, while immigrants of European background generally receive above-average income for their educational level. As groups, however, foreign-born visible minorities and Aboriginal people earn incomes considerably below the national mean, while the incomes of Canadian-born visible minorities are somewhat closer to the mean but not as high as those of Caucasians, whether foreign- or native-born (with the exception of Southern Europeans).[19]

RESEARCH CLIP 3.2	Inequality among Persons of Caribbean Origin in Toronto

Approximately three quarters of all Caribbean-born persons in Canada live in the province of Ontario, with most living in Metropolitan Toronto and the surrounding areas of Mississauga and Brampton. There is increasing residential concentration of Caribbean immigrants in these cities.

Inequality among these Caribbean immigrants is manifested in what Francis Henry identifies as *differential incorporation*. As a whole, the primary reason that persons of Caribbean origin are not structurally integrated into the mainstream of Canadian society is their inability to gain full access to the economic, social, and cultural rewards of the society. While they are part of Canadian society in a broad sense, there are both internal and external factors which create barriers to their full participation in the society.

The most significant internal factor is that the Black community is segmented into two classes: working class and middle class. But there is also a growing underclass of youth born to working-class parents and/or single mothers; these young people frequently drop out of school and experience significant frustration because of poverty and racism in the surrounding environment. While coping mechanisms, such as entrepreneurship, support groups, and island associations, have developed, varying degrees of marginalization and internal class divisions continue to fragment the community and prevent more cohesive political mobilization.

The major barrier to integration into Canadian society, however, is racial discrimination, expressed through various forms of exclusionary behaviour. The strongest evidence of differential incorporation is found in matters of employment. Persons of Caribbean origin are poorly represented in managerial and supervisory positions and overrepresented in skilled, semi-skilled, and manual occupations.

Source: Based on Frances Henry, *The Caribbean Diaspora in Toronto: Learning to Live with Racism* (Toronto: University of Toronto Press, 1994).

It may well be asked whether the barrier to equality is ethnic status or whether it is a societal structure that creates discrimination against particular ethnic groups. In other words, are the ethnic group's characteristics the problem or is the host society's response at fault? The answer appears to depend upon the ethnic group in question. For example, the incomes of Italians and Portuguese are higher than their relatively low levels of education and occupational status might suggest; on the other hand, Chinese and South Asians have higher levels of educational attainment than their incomes would suggest. Hou and Balakrishnan argue that ethnic differences in socio-economic status still exist within Canadian society but manifest differently among diverse groups.[20] In that sense, the structure of society gives evidence of *systemic discrimination*—institutionalized practices that are arbitrary and exclusionary and that contribute to ethnic inequality. The devaluing of foreign credentials is one example of systemic discrimination, and the lack of employment networks for top jobs may be another.

It is important that the complexity of these questions be acknowledged, for although ethnicity is sometimes viewed as a cause of inequality, in reality it is intimately connected to other factors, such as occupation, educational opportunity, gender, and age. Peter Li has concluded, in contrast to the argument of *The Vertical Mosaic*, that there is not a strong relationship between ethnicity and class position; ethnicity, he argued, must be understood not as in itself causing inequality but as combining with additional factors to give some groups advantages over others. [21] Not only race/ethnicity but length of residency in Canada and cultural accommodation are important variables in whether and how inequality will be experienced. Race/ethnicity is still an important variable in inequality, but its precise role is not always clear—particularly after several generations.

Regional Inequality

Another historic dimension of inequality in Canadian society is based on regional economic differences. Mildred Schwartz has described regionalism as a form of "institutionalized inequality" between the various parts of the Canadian entity.[22] While this inequality may be a consequence of the power relationships between regions, regional inequalities may also be viewed as a consequence of the class structure that cuts across regions.

The traditional view of regional disparities stresses the importance of geographical causes, such as distance from markets or transportation problems, as the basis of inequality; according to this view, some regions of the country are less developed than others because these difficulties made them less competitive. The point is that regional disparities were considered more or less natural; any regional differentials in power and development were attributed to the fact of some regions having more people, industry, and resources. From this perspective, it is seen as the government's role to correct normal market forces by using stimulants to create jobs and grants to equalize the standard of living across the society. However, Brym has pointed out that in spite of such government interventions, the per capita income gap between regions has actually increased.[23]

The *political economy perspective* suggests that those who own and control the means of production (i.e., the capitalist class) enlarge their activities in those locations where profit-making potential is greatest.[24] Profit-making, in turn, is more likely to occur in places close to markets, large pools of labour, other members of the decision-making capitalist class, and transportation nerve-centres. This has encouraged *centralization* and *concentration* of business activity, which have helped to produce regional differences in wealth. The hinterland resources in outlying regions of Canada are important to the industrial economy of central Canada and foreign markets. Extraction of these resources requires a hinterland working class, whose employment cycle is heavily dependent on forces external not only to their region but also to their class position. In other words, decisions made by the economic elite, who have interests in other regions or countries, effectively control the nature and existence of resource-based jobs. Workers in the resource industries continually face the threat of mine or mill shutdown as a result of escalating production in competing regions or reduced market demand.

Wherever the concentration of corporate capitalism occurs, an infrastructure of manual workers, a middle class of technocrats and managerial workers, and a capitalist class of owners with higher levels of income will develop. This development will effectively increase regional disparities in income. Poorer regions will experience a drain on their best people to regions with greater income potential. When hinterland economic activity requires corporate-office participation, centrally located corporations send representatives from the industrial heartland to the hinterland as managers and supervisors; in consequence, residents of outlying regions are confined to jobs providing manual labour, with little opportunity for advancement. Thus the centralization of capitalist activity both reflects and contributes to regional disparities.

Just as ethnic inequalities have a strong economic basis, so too must regional inequalities be grounded in economic realities. But just as we debated whether and to what extent ethnic inequality may be rooted in the class structure, we can also debate whether regional inequality may be not the natural result of economic differences but a consequence of decisions made in the interests of the dominant class. Are there indeed economic differences between the regions?

Table 3.1 (page 90) revealed significant differences in provincial levels of educational attainment. Nunavut (41.3%) has the highest percentage of residents with less than a Grade 9 education; Newfoundland (27.6%), Quebec (27.2%) and New Brunswick (25%) also have significant proportions of residents with a comparable level of schooling. These numbers can be compared with a much lower percentage for the Yukon (8.4%), British Columbia (10.6%), and Alberta (9.9%). On the other hand, the percentage of persons holding university degrees is highest in Ontario (38.4%), British Columbia (36.2%), Alberta (34%), and the Yukon (39%); the percentage having completed university is lower in New Brunswick (24.6%), Saskatchewan (24.3%), and Newfoundland (20%). This is not to imply that areas with less-educated populations lack good educational systems but rather that the better educated tend to live where employment opportunities requiring certification are more likely to be concentrated. Therefore we would expect regions with stronger economies to have the best-educated labour force.

Table 3.5 shows that the lowest unemployment rates are in the area from Ontario westward, though British Columbia's unemployment rate spiked in the years preceding 2001. Median family incomes are highest in Ontario and Alberta; the percentage of families with incomes over $100 000 is highest in these provinces as well. The Atlantic region has higher unemployment rates and lower median incomes. Quebec does better in employment and in median family income than the Atlantic provinces but not nearly as well as Ontario; the differences between the two provinces are striking. In the West, Alberta differs significantly from the two other Prairie provinces and even from British Columbia, having lower unemployment, higher median family income, and a higher percentage of residents with incomes over $100 000. It is not surprising that the provinces with the biggest cities are

TABLE 3.5	Unemployment Rates, Median Income, and Percentage of Population with Incomes over $100 000, by Province		
	Unemployment Rate	Median Family Market Income	% with Family Income over $100 000
Newfoundland	21.8	$25 600	6.7
Prince Edward Island	13.2	29 500	5.6
Nova Scotia	10.9	32 700	7.6
New Brunswick	12.5	31 600	7.4
Quebec	8.2	34 700	9.1
Ontario	6.1	48 600	16.8
Manitoba	6.1	38 200	8.8
Saskatchewan	6.3	34 900	7.9
Alberta	5.2	47 400	15.5
British Columbia	8.5	40 300	12.8

Source: Statistics Canada, 2001 Census, Catalogue No. 93F0053XIE and CANSIM Table 202-0201.

also those in which these indices of economic health are the strongest (although Quebec is something of an exception).[25] In general, lack of job availability, particularly in the Atlantic provinces, suppresses median income and exacerbates regional inequalities.[26]

Canada's core regions are highly urban industrial areas; hinterland regions are peripheral to the core.[27] A *metropolis* is a centre of political and financial power, and it is from Canada's metropolises that the elite engage in decision making that affects the rest of the society. The *hinterland* essentially plays a supporting role to the metropolis by providing raw materials and labour as needed. The relationship between the metropolis and hinterland is *symbiotic* (i.e., one needs the other); however, it is *unbalanced*: The metropolis tends to dominate and exploit the hinterland. The appearance of opposition between regions may be primarily a result of the fact that one region's decision-making elite is in a position to exercise control over subordinate regions. Subordinate regions may thus have the perception that their fate is controlled by sinister powers in dominant regions. In the 1920s and 1930s, for example, the farmers' movements of the West were built upon regional perceptions of control by an elite, identified as Toronto's "Bay Street Barons." In a similar vein, Pierre Vallières termed Québécois "white niggers" because of their subordination to the anglophone industrial elite.[28]

Region can thus be understood not only as a demographic or territorial construct but as a class relationship. Regions can be analyzed in terms of their common class basis (e.g., the petit-bourgeois farmers of the West) and opposition to elite control (e.g., of credit, markets, transport policy) based in central Canada.[29] Alternatively, in order to maintain hierarchical interregional relationships, regions might be examined in terms of their class structure so as to identify which elites operate in more than one region. Struggles for control of a regional resource (e.g., fish) by large extraregional capitalist entrepreneurs in competition with regional capital or local residents also reflects the class context of

| RESEARCH CLIP 3.3 | Life Satisfaction in Marginal Regions |

Disparities in levels of economic development do not imply superior or inferior lifestyles. In fact, one study of an underdeveloped region, the Great Northern Peninsula of Newfoundland and Labrador, found that residents' level of life satisfaction was high because, thanks to the informal exchange of labour within the community, they could own their own residences without a mortgage. Leaving the community to seek better work elsewhere would inevitably mean a higher cost of living, as well as loss of meaningful friendship-networks. People therefore deal very constructively with marginal economic environments.

Source: Lawrence F. Felt and Peter R. Sinclair, "Home Sweet Home: Dimensions and Determinants of Life Satisfaction in an Underdeveloped Region," *Canadian Journal of Sociology* 16 (1991): 1-21.

regionalism.[30] The dynamics of regionalism will be the subject of Chapter Four; for the time being, it is sufficient to note that inequalities based on region are an important dimension of Canadian society.

Gender Inequality

A third and highly important dimension of inequality is gender. In fact, it has been argued that most of our analyses of hierarchical social ranking need to be virtually redone in view of the traditional neglect of gender in studies of inequality.[31] It is perhaps only in the last 20 or 30 years that consciousness-raising has taken place about the socio-economic importance of gender differences.

Whatever the biological differences between men and women may be (to which we refer using the term "sex"), there are also social/cultural differences, to which we attach the term "gender." By focusing on gender differences, we come to see how differences between men and women are *socially constructed*—that is, how our society establishes roles and expectations for people based on their gender.[32] Why is it that secretaryship is considered a feminine domain and management a masculine one? Men are just as capable of filing or typing as women, yet society traditionally defines certain jobs as appropriate for women, even restricting women to those roles. When these societally defined roles involve being subordinate to men, the result is gender inequality, or what is known as a *gendered division of labour*.

What evidence is there of gender inequality? Let's go back to tables presented earlier in this chapter and review the data, which we deferred for discussion until now. Table 3.1 reveals that there is very little difference between the levels of educational attainment of men and women. Men were slightly more likely than women to have a university degree. In 1980, women made up the majority of university undergraduates for the first time; significant changes have clearly taken place since then, bringing women to higher levels of educational attainment than ever before.[33]

Do similar levels of education lead to equal pay? Table 3.2 suggests that at all levels of education, men earn considerably more than women; the gap is especially wide for those with university degrees. Table 3.4 shows that men are overwhelmingly better represented in the highest-paying professions, whereas women are the overwhelming majority in the lowest-paying occupations (except manual labour). In all professions, men earn more than women. The gender gap in earnings is measured by the female-to-male earnings ratio. In 2002, women employed full-time earned 71.3% of what men earned, and women employed part-time earned 79.4%; overall, women earned 65.2% of what men earned. Although Figure 3.3 indicates that women have made significant progress since 1980, when they earned 51.3% of what men earned, the gender gap is still very much present. Not shown in the data presented is the fact that single women are the only group to approximate men's earnings (at 92%).

It has already been suggested that the gender gap in earnings has been a relatively recent societal issue. The reason for the emergence of this issue has been the dramatic increase in women's labour-force participation. In 1901, 16% of Canadian women participated in the labour force. That number edged up by only eight percentage points in 50 years (to 24% in 1951).[34] Since 1961, women's labour-force participation rates have increased phenomenally, from 29% to 40% between 1961 and 1971, to 51% by 1981 and up to 57% by 2003. Ironically, men's labour-force participation, while still substantially higher than women's, has declined in recent years—from 78% in 1975 to 68% in 2003. Forty-seven percent of all employed persons are now women.[35] Whereas in 1976 only 39% of women with children under the age of 16 were in the paid labour force, that number jumped to 72% by 2003 (though a significant percentage were part-time). Clearly, the traditional view of women as solely homemakers is out of date. What is remarkable is how relatively recent these changes are!

Two observations must be made about the altered character of the Canadian labour force. One is that women's employment roles are concentrated in specific sectors. Men work in a broader range of occupational sectors, whereas women are clustered in clerical and service industries, with a smaller number concentrated in the health and education fields (in which areas some build management and administrative careers). The concentration of females into

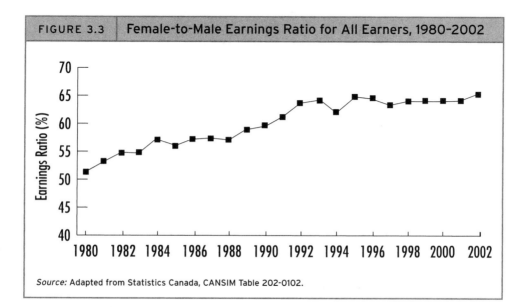

FIGURE 3.3   Female-to-Male Earnings Ratio for All Earners, 1980–2002

Source: Adapted from Statistics Canada, CANSIM Table 202-0102.

a narrow range of occupations is known as *crowding*, an indication of a *dual labour market* (i.e., one in which women's employment spheres are almost distinct from men's).

The second observation is that even in the relatively short time from 1982 to 1993, women made some impressive gains. For example, while women represented 29.2% of all persons in the managerial/administrative category in 1982, they accounted for 42.2% of that category by 1993.[36] In the period from 1987 to 2003, women's representation in senior management positions had improved from 16.9% to 24.2%, and in professional roles in the natural sciences and engineering, from 16.7% to 22%.[37] Despite such progress, there are still domains, such as the clerical and nursing fields, in which women dominate. Thus, although (as has already been noted) the female-to-male earnings ratio has improved, gender equality is still far away.[38]

Important changes are taking place, and it is true that some women have moved into traditionally male professions. But as Armstrong and Armstrong have pointed out, two thirds of women are in jobs where 70% of the workers are female.[39] Women workers are concentrated in only 35 of the 200 occupations listed by Statistics Canada. Although the gender wage gap (among all workers, regardless of education) is decreasing, this decrease is primarily due to a decline in male employment income; furthermore, the wage gap between the most highly educated, highest-earning men and women seems to be increasing. Women continue to be crowded into low-paying employment sectors; the percentage of women in clerical careers, for example, shows no sign of abatement at all.

Women from visible minorities face problems related not only to the gendered division of labour but also to the *racialized* division of labour.[40] Immigrant women from visible minorities often deal with huge cultural differences in role expectations and often find themselves doing menial or part-time work for wage labour. These women are thus doubly disadvantaged.

Explanations How can gender inequality be explained?[41] A structural-functional explanation would assert that women and men each have their different roles to perform and functions to fulfill, and therefore whatever inequality exists is *natural*. For example, the fact that men are more active in the economic sphere and women more active at home would be seen as reflecting a natural division of labour in which different roles are played by different members of society. Yet the reality is that only one third of married women with children under 16 are full-time housewives.[42] The economic realities of the cost of living and/or of contemporary lifestyle preferences increasingly make a dual income a necessity. The evidence, then, suggests that the traditional family pattern has changed significantly and that gender roles are not fixed.

A conflict type of explanation looks at the structural basis for inequality and roots it in *patriarchy*. Central to the concept of patriarchy is the idea that males have supported or created a social structure in which they have greater power and economic privilege. Patriarchy leads to inequality in two ways. First, since men are the primary breadwinners, women's work can be trivialized and women relegated to temporary, part-time, or seasonal activity in low-paying jobs that lack the security, benefits (e.g., pensions), and higher pay of full-time jobs. When women do work full-time, it is most likely to be in the clerical and service sectors, where pay is relatively low. Second, even when women upgrade their skills and education, they are confined by traditional practices and attitudes to lesser roles in male-dominated professions or occupations. Either way, men retain their position of dominance, consciously or unconsciously preventing women from reaching their potential.

Another conflict-based interpretive scheme ties women's work into the capitalist economy. While it is true that some women wish to only work part time, it can be argued that this flexible labour pool is of significant benefit to profit making. Women make up 72% of the part-time labour force, and employers can cut costs by hiring more part-time employees. Furthermore, women engage in domestic labour which goes unrewarded although it is essential to the maintenance of the paid labour force.[43] In raising the dependent children who become tomorrow's work force, as well as being caregivers to all family members, women perform work which is considered economically valueless but is necessary to sustain the economy. Women then, remain highly dependent on men because their own work keeps them economically subservient (as a kind of proletariat),[44] without pensions and with poor remuneration. Thus women play a critical role in supporting the capitalist system but are excluded from its benefits through structural subordination.[45]

As women have entered the workforce in greater numbers (primarily out of economic necessity), one thing that has changed but little is women's responsibility for domestic labour. Women who do paid work outside the home must also do unpaid work inside the home—the so-called "*second shift*," which massively increases their workload.[46] This dual segregation of women into the so-called *pink ghetto* of paid labour and the domestic ghetto of unpaid labour is referred to as the *double ghetto*.

Transforming the Status of Women The *feminist movement* arose as a response to gender inequalities. It has a descriptive and interpretive objective (i.e., evaluating and explaining evidence), but it also has an activist agenda of bringing about change. Within feminism, three streams or approaches can be identified. *Liberal feminism* tends to accept the fact that men and women differ but lobbies for laws and policies which, by eradicating inequality and promoting equal opportunity, may produce a more just society. *Socialist feminism* views capitalism as the structural cause of oppression in both class and gender dimensions and therefore desires to change the capitalist structure whereby inequities in both domains are perpetuated. *Radical feminism* understands the ideology of male superiority as the fundamental source of oppression and exploitation and seeks to replace this dominant ideology. Strains of all three can be found in Canadian society, and the different feminist approaches are frequently expressed in ways that are not mutually exclusive.

Roberta Hamilton has argued persuasively from a feminist perspective that the Canadian state itself has been patriarchal. She asserts that despite some changes, the status quo of male dominance has been maintained by means of, for example, the lack of gender equity among political decision-makers and the undervaluing of women's work.[47]

At the turn of the century, women's quest for gender equality in Canada focused on the right to vote, or *suffrage*[48]; women finally won that right in 1918. However, it was not until the late 1960s and 1970s that women's groups began to put pressure on the government for other forms of equality. Among the most significant events in the evolution of the Canadian women's rights movement were the appointment of a Royal Commission on the Status of Women in 1967; the formation of a coalition of 170 women's groups, the National Action Committee, in 1972; and the creation of a public-policy advisory group, the Canadian Advisory Council on the Status of Women, in 1973.

Perhaps the most significant indicator of the changing social structure was the appointment, in 1983, of the Royal Commission on Equality in Employment. While the Commission was created in response to the entry of large numbers of women into the labour force, it also identified other disadvantaged groups, including visible minorities,

REAL PEOPLE 3.1	Gendered Inequality in Leadership: Selected "Occupational Firsts" for Canadian Women

1957	First woman federal cabinet minister	Ellen Fairclough
1973	First woman president of a coeducational university	Pauline Jewett
1975	First woman federal deputy minister	Sylvia Ostry
1975	First woman president of a major union	Grace Hartman
1980	First woman Speaker of the House of Commons	Jeanne Sauvé
1982	First woman appointed to the Supreme Court of Canada	Bertha Wilson
1984	First woman Governor General of Canada	Jeanne Sauvé
1991	First woman premier	Rita Johnson
1991	First woman president of the Canadian Medical Association	Carol Guzman
1992	First woman president of the Canadian Bar Association	Paule Gauthier
1992	First Canadian woman in space	Roberta Bondar
1993	First woman prime minister	Kim Campbell

Source: Compiled from *Woman in the Labour Force*, 1994 Edition, Statistics Canada Catalogue 75-507, 65-67; Library and Archives Canada, *Celebrating Women's Achievements*.

people with disabilities, and Indigenous peoples.[49] The Commission identified the cause of inequality as *systemic discrimination*, meaning that most employment barriers were hidden (usually unintentionally) in rules, procedures, or traditions which encouraged or discouraged individuals on the basis of their membership in a particular group rather than on their ability to do the job. A new federal policy, *employment equity* (less coercive than the quotas dictated by earlier affirmative-action policies) was implemented to correct discrimination in the workplace. The objective of the employment-equity policy was to ensure that employers (beginning with those doing business with the federal government) worked towards a *representative work force* (i.e., one roughly demographically representative) and demonstrated *reasonable accommodation* (flexibility in striving to accommodate disadvantaged groups, including women).

The quest for gender equality is fraught with controversy because of entrenched values and cultural norms that are not always amenable to change.[50] The strategies that have been implemented to achieve employment and pay equity have had limited success; the uneven distribution of domestic labour also remains an unresolved issue.[51] Yet public opinion and support for gender equality have increased dramatically since the 1970s, particularly among younger cohorts.[52] There is no denying that significant social structural changes have already occurred to which our institutions and practices are being challenged to adjust.

SOCIAL MOBILITY

The suggestion that class position is not fixed and that for some people, at least, it may change, can only be true in a society that possesses a relatively open class system. In societies with a caste system, one is locked into a class position and there is virtually no possibility of changing it as long as one remains a member of that society. In such a society, status is *ascribed* or assigned; in more open class societies, status is *achieved*; i.e., it may be earned through personal effort. Even in more open societies such as Canada, there is an ascriptive dimension to status in that it may be derived from parental background, age, sex, race, or even ethnic origin. To be born into a working-class home does not prevent a person from dreaming of becoming president of a major corporation and perhaps even eventually attaining that goal. Unfortunately, in spite of well-publicized exceptions, the likelihood of such a status-transformation is not great.

Social mobility is the term used to designate movement within the stratified social system. In a society where the boundaries separating social strata or occupational groups are not completely rigid, any change in social position produces social mobility. While mobility may be either upward or downward (i.e., *vertical mobility*), it is most common in our society to speak of *upward mobility*. If change in social class occurs within one person's lifetime, it is known as *intragenerational mobility*; if it occurs within a family from one generation to the next, it is known as *intergenerational mobility*. Changing one's occupation or role for another of similar status is referred to as *horizontal mobility*.

One of the issues that must be addressed is how much mobility or change in class position actually has occurred in Canadian society. Conflict theorists, in particular, feel that the evidence indicates that very little mobility has taken place, and that the gap between the rich and the poor is possibly even increasing (i.e., that the classes are becoming more *polarized*). Before proceeding with that discussion, we will examine the classic argument about the changing Canadian social structure.

Education and Social Mobility

In an industrial society, education is viewed as the primary mechanism for generating social mobility. Regardless of the status of your parents, it is argued, you can, through your own efforts, obtain the educational credentials to become a lawyer, a nuclear engineer, or anything else you want to be. This view of a stratified society suggests that class position and social mobility are predominantly related to personal achievement. If this is the case, personal initiative should be the only variable that determines rank in the stratification system.

It has already been shown that ascribed characteristics, such as sex and ethnicity, influence social mobility. Although education is a factor in social mobility, there are two arguments against the claim that achievement is a simple panacea for improving class or status position. The first argument (the macro view) is rooted in the historical position of education in Canadian society; the second argument (the micro view) concerns itself with the student's home background and school experience.

The Macro View Based on data gathered in the 1950s, John Porter stated in *The Vertical Mosaic* that in the post-war period Canadians did not experience the kind of upward mobility that they should have. His *mobility deprivation thesis* explained this fact as the result of a general societal failure in education.[53] The expansion of the urban labour force through post-war industrialization created numerous new occupational opportunities which, argued Porter, could have led to considerable upgrading of the labour force. However, because post-war Canada's conception of education was traditional and rather elitist, encouraging advanced education for only a small number of people, social mobility was impeded. The problem was exacerbated by the perception that the United States had better opportunities for advancement, which led to a *brain drain* and *labour drain* of those particularly eager for upward mobility.[54]

The resulting labour-force shortages found a rather quick resolution through immigration, noted Porter. Canada found it much easier to import needed skilled and professional people through preferred-immigration regulations (a so-called *brain gain*) than to insist on educational reform. Thus Canada was both donor and recipient in what has been labelled the *brain trade*. The emigration of some of the most highly skilled persons, coupled with the growing demand for new skilled and professional workers, should have meant greater opportunities (i.e., upward social mobility) for Canada's resident population; however, large-scale immigration and an outdated, elitist model of education greatly reduced the potential for social mobility. Porter conservatively estimated that between 1950 and 1960, immigrants filled 50% to 60% of the new skilled jobs that resulted from the nation's industrial development. At that time, advanced education was neither encouraged nor universally available; the social structure, therefore, remained relatively fixed, producing *mobility deprivation*. There was more movement in and out of the stratified system than movement within it. Rather than entering Canada primarily at lower social-class levels and pushing the resident working class up the social strata, skilled immigrants filled the specialized needs of the workforce because of the resident population's lack of preparedness for mobility.

It is important to note that Porter was not saying that no upward mobility occurred, nor that immigrants (particularly skilled immigrants) were detrimental to Canadian society. Even though urbanization was producing a massive shift from manual to white-collar occupations (i.e., from farming to office work) in the Canadian labour force, this shift, in itself, did not represent vertical mobility (although some mobility obviously did take place once workers acquired necessary skills). However, what disturbed Porter was that immigration was used as a convenient substitute for educational reform and that this substitution retarded both the demand for education and the development of fuller educational participation. In addition, a potentially dynamic social structure remained relatively static because Canada was not a "mobility-oriented society."[55]

Porter analyzed the evidence in the early 1960s, just as educational change really began to take place in Canada. Throughout the 1960s and even into the 1970s, university attendance increased dramatically, and post-secondary schools of technology were built. Post-secondary enrollment almost tripled by 1970, with close to 20% of the 18–24 age group enrolled at post-secondary institutions. In addition, the rate of increase in the number of undergraduate students was 10%–15% annually, and graduate enrollment increased sixfold.[56] Therefore, even though skilled and professional immigrants were still given entrance priority, the Canadian labour force was in a much better position to compete than it had been. In fact, by the mid-1970s, Canadians' concern about employment produced a move to reduce immigration to its barest minimum. Notwithstanding these changes and the fact that other factors besides education affect mobility, Porter's analysis highlighted the fact that the accessibility of advanced education and its relationship to immigration policy were important factors influencing the potential for social mobility.[57]

The expansion of educational opportunities was based on the *human capital theory* that a better-educated labour force would be a more productive one. Consequently, the emphasis in the ensuing decades has been on improving the accessibility of advanced education. It was thought that post-secondary educational institutions in particular should be conveniently located and relatively inexpensive, and that more institutions should be available so that more students could be admitted. Governments poured large sums of money into educational endeavours so as to build human capital, which would then have a positive effect on employment and the Gross National Product. Thus education, by creating equality of opportunity so that upward mobility could take place, was to be the means of equalizing the effects of the existing social structure.

Equality of opportunity suggests that all people have an equal chance to take advantage of opportunities. In reality, by virtue of more advantageous family background, personal aptitudes, and personal circumstances, some people are more able than others to take advantage of available opportunities. In the absence of *equality of condition,* mobility through equal opportunity will be restricted or conditioned by other factors.

The Micro View The analysis of equality of condition has resulted in a clearer picture of the factors that lead specific individuals to take advantage of educational opportunity. One perspective emphasizes the role of schools themselves (particularly junior- and senior-high schools) in sorting students into program *streams*. While the criteria upon which streaming is based are normally perceived to be students' intellectual capacities and aptitudes, research has found that the most important factor behind students' academic performance is familial expectations. For example, a home environment in which learning is devalued has a strong negative influence on academic performance. The family also exerts a significant, albeit indirect, influence on program selection, in that a person's concept of his or her own ability is related to family socio-economic status. Thus the role of the school in streaming students is strongly associated with family influence.[58] The results of considerable sociological research (including later work by Porter) indicate that the pursuit of higher education is indeed related to social class.[59] In general, the higher the social-class position of the parents, the greater the expectation that the child will obtain a higher education and the greater the likelihood of that outcome. But even though lower parental social status may negatively affect the likelihood of the child's attending university, higher education is indeed an important mechanism of upward mobility for some students of lower social-class background. Foreign-born youth or children of foreign-born parents, for example, tend to view education as the primary instrument of upward mobility.

Regardless of these tendencies, it is true that more people, regardless of background, are attaining higher levels of education, and that the educational system can be *meritocratic* (i.e., tending to award people on the basis of merit) even as it is influenced by students' social class. Education can be the way in which some disadvantaged persons overcome their origins, but education (or the lack thereof) is also the way parents transmit their status to their children.[60]

Does Your Parents' Education Matter to You?

About one half of Canadians ages 26 to 35 report having a higher level of education than their parents. This general rise in levels of educational attainment has been going on for some time and improves the level of *intellectual capital* available to the next generation.

Nevertheless, the higher the parents' level of education, the more likely that the child will pursue higher education. Young adults ages 26 to 35 whose parents had a post-secondary education are almost three times more likely to earn post-secondary credentials than those whose parents had not completed high school.

The father's socio-economic status is also associated with his children's higher educational attainment. So it is not just parents' education that is important but the role parents play in creating *family intellectual capital* by passing on positive attitudes (e.g., self-direction, independence, curiosity) and expectations regarding advanced learning, as well as by modelling the difference education made in their own self-concept and careers.

In this regard, your future is in the hands of your parents.

Source: Based on Patrice de Broucker and Laval Lavallée, "Does Your Parent's Education Count?" *Canadian Social Trends* (Summer 1991), Statistics Canada Catalogue 11-008XPE, 11-15. See also M. Reza Nakhaie and James Curtis, "Effects of Class Positions of Parents on Educational Attainment of Daughters and Sons," *Canadian Review of Sociology and Anthropology* 35, 4 (1998): 483-515.

Evaluating Mobility

In order to evaluate whether real mobility has occurred at all, we need to distinguish between two types of mobility. The first, called *circulation mobility* or *exchange mobility*, is based on individual achievement. This model of mobility suggests that the upgrading of skills, acquisition of knowledge, and hard work will result in some change in social position from parent to offspring.[61]

The second type is called *structural mobility*. It is related not to individual effort but to changes in a society's occupational structure. Macro-level factors, such as economic depressions or booms, corporate restructuring, technological changes (e.g., computers, robotics), or the entrance of new groups (e.g., women, immigrants) into the labour force create new conditions which affect opportunities. For example, the shift from a rural agricultural population to an urban industrial population in the post-war period led a whole generation to strong perceptions of upward mobility. They exchanged their blue-collar agricultural positions (which, although they came with considerable equity, also came with little surplus cash and high indebtedness for land and machinery) for white-collar work, regular paycheques, and suburban living. This massive rural–urban shift is best described in terms of structural mobility. Whether or not it necessarily represents a significant change in social position is debatable.

The whole range of new white-collar jobs now available, some of which have become increasingly routinized and supervised, suggests that class position may have changed little.[62] In fact, the evidence is that while incomes may have increased, there is now just as wide a spread or disparity among incomes within the society as there was 40 years ago.[63]

There has been a proliferation of white-collar jobs that entail menial work (e.g., record keeping), supervision (i.e., bureaucratic procedure), and mechanization (e.g., computers, robotics), reducing the freedom, creativity, and control of the employee. This trend is frequently disguised by the image of higher credentials and gleaming office towers, or by the white-collar nature of the jobs. This shift from more independent craftsman-like work to routinization and supervision is called *deskilling*.

Thus, from one perspective, it would appear that mobility has occurred in real ways and that Canada is a reasonably open society. The more critical perspective, on the other hand, suggests that although most of the new range of jobs may require higher levels of education, they are increasingly confining and controlled by machines or bureaucratic policy—a fact that has its own proletarianizing effects. If the shift from rural to urban employment was one major structural change in Canadian society, another has been the shift from an industrial to a *post-industrial society* in which the service sector predominates. Jobs in agriculture and manufacturing have seen steep declines, and the service sector now employs close to three quarters of the labour force. In conjunction with this transformation, there has been a the shift away from full-time, full-year, permanent employment to part-time, short-term, temporary employment, known as *non-standard employment*. One third of all jobs are now of this type, and most of them are in the service industry, with lower wages and fewer benefits.[64] While it is too early to assess the full outcome of this trend, some fear that it will contribute to some forms of downward mobility and create new forms of inequality.

Creese, Guppy, and Meissner have published an important study evaluating the evidence about mobility in Canada.[65] They found that the educational level of nearly two thirds of Canadians is higher than that of their parents. Half of this educational mobility reflects individual achievement (circulation or exchange mobility) and half is due to the overall upgrading of the labour force (structural mobility). Men's mobility is more likely to be of the exchange variety, while women's is more likely to be structural in nature (e.g., women entering the labour force in greater numbers and largely finding employment in white-collar clerical jobs). Gender makes little difference to educational mobility but it does to occupational mobility; women experienced less upward mobility from their first to their current job than did men.

Several concluding points need to be made. First, education, as a vehicle of personal achievement, can modify the ascribed status we inherit from our parents, although it does not necessarily do so.[66] For middle-class people in particular, education is the primary means of maintaining class position relative to other workers. Second, while there has been a significant reduction in educational inequality, income inequality continues to exist, suggesting that education is no guarantee of other forms of equality.[67] And third, however one interprets the mobility or structural change, direct comparison of Canada with other countries indicates that Canada is no less mobility-oriented than other industrial societies.[68] In fact, Wanner has argued that the association between status origins and class destination is fairly low in Canada, particularly in comparison to the United Kingdom, France, Sweden, and the Netherlands; this fact suggests that we are a reasonably open society.[69]

SOCIAL POWER

Stratification and inequality imply more than the mere fact that some people have higher incomes and better education, or bigger homes and fancier cars, than other people; with these differential indicators of social status come differences in power and control. Because money is a scarce resource, those who have it and use it can control, directly or indirectly, those who do not have it but need it. There is thus a relational aspect to inequality: Groups of people who have more money have an advantage over those who have less, and can compete more successfully against them.

Power implies control over decisions that affect other people. We like to think that in a democracy power is shared and held by all. Yet when we vote, we are conscious that our choices have are already been circumscribed by groups within the society that control political parties or have sufficient financial resources to promote particular candidates. Thus we are at the very least aware that power is wielded by a variety of competing groups (e.g., the corporate sector, labour unions, farmers' groups) that vie for public support. The diffusion of power among many interest groups is known as *pluralism*. Power can also be wielded by *elites*, that is, small minorities who make decisions on behalf of the majority. Elitist power can be formalized through the election or appointment of select individuals to governmental positions of authority, or it can be informal and in some ways invisible, as in the use of economic power. Clement and Myles refer to such invisible elites as "unelected economic rulers" who have considerable power over society at large.[70]

Elites exist in each sector of society (e.g., politics, media, finance), but there has always been a particular fascination with the *economic elite*. The political-economy perspective maintains that the nature of economic relations within a society is fundamental to understanding how that society operates, and economic elites naturally wield unusual influence in a capitalist society. Political economy refers to the economic elite as the *capitalist class* because it comprises employers or major investors who own the means of production and employ others to make a profit.

One attempt to explain how Canadian society has developed finds the answer in the actions of the economic elite. In a thesis known as *merchants against industry*, Naylor argued that around the time of Confederation, the Canadian capitalist class chose finance, commerce, and transportation rather than industry as the focus of their investments.[71] The result was a society with truncated industrial development—all because the commercial elite profited more significantly from a staples economy and squeezed out industrial capital, later mediating the importation of more profitable American branch plants. This thesis placed the Canadian commercial elite squarely in the context of continental capitalism, seeing them as having created and profited from Canadian dependency on the United States.

Key to Naylor's argument is the understanding that the capitalist class can be split into merchant and industrial factions which are distinct and antagonistic. It was in the best interests of the government-protected banking cartel, for example, to perpetuate a staples economy that inhibited or distorted industrial capital. But in an empirical examination of Naylor's argument, Richardson concluded that the boundaries between these class factions were actually not strong.[72] In fact, in the 1920s only 51% of the directorships of banks and insurance companies were held by financiers; this suggests that members of the economic elite belonged to both class factions. Richardson suggests that rather than antagonism between class factions, considerable capital integration existed within the elite.

This discussion raises fundamental questions about the concentration of power. Is power in Canadian society best understood in terms of a plurality of competing groups and their elites, or is power best understood as being concentrated in a single elite? John Porter, Wallace Clement, and William Carroll offer contrasting points of view in this debate.

Elites—in Porter

The second half of John Porter's *The Vertical Mosaic* attempts to establish the characteristics of the Canadian elite. Porter was able to identify elites in a variety of sectors of the society—from the economic elite to the media, political, and bureaucratic elites. For example, in studying the economic elite, Porter determined that in the early 1950s, there were 985 men holding directorships in 170 dominant corporations, banks, and insurance companies. He noted that it was largely this same group which held most of the common stock (and thus received most of the dividend income)—meaning that both ownership and management were concentrated in the hands of a few individuals rather than widely dispersed to many shareholders.

The social homogeneity of this economic elite developed as a result of a number of factors. First, members of this elite recruited internally, serving on each other's boards of directors in what are called *interlocking directorships*. Second, as Porter discovered by constructing biographical sketches of this elite, family continuity was a dominant pattern. Third, many members had a university education, and many had attended the same private schools as youngsters. Fourth, members of this group were predominantly of British descent; very few persons of French-Canadian descent or Catholic affiliation were included. Fifth, the economic elite socialized among themselves through membership in private clubs and held prominent positions on the boards of charitable organizations, educational institutions, and trade associations.

Although the economic elite is clearly the most fundamental segment, Porter recognized that other elites also have important decision-making roles. Of all elites, the elite of organized labour had the highest proportion of foreign-born and the lowest level of education, and members tended to come from working-class backgrounds. The political and the federal bureaucratic elites were very similar in having the highest proportions of native-born and university-educated members and tending to be of British, Protestant, and professional backgrounds. Ontario as a region was overrepresented in this elite. The mass-media elite was a smaller group, in which ownership was shared among only a few families; the media in French Canada were an exception because they were independent of syndicates and chains. Lastly, Porter identified the intellectual and religious elite—a much less homogeneous group.

For Porter, power was a response to the general social need for order.[73] Elite groups each coordinated and directed their own institutional orders and sought an equilibrium between themselves, though this did not mean that all elite groups were equally powerful. The emphasis in Porter's analysis was on internal recruitment, cross-memberships, and collegiality among elites as a relatively small group. The plurality of elite dominance is best expressed in a phrase Porter used several times, "the confraternity of power." What Porter argued for, however, was greater mobility into the elite so that it did not become a closed domain of power.

Elites—in Clement

In the 1970s, Wallace Clement, one of Porter's students, sought to bring Porter's 1950s data up to date but with a focus on the corporate or economic elite. Clement pointed out that as a result of the growth of complex subsidiaries, the number of dominant corporations had been reduced from 170 (at the time of Porter's study) to 113.[74] Interlocking directorships were again a dominant feature: Of the 113 dominant corporations, 1 848 directorships were interconnected, with the Canadian Imperial Bank of Commerce, the Bank of Montreal, the Royal Bank, the Canadian Pacific Railway, and Sun Life most closely interlocked. Significantly, 29% of this total elite of 113 dominant corporations held 54% of all directorship positions. In sum, Clement found that the concentration of power had become tighter and access into the elite more difficult.

In a second study, published two years later, Clement showed how Canadian and American economic power were inextricably linked.[75] He did this by distinguishing three types of elites: the *indigenous elite* of Canadian-controlled corporations (particularly in transportation, finance, and utilities); the *comprador elite,* comprising native-born directors and management personnel of foreign-controlled corporations operating in Canada (particularly in resources and manufacturing); and the *parasite elite*, based largely outside Canada, who control the multinational corporations operating in Canada. Therefore, to understand Canadian economic power adequately, one must place it within a continental framework.

Clement differs from Porter in giving the economic elite absolute primacy over all other elites and over society in general. The concentration of elite power occurs via dominant corporations' links with other sectors such as the media, which the economic elite owns and controls and uses to propagate its dominant ideology. There are also linkages between the corporate elite and the state that support the objective of profit-making; boundaries between the economic and political sectors are removed by means of advisory-council participation, political appointments, and the funding of political parties.[76] In sum, Clement rejects a pluralist notion of power.

Re-evaluating the Corporate Elite

Porter and Clement's work served as the benchmark for research on the corporate elite over the next two decades. One study pointed to family ownership groups and showed how they had grown.[77] It was demonstrated that more than 76% of the 170 largest Canadian non-financial corporations were controlled by 17 dominant enterprises, of which 11 were single-owner or family-owned. Names like Reichmann, Bronfman, Weston, Thomson, Irving, and Desmarais dominated; some new upwardly mobile non-British families were also moving into this group. Thanks to "control pyramid structures," families like the Bronfmans could own parts of hundreds of companies and have controlling interest over all of them.[78] Only 53 of the 246 largest public firms were actually largely publicly owned; the rest had controlling shareholders, often in family-owned firms.

Other research found that large-scale capital was socially integrated in a densely connected network of directorship interlocks.[79] One study of 250 large Canadian corporations concluded that Canadian firms had more interlocking directorships than American firms did, suggesting a tighter circulation of power.[80] Financial companies, especially banks, occupied the most central position in the network, linking foreign- and domestically controlled companies. Commercial capital and industrial capital, therefore, had close ties or were so linked as to be much more independent from external capital than had previously been thought. An inner circle of closely interlocked capitalists controlling super-blocs of indigenous finance capital made these linkages possible.[81] Yet the direct links between corporations and the state, while present, were not as strong as expected, with elite involvement highest in university and hospital boards and lowest in federal and provincial bureaucracies.[82] In fact, Ornstein's research demonstrated that there was significant ideological conflict between the capitalist class and the state.[83]

While the existence of an elite is not in doubt, questions have also been raised about its composition. Porter, for example, had argued that the elite was a homogeneous British upper class. But Ogmundson challenged that view with more recent data indicating that British domination was drawing to a close because of the growing permeability of the elite, in contrast to its former social exclusivity and homogeneity.[84] Nakhaie has countered this conclusion by pointing out that the decline in the numbers of persons of British descent in the elite is only an absolute numerical decline, not a decline relative to their proportion of the population.[85] Persons of British descent still have effective control of all categories of the elite, despite the fact that the political and bureaucratic elite was less exclusive than the economic one; in the Ontario civil service, for example, persons of British ancestry were overrepresented in positions earning over $100 000. On the other hand, it has been shown that the labour elite was much less British and more French Canadian and female.[86] In general, researchers agreed that the relationship between ethnic origin and elite position was in flux.[87]

Carroll's Recent Work on Elites

Based on his comprehensive study of the corporate elite existing in Canada in 1976 and 1996, Carroll, rather than viewing the elite in simplistic terms, distinguished three types of corporate power.[88] *Operational power* is essentially the power of management to control the labour process. *Strategic power* is the power to establish business strategy, usually represented by ownership of the largest bloc of shares. *Allocative power* is held by those who control the line of credit or supply the financing. Most boards of directors now involve persons representing all three forms of power.

In examining Canada's 250 largest corporations, Carroll found that the corporate elite's exclusivity had diminished considerably, partly as the result of reforms in board governance made in the mid-1990s to protect public shareholders. Here are some of the changes Carroll observed. First, women represented a greater percentage of the corporate elite—although that percentage was still small (10%). Second, although persons of British ethnic origin were still overrepresented, the corporate elite was much more ethnically diverse than before, with particular strides having been taken by persons of French and Jewish descent. Third, there was a striking decrease among the elite in participation in elite clubs, with almost half reporting no elite club memberships. Fourth, the economic elite was older and was more likely to have educational credentials. Fifth, the number of "big linkers" holding four or more directorships had shrunk from 128 to 82, at least partially because the size of boards had been reduced over that 20-year period. Bank boards, however, involved persons who usually did hold other directorships (although not with other banks, which is prohibited) and composed a core elite. In general, there was a thinning of interpersonal contacts among the corporate elite.

On the other hand, Carroll found that in the 20 years from 1976 to 1996, there was an important shift to corporate control by a controlling shareholder; by 1996 less than 20% of the 250 largest firms did not have a controlling shareholder. The largest proportion of such control was held by families such as the Westons and Bronfmans, but controlling shareholders also included some government investment and some non-proprietary interests (such as insurance policy holders) or workers' unions (e.g., the Ontario Teachers Pension Fund).

The number of interlocking directorships declined from an average of five to three per corporate board, a loss of 649 interlocks from 1976 to 1996. Carroll noted that the number of *primary interlocks* (i.e., officers of one company sitting on the board of another company) had declined, as had *secondary interlocks* (i.e., outsider directors of one board sitting on the board of another company). Instead of thinking in terms of an internal capitalist class, Carroll argues that the economic elite have become much more transnational, centred around a core of 26 corporations with high secondary interlocks of outside directors (Figure 3.4). Seven transnational financial corporations, including all the major banks plus 19 industrials (e.g., Bombardier, Falconbridge, Amoco, Seagram, and Thomson) may have loosened the interlocks somewhat, changing their focus from solely Canadian to transnational interests. Accordingly, the Canadian corporate elite can no longer be understood purely in nationalist terms.

FIGURE 3.4	The Interlocks Between the Dominant Canadian Transnational Corporations

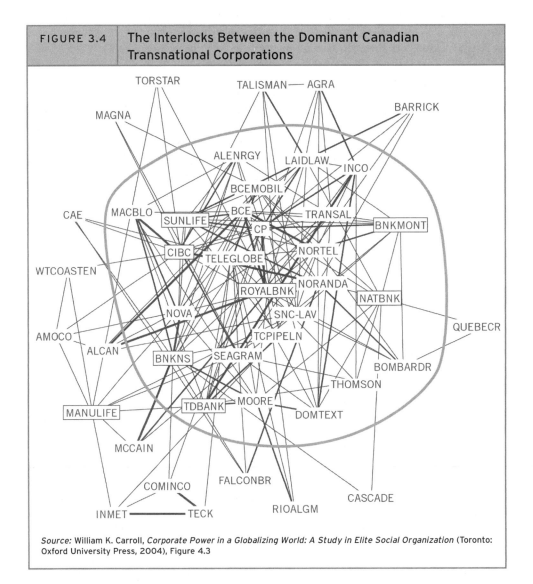

Source: William K. Carroll, *Corporate Power in a Globalizing World: A Study in Elite Social Organization* (Toronto: Oxford University Press, 2004), Figure 4.3

Carroll concludes that corporate power is now in a period of transition. Foreign ownership in Canada has not increased and neither have Canada–US board interlocks, the Montreal–Toronto axis of corporate power has focused more on Toronto, there has been some shift to Calgary and Vancouver, and finance capital is centered in Toronto while having a more global focus. Interlocks with Europe are more significant than with Asia; in general, however, Canadian capital is not a major global player. Yet the largest corporations are all transnational and the trend is towards more transnational links expanding beyond national borders. In short, a Canadian corporate elite does exist, but its characteristics are more complex and global than previously thought.

Evaluating Elitism

Some people view elitism as an inevitability. The iron law of oligarchy suggests that there will always be a tendency, in every society, for a small elite to dominate the masses.[89] The reason for this tendency is that people tend to passively accept the flow of power to a few persons at the top. For believers in democracy, however, the long-term perpetuation of elite decision-making weakens the general belief in equality and also reduces public participation in decisions affecting the lives of many people.

On the other hand, some argue that elite control has been greatly exaggerated. A focus on boards of directors of corporations, for example, may miss the fact that persons who serve on boards exercise little formal control. Corporate board meetings are short and infrequent, and the directors are often only advisors. So while formal power may be legally vested in the board, actual control is held by managers, owners, and those who prepare corporate information.[90] It has also been argued that elites are neither monolithic nor completely impenetrable. The maturation of Canadian capitalism may, for example, give rise to the emergence of new elite factions, which may compete against established elites (and each other) rather than form a common class front. Moreover, a distinction has been made between *strategic* and *core elites*— the former made up of those who have achieved key functional roles, the latter of those who have inherited wealth and status. While access to the core elite may remain virtually closed, the strategic elite may be more open to persons of demonstrated competence and skill.[91]

There is also some evidence which might point to the role of the strategic elite in changing the overall ethnic composition of the upper stratum of society. For example, while francophones were previously underrepresented in virtually every elite, there has been increasing francophone participation in the federal bureaucratic and political elite, and a stronger French-Canadian economic elite has emerged as well.[92]

In concluding this discussion, we should note that although many observers are concerned with "access" to the elite, others find the mere existence of an elite distressing.[93] We will return to this issue at the end of the chapter.

POVERTY

We have already seen in Figure 3.2 that the quintile of the Canadian population with the lowest incomes (i.e., the bottom 20% of the population) receives about one third of their income from employment earnings and almost two thirds from government transfers. But at what income level do we define someone as poor? Does a hierarchy of incomes necessarily mean that those with the lowest income are poor?

To answer this question it is important to distinguish between absolute poverty and rel-ative poverty, for these two measures make use of different assumptions. *Absolute poverty* refers to the income level needed for basic subsistence (i.e., food, clothing, shelter). By this standard, anyone without sufficient income to buy what is essential for survival is consid-ered poor. *Relative poverty*, on the other hand, acknowledges that the definition of poverty is dependent on community standards. If, for example, a car is a necessity for transporta-tion to work or school or for participation in community life, then a person who cannot afford a car may be considered poor. Because most other persons in the community use automobiles in their daily life, owning a car may become a norm against which poverty can be measured. Both concepts of poverty involve value judgements which make their definitions of poverty somewhat controversial. For absolute poverty, how is basic subsis-tence defined and what is the minimum threshold for spending on food, shelter, and cloth-ing? For relative poverty, what is the community standard? Should the minimum be the full community standard? half of it? a third? Clearly, what one person considers an absolute necessity or normative in a community, another might consider non-essential or a luxury.

For many years, Statistics Canada has been calculating what they call Low Income Cut-Offs (LICO).[94] The low income cut-off is calculated by identifying the income-levels of those who spend more than 64% of their income on the basic necessities of life; the allowance varies by size of family and place of residence. For example, in 2002, the low income cut-off for a single person was $15 907 in cities of over 500 000 and $10 429 in rural areas; for a family of four, it was $30 576 in large cities and $20 047 in rural areas. Most social-policy agencies, such as the National Council of Welfare, use LICO as the measure of poverty, whereas Statistics Canada has claimed that it is not necessarily a meas-ure of poverty but only a means to identify those who are substantially worse off than the average.

Figure 3.5 shows that the incidence of low income varies somewhat from year to year, and also is different depending on whether income is considered before or after tax. As

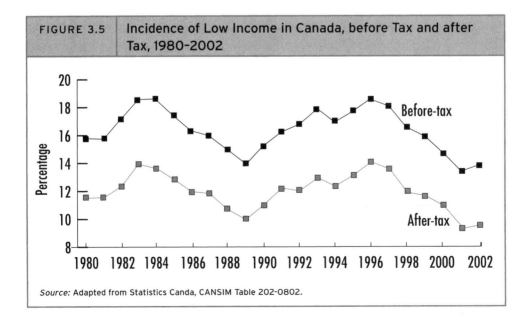

| FIGURE 3.5 | Incidence of Low Income in Canada, before Tax and after Tax, 1980-2002 |

Source: Adapted from Statistics Canda, CANSIM Table 202-0802.

RESEARCH CLIP 3.4	Understanding Power in Advanced Capitalist Societies

There are two main expressions of power in advanced capitalist societies. One is *decision making,* and has to do with when and where and how much capital is invested in the production process. The other is *authority,* which has to do with the direction or disciplining of labour. Another way to describe this difference is that the former type of power is *strategic,* pertaining to long-term planning, and the latter is concerned more with the *tactical* decisions of day-to-day operations. Decision-making and strategic roles are identified with the *capitalist–executive class,* and authority over labour is the responsibility of the *new middle class.*

The new middle class lacks real ownership of the means of production but is given the responsibility of the control and surveillance of labour on behalf of capitalists. In that sense, the new middle class is neither working-class nor capitalist–executive but is intimately related to both. The old middle class, in contrast, was more independent and individualistic, with direct entrepreneurial ownership of their own enterprise. The new middle class is characteristic of large bureaucratic enterprises.

Defined as persons who have *both* decision-making power and labour power over three or more persons, the capitalist–executive class in Canada accounts for about 6% of the population.* The new middle class of managers (administrative, budgeting, and personnel) makes up about one quarter of the labour force. In comparison, in the United States the capitalist–executive class and new middle class make up slightly higher proportions of the population. Finland, in contrast, has a smaller new middle class and larger working class.

*Obviously, the size of the capitalist-executive class would be reduced significantly if it were redefined to include only large operations (such as those with 10 000 or more employees) in which power is much greater.

Source: Based on Wallace Clement and John Myles, *Relations of Ruling: Class and Gender in Post-Industrial Societies* (Montreal: McGill-Queen's University Press, 1994), Chapter 1.

expected, the incidence of poverty is lower when after-tax income is considered, but even then the poverty rate is about 10%. It is clear that poverty is related to unemployment, because about one third of those in the low income category one year were not in poverty the following year, a fact that suggests some turnover from one year to the next.[95] Others were not so fortunate and experienced more enduring low income. The most important determinant of poverty is family type: the poverty rate is lowest among two-parent families and highest among single-parent families with children under 18. Poverty rates are higher in large cities and among those with less schooling; poor education can be both a cause and an effect of poverty. Poverty rates are higher for women than for men;[96] women, however, play a key role in keeping families out of poverty, as the poverty rates among families drop when wives are working. Immigrants, particularly visible-minority women, are also consistently over-represented among the poor.[97] There are also some regional differences: the highest poverty rates are found in British Columbia and Newfoundland, and the lowest in Prince Edward Island. Perhaps the most dramatic shift over time has been the significant decline in poverty rates among seniors. In 1980 the poverty rate for the elderly was 19.2%, but it had dropped to 6.9% by 2002. The role of government, corporate, and personal pension programs was making a big difference for this age group.

It has already been noted that poverty is closely linked to unemployment. In the early 1980s (as Canada shifted from a goods-producing economy to a service economy) and in the 1990s (as a result of free trade), large numbers of jobs were lost, particularly in central Canada.[98] One study conducted in London, Ontario, has traced the social psychology of being unemployed from the victim's perspective.[99] The unemployed, a largely invisible minority, may be said to suffer the ultimate condition of powerlessness; the rising poverty rates of the 1990s were related to their increasing numbers. There are also the large numbers of working poor, who, although part of the work force, work part time and/or at minimum-wage jobs that keep them in poverty. Perhaps one of the most startling indicators of poverty is the rise of homelessness—a phenomenon seldom heard of 20 years ago.[100]

Statistics Canada has gone on record as noting that income inequality before transfer payments has grown significantly and continues a trend that began in the early 1980s. From 1996 to 2002, the employment income of the lowest quintile increased by only $3 200, whereas that of the highest quinitile rose by $21 100.[101] This is why the debate about the meaning and measurement of poverty is so important. For example, the richest 20% spend a lower percentage of their incomes on food and shelter than the poorest 20%, and yet the wealthiest eat much better and live in nicer homes.

Given the difficulty of establishing poverty lines using the old methods, a new method utilizes the *market basket* approach. The idea is to draw up a specific list of goods and services required by all people and to price them in a variety of locations (the cost of the "market basket" would thus differ from city to city). By adding up the total cost of all items on this list, a low-income baseline can be established. The big question is, What items should go in the market basket? How many rolls of toilet paper or paper towels? Are allowances to be made for taxis or just for buses? Are first-aid supplies included in the shopping list? How about dental checkups, and if so, how many? Is only a cheap basement apartment with few windows acceptable, or may a more expensive apartment on a higher floor be a necessity? And what about the need for discretionary income whereby the person can make some additional choices? How much discretionary income is allowable for buying a magazine, eating out, or taking a vacation for your mental health? These are the kinds of questions that lead to wide variations in the total value of different market baskets. For an excellent discussion of the issues and a feel for the controversy surrounding this issue, compare the work of Christopher Sarlo with that of the National Council of Welfare (NCW).[102] Sarlo, from his market-basket calculations, arrived at a poverty line much lower than that identified by the NCW. He declared that poverty is not a significant problem in Canada and probably only affects about one million people, claiming that the NCW's assessment includes students or people underreporting their incomes and does not take into consideration the fact that other forms of assistance (i.e., charity) are available. The NCW, on the other hand, argues that people have a right to their dignity, should not be visibly poorer than the rest of society, and should not be treated like social pariahs. From this perspective, it is feared that the market-basket approach might lower the poverty lines to the point that the problem of poverty is defined out of existence. This is where ideology comes into play, as those who want to minimize the problem clash with those who want to mobilize the government to action in defence of the poor.

In 1996, the federal government made a significant change in the way it allocated funding to furnish aid to the poor and provide for the health, education, and assistance needs of all Canadians.[103] The previous mechanism, known as the Canada Assistance Plan, required provinces to provide welfare assistance (without provincial residency requirements); the program was maintained with financing from Ottawa and also cost-shared by the provinces. With the new Canada Health and Social Transfer (CHST), the federal contribution to such assistance was reduced and provinces were given more control over how the federal funds was used. All of this took place in a climate of deficit reduction at both federal and provincial levels that threatened the existence of a clear proactive national policy for dealing with income inequalities.

THE STATE AND INEQUALITY

In contrast to the United States, where poverty rates are the highest among industrialized countries,[104] Canada has historically tended to use government programs to reduce inequalities in what is called the *welfare state*. Essentially a post-war phenomenon that became well established by the 1960s, the welfare state entailed social policies—from medical care to old age security to family allowance— to provide for human needs that the capitalist mode of production would not cover.[105] From its original focus on the poor or those who qualified under income tests, the welfare state broadened its objective to the provision of such programs for all socio-economic groups (although it was clear that need was most acute among those of low income). A second way in which the state attempted to deal with inequalities was to establish publicly owned businesses, called *Crown corporations,* to provide basic services for a young and sparsely populated country, to stimulate regional economic development, or to build a more diversified economy beyond resource dependence. Crown corporations were set up for utilities and telephones, airlines, and railroads, and even for the development of resources such as oil (e.g., Petro-Canada).[106]

A third way in which the state has responded to inequalities (particularly regional inequalities) has been through *equalization grants*. In 1937, the Rowell-Sirois Royal Commission on Dominion–Provincial Relations, noting the income and employment inequalities existing at that time, advocated a more equitable distribution of social-service benefits. By 1957, the government had established equalization grants, which redistributed tax revenues so that regions of Canada with incomes lower than the national average would be able to provide education and health facilities at the same levels as regions with higher incomes. Sensing that a more comprehensive program of development was needed, the government created the Department of Regional Economic Expansion in 1969, but the Department's successes were limited because of the ensuing dependence on heavy government tax-incentives. As Acheson pointed out, the net effect of these efforts was that underdeveloped areas virtually became "client-states" of the federal government, a consequence of their dependence on federal handouts in the form of either grants or transfer payments (e.g., unemployment insurance or income supplements to raise residents' standard of living).[107] Matthews labels this same phenomenon *transfer dependency*.[108]

The shift to neo-liberalism in the 1990s has somewhat changed the priorities of the state and its response to inequalities. Themes such as the privatization of public companies and public-sector downsizing have changed the role of the state, in a shift away from reliance on the public sector to respond to societal needs. Most importantly, fiscal cutbacks and tax reductions eliminate the state's ability to respond as it once did. Li refers to these factors, in combination with the aging of the population and the shrinking of the labour force relative to the growing aging population, as the *fiscal crisis of the state* because of the threat they pose to social programs.[109] Universal medical care still remains a distinctive feature of Canadian society but is under significant duress. In general, the focus of social programs is now primarily on the poor, and even here severe cutbacks are being experienced. It has also been shown that government cutbacks affect the genders differentially: Women have been particularly negatively affected by layoffs, the decline of public-sector employment, and the reduced availability of government services.[110]

How successful is the state in reducing inequality? It is clear that income inequality in Canadian society has continued to grow, even though government transfer programs have provided minimal supports for the very poor.[111] But should we expect the state to perform this function, and will it really be successful in mitigating inequality? The answers to these questions depend on your concept of the state and of who controls it.

The *institutional approach* views the state as an independent body meant to serve as the arbiter between different groups and opposing interests in a society. The focus in this approach is on constitutions, laws, policies, and rights enshrined in government documents and operationalized in government structures. The *instrumental approach* suggests that the state is intimately linked to capitalist interests.[112] In its strongest form, instrumentalism contends that the state is dominated by business interests. This view focuses on the imposition of capitalist requirements on state policies. The *structuralist approach* maintains that the state, while more or less structurally independent, embodies and supports the assumptions of the capitalist society (as the phrase "relative autonomy" suggests).[113] The latter two approaches attempt to more clearly explain how the state operates by considering socio-economic forces rather than by merely evaluating policy.

The question of the state's degree of autonomy or independence from capitalist interests is extremely important. There is no question that the state underwrites the capitalist economy through the provision of labour-power via immigration, education, and health-care policies. It also provides loans, depreciation allowances, and direct and indirect subsidies (through various forms of write-offs and employment incentives).[114] Governments also support labour flexibility for corporate profit-making by providing a "safety net" of social programs for citizens when corporations lay them off. As political economy points out, monopoly capitalism thus benefits as the state pays for labour costs (e.g., education, medical care, provisions for the unemployed or laid-off, labour relocation) through the taxpayer while the private sector retains the profits.[115] It has been argued that more attention has been paid to investment and policing than to welfare.[116] These issues are endemic to any capitalist society, but it is clear that although the Canadian state plays a direct and indirect role in the economy to ensure the well-being of its citizens, it does so in a way that is particularly supportive of the interests of the capitalist class.

On the other hand, the state does maintain some distance from capitalist interests. Indeed, without that distance, political action by others would be futile. Publicly accountable government bodies and public pressure groups interact to modulate the influence of the business elite. The state itself has its own interests. The facts that 16% to 21% of the labour force (depending on how the figure is calculated) work in the public sector and that public bureaucracies have their own agendas suggest that corporate economic power is far from absolute.[117] One study of political and business elites demonstrated that although state elites have more contact with the business elite than with any other elite group, such contact has little effect on the policies of business leaders.[118] This suggests that business may have more

The Quicksand Effect

Since the early 1980s, the policy of member-countries of the Organization for Economic Co-operation and Development (OECD), of which Canada is one, has been to promote economic growth through monetary restraint (low inflation) and fiscal retrenchment (lower state expenditures), as well as through globalization of production and distribution. Much to these countries' alarm, these policies have produced increasing income polarization, high unemployment, and lives of instability for various social groups. Thus, building on the economic growth achieved by such policies has been somewhat like building on quicksand: At the very time that people need more support in order to cope with the new flexibilities demanded by the market, that support has been taken away.

Key to the cohesion of societies is the state's role in providing social protection (e.g., the law) and services (e.g., medical care, education) which not only give members a sense of personal and collective security but also provide a reason for their feeling of commitment to the society in which they live. Perhaps the most basic thing a society can give each member is the sense of worth and place that come from employment and adequate income. As all OECD countries are now recognizing more clearly, a competitive, globalized market economy has made these things much more precarious for segments of society.

To Ponder:

Do you agree that reducing the role of the state could have the ultimate effect of reducing residents' commitment to the state? Is this another reason why Canada is becoming so precarious as a society?

Source: Organization for Economic Co-operation and Development, *Societal Cohesion and the Globalising Economy* (Paris: 1997).

of an impact on government than vice versa. To expect the state to always be an instrument of the people is naive and idealistic; on the other hand, to view the state as solely an instrument of capitalist interests leads to cynicism and despair. A more realistic view, perhaps, is that the state does support inequality but at the same time attempts to mitigate some of its harshness. How we respond to this situation is the subject of our final section.

RESPONSES TO INEQUALITY

The use of the term "inequality" suggests that we all agree that equality is the normative or moral condition. The fact is, however, that Canada remains a stratified society, and there is no ideological consensus as to whether that inequality is necessary or unnecessary, or, indeed, on the meaning of "equality" itself (to believe in equality at the ballot box, for example, is certainly not the same as to believe in equality in economic matters). At the same time, the reality of individual differences must be integrated into our conceptions of what Canadian society should or could be.

As each of us encounters social reality, we employ interpretive lenses that help us to understand what we see. These lenses can be called *ideology*, or the complex of values, assumptions, and beliefs that help us interpret the social phenomena we observe. Ideology also supplies "selectivity," allowing one person to perceive one aspect of a phenomenon and another person to see something different. Above all, ideology provides the interpretive apparatus that helps us evaluate and judge social reality. It is not surprising, then, that each of us uses different lenses according to our different experiences, our family background, our class interests, and the values we personally cherish. Thus inequality, the objective reality of which has been established in this chapter, will be perceived, interpreted, and evaluated from many different perspectives. While there are considerable individual variations in ideological perspective, ideologies tend to cluster into several categories.

In an erudite presentation of ideologies in Canada, Marchak argues that there are two fundamental ideological continuums.[119] The *individual–collectivist continuum* ranges from extreme individualism (a belief in the absolute freedom of the individual, essentially untrammelled by constraints or pressure to conform) to extreme collectivism (a belief in the precedence of the social good and in conformity in the service of society's unity and well-being), with many intermediate points in between. The *egalitarianism–elitism continuum* ranges from extreme elitistism (a belief in giving complete power to those who rule) to extreme egalitarianism (belief in absolute equality of condition and opportunity), also with many points in between.

Without dealing with the extreme positions (which have small but sometimes vocal followings), we can identify three dominant ideologies in Canada. By arranging one continuum horizontally and the other vertically so that they intersect, it is possible to combine

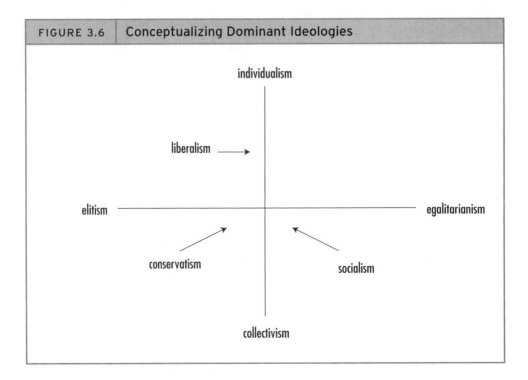

FIGURE 3.6   Conceptualizing Dominant Ideologies

elements from both (Figure 3.6). When egalitarianism and collectivism are combined, the result is an ideological position known as *socialism*. Socialism advocates the unity of society amidst conditions of full equality, condemning any practices that exploit some people for the advantage of others. The combination of elitism and collectivism produces the ideology known as *conservatism*. Conservatives also advocate a unified society, but one in which everyone has an assigned place in the social hierarchy; the government's role is to preserve the hierarchy and maintain order. In the third case, individualism intersects with elitism to produce the ideology known as *liberalism*. In liberalism, society is not so much seen as a unity as it is seen as a collection of individuals whose rights and freedoms must be protected. The role of government is to ensure that there is sufficient equity in the structure of society to allow individuals to achieve their own objectives.

Socialism continues to have some influence in Canadian society, primarily through the social-democratic tradition that argues for strong government, acting democratically for the general good, to intervene in the economy (e.g., by ownership of strategic industries and resources). Conservatism stands at the other end of the continuum, either opposing government intervention or advocating its defence of elite interests (which it portrays as ultimately serving the public good). It is not surprising that much of federal life has been controlled by the more intermediate position of liberalism. In recent years, however, new variants have emerged: neo-liberalism and neo-conservativism.[120] *Neo-liberalism* champions individual liberty and eschews any state interference. Whereas the old liberalism was more of a welfare liberalism, neo-liberalism perceives the welfare state as costly, inefficient, and culpable in the creation of economic dependencies. *Neo-conservativism*, on the other hand, has a moral-political agenda in which excessive individualism is understood to be problematic for the public good. Many of the battles being fought in Canadian society revolve around issues of family, law, sexuality, and crime, in which the moralities of these two points of view repeatedly clash. In any case, all ideologies are straining towards individualism, which seems to be the dominant thinking of our era.

The search for a just society is unending because there are different conceptions of what is just. For this reason, we can see responses to inequality as a matter of ideological conflict. However, ideological conflict is more than a matter of differences of opinion. It is necessary to analyze how these ideological positions reflect class, regional, ethnic, or gender interests and how they prevent some people from realizing their potential. This analysis requires careful scrutiny of all factors rather than sloppy generalizations or stereotypes. By conducting such an analysis, we can uncover important dynamics that tell us a lot more about Canadian society.

FURTHER EXPLORATION

1. Why is the issue of inequality controversial? Choose one form of inequality and explain the forces at work in sustaining and disrupting it.

2. Which dimension of inequality is most problematic for you? What suggestions do you have for reducing it? Why are some forms of inequality more acceptable than other forms of inequality?

3. Look for evidence in the print media of the shift to the right and the movement away from attention to the issue of inequality. What are the advantages and disadvantages of this shift and how are people affected?

SELECTED READINGS

Armstrong, Pat and Hugh Armstrong. *The Double Ghetto: Canadian Women and Their Segregated Work.* 3rd ed. Toronto: McClelland and Stewart, 1994.

Beaujot, Roderic P. *Earning and Caring in Canadian Families.* Peterborough: Broadview, 2000.

Brodie, Janine M. *Women and Canadian Public Policy.* Toronto: Harcourt Brace, 1996.

Clement, Wallace and Leah F. Vosko, eds. *Changing Canada: Political Economy as Transformation.* Montreal: McGill-Queen's University Press, 2003.

Curtis, James, Edward Grabb, and Neil Guppy, eds. *Social Inequality in Canada,* 4th ed. Toronto: Pearson Prentice Hall, 2004.

Hamilton, Roberta. *Gendering the Vertical Mosaic,* 2nd ed. Toronto: Pearson Prentice Hall, 2005.

Li, Peter S. *The Making of Post-War Canada.* Toronto: Oxford, 1996.

Nakhaie, M. Reza, ed. *Debates on Social Inequality: Class, Gender, and Ethnicity in Canada.* Toronto: Harcourt Brace, 1999.

Satzewich, Vic, ed. *Racism and Social Inequality in Canada.* Toronto: Thompson, 1998.

Zwilski, Valeria, and Cynthia Levine-Rasky, eds. *Inequality in Canada: A Reader on the Intersections of Gender, Race, and Class.* Toronto: Oxford University Press, 2005.

ENDNOTES

1 The difficulty people have in placing themselves within a class or the tendency for people to see themselves as middle class is documented by John Goyder and Peter Pineo, "Social Class Self-identification," in James E. Curtis and William G. Scott, eds., *Social Stratification in Canada,* 2nd ed. (Scarborough: Prentice Hall, 1979), 434.

2 For a review of these approaches and their critics, see Edward G. Grabb, *Theories of Social Inequality: Classical and Contemporary Perspectives* (Toronto: Holt Rinehart and Winston, 1990).

3 For examples of work in this tradition, see Wallace Clement, T*he Challenge of Class Analysis* (Ottawa: Carleton University Press, 1988); and Henry Veltmeyer, *The Canadian Class Structure* (Toronto: Garamond, 1986).

4 Michael Ornstein, "Social Class and Economic Inequality," in James Curtis and Lorne Tepperman, eds., *Understanding Canadian Society* (Toronto: McGraw-Hill Ryerson, 1988), 185–221.

5 Wallace Clement, "Comparative Class Analysis: Locating Canada in a North American Context," *Canadian Review of Sociology and Anthropology,* 27 (1990): 462–86.

6 For an application of class analysis and political economy to Canadian society, see Wallace Clement, *The Challenge of Class Analysis* (Ottawa: Carleton University Press, 1988). See also Patricia Marchak, "Canadian Political Economy," *Canadian Review of Sociology and Anthropology* 22 (1985): 673–709; Special Issue on Comparative Political Economy, *Canadian Review of Sociology and Anthropology* 26 (1989), No. 1; Wallace Clement and Daniel Drache, eds., *The New Practical Guide to Political Economy* (Toronto: Lorimer, 1985); and Wallace Clement and Glen Williams, *The New Canadian Political Economy* (Montreal: McGill-Queen's University Press, 1989). See also the journal *Studies in Political Economy.*

7 For an excellent analysis of Canadian society from a political-economy perspective, see Peter S. Li, *The Making of Post-War Canada* (Toronto: Oxford, 1996). For a more specialized analysis, see Julie White, *Sisters and Solidarity: Women and Unions in Canada* (Toronto: Thompson, 1993).

8 S.H. Milner and H. Milner, *The Decolonization of Quebec* (Toronto: McClelland and Stewart, 1973), chap. 3.

9 Jacques Dofny and Marcel Rioux, "Social Class in French Canada," in Marcel Rioux and Yves Martin, eds., *French-Canadian Society*, vol. I (Toronto: McClelland and Stewart, 1971), 307–18.

10 See Anthony Richmond, *Post-War Immigrants in Canada* (Toronto: University of Toronto Press, 1970), 3–26, for a brief sketch on immigration policy.

11 See, for example, Monica Boyd, "Status Attainment in Canada: Findings of the Canadian Mobility Study," *Canadian Review of Sociology and Anthropology* 18 (1981): 657–73.

12 Wsevolod W. Isajiw, Aysan Sev'er, Leo Driedger, "Ethnic Identity and Social Mobility: A Test of the Drawback Model," *Canadian Journal of Sociology* 18 (1993): 177–96; Edward N. Herberg, "The Ethno-Racial Socio-economic Hierarchy in Canada: Theory and Analysis of the New Vertical Mosaic," *International Journal of Comparative Sociology* 31 (1990): 206–21.

13 Jason Z. Lian and David Ralph Matthews, "Does the Vertical Mosaic Still Exist? Ethnicity and Income in Canada," *Canadian Review of Sociology and Anthropology* 35, 4 (1998): 461–81.

14 Richard A. Wanner, "Expansion and Ascription: Trends in Educational Opportunity in Canada 1920–1994," *Canadian Review of Sociology and Anthropology* 36, 3 (1999): 409–42.

15 Hugh Lautard and Neil Guppy, "Revisiting *The Vertical Mosaic*: Occupational Stratification Among Canadian Ethnic Groups," in Peter S. Li, ed., *Race and Ethnic Relations in Canada*, 2nd ed. (Toronto: Oxford University Press, 1999), 219–52.

16 Carol Agocs and Monica Boyd, "The Canadian Ethnic Mosaic Recast for the 1990's," in James Curtis, Edward Grabb, and Neil Guppy, eds., *Social Inequality in Canada: Patterns, Problems, Policies*, 2nd ed. (Scarborough: Prentice Hall, 1993), 332. For the "new" vertical mosaic, see 337.

17 J.A. Geschwender and N. Guppy, "Ethnicity, Educational Attainment and Earned Income Among Canadian-Born Men and Women," *Canadian Ethnic Studies* 27, 1 (1995): 67–84; Lian and Matthews, "Does the Vertical Mosaic Still Exist?"

18 Richard A. Wanner, "Prejudice, Profit or Productivity: Explaining Returns to Human Capital Among Male Immigrants to Canada," *Canadian Ethnic Studies* 30, 3 (1998): 6–23.

19 Peter S. Li, "The Market Value and Social Value of Race," in Vic Satzewich, ed., *Racism and Social Inequality in Canada* (Toronto: Thompson, 1998), 115–30.

20 Feng Hou and T.R. Balakrishnan, "The Integration of Visible Minorities In Contemporary Canadian Society," *Canadian Journal of Sociology* 21, 3 (1996): 307–26.

21 Peter S. Li, *Ethnic Inequality in a Class Society* (Toronto: Wall and Thompson, 1988). See also Raymond Breton, Wsevolod W. Isajiw, Warren Kalbach, and Jeffrey G. Reitz, *Ethnic Identity and Equality: Varieties of Experiences in a Canadian City* (Toronto: University of Toronto Press, 1990), who argue that the relationship between ethnic persistence and equality can be both an asset and a liability and therefore is highly variable.

22 Mildred A. Schwartz, *Politics and Territory: The Sociology of Regional Persistence in Canada* (Montreal: McGill-Queen's University Press, 1974), 336.

23 Robert J. Brym, ed., *Regionalism in Canada* (Toronto: Irwin, 1986), 4–18.

24 This argument is developed in some detail by Carl Cuneo, "A Class Perspective on Regionalism," in Daniel Glenday, Hubert Guidon, and Allan Turowetz, eds., *Modernization and the Canadian State* (Toronto: Macmillan, 1978).

25 R. Keith Semple, "Urban Dominance, Foreign Ownership, and Corporate Concentration," in James Curtis et al., *Social Inequality in Canada: Patterns, Problems and Policies* (Scarborough: Prentice Hall, 1988), 343–56; and Benjamin Higgins, *The Rise and Fall of Montreal* (Moncton: Canadian Institute for Research on Regional Development, 1986).

26   Neil Swan and John Serjak, "Analysing Regional Disparities," in James Curtis, Edward Grabb, and Neil Guppy, *Social Inequality in Canada*, 2nd ed., 430–48.

27   For a presentation of the metropolis–hinterland thesis, see Arthur Davis, "Canadian Society and History as Hinterland and Metropolis," in Richard J. Ossenberg, ed., *Canadian Society: Pluralism, Change and Conflict* (Scarborough: Prentice Hall, 1971), 6–32.

28   For one account of the agrarian reaction, see John A. Irving, *The Social Credit Movement in Alberta* (Toronto: University of Toronto Press, 1959). Pierre Vallières's book is entitled *White Niggers of America* (Toronto: McClelland and Stewart, 1971).

29   For an example of this kind of regional class analysis, see Peter Sinclair, "Class Structure and Populist Protest: The Case of Western Canada," *Canadian Journal of Sociology* 1 (1975): 1–17.

30   Ralph Matthews, "Class Interests and the Role of the State in the Development of Canada's East Coast Fishery," *Canadian Issues: Journal of the Association for Canadian Studies* 3 (1980): 115–24.

31   Bonnie J. Fox, "The Feminist Challenge," in Robert J. Brym, *From Culture to Power*, chap. 5, 32 E.D. Nelson and Barrie W. Robinson, *Gender in Canada* (Scarborough: Prentice Hall, 1999), chap. 1.

33   Roderic P. Beaujot, *Earning and Caring in Canadian Families* (Peterborough: Broadview Press, 2000).

34   Women in Canada: Work Chapter Updates 2003, Statistics Canada Catalogue 89F0133.

35   Ibid.

36   *Women in the Labour Force*, 1994 Edition, Statistics Canada 75-507, tables 2.8 and 4.4.

37   Ann DuVy, Nancy Mandell, and Norene Pupo, *Few Choices: Women, Work and Family* (Toronto: Garamond, 1989), 18.

38   Women in Canada. Work Chapter Updates 2003. Statistics Canada, Catalogue No. 89F0133, Table 11.

39   Pat Armstrong and Hugh Armstrong, *The Double Ghetto: Canadian Women and Their Segregated Work* (Toronto: McClelland and Stewart, 1994), 9.

40   Vijay Agnew, *Resisting Discrimination: Women in Asia, Africa, and the Caribbean and the Women's Movement in Canada* (Toronto: University of Toronto Press, 1996).

41   For a good review of the approaches discussed here, see Eileen Saunders, "Theoretical Approaches to the Study of Women," in Curtis, Grabb, and Guppy, *Social Inequality in Canada*, 3rd ed., 168–85.

42   DuVy, Mandell, and Pupo, *Few Choices: Women, Work and Family*, 46.

43   Margrit Eichler, "The Connection Between Paid and Unpaid Labour and Its Implications for Creating Equality for Women," in *Research Studies of the Commission on Equality in Employment*, 539–45. See also Ann Duffy and Norene Pupo, *The Part-time Paradox: Connecting Gender, Work and Family* (Toronto: McClelland and Stewart, 1992).

44   Carl J. Cuneo, "Have Women Become More Proletarianized Than Men?" *Canadian Review of Sociology and Anthropology* 22 (1985): 465–95 and William K. Carroll, "Which Women Are More Proletarianized? Gender, Class and Occupation in Canada," *Canadian Review of Sociology and Anthropology* 24 (1987): 571–85.

45   Paul Phillips and Erin Phillips, *Women and Work: Inequality in the Labour Market*, rev. ed. (Toronto: Lorimer, 1993); Pat Armstrong and Hugh Armstrong, *The Double Ghetto*, rev. ed. (Toronto: McClelland and Stewart, 1984); Meg Luxton and Harriet Rosenberg, *Through the Kitchen Window: The Politics of Home and Family* (Toronto: Garamond, 1986); Carl Cuneo, *Pay Equity: The Labour/Feminist Challenge* (Toronto: Oxford, 1990); and Jane Jenson, Elisabeth Hagen, and Ceillaigh Reddy, eds., *Feminization of the Labour Force: Paradoxes and Promises* (New York: Oxford, 1988).

46 Meg Luxton, Harriet Rosenberg, and Sedef Arat-Koc, eds., *Through the Kitchen Window: The Politics of Home and Family* (Toronto: Garamond, 1990); Kevin McQuillan and Marilyn Belle, "Who Does What? Gender and the Division of Labour in Canadian Households," in Curtis, Grabb, and Guppy, *Social Inequality in Canada*, 3rd ed., 186–98.

47 Roberta Hamilton, *Gendering the Vertical Mosaic,* 2nd ed. (Toronto: Pearson Prentice Hall, 2005).

48 S.J. Wilson, *Women, the Family and the Economy*, 3rd ed. (Toronto: McGraw-Hill Ryerson, 1991). See also Sandra Burt, Lorraine Code, and Lindsay Dorney, eds., *Changing Patterns: Women in Canada*, 2nd ed. (Toronto: McClelland and Stewart, 1993).

49 *The Report of the Royal Commission on Equality in Employment* was published in 1984 and *The Employment Equity Act* was passed in 1986. The results of the research reports done by the Commission were published in 1985 as "Research Studies of the Commission on Equality in Employment."

50 For good discussions of gender relations and gender socialization, see Marlene Mackie, *Gender Relations in Canada: Further Explorations* (Toronto: Butterworths, 1991) and *Constructing Men and Women: Gender Socialization* (Toronto: Holt Rinehart and Winston, 1987).

51 Gillian Creese and Brenda Beagan, "Gender at Work: Seeking Solutions For Women's Equality," in Curtis, Grabb, and Guppy, *Social Inequality in Canada*, 3rd ed., 199–211. See also Janine Brodie, *Women and Canadian Public Policy* (Toronto: Harcourt Brace, 1996) and Caroline Andrew and Sanda Rodgers, eds., *Women and the Canadian State* (Montreal: McGill-Queen's University Press, 1997).

52 Joanna Everitt, "Public Opinion and Social Movements: The Women's Movement and the Gender Gap in Canada," *Canadian Journal of Political Science* 31, 4 (1998): 743–65.

53 John Porter, *The Vertical Mosaic* (Toronto: University of Toronto Press, 1965), 38–59. For a good review of the legacy of *The Vertical Mosaic*, see Rick Helmes-Hayes and James Curtis, eds., *The Vertical Mosaic Revisited* (Toronto: University of Toronto Press, 1998).

54 For an excellent discussion of the nature and significance of the brain drain, see Walter Adams, ed., *The Brain Drain* (Toronto: Macmillan Co. of Canada, 1968); also K.V. Pankhurst, "Migration Between Canada and the United States" in *The Annals of the American Academy of Political and Social Science* 367(1966): 53–62.

55 For an assessment of John Porter's analysis of class, mobility, education, and power in Canadian society, see a special issue (No. 5) of the *Canadian Review of Sociology and Anthropology* 18 (1981), issued in memory of John Porter.

56 Economic Council of Canada, Seventh Annual Review, 1970, 56–61; and Max Van Zur-Mehlen, "The Ph.D. Dilemma in Canada," in Sylvia Ostry, ed., *Canadian Higher Education in the Seventies* (Ottawa: Economic Council of Canada, 1972), 79.

57 Michael D. Ornstein argues that the extent of mobility must be related to features of the labour market, such as employment opportunities or the hiring and promotion policies of corporations. "The Occupational Mobility of Men in Ontario," *Canadian Review of Sociology and Anthropology* 18 (1981): 183–215. See also Harvey Rich, "The Vertical Mosaic Reconsidered," *Journal of Canadian Studies* 11 (1976): 14–31, who argues that Porter described an archaic rather than contemporary view of Canadian society.

58 Sid Gilbert and Hugh A. McRoberts, "Academic Stratification and Education Plans: A Reassessment," *Canadian Review of Sociology and Anthropology* 14 (1977): 34–47.

59 John Porter, Marion Porter, and Bernard R. Blishen, *Stations and Callings: Making It Through the School System* (Toronto: Methuen, 1982), 311–15; and Neil Guppy and Bruce Arai, "Who Benefits from Higher Education? Differences by Sex, Social Class, and Ethnic Background," in Curtis, Grabb, and Guppy, eds., *Social Inequality in Canada*, 214–32.

60 Monica Boyd, "Status Attainment in Canada: Findings of the Canadian Mobility Study," *Canadian Review of Sociology and Anthropology* 18 (1981): 670.

61 Monica Boyd et al., *Ascription and Achievement: Studies in Mobility and Status Attainment in Canada* (Ottawa: Carleton University Press, 1985), 517–23. For an interesting historical study of the role of achievement in the growth of the Canadian middle class, see Robert Lanning, *The National Album: Collective Biography and the Formation of the Canadian Middle Class* (Ottawa: Carleton University Press, 1996).

62 Harry Braverman, *Labour and Monopoly Capital: The Degradation of Work in the Twentieth Century* (New York: Monthly Review, 1974).

63 Alfred A. Hunter, *Class Tells*, 2nd ed., 63.

64 Graham S. Lowe, "Labour Markets, Inequality, and the Future of Work," in Curtis, Grabb, and Guppy, eds., *Social Inequality in Canada*, 113–27. See also Harvey Krahn and Graham Lowe, *Work, Industry and Canadian Society*, 3rd ed. (Toronto: Nelson, 1998).

65 Gillian Creese, Neil Guppy, and Martin Meissner, "Ups and Downs on the Ladder of Success: Social Mobility in Canada," Statistics Canada Catalogue 11-612E, 1991.

66 Edward B. Harvey and Ivan Charmer, "Social Mobility and Occupational Attainments of University Graduates," *Canadian Review of Sociology and Anthropology* 12 (1975): 134–49; John C. Goyder and James E. Curtis, "Occupational Mobility in Canada over Four Generations," *Canadian Review of Sociology and Anthropology* 14 (1977): 303–19. For a good review of the recent evidence relating stratification to accessibility, see Paul Anisef and Norman Okihiro, *Losers & Winners: The Pursuit of Equality and Social Justice in Higher Education* (Toronto: Butterworths, 1982).

67 Alfred A. Hunter, *Class Tells*, 83–84.

68 Michael Ornstein, "The Occupational Mobility of Men in Ontario," *Canadian Review of Sociology and Anthropology* 18 (1981): 193–215. See also Robert Brym, *From Culture to Power*, 93–95.

69 Richard A. Wanner, "Social Mobility in Canada: Concepts, Patterns, and Trends," in Curtis, Grabb, and Guppy, eds., *Social Inequality in Canada*, 144. See also Edward N. Herberg, op. cit., who argues that a contest model of mobility is more appropriate to Canada than an ascriptive model.

70 Wallace Clement and John Myles, *Relations of Ruling* (Montreal: McGill-Queen's University Press, 1994), 4.

71 Tom Naylor, "The Rise and Fall of the Third Commercial Empire of the St. Lawrence," in Gary Teeple, ed., *Capitalism and the National Question in Canada* (Toronto: University of Toronto Press, 1972), 1–41.

72 R.J. Richardson, "Merchants Against Industry: An Empirical Study of the Debate," *Canadian Journal of Sociology* 7 (1982): 279–95.

73 John Porter, *The Vertical Mosaic*, chap. 7.

74 Wallace Clement, *The Canadian Corporate Elite: An Analysis of Economic Power* (Toronto: McClelland and Stewart, 1975).

75 Wallace Clement, *Continental Corporate Power* (Toronto: McClelland and Stewart, 1977), chaps. 6, 7, and 8.

76 See also Dennis Olsen, *The State Elite* (Toronto: McClelland and Stewart, 1980).

77 R. Jack Richardson, "Economic Concentration and Social Power in Contemporary Canada," in James Curtis and Lorne Tepperman, eds., *Images of Canada: The Sociological Tradition* (Scarborough: Prentice Hall, 1990), 341–50.

78 The conclusion of this study was that countries in which billionaire heirs' wealth was large relative to GDP (in contrast to self-made billionaires' wealth) grew more slowly economically because billionaire heirs spent less on innovation and their preferential access to capital helped preserve less

competitive firms. Randall Morck, David A. Strangeland, and Bernard Young note that free trade might change this traditional pattern in Canada. "Inherited Wealth, Corporate Control and Economic Growth: The Canadian Disease?" (University Of Alberta, Institute for Financial Research, Working Paper 4–98, 1998).

79 William K. Carroll, John Fox, and Michael D. Ornstein, "The Network of Directorate Links Among the Largest Canadian Firms," *Canadian Review of Sociology and Anthropology* 19 (1982): 44–69.

80 Michael D. Ornstein, "The Boards and Executives of the Largest Canadian Corporations: Size, Composition, Interlocks," *Canadian Journal of Sociology* 1 (1976): 411–37 and "The Social Organization of the Canadian Capitalist Class in Comparative Perspective," *Canadian Review of Sociology and Anthropology* 26 (1989): 151–77.

81 See the work of William K. Carroll, *Corporate Power and Canadian Capitalism* (Vancouver: University of British Columbia Press, 1986) and "The Individual, Class and Corporate Power in Canada," *Canadian Journal of Sociology* 9 (1984): 245–68.

82 John Fox and Michael Ornstein, "The Canadian State and Corporate Elites in the Post-War Period," *Canadian Review of Sociology and Anthropology* 23 (1986): 481–506.

83 Michael Ornstein, "Canadian Capital and the Canadian State: Ideology in an Era of Crisis," in Robert J. Brym, ed., *The Structure of the Canadian Capitalist Class* (Toronto: Garamond, 1985).

84 R. Ogmundson, "Perspectives on the Class and Ethnic Origins of Canadian Elites: A Methodological Critique of the Porter/Clement/Olsen Tradition," *Canadian Journal of Sociology* 15 (1990): 165–77; and R. Ogmundson and J. McLaughlin, "Trends in the Ethnic Origins of Canadian Elites; The Decline of the Brits?" *Canadian Review of Sociology and Anthropology* 29 (1992): 227–42.

85 M. Reza Nakhaie, "Vertical Mosaic Among the Elites: The New Imagery Revisited," *Canadian Review of Sociology and Anthropology* 34, 1 (1997):1–24; and "Ethnic Inequality: Well-Paid Employees of the Ontario Public Bureaucracy," *Canadian Ethnic Studies* 30, 1 (1998):119–39.

86 R. Ogmundson and M. Doyle, "The Rise and Decline of Canadian Labour 1960–2000: Elites, Power, Ethnicity, and Gender," *Canadian Journal of Sociology* 27, 3 (2002): 413–54. Ogmundson and Doyle point out the significant shift to unions being much more female, white-collar, and public-sector based.

87 M. Reza Nakhaie, "Ownership and Management Position of Canadian Ethnic Groups in 1973 and 1989," *Canadian Journal of Sociology* 20, 2 (1995): 167–92.

88 William K. Carroll, *Corporate Power in a Globalizing World.* (Toronto: Oxford University Press, 2004).

89 Robert Michels, *Political Parties: A Sociological Study of the Oligarchical Tendencies of Modern Democracy* (New York: Free Press, 1966).

90 See, for example, D.W. Dimick, and V.V. Murray, "Career and Personal Characteristics of the Managerial Technostructure in Canadian Business," *Canadian Review of Sociology and Anthropology* 15 (1978): 372–84; and Terence H. White, "Boards of Directors: Control and Decision-Making in Canadian Corporations," *Canadian Review of Sociology and Anthropology* 16 (1979): 77–95.

91 Merrijoy Kelner, "Ethnic Penetration into Toronto's Elite Structure," *Canadian Review of Sociology and Anthropology* 7 (1970): 128–37.

92 See Jorge Niosi, *Canadian Capitalism: A Study of Power in the Canadian Business Establishment* (Toronto: James Lorimer, 1981). For a discussion of the issue of francophone participation in the federal bureaucracy, see Christopher Beattie, Jacques Desy, and Stephen Longstaff, *Bureaucratic Careers: Anglophones and Francophones in the Canadian Public Service* (Ottawa: Information Canada, 1972); and Christopher Beattie, *Minority Men in a Majority Setting* (Toronto: McClelland and Stewart, 1975).

93 For a discussion of the ideological use to which elite analysis may be applied, see Harvey Rich, "John Porter's Sociology and Liberal Democracy," *Canadian Journal of Sociology* 17 (1992): 193–98.

94 See Statistics Canada, Catalogue 13-207.

95 *Income in Canada 2002*, Statistics Canada, Catalogue 75-202-XIE

96 This is understood as the feminization of poverty. For a discussion of women and poverty, see Morley Gunderson, Leon Muszynski, and Jennifer Keck, *Women and Labour Market Poverty* (Ottawa: Canadian Advisory Council on The Status of Women, 1990).

97 Abdolmohammad Kazemipur and Shiva S. Halli, "The Changing Colour of Poverty in Canada," *Canadian Reviw of Sociology and Anthropology* 38, 2 (2001): 217–238.98; Garnett Picot and Ted Wannell, "Job Loss and Labour Market Adjustment in the Canadian Economy," The Labour Force 1987: 85–135 (Statistics Canada); and David Sobel and Susan Meurer, *Working at Inglis: The Life and Death of a Canadian Factory* (Toronto: James Lorimer, 1994).

99 Patrick Burman, *Killing Time, Losing Ground: Experiences of Unemployment* (Toronto: Wall and Thompson, 1988).

100 Tracy Peressini, "Canada's Homeless: Patterns and Policies," in Curtis, Grabb, and Guppy, *Social Inequalities in Canada,* 4th ed., 382–92.

101 *Income in Canada 2002*, Statistics Canada, Catalogue 75-202.

102 Christopher Sarlo, *Poverty in Canada* (Vancouver: Fraser Institute, 1992); and National Council of Welfare, *A New Poverty: Yes, No, or Maybe?* (Ottawa, 1998–99)

103 Therese Jennissen, "Implications for Women: The Canadian Health and Social Transfer," in Raymond B. Blake, Penny E. Bryden, J. Frank Strain, eds., *The Welfare State in Canada: Past, Present, and Future* (Toronto: Irwin, 1997).

104 Poverty rates among non-elderly families for the following countries are as follows: United States 18.7%, Canada 15.7%, Australia 15.4%, France 8.9%, Germany 8.5%, Belgium 5.4%, Netherlands 4.7%. Ross, Shillington, and Lochhead, *The Canadian Factbook on Poverty 1994*, 111.

105 See Gary Teeple, "The Decline of the Canadian Welfare State: Policies and Implications of Retrenchment," in B. Singh Bolaria, ed., *Social Issues and Contradictions in Canadian Society*, 3rd ed. (Toronto: Harcourt Brace, 2000), 434–68; and Blake, Bryden, and Strain, eds., *The Welfare State in Canada*.

106 G. Bruce Doern and Richard W. Phidd, *Canadian Public Policy: Ideas, Structure and Process* (Toronto: Methuen, 1983), chap. 1; and Allan Tupper and G. Bruce Doern, eds., *Public Corporations and Public Policy in Canada* (Montreal: Institute for Research on Public Policy, 1981), chap. 1.

107 T.W. Acheson, "The Maritimes and 'Empire Canada'," in David J. Bercuson, ed., *Canada and the Burden of Unity* (Toronto: Macmillan, 1977), 103.

108 Ralph Matthews, *The Creation of Regional Dependency* (Toronto: University of Toronto Press, 1983), 69–76.

109 Peter S. Li, *The Making of Post-War Canadian Society* (Toronto: Oxford, 1996), 91.

110 Patricia M. Evans and Gerda R. Wekerle, eds., *Women and the Canadian Welfare State: Challenges and Change* (Toronto: University of Toronto Press, 1997); and Janine M. Brodie, *Politics on the Margins: Restructuring and the Canadian Women's Movement* (Halifax: Fernwood, 1995).

111 Keith G. Banting, "The Welfare State and Inequality in the 1980s," *Canadian Review of Sociology and Anthropology* 24 (1987): 309–38.

112 Ralph Miliband, *The State in Capitalist Society* (London: Weidenfeld and Nicolson, 1969).

113 Nicos Poulantzas, *Political Power and Social Classes* (London: Verso, 1975).

114 Gregory Albo and Jane Jenson, "A Contested Concept: The Relative Autonomy of the State," in Clement and Williams, *The New Canadian Political Economy*, 180.

115 Peter S. Li, *The Making of Post-War Canadian Society*, chap. 5.

116 Cf. Leo Panitch, ed., *The Canadian State: Political Economy and Political Power* (Toronto: University of Toronto Press, 1977), 18–19.

117 John Calvert, "Government Policy and Economic Crisis," in James Curtis et al., *Social Inequality in Canada*, 423.

118 A. Paul Williams, "Access and Accommodation in the Canadian Welfare State: The Political Significance of Contacts Between State, Labour, and Business Leaders," *Canadian Review of Sociology and Anthropology* 26 (1989): 217–39.

119 Much of the following discussion is based on M. Patricia Marchak, *Ideological Perspectives on Canada*, 3rd ed. (Toronto: McGraw-Hill Ryerson, 1988). It is interesting to read of Marchak's own ideological pilgrimage in the book's introduction, from reformist liberalism to neo-Marxism to a contemporary search for a better theoretical perspective.

120 For a good discussion comparing these two ideas, see Linda Trimble, "Women and the Politics of Citizenship," 143–46, in Janine Brodie and Linda Trimble, eds., *Reinventing Canada* (Toronto: Prentice Hall, 2003).

WEBLINKS

www.ccsd.ca

The Canadian Council on Social Development provides data and discussion papers on the various dimensions of poverty in Canada.

www.hc-sc.gc.ca/seniors-aines

Health Canada's Division of Aging and Seniors provides access to research, educational activities, and policy issues related to aging in Canada.

www.cmec.ca

Council of Ministers of Education (Canada) is the national voice for education in Canada. The site includes reports about education in Canada and around the world.

www.swc-cfc.gc.ca

The Status of Women Canada (SWC) is a federal organization committed to promoting gender equality and the full participation of women in every aspect of daily life.

chapter four

The Issue of Regionalism

The economic history of Canada has been dominated by the discrepancy between the cen-
tre and the margin of western civilization. Energy has been directed toward the exploita-
tion of staple products and the tendency has been cumulative.

–Harold A. Innis, acclaimed University of Toronto political economist,
early leader of the social science community, and originator of the
staples thesis, in his *The Fur Trade in Canada* (1930), 385

It should not be surprising that regions should be important in a country as large as Canada. Because segments of the society are separated by huge geographical distances, regions develop quite naturally. But vast territory is not in itself a sufficient explanation for why regions develop, because we know that even in relatively small countries like Switzerland coherent regions have emerged (see Chapter Six). Regions must be understood as the product of people in interaction—people sorting themselves out in space and creating their own cultures; to understand regions, we must understand how this interaction, rooted in local conditions, helps people of one region to differentiate themselves from other people of other regions. It is not just physical features (e.g., mountains, rivers) which divide up space, but the activity of people creating their own communities. This is why it makes a difference whether you live in Grand Falls, Newfoundland; Trois Rivières, Quebec; Regina, Saskatchewan; or Victoria, British Columbia. It is because people who share a territory interact with each other and share a local history, climate, and economy that they produce their own traditions, social structure, and culture. In short, *regions are social constructions,* because people both respond to the elements of their surroundings and initiate action to transform them, thereby creating their own local communities.[1]

Chapter One examined some of the problems of defining a region, and the reader may want to review that material. In that chapter, our concern was to show the demographic differences between areas of Canada. Chapter Three demonstrated the existence of regional inequality using several key indicators. The treatment of the issue in the earlier chapters was descriptive, with little explanation of what regional differences meant, why they existed, or their consequences. We now turn our attention to the dynamics of regionalism, its causes and consequences, and try to understand why it is such an important factor in Canadian society. The chapter concludes with an illustrative discussion of three Canadian regions: the West, the Atlantic region, and the North.

REGIONALISM AS A SOCIAL FACTOR

Regions are always related to geography. Typically, we look for areas with similar topographical features and note how these areas are demarcated from others by mountains, bodies of water, or changes in foliage. Regions can be distinguished by types and amounts of precipitation and variations in temperature, soil conditions, and plant life.

Geographical features are more than a critical basis for identifying a region; such features as soil conditions and climate, for example, have a major role to play in the attractiveness of an area as a place to live and in its ability to support a population economically. Thus, if the first dimension of regionalism is *geographic*, the second dimension is *economic*; i.e., what do people do to earn a living? The rocky soil of much of the Atlantic region does not allow the grain farming endemic to the Prairies, nor do the landlocked Prairies support the fishing and marine industries common to the Atlantic area. What people do for a living—its importance and economic value—shapes the nature and quality of their lives and gives a region a distinct identity. Social institutions (e.g., grain growers' groups, fish cooperatives, manufacturing unions) grow up around these economic activities, helping to produce a regional culture, a similar view of the world, a folk culture of customs and traditions, a common history, linguistic idioms, and, consequently, a personal attachment to an area and group identity.

While homogeneous regions may exist in theory or reflect images propagated by the media, modern societies are far too complex for our use of simple regional distinctions. People outside central Canada usually think of Ontario as the industrial heartland of the nation, yet Ontario also possesses a strong mixed-farming sector. Similarly, the stereotype of the Prairies as a wheat-farming region ignores the fact that the population of the Prairie provinces is now overwhelmingly urban. The point is that changes resulting from urbanization and other socio-technical changes have blurred the simple distinctions that may have once existed between the regions. Nevertheless, it is still possible to say that the dominant oil and gas industries of Alberta and Saskatchewan, for example, give those provinces a significantly different cast from the strong manufacturing sectors of Ontario and Quebec. Similarly, the mining, lumbering, and shipping industries of British Columbia clearly distinguish that region from the Prairies and help to explain why the Prairies and British Columbia resist being lumped together into one homogeneous western region. Although regions may not be easy to distinguish, a region's distinctive economic components do combine with other factors (e.g., a sense of history or ethnic composition) to assist in the creation of a regional culture.

It is not without significance that the first modern sociologists to take up the study of regionalism were prompted by the negative comparisons made in distinguishing their region from other regions in the national whole. Sociologists Howard Odum and Rupert Vance of the University of North Carolina noted how the American South in the 1920s and 1930s had not participated in the industrialization that characterized the North.[2] The South's comparative disadvantage led them to seek a material and cultural renaissance of the regional South. Even though industrial expansion in the American South over the last few decades has removed some of the economic differences, it has been argued that Southerners still possess a strong regional identity and culture.[3] Thus, looking at regions may be an important way to analyze a society because of the comparisons that can be made *between* regions.

Does region of residence help explain people's behaviour or illuminate the dynamics of a national society? There is considerable debate on this issue; some social scientists believe social class, occupation, or ethnicity to be more powerful determinants of behaviour,[4] and think of region as a mere container which in itself does not explain anything. And yet why do we continually refer to region as an important variable in understanding Canadian society? The answer is to be found in the fact that people who share a territory create their own localized society. This regional society may have all kinds of external links and the boundaries may be imprecise. Regions also interact with each other and through this interrelationship become aware of their distinguishing characteristics. Normally, however, regions are not actors but their constituents are, and it is always intriguing to see how residents may be mobilized into action when territory is invoked as the basis for unity. This is where region and regionalism come together.

Region, then, is the result of people who share a territory creating their own society with its own unique culture and social structure. The dimensions and characteristics of that region can be catalogued using a wide variety of indicators, from per capita income to unemployment rates and from occupational structure to ethnic origins, as well as community and institutional components. From these elements, a population sharing a territory create their own *regional society. Regionalism*, on the other hand, is the politicization of these local traits into a consciousness of kind or regional identity. It is the mobilization of key elements of regional culture (e.g., dominant occupational groups, significant natural resources, aspects of the economy) and the attempt to translate them into a coherent worldview with which residents of a region encounter other regions.[5] The important idea here is that the contents of this regional ideology or interpretive apparatus may change over time, and the ideology itself may wax and wane according to circumstances. So although *region* itself is just a descriptive category, it becomes dynamic when it is transformed into a relationship between regions, thereby prompting the emergence of *regionalism*. Thus, for example, if one region of a country has a strong manufacturing sector and another region has virtually none, that fact reflects a relationship between the two regions that must be explored and explained. But that fact may also potentially arouse strong feelings or perceptions in residents within (internal) and between (external) regions. Such interregional defence of territorial interests is the stuff of regionalism. Region, then, is a neutral concept, whereas regionalism is always dynamic and volatile.

In our study of regionalism we must attempt to understand the constitutive elements of a region while keeping an eye on how regional traits contribute to a way of understanding the world (or at least other regions within the national society). Before we engage in case studies of regionalism in Canada, it is important to examine explanations for why regionalism persists as a societal issue.

WHAT CAUSES REGIONALISM?

The *dynamic approach* to regionalism views regions not simply as territories with different names and characteristics but as units that must be understood in relation to one

Differing Perspectives

Structural Functionalism

The structural functionalist perspective understands regions as part of the unique tapestry of Canadian society. While regions have different histories, cultures, economies, and populations, these differences are not so much problematic as reflective of how each region contributes differently to Canadian society as a whole. Regional differences are seen as the natural result of differing locations and opportunities. Some regions will play more dominant roles because they are more centrally located or more populous; others may have less industry or a shrinking employment base due to their hinterland location. When disparities exist, the society as a system will develop ways to provide support for less prosperous regions in order to maintain the status quo and keep the society intact.

Conflict

The conflict perspective places particular emphasis on how regions are created by differential access to economic resources. The dominance of any one region occurs at the expense of other regions. The concentration and centralization of regional power are primarily reflective of the capitalist system, which conceives of the whole country as its market and enhances profit by centralizing its operations, making some regions hinterlands for the products of economically dominant regions. Regional elites may attempt to challenge the elites of dominant regions; in so doing they may enlist grassroots regional support, which may produce regional movements. Regional feeling develops as a result of collective resistance to regional disparities, perceptions of regional superiority, and elites' use of political power to create regional confrontations. Regions are therefore the end result of power struggles, either overt or covert.

Symbolic Interactionism

The symbolic interactionist perspective focuses on how people sharing a regional territory create meaning and develop a sense of community. The emphasis is on how people construct regional traditions, institutions, and other symbols of regional sentiment that are unique and not shared with people in other regions. The way people come to understand themselves in terms of their regional identity can be compared with the way they view people in other regions. The focus is on how specific locale and shared experiences give local people a unique identity. Region is understood as a lived part of daily life which in a real sense becomes part of who a person is as an individual and also provides a perspective on the world outside.

another. By analyzing how regions relate to one another within a country, we understand more clearly how power is distributed throughout that society. Regional characteristics remain benign descriptors unless people within the various regions become aware of the meaning of their regional differences. What transforms neutral understanding of regional characteristics into the more politicized form of regional awareness which is the essence of regionalism? Five factors can be identified.

1. Uneven Development

One of the most dramatic causes of Canadian regionalism has been the unevenness of economic development in different parts of the society. For example, the original industrial strength of the Maritime region was superseded by greater industrial centralization in Central Canada; consequently, the Atlantic provinces went into a decline from which they have never recovered.[6] On the other hand, the industrial strength of Ontario and Quebec gained new momentum in the post-World War II era, during which 75% of the leading Canadian corporations and 85% of the major financial institutions established their head offices in Toronto or Montreal.[7] Using the protective tariff to guarantee a Canadian market for their products, these industries felt little need to develop elsewhere, and the rest of Canada became a market hinterland to Central Canadian industries. Freight-rate squabbles and animosity regarding mortgages held by Central Canadian financial institutions frequently became symbolic of hinterland resistance to regional dominance.

While Ontario and Quebec have been the beneficiaries, it is clear that the foci of economic development were the metropolitan galaxies of Toronto and Montreal. Both cities spawned an elaborate suburban system and drew supporting cities into their orbit. For example, while Toronto and Hamilton were once distinct cities separated by considerable green space, they are now linked in an almost continuous megalopolis as a consequence of the growth of new interstitial cities, such as Burlington, Oakville, and Mississauga.

From a national point of view, what is significant is that disproportionate economic and population growth took place within these two metropolitan areas. Vancouver, as a Pacific port city with a coastal climate, experienced some growth, but the foci of Canadian economic development were clearly Toronto and Montreal. These are *primate cities*—a term used in cases where one or two surpassingly large cities dominate the rest of a country and have developed at such a pace that significant socio-economic and even cultural differences emerge between them (and their supporting regions) and the rest of the nation. The overdevelopment of these metropolitan areas, as compared to the underdevelopment of urban centres in other regions, has become an important aspect of Central Canada's dominance. The concentration of employment opportunities in the industrial regions has meant that persons seeking work or career advancement are forced to leave the hinterland regions and move to Ontario or Quebec; this movement contributes to further population imbalances. Chapter Three examined how important socio-economic indicators, such as income, education, and unemployment, reveal the existence of significant regional disparities.

To emphasize that regional identities are the result of interregional relationships, Clement has argued that the overdevelopment of one region can take place only at the expense of the underdevelopment of others.[8] This assertion is based on the assumption that national societies with closed boundaries force regional units into a power struggle in which some regions win and others lose. One study of import–export trade ratios between other provinces and Ontario demonstrated that, whereas Quebec's ratio with Ontario was quite close (4:5), Alberta's and Saskatchewan's were unbalanced (at 1:8 and 1:15 respectively), while Prince Edward Island's (2:47) and Newfoundland's (3:1 000) were even more unbalanced in Ontario's favour.[9]

The dominance of Central Canada does not mean that all other regions are equal. On the contrary; regions with raw materials or resources the industrial centre needs have a more favourable exchange ratio than regions with less to exchange. Yet it is precisely this exchange of finished goods for raw materials that ensures the continued dominance of the

REAL PEOPLE 4.1	Call Centres: A New Form of Regional Economic Development

Moncton, New Brunswick

Bill (to cousin Joe, formerly from New Brunswick, but who now lives in Peterborough, Ontario, to whom Bill talks to on the phone two or three times a year):

"You wouldn't believe what they are saying about this province where you grew up. Yup, they are calling it the 'Call Centre Capital of North America.' Sounds pretty important, doesn't it? That's something new we have around here. We never thought that the day would come when people in this province would work for the big fancy corporations. We were more used to agriculture and small businesses. Now it's Fedex, Xerox, Royal Bank, and UPS, plus airlines and car rental companies and hotels and lots more. The paper the other day said there were over 80 call centres in New Brunswick now, employing close to 9 000 people."

Joe: "I never knew what a call centre was until last year when I called to make a reservation with a hotel chain. I commented about the weather and the representative said she was not in my city or even in Ontario but in Saint John, New Brunswick. Now every time I make a reservation for anything, I ask where they are answering the phone at. You never know, it might be someone I know or whose parents I grew up with if they are answering in New Brunswick."

Bill: "Yeah, you know those 1-800 numbers. I guess they handle calls from all over North America. It is really great. It provides lots of jobs in clean offices. Better than industries that pollute the environment or unpredictable resources."

Joe: "I wonder what kind of jobs these are? I mean it is good that the unemployed and especially the young have a chance at jobs in the province so that they don't have to go elsewhere like I did. But I hope these jobs really use the skills of your people and give them some opportunity for advancement."

Note: New Brunswick has developed an explicit strategy to attract call centres, which are customer-contact facilities that deal largely with incoming telephone inquiries from all over Canada and often the United States (and sometimes the world). This strategy attempts to address an unemployment rate in the 11% range and promises corporations a skilled and knowledgeable work force which can deal with customers in one central location. In some ways, call centres have the appearance of a high-technology assembly line—which implies many low-paying jobs. Yet the government argues that these are indeed good jobs with a pay rate above the average salary in New Brunswick.

industrial regions. It is for this reason—i.e., in order to participate in the employment and technological growth that could result—that the West, particularly Alberta, has attempted to use its resources as a basis for industrial development. It is also for this reason that Newfoundland attempted to use the development of its own offshore oil as an employment opportunity for Newfoundlanders first, rather than for any other Canadians who might apply. All of these developments, and others which are likely to follow, represent efforts to rearrange the old imbalances which have been such a major part of regional inequalities.

Uneven development causes regionalism in that it creates economic winners and losers in a spatial system. It is for this reason that some have defined *regionalism as the result of inequality.*[10] Whether regionalism would go away under conditions of equality is certainly debatable, but there is a strong sense that regionalism is more easily mobilized in the presence of inequality. The defence of territorial advantage is a major issue, and efforts to seek redress for territorial disadvantage often successfully mobilize regional feeling.

Development imbalances do not just happen. They are the result of human actions which will be delineated in our next three points. First let us consider state action.

2. State Policy

The policies of the Canadian state which promote economic growth are normally designed to directly stimulate growth in specific places or to have indirect effects on specific places. For example: By altering its energy policy in creating the National Energy Policy of 1980, the state negatively affected oil-producing regions at the same time that it positively impacted oil-consuming regions. Although its name implies that it was in the "national" interest, the National Energy Policy had a differential regional impact. In a more recent example, the Kyoto Accord will potentially have a more negative economic impact on the oil-producing than the oil-consuming regions. Government policies are seldom regionally neutral; they may affect some regions more than others, or what is helpful to one region may be harmful to another. Even ostensibly neutral policies pertaining to matters such as the environment or minimum wage have differential effects on regions.

Brodie has argued that this regionalizing impact of state policies was evident in *three national policies* which the government developed at different points in its history.[11] The first was the National Policy of 1879, which sought to build a transcontinental economy to the West (see the discussion later in this chapter). The protective tariff was applied at all borders, with the eventual effect that Central Canadian industries flourished, the Maritimes became deindustrialized, and the West was limited to providing primary products as an exporting hinterland. This policy indeed tied Canada together, but with significantly different regional impacts.

The second state policy was the post-Depression/post-World War II shift towards the encouragment of more American direct investment in order to strengthen the economy. This was the era of the American branch-plant subsidiary, and American development especially benefited Ontario. This in turn led to efforts to redistribute some of Central Canada's economic good fortune to other regions through regional development grants and equalization grants—which, though intended to support social-welfare policies, only sustained regional hegemony. Thus clear regional disparities emerged from this policy.

Free trade, the third national policy, began in the late 1980s. Free trade policies supported the elimination of a protected economy in favour of global competition, hemispheric integration, reducing the role of the state, increased privatization, and market-driven values. Again, some regions were better able to take advantage of integration into the global economy than others, and other regions were not only hurt by their inability to do so but were further disadvantaged by the lack of federal transfer payments to support their services infrastructure. In one illustration of the changed mode of thinking that has accompanied free trade, it has been argued that the federal state was the cause of the disparities between rich and poor regions because the transfer payments it provided encouraged people to stay where they were rather than migrate to regions where the economy was stronger;[12] in other words, blame for the exacerbation of regionalism has been laid upon state policies.

In fairness, however, it must be pointed out that a tenet of the state's national unity policy has been to take action to attempt to reduce regional disparities. In post-war Canada, the government established a range of agencies whose mandate was to do so; the most well-known was the Department of Regional Economic Expansion (DREE) in 1968, followed by others, such as Western Diversification (WD) and Atlantic Canada Opportunities Agency (ACOA). While these may have had some limited successes, regional disparities remain.[13]

3. Elite Control and Capital Flows

The next and related cause of regionalism linked to human action is decision making by capitalist elites. As we will see, these elites work closely with political elites to create state policy. As noted in Chapter Three, Porter and Clement demonstrated that Canada's economic elite have resided primarily in Ontario and Quebec. To reduce competition, Central Canadian corporations either bought out weaker corporations in other parts of Canada or subjected them to price wars which the dominant corporations usually won.[14] Such *consolidation* meant that capital, control, and power became regionally concentrated and centralized. But by focusing on elite control, we soon realize that it is not so much the geopolitical units themselves (i.e., Ontario and Quebec) that maintain regional dominance over the rest of Canada, but the *capitalist class,* which resides primarily in the two primate cities of Toronto and Montreal, whose activities result in dominance that extends even beyond Canada's borders to external capital markets and foreign centres of capital control.[15] The desire of the economic elite to expand markets and maintain production efficiency is driven by the desire to maximize profits, an objective that often has regional effects. Corporations will only build plants in regions where the unemployment rate is high, labour is cheap, and tax incentives are provided as long as doing so fits corporate objectives. Corporate owners who shut down unprofitable plants have little concern for regional disparities.

Because of their power and interrelatedness with other elites, the economic elite is able to lobby for federal and provincial policies that support its interests. A protective tariff is an example of an economic mechanism that would not exist without legislative decree; accordingly, in order to obtain political support for a proposed tariff supporting a Central Canadian industry, the capitalist class would have to demonstrate to the political elite why such legislation would be in the national interest (rather than just in the capitalist interest). The support of labour unions and their elite, as well as of the Central Canadian voting public, would then be enlisted, as such a policy would protect both the jobs and the capital of supporting services and industries. The problem is that because capital investment and control are regionally concentrated, hinterland regions seldom share directly in the benefits of such national policies. Instead, the centralization of capital and political control is more likely to lead outlying regions to discussions about the cost of Confederation. In the past, such discussions have often centred around the higher price of manufactured goods charged by protected, monopolistic industries located far from their captive markets.

The traditional strength of the capitalist class in Ontario and Quebec does not mean that there is no economic elite in other regions. In fact, each region has its own local elite, which, as agent for the central elite, may benefit from the regionalization of Canadian society. In other situations, the local elite may even try to challenge the capitalist class of other regions; regionalism can provide a range of populist symbols that are appealing to regional residents. However, it has also been argued that regionalism can be an ideology that disguises the process of capitalist concentration on the periphery.[16] The regional capitalist class, while benefiting, may also be vocal advocates of regional policies (such as equalization grants) to national political elites in order to reduce the effect of regional disparities.

Efforts by regional elites to marshall regional powers through a province's political apparatus have been called *province building*.[17] The goal of province building is to use the legislative power of the province to provide tax incentives, grants, or challenges to the policies of other regions in order to establish a more favourable environment for capital formation and economic development in a particular region. Regions thus may compete against each other, as happened in 1980 when Alberta unsuccessfully attempted to wrest some economic activity away from Ontario and Quebec. Clearly, then, within a national state, regional units struggle against each other for development, and it is the economic and political elite in each region who are frequently at the centre of the heightened competition and struggle. Because federal elections are usually won or lost in Ontario and Quebec (which have the greatest number of parliamentary seats), the elites of this region have inordinate control over national policy.

If the dominance of Central Canada is supported by a symmetry between this regional elite and the federal elite, then effective challenges to this regional dominance require an alternate legislative vehicle. Thus capitalist classes in other regions will form alliances with their local provincial governments to challenge the dominance of the national–Central Canadian bourgeoisie. Because the local economic and political elites use the province to challenge federal control and to promote local development, regionalism has become equated with provincialism. Federal–provincial hostilities and confrontations reflect the interests of the regional elite, and long-standing popular sentiment may even be manipulated in order to create regional solidarity.[18] Some politicians have successfully won provincial elections precisely by accentuating regional–national cleavages.

In short, regionalism is intimately related to internal power (and power struggles) within a national society. Elites both internal and external to a region play a significant role in charting the course of regional economies and regional relationships.

4. Political Structures

Another way in which human action contributes to regionalism is in the creation and operation of the political system. Canada's principle of *representation by population* provides for greater political representation for areas with a larger population.[19] Consequently, population imbalances within the nation (e.g., almost two thirds of the population live in Ontario and Quebec) result in an awesome concentration of power. The votes of persons in regions other than Ontario and Quebec are seldom vital to the outcome of an election; elections are essentially decided in those two provinces, a fact that leads residents of other regions to feel disenfranchised. If those in Quebec and Ontario cast their vote with the party that is ultimately elected, the rest of Canada feels that the government will cater to the majority in Central Canada; if residents in less populous regions elect a Member of Parliament whose party forms the opposition, they realize that their representative has no input into the formulation of the ruling party's policy. In either case, many regions feel that the federal government has little sympathy with, or motivation to, address their needs.[20]

Furthermore, the strong *party discipline* required by the parliamentary system allows little opportunity for the expression of regional interests.[21] These factors, combined with the perception that the major national parties are controlled by Central Canadian interests, lead the hinterland regions to a sense of futility about the political process. Occasionally, this sense of futility erupts into anger, and a "protest party" (or "third party") with a strong regional basis may emerge on the national scene to challenge the major parties. These protest parties have been particularly successful in the West, where their ideologies have been characterized by strong anti-Central Canada sentiment. As yet, however, there is no federal vehicle (such as a regionally apportioned Senate) to enable regions to encounter one another on an equal footing.

Another way that political structures perpetuate regionalism is through the actions and rhetoric of provincial governments. Territorially based discussions in relation to other territorial units are made possible by provincial boundaries. Interest groups within each territory can use the provincial government as the vehicle for striking out at interest groups in other regions. Provincial political parties may fight elections on a platform of defending regional interests against competing regional interests or of seeking regional solidarity in the face of external threat. Governments then confront other governments as large and powerful institutions—each with its own civil service personnel, each concerned about survival, and each struggling to establish or retain jurisdictional competence over their territory. Cairns has called this form of regionalism *governmentalized societies*.[22] The relationship between intergovernmental conflict and elite control becomes clearer as peripheral political and economic elites become frustrated with their hinterland position and, through a policy of economic provincialism, give priority to development within their particular region.[23] Such a policy was exemplified in 1981, when Newfoundland argued that Newfoundlanders should receive priority above other Canadians in any employment created by an offshore oil boom. Regional confrontations are produced by the attempts of hinterland regions to challenge the status quo; thus, the more regions seek equality through industrial development, the more they struggle and compete over scarce commodities, and the more this struggle intensifies the regional conflict.[24] It is for these reasons that regionalism is, at least in part, politically propagated.

5. North-South Linkages

Another explanation of regionalism is based on Canada's intimate relationship with the United States. Natural alliances and mutual interests are viewed as emerging from geographical proximity of Canadian and American regions. Stevenson has argued that regionalism in Canada must be seen in its continental context, as Confederation and the National Policy of 1879 sought to obliterate the north–south cross-border regional relationships that had existed long before 1867.[25] He noted that some opponents of Confederation in the Maritimes based their opposition on the fact that they felt closer attachments to the New England states than to Canada and feared the dominance of Central Canada. Similarly, some people in the southwest peninsula of Ontario felt very strong ties with residents of New York and Michigan.

If these north–south linkages were undermined by the National Policy, Stevenson demonstrates that they have been revived as a consequence of the decline of European ties and of the shift of people and economic power away from the American Northeast and Central Canada and towards the West (and, in the case of the US, towards the South). Neighbouring provinces and states have begun to look to each other in an effort to find cooperative solutions to mutual problems (e.g., energy, the environment). For example, the New England Governors and Eastern Canadian Premiers (known as NEG/ECP Conference) meet regularly and form agreements on important issues.[26] In the West, a new form of binationalism has formed in the Pacific Northwest, linking Alaska, the Territories, British Columbia, Alberta, Montana, Idaho, Washington, and Oregon in what is known as

"Cascadia" or the "Pacific Northwest Economic Region" (PNWER). Each Canadian region is thus developing its own pattern of interrelationships with an allied American region, based on economic development, travel, and even cable TV and professional sports. Energy agreements (e.g., the Columbia River Treaty, Quebec–New York power grid), industrial development (e.g., the automobile industry that links Ontario and Michigan), religious ties (e.g., Mormons of Utah and Alberta), and sports (e.g., hockey and baseball divisions) are all based on north–south links; each of these links can detract from, or compete with, national ties.

One way to understand regions that traverse borders is as *natural economic zones* that create their own sense of community and have their own political agendas. The political will of the region may be presented to the host nation(s) as a challenge to other regional interests; or, in a globalized world, the region may try to avoid the state altogether. Free trade has the potential to lower border barriers and amplify regionalist trends across the American border to an even greater extent.[27]

Regionalism has also been exacerbated by the proximity and accessibility of regionalized American corporate activity that carries over into specific regions of Canada. For example, many US subsidiaries in British Columbia have headquarters in California, subsidiaries in Alberta are tied to American southwestern multinationals, corporations based in Michigan, Illinois, or New York have been more likely to choose Ontario as the location for their Canadian activity, and Quebec business activity is more likely linked to Massachusetts, New York, or New Jersey. The fact that the traditional centre of American industrial strength has been the Northeast has meant that Ontario and Quebec have been more likely to benefit from their proximity than other regions, a fact that has also contributed to uneven economic development.[28]

It is not so much that American investment caused regionalism as that it sustained regional imbalances that already existed.[29] Regions with a manufacturing industry, competing strongly to retain their leadership, were successful in attracting American industries. Regions with little manufacturing but a strong resource base also attracted American capital—but only for the extraction of resources. Thus, US investment in Canada retained regional patterns already established and, furthermore, brought Canadian regions into closer contact with similar American regions. If it is manufacturing that drew together Toronto, Cleveland, and Detroit, it is energy that links Calgary, Denver, and Dallas.

Because this foreign investment is so important to the regional economy, the host region will be far more sympathetic to foreign investment than other regions might be. Ontarians may ridicule the American multinational oil companies in Alberta, but Westerners are quick to point out that it is American firms that provide employment for thousands of Ontarians in the manufacture of vehicles and appliances. Thus, north–south linkages help accentuate regional disparities and hostilities.

The Region/Class Debate

No explanation for the persistence of regionalism can rest on a single factor. Regionalism is a complex phenomenon, and we have only sketched the dominant structural conditions that have the potential to change a region from a unit of analysis to an element of social structure. But regionalism is produced by human responses to these underlying conditions. Wheat farming in Saskatchewan may be little more than a typical occupation in that region, until the particular farmer begins to compare his position with that of farmers or other occupation groups in other regions, attempts to ascertain the impact on farmers of federal economic policy, or seeks an explanation for spiralling costs that jeopardize agrarian operations. It is thus the *interpretation* farmers give to their position, in the nation as a whole and as a dominant regional group, which creates regionalism. Again, regional differences are benign until interpreted and articulated as a factor in interregional relations. If people in a predominantly agricultural area feel that the interests of other regions are given priority within the society as a whole, then the interests of farmers will be defined as a regional issue in opposition to the interests of other regions.

The above example illustrates a major debate in regional analysis. Do people really possess a regional identity which guides and directs their actions, or is the regional identity only a mask for class interests? Could it be that farmers in Ontario, Nova Scotia, and Saskatchewan have far more in common than all the people who live on the Prairies and form a geographic region? The region/class debate thus focuses on the question of whether geography is an appropriate unit for analysis or whether social class is a more basic structural condition. If we take the regional approach, *Prairie* farmers are opposed to *Central Canadian* industry (with the emphasis on location). If we take the class approach, Prairie farmers as small independent producers are opposed to large Canadian and multinational corporate capitalists located in Central Canada (with the emphasis on position in the capitalist system).

Analysts taking the class position tend to devalue the significance of regions on the grounds that what passes for regionalism is primarily an expression of class struggle.[30] Regionalism is regarded as a consequence rather than a cause, as class is considered the prior and more important condition. What is at issue is not "the Prairies versus Central Canada" but "the interests of small entrepreneurs versus the interests of the capitalist class." The class perspective is penetrating because it forces us to look beyond regions as homogeneous geographic units, to the divisions that may exist both within regions and between regions of competing economic interests. From this perspective, regionalism is more likely to be understood as an ideology that masks real class interests.

On the other side are analysts who continue to view region as an important unit of analysis. These point to the existence of regional cultures and regional identities that may even have stronger explanatory power than status, class, or ethnicity.[31] Sharing a common political and economic environment may give people a unique lens for interpreting what is happening in their society; as a result, they may identify with their region and feel a commitment to it as a place that is not only personally meaningful but different from other regions in the society.

The region/class debate is not easily resolved, except to say that both perspectives make valid points. Class analysts stress the material basis of regionalism; though they may deny that they are advocating an economically determinist position, they make little effort to discuss the cultural side of regional life. The region analysts, on the other hand, may borrow freely from class analysis to stress the impact of dependency and capital control, but also acknowledge that other factors, related to history or regional collective consciousness, help build regional culture.

Regional Culture

The region/class debate serves as an appropriate caution that regions, just like countries, are divided by class and other interest groups. Therefore, to speak of a regional culture as though it were an undifferentiated monolith can ignore important class-based realities or even sub-regional differences. However, when regions are separated by thousands of kilometres, as they are in Canada, with different histories, economies, and settlement patterns, it is possible to speak of regionalized cultures, though these these cultures may not be as sharply distinctive or unique as some might expect.[32]

A *culture* refers to the complex of beliefs, morals, customs, laws, and habits which people share as a consequence of their group experiences. Culture also includes material aspects such as art, technology, and objects which represent a people's struggle with their physical and socio-economic environment.

As a population tries to adapt to that region's topographical and climatic features and responds to its own economic challenges, it produces its own unique matrix of traits. Such traits are reflected in its literature, folklore, self-understanding, and perception of itself in relation to other regions of Canada. The media frequently pick up symbols of regional character (e.g., the idyllic fishing village of Peggy's Cove, the skyscrapers of Toronto in the shadow of the CN Tower, the Prairie grain elevator surrounded by flat land and open skies), which help perpetuate regional images. Institutions, traditions, and social movements develop within this regional context, often with features that are distinguishable from those of other regions. What makes culture regional is its contrast with the whole, or with other units of the whole. Although there are many influences contributing to the de-emphasis of regional cultures and the promulgation of a national or continental culture (e.g., television, urbanization, federal efforts to promote a national identity), the history, population composition, and political economy of a region provide the cultural matrix that allows regional distinctions and identities to develop.

If regional cultural differences exist, these differences should be reflected in the attitudes of individuals. For this reason, virtually every national study of the opinions, attitudes, and behaviour of Canadians breaks down the responses by region in order to identify regional differences, which frequently do exist. We know, for example, that there are regional differences in church attendance rates, attitudes towards gun control, acceptance of multiculturalism, perceptions of the federal government, and identification with region. Of course, differences across regions do not necessarily mean that region is a more powerful explanatory variable than other variables, such as occupation, education, or gender, but it does suggest that region may be a factor.

In Canada, the most typical product of regional cultures is the stereotypical evaluation of other regions. The devaluation of other regional cultures on the basis of the presumed superiority of one's own is known as *ethnocentrism*; however, the negative attitude or feeling of distance and detachment resulting from unbalanced interregional interaction is know as *alienation*. Some regions maintain cultural or economic superiority to others while others feel dominated or exploited. Regional attachments are thus accompanied by perceptions and attitudes about other regions, with whom relationships are usually unequal. It is this inequality that usually heightens the regionalization of attitudes.

There is some question about whether regional and national identities and attitudes mutually exclusive—in other words, can national and regional loyalties coexist? [33] To assess this, respondents are often asked whether they self-identify in terms of their region or province first or as Canadian first.[34] While there is some variation in responses, Ontarians are the most likely to see themselves as Canadian first, while Quebecers and Newfoundlanders are least likely to see themselves as Canadian first. Maritimers and Westerners are found somewhere in between, depending on current issues and debates.

There is a danger in assuming that national and regional identities are exclusive, or that both identities are equally important, or that regional identities are always less important than national ones. In reality, identities may vary with the issue and the person, and may vary over time depending on circumstances. Nevertheless, differences in identity and culture are not in themselves adequate explanations for regionalism. Perhaps at its deepest level, regional identity is intimately tied to regional economy. But without a consciousness-raising about the meaning and interpretation of regional differences within the context of the wider society, regionalism does not exist. For that reason, to understand why regionalism exists we must look beyond the structural conditions to the human responses to those conditions.

We can now move on to an examination of how these factors have operated in specific regional situations. Three regions have been selected for closer analysis. The first case study will deal with the Prairies and the New West; next, we will turn to the Atlantic region, and finally, to the North. All three areas have had relatively high visibility and recognition as peripheral regions to Central Canada. They are well-suited for the purpose of comparative study because their geographic and economic contexts support different social worlds.

The Case of Quebec

Before we move on to our specific regional analysis, we should note that no discussion of regionalism in Canada would be complete without a rather lengthy analysis of Quebec. In fact, it could reasonably be argued that the salience of regionalism in the society as a whole is at least partially a consequence of the regional solidarity of Quebec. This solidarity is based upon a linguistic and ethnic commonality grounded in a historical group perception. This commonality, in combination with territorial dominance and political control in the province, has led some francophone Quebecers to argue that Quebec is *not just a region* of Canada, but a *distinguishable nation*. As long as Quebec remains a part of Canadian society, its socio-cultural attributes make it perhaps the most distinctive region of all. Most Quebecers share a language and an ethnic heritage quite different from those of most other Canadians.

Since Confederation, Quebec has been rather successful in negotiating special considerations from the federal government that accommodate its own cultural needs. This fact has not gone unnoticed by other regions, which have periodically demanded special concessions for their own regional aspirations. In this way, the example of Quebec has been instrumental in heightening regional desires for more localized control and more equitable economic policies and in modelling the use of provincial power to obtain desired ends. Thus, from at least one perspective, Quebec has helped contribute to the regionalization of Canadian society. Other regions may lack an ethnic basis for their regional community, but the large economic gap between their regions and Central Canada has accentuated their regional grievances.

A more detailed discussion of Quebec will be left for the next chapter, even though many of the same regional dynamics discussed in this chapter apply. The importance of Quebec as a significant region in Canada, however, needs to be acknowledged at the outset, and the decision not to discuss it in detail at this point should in no way be construed as an underestimation of Quebec's critical position as a powerful and distinctive region of Canada.

REGION STUDY I: THE PRAIRIE WEST AND THE NEW WEST

No one who has driven from Winnipeg to Calgary can forget the wide open spaces, marked only by grain elevators jutting up into the sky to remind one that indeed, far up ahead, another town is situated. Bounded by the tundra of the three territories to the north, the Prairies are intimately tied to the Great Plains of the Dakotas and Kansas to the south, where grain remains a staple crop. A regional culture has emerged in this geographical area, reflecting a people's social and economic adaptation to a particular environment.

Separated from Central Canada by the Canadian Shield, the West had no natural ties with the East; the Rockies prevented continuity with the coastal communities of British Columbia to the west. If the space between Vancouver and Toronto was to be claimed and held as Canadian territory, deliberate steps would have to be taken to integrate the Prairie region and thereby prevent British Columbia from being totally isolated. The program established by the federal government to accomplish these objectives was known as the *National Policy*.[35] This policy had three main features: the settlement of the Prairie region through encouragement of immigration and implementation of *The Homestead Act*, which provided land for settlement at an extremely low price; the establishment of an east–west transportation system, the Canadian Pacific Railroad, to link Vancouver with Toronto, thereby facilitating the movement of persons and goods needed by the Prairie community and reversing the more natural north–south ties; and the legislation of a protective tariff to ensure a market for Central Canadian manufactured goods. In this way, the National Policy succeeded in settling, claiming, and integrating the Prairie region into the Canadian fabric.

The society that grew up in this regional territory was an extension of Central Canada, yet also separated from it. The burgeoning and aspiring industrial economy of the "centre" was easily distinguished from the single-industry agricultural economy of the Prairies, and a metropolis–hinterland relationship developed. While it is clear that both regions needed each other, the tariff—by inhibiting the purchase of cheap machinery or goods from the United States—created regional resentment: Prairie people came to view their inter-regional Canadian relationship as one of exploitation. Almost from the beginning, then, an attitude of regional alienation developed among residents of the Prairies.[36] That attitude was the outcome of a political economy of dependency.

Regional discontent became widespread because this dependency touched everyone. Mortgages were held by Central Canadian banks; appliances, farm implements, and auto-mobiles were manufactured in the "East"; canned goods came from Ontario. Virtually everything was imported into the region, and the region had little to exchange except grain, which was sold primarily on international rather than national markets. The instability of international prices for this grain was even more problematic because of crop-production uncertainties, insect infestations, and drought. The unbalanced import–export situation made Prairie residents realize that they had become captive to national policies. This realization was heightened during the Depression, as frustrated and economically beleaguered Prairie farmers struggled to pay their Central Canadian creditors.

The *J-curve theory* suggests that social unrest is most likely to occur when rising expectations are frustrated and conditions become worse rather than better.[37] The new settlers on the Prairies were prepared for hard work because they ultimately expected prosperity; however, these expectations were frustrated—not only by climatic conditions but by market and general economic conditions over which they had little control; control was exercised by a dominant Central Canada. The Prairies then produced a series of reform movements, such as the Non-Partisan League, United Farmers of Alberta, Social Credit, and the Co-operative Commonwealth Federation, which were based to a large extent on the hostilities felt towards Central Canada and monopoly capital.[38]

Western alienation, then, has a unique history based on agrarianism in the Prairie provinces. Sometimes this alienation has been expressed in the perception of a regional conspiracy against the West. Most frequently, however, alienation focuses on elite control from Central Canada, whether it be of large corporations, banks, or political parties. Gibbins speaks of this attitude as a *regional ideology* because it is a socially shared set of beliefs with a recognized history and constituency, all based on estrangement from the Canadian heartland.[39]

The Prairies were the last large area in Canada to be settled in which land was still available for agriculture, with most of this settlement occurring from 1870 to 1920. The source of immigration and pattern of settlement helped make the Prairies unique. For one thing, the federal government encouraged large numbers of Europeans to settle in the West. Many of these settlers came directly from Europe and organized their relocation in a bloc settlement. Other immigrants came individually from Ontario, the United States, or England and settled next to people with whom they had little in common. The result was that the Prairies became an interesting, multi-ethnic, agricultural community without parallel in rural Canada.[40] For this reason, many Prairie residents were later offended by proposed federal policy on bilingualism and biculturalism.

Transition from the "Old West" to the "New West"

The newly settled population struggled to survive during the difficult Depression years, but the post-war experience totally changed the face of the Prairie population as agriculture went through a significant consolidation. From 1941 to 1966, the number of farms on the Prairies fell by one third, the average farm increased in size by 80%, farm land was used more intensively (cow herds increased by 72%), and the number of farmers and farm labourers decreased substantially.[41] People moved to Prairie cities, then frequently moved on to Toronto or Vancouver for the employment available in those booming cities. Thus the changes that took place between the 1940s and 1960s meant that it was no longer possible to speak of the people of the Prairies as primarily an agrarian population.

As the rural–urban balance shifted so that the majority of the people were living in urban centres, the economy of the region shifted from agriculture to service, retailing, administration, and a small amount of manufacturing.[42] Perhaps most significant was the discovery of oil at Leduc in 1948, which inaugurated the modern era of energy production in Alberta. The discovery of oil and gas at various locations in Alberta led to the development of an active petroleum industry, with strong linkages to American capital and corporate expertise. Thus, the north–south ties which were natural when the province was primarily agrarian were reinforced by energy-industry relationships. Calgary became the administrative centre for this development; because the provincial government was considered the owner of these resources, the province enjoyed a new-found prosperity from the rents and royalties accruing from energy development. For this and a variety of other reasons, Alberta developed an economic edge over the other Prairie provinces.

The discovery of gas in British Columbia and of both conventional and heavy oil in Saskatchewan has contributed to a "New West." Whereas in the early years wheat farming had created a commonality among the three Prairie provinces of Manitoba, Saskatchewan, and Alberta, these later years have seen the development of a commonality among the energy-producing provinces of British Columbia, Alberta, and Saskatchewan. But, just as grains were a staple extracted from Prairie soil and shipped and processed elsewhere, so energy became a staple extracted in the West and marketed in the industrial centres of Canada and the United States. In both cases, the raw material was taken out of the region, and the West essentially remained a hinterland. This fact did not go unnoticed, and Western perceptions of dependency and truncated regional development amidst potential prosperity evoked lingering alienation.[43]

As energy became an even more valuable commodity through the 1970s (as OPEC countries threatened the industrial countries with cutbacks and price increases), it became increasingly clear that its supply of energy could give the Western region enormous advantages. Instead of remaining resource-rich hinterlands for industrial markets elsewhere, governments in possession and control of such resources sought to use them as the basis for greater regional development. Furthermore, the significant economic advantage provincial governments gained from energy income threatened to change the whole balance of power in Canadian society.[44] Some of the proceeds from these oil revenues, for example, were placed in the Alberta Heritage Trust Fund, which made the Alberta government a major creditor and investor within Canada; more importantly, it was thought that this money could be a means of fostering regional economic development.

The matter most symbolic of the West's hinterland position through the years has been a "discriminatory" freight rate, frequently referred to as the *Crow rate*. In keeping with the Crow's Nest Pass Agreement of 1897, the federal government approved the movement of grain by railroad at rates below cost in order to assist farmers to get their product to market.[45] The fact that this low rate only applied to grain, however, discouraged the shipment of other products processed in the West. Furthermore, a higher rate prevailed for shipping manufactured goods into the West, and Westerners were constrained to buy these products because of

Is the Prairie Region One Region or Two?

A *strong staple* is a resource with high demand and limited supply, which consequently yields greater revenue (e.g., oil). A *weak staple* is a resource with lower demand and greater availability, which consequently yields smaller revenues (e.g., wheat).

While agriculture is a common staple activity throughout the Prairies, the three Prairie provinces can be divided into the western part (Alberta and western Saskatchewan), where a strong staple (oil) is present; and most of Saskatchewan and southern Manitoba, where a weak staple (wheat) predominates.

Initially, the Prairie region was focused on Winnipeg, the "Gateway to the West," as the centre of commerce, industry, and transportation. Manitoba's former role is now totally eroded, except in manufacturing, where its output exceeds that of the other three provinces. Not only has the wheat economy declined there but Manitoba has had little participation in the new strong staple. As the eastern terminus for wheat exports, Manitoba is no longer as pivotal as it once was, as Churchill and Thunder Bay are now shipping only a fraction of the wheat exported out of the region.

Source: Based on Paul Phillips, "The Canadian Prairies—One Economic Region or Two?" in James McCrorie and Martha C. MacDonald, eds., *The Constitutional Future of the Prairie and Atlantic Regions of Canada* (Regina: CPRC, 1992), 37–49.

the protective tariff. While the Crow rate was beneficial to farmers in one way, it created higher prices for durable goods. As the population in the West became less agrarian and more urban, the new urban middle-class Westerner tended to favour the abolition of the Crow rate, recognizing that industrial development in the West would provide new opportunities for employment and upward mobility. The tensions and disagreements produced by the elimination of the Crow rate in 1995 reflected Westerners' concern about maintaining their solid agricultural base while participating in new prospects for economic development.

It was the expanding middle and upper classes of urban professionals, entrepreneurs, and provincial civil servants, particularly in Alberta, that began to look to the province to help diversify and strengthen the local economy.[46] Small Canadian energy companies emerged in the West to take advantage of the boom, along with a new regional bourgeoisie. The availability of jobs in the West, combined with an industrial slowdown in Ontario and Quebec, resulted in heavy shifts of population to the West in the late 1970s and early 1980s. These events had widespread societal significance because they indicated a potentially dramatic alteration of the traditional metropolis–hinterland relationship. The regional elite and the ascendant regional middle class formed a coalition that sought to use the provincial government as the vehicle to protect and advance regional interests.

A Western separatist movement burst on the scene in the early 1980s as a direct consequence of Westerners' new expectations of regional economic development.[47] The February election of 1980 was decided in the "East" before many Westerners even voted; this, coupled with the fact that only two members of the governing Liberal party were elected in the entire West, reawakened Westerners' old sense of disenfranchisement. Federal–provincial confrontations over energy revenues—and particularly over the National Energy Policy, which removed the energy dynamic from the West in the "national" interest—suggested to Westerners that federal assertiveness in the face of Western aspirations was really another expression of Central Canadian control.

In any event, important forces had been set in motion that might have contributed to a change in traditional Central Canadian–Western relationships. Yet the principle enunciated earlier—that the growth of one region usually takes place at the expense of another—helps to explain why there was resistance to any significant shift in regional relationships. In fact, while Toronto and southern Ontario were booming in the mid-1980s, the West (particularly Alberta) was in a significant recession.[48] For this reason, support for free trade has been generally strong in the West, as the region's inability to diversify within Canada has encouraged the search for participation in a larger continental market. To the extent that diversification of the economy away from the staples industries remains an issue, the West is likely to generate continuing regional conflict.

The economic and demographic expansion of British Columbia and Alberta through the 1980s and 1990s distinguishes the urban West from the more agrarian West. Whereas Manitoba and Saskatchewan have had little new population growth, the cities of Vancouver, Calgary, and Edmonton have not only attracted population but have also served as growth poles for new employment, primarily in the service industry. The Alberta government in particular has used lower costs and business-friendly taxation as a means of attracting economic opportunities to the province, promoting what it calls the "Alberta Advantage."[49] Interestingly enough, Ontario has fought back with its own lowered tax rates to prevent the erosion of its traditional dominant position.

The "New West" is clearly different, in that Alberta has taken on a new sense of power. The economic energy displayed in the province has taken it to new levels of prosperity for both the region and the country. This has intensified since 1996, partly because of the thriving oil and gas industry but also partly as the result of the "Klein Revolution" (which defined Alberta as economically right-wing, in contrast to other western provinces with left-leaning governments). Problems in British Columbia during the early part of this period also helped elevate Alberta to a more powerful position and contributed to growth through interprovincial migration. The shift of several corporate head offices to Calgary (for example, Canadian Pacific from Montreal and Imperial Oil from Toronto) seemed to confirm the sense that Calgary was becoming "the heart of the New West." In that regard, Calgary can be differentiated from Vancouver, which has become more important as a Pacific Gateway. In spite of these developments, economic, demographic, and political power at the national level is still located in Central Canada.

It may be Canada's inability to resolve Quebec's aspirations for recognition as a distinct society that contributes to the West's repeated expressions of regional alienation. Provoked to anger by the fact that Quebec (a Central Canadian province) controls the national agenda and is able to wrest compromises from Ontario (the other Central Canadian province), the West has birthed a distinct regional vision for a reformulated Canadian society.[50] Based on the notion of political equality (not to be confused with economic equality), several western-based political parties (e.g., Reform, Canadian Alliance)

RESEARCH CLIP 4.1	**Fighting for a Western Voice: Federal Political Innovations**

The Reform Party was formed in 1987 by Preston Manning, son of a former Premier of Alberta, in an attempt to bring western political ideas into national debate. In the federal election of 1993, Reform won 52 seats, most from British Columbia and Alberta but some from Manitoba and Saskatchewan as well. In the 1997 election, the Reform Party, with its base in the West, became the Official Opposition in Parliament

If the Reform Party ever hoped to govern Canada, it was crucial that it make inroads into vote-rich Ontario. In 2000, although the party's name had been changed to the Canadian Alliance, only two seats were won in Ontario. In 2003, a concerted effort was made to unite all conservatives in the country through the creation of a merger known as the Conservative Party of Canada;

this still did not suffice to topple the Liberal government in 2004.

The Conservative Party is a national party, yet there is no doubt that its roots and greatest strength are in the West—particularly farther west, where people felt they lacked power in defining what Canada should become. Ironically, 1993, the year of the breakthrough election for the West, was also the year that the Bloc Québécois (with representatives from Quebec alone) became the Official Opposition; although it remains strong, the Bloc was replaced by Reform in 1997. These strong political expressions of regionalism speak volumes about the regionalization of Canadian society.

Reference: For a good analysis of the populist base of the Reform Party in the West, see Trevor Harrison, *Of Passionate Intensity: Right-Wing Populism and the Reform Party of Canada* (Toronto: University of Toronto Press, 1995).

have taken a position against the accommodation of "special interest groups" (such as Quebec). They have called for a single national community, "One Canada," and gained renown for demanding a Triple E Senate (**e**lected, **e**qual, **e**ffective) to serve as a countervailing force to Central Canadian dominance in Parliament. The slogan "The West Wants In!" articulates Westerners' perception that the status quo marginalizes them, and expresses their desire for redress.

REGION STUDY II: THE ATLANTIC REGION

In our examination of the West, we have seen how agriculture and energy have provided the stimuli for regional identities and the establishment of socio-economic structures and traditions. Shifting focus to the eastern end of the country, we note that fishing serves as the backbone of regional identity. As Prairie residents are "people of the land," Atlantic residents are "people of the sea." The ocean has inspired shipbuilding and overseas transportation, which have facilitated regular contact with international trading partners. The ocean, too, has provided seafood as part of the regular diet, and mist and fog as part of the climate.

The relationship of this region to the sea has led to its designation as "the Maritimes." It is significant to note, however, that just as British Columbia in the West has a somewhat different history and settlement experience from the Prairies, so Newfoundland at the eastern extremity of Canada possesses its own unique identity and heritage quite apart from the provinces of Nova Scotia, New Brunswick, and Prince Edward Island. While the body of water (Cabot Strait) separating Newfoundland from these provinces symbolizes significant distinctions in geography, culture, and politics, it is possible nevertheless to speak of this cluster of provinces as one Atlantic region, for there is much in their socio-economic condition they hold in common.

The "fishing-village" image of the region is unfortunate in one respect, because it is based on a worn stereotype. In the first place, the proportion of the population engaged in commercial fishing is declining; the majority of the population is urban. Second, the image is essentially pre-industrial and implies that the region has never embraced the process of industrialization. In point of fact, the region did have a thriving industrial base at one time and then lost it through a process of interregional transfer.

The long stretches of Atlantic coastline characteristic of the region have meant close contact with ocean-going vessels. This contact has resulted in regular interaction with Europe (particularly Britain) and the New England states. Early settlers came from Britain and France (*les Acadiens*). Later, with the arrival of the Loyalists from the United States, the period from 1815 to 1860 became known as a time of considerable prosperity: The shipping industry grew rapidly, the merchant marine expanded to rank fourth in the world, and banks and insurance companies were established to finance and protect capitalist expansion. Rawlyk and Brown refer to the eve of Confederation as the "Golden Age" of Atlantic Canada, when prospects of an industrial future were bright indeed.[51] The Atlantic region was not oriented towards the interior of the continent but to trading links with the eastern-US seaboard and Britain. Nova Scotia, in particular, developed industries around iron, steel, textiles (including cotton mills), rope factories, glass works, and sugar refineries.

The prospect of participating in Confederation was met with mixed feelings.[52] On the one hand, there was the "beachhead" possibility, i.e., that the Atlantic region might serving as the key trading centre between the interior provinces and Europe. There were also potential markets for local products in the Canadian interior. On the other hand, there was a legacy of fear concerning Central-Canadian ambitions and politics. The breakdown of reciprocity negotiations with the US, however, and the failure of railway development (the Intercolonial Railway was not completed until after Confederation), together with a sense of the inevitable, led the Atlantic provinces to join Confederation in 1867 (with the exception of Newfoundland, which joined much later, in 1949).

Some regret about that decision has always remained—particularly in Nova Scotia, which spawned an anti-Confederation movement in the 1860s and considered secession in the 1880s.[53] Perhaps most notable was the post–World War I Maritime Rights Movement, which was essentially a regional protest against the inequities of Confederation. What were the long-term effects of Confederation for the region?

Perhaps the most salient fact about the post-Confederation years was that the anticipated industrial expansion of the region never materialized; in fact, recession took place. One reason for this decline was a drop in the overseas staples trade (e.g., fish and lumber), but a second problem was that the region was unable to compete with Central Canadian industries. While the Intercolonial Railway initially provided Maritime industries' access to Western markets, a change in the freight-rate structure (which had originally made it cheaper to ship goods to the West than to the East) took away the Maritime industries' advantage and they were never able to recover.[54] Third, the lack of both capital and markets forced many Maritime industries to sell out to Central Canadian interests. This fostered a continual process of *consolidation* and *centralization* of industry in Central Canada.[55] Fourth, federal policy became preoccupied with the problems of the West, and this put the Atlantic region in competition for federal attention. The addition of the Western provinces to Confederation meant that the strength of the Maritime provinces in political decision making was diminished considerably.

The end result of this process was the industrial decline of the Maritimes. The Maritime Rights Movement (1919–1927) was a protest against the region's declining status as a result of the growing dominance of Central Canadian metropoles and the rise of Western competition.[56] The growing weakness of one region was clearly related to the increasing strength of another, as the National Policy produced net benefits to Central Canada at the expense of other regions, such as the Prairies.[57] The Prairies, however, had no industry, whereas Maritime industries at one time had thrived. As the Maritimes grew weaker, a process of *deindustrialization* occurred. Symbolic of this reversal was the significant emigration of population between 1900 and 1930; most of these people went to the industrial centres of New England.[58] A pattern of regional exploitation was established, whereby Central Canada marketed its consumer goods in the Maritimes but in turn did little to provide a strong economic base for the region. The Maritimes reverted to exporting staples, such as coal, potatoes, wood and wood products, apples, and fish, and returned to a position of economic dependency on Central Canadian metropoles.

Conrad speaks of the ongoing struggle between Ottawa and the Atlantic provinces in the mid-1950s to mid-1960s as the *Atlantic revolution*.[59] Within the region, a new group of middle-class professionals and bureaucrats responded to post-war economic decline and the demand for expansion of state services. Their negotiations with Ottawa for a more meaningful federalism won recognition of the principles of *equalization* and *regional development assistance,* which remain in place as institutionalized themes in Canadian society, but which perpetuate *dependency*. It has also been argued that the collapse of the regional economy produced a concentration of regional capital in the hands of several key families (e.g., McCain, Sobey, Irving), who monopolized and expanded their regional control of trade.[60] For example, New Brunswick potato-farming operations were transformed from independent businesses to agribusinesses dominated by one company, which told them what to plant and how much to plant. In any case, staples remained the backbone of the economy and little new development occurred.

Newfoundland's relationship to Canadian society is particularly interesting because of that territory's relatively late entry into Confederation and the circumstances under which it occurred. The initial settlements on the eastern shores of the island were based on a fishing economy, with markets in Britain and also more distant places, such as Spain and Brazil.[61] Newfoundland obtained responsible government in 1855 and actually entered into treaties and agreements with other countries in subsequent years. However, the volatility of foreign markets, in combination with over-expansion in earlier years, led to a financial crisis in 1931 (it should be noted that many other governments faced similar situations, without the same result), which resulted in the replacement of responsible government by a commission government under British sponsorship.[62] Newfoundland's strategic location as a military base and stopover for trans-Atlantic flights during World War II and in the

Comparing the Prairie and Atlantic Regions

Similarities:

* High dependence on primary industries, whether fishing, lumbering, agriculture, or natural resources
* Staple products exported from region in raw or semi-processed state
* Dependence on industrial heartland for finished goods, finance, and commercial direction
* Perceptions of hinterland status sustained by design and supported by federal policies. Regional sense of political and economic powerlessness

Differences:

* Greater ethnic heterogeneity in the West and sense of openness as a more recent frontier; greater ethnic homogeneity in Atlantic region and lengthier settlement history
* Successful history of third ("protest") parties in West that have thrived on protest ideology; greater political conservatism in Atlantic region
* A mix of both strong and weak staple resources, an entrepreneurial spirit, and larger cities give the Prairies a stronger economic dynamic; in the Atlantic region, agriculture is less important, shipping and fishing are historically important but currently less so; there is offshore oil potential

Source: Based on Thérèse Arsenau, "The Prairies and Atlantic Canada: Constitutional Common Ground," in J. McCrorie and M.L. MacDonald, eds., *The Constitutional Future of the Prairie and Atlantic Regions of Canada* (Regina: CPRC, 1992), 326–30.

years thereafter led to significant prosperity, which helped prepare the way for the consideration of union with Canada.

The decision to join Canada was far from unanimous; many resented the loss of independence and questioned the "engineering" of the referendum.[63] In fact, two referendums were held, with the final result in 1948 showing 52.3% in favour of joining Confederation. Clearly, many were apprehensive about losing their earlier independence and questioned the benefits they would receive. If Newfoundland experienced no significant improvement in its economic conditions as a result of its union with Canada, dependency and underdevelopment would remain. This is precisely what has occurred, in a process known as *transfer dependency* whereby "Uncle Ottawa" (directly and indirectly through federal subsidies to the provincial government) has been responsible for a majority of the spending in the province.[64] A high birth rate (the highest in Canada for much of the post-war period), a declining fishery, and a resettlement program[65] aimed at providing better services (e.g., schools, water systems) to a previously dispersed population all contributed to an increasingly urbanized population, but with little increase in employment opportunity. What new industries were established, such as mining and pulp and paper, were still staple-based and subject to enormous fluctuations in demand. In sum, Newfoundland's quality of life improved in many ways, but the economic indicators of lower per capita income, high unemployment and underemployment, and lack of industrialization demonstrate that dependency and underdevelopment are substantial and perpetual.

It is clear from the above discussion that the Atlantic region has not fared well within Canadian society, at least in terms of economic indicators.[66] Rawlyk refers to the feelings engendered by this fact as "a paranoid style of regionalism," sustained by a conspiracy theory focused on Central Canada.[67] The federal approach to rectifying economic disparities has been to use transfer payments or equalization grants (unemployment insurance and grants for hospitals, roads, and universities) to ensure a higher standard of living for the region. In the early 1990s, federal transfer payments made up 37% to 40% of Atlantic provincial revenues, and government employed a higher share of the regional workforce than elsewhere.[68] Some incentives have also been provided to private enterprise (e.g., Bricklin, Michelin Tire), and the Atlantic Canada Opportunities Agency (ACOA) was established, but these measures have been marginally successful at best.[69] Of most significance to other centres of economic growth in Canada, the Atlantic region has provided a large reverse labour pool of short-term and long-term migrants to other regions where labour is needed.[70] On the other hand, the Halifax metropolitan area has shown significant population and employment growth, having become the dominant commercial and technological centre for the region.

Given the Atlantic region's peripheral condition, it was not surprising that the prospects of offshore oil awakened hope of new opportunities for regional development, particularly for Nova Scotia and Newfoundland.[71] Three problems arose from these expectations. In the first place, offshore oil was under federal jurisdiction, so provincial governments would have no chance to derive the level of economic benefits that production had brought to the Western provinces without a confrontation with the federal government. Premier Peckford of Newfoundland engaged in a particularly protracted battle, sometimes presented as a hinterland revolt, with the federal government over this issue. Second, conflicts developed between the traditional industry, fishing, and the new industry, oil. Oil can be characterized as a strong staple, because it is in high demand in world markets and is tied to large capital and corporate conglomerates, whereas fish is a weak staple because of lower demand and its less organized commodity sector.[72] Whenever the two are co-present, the oil industry tends to dominate the fishery industry to the point that the fishery will be disturbed or restructured and fishing cultures and communities eroded or transformed. Third, oil is still only another staple, albeit in higher demand, but also subject to depletion and to exportation in its raw form with little benefit to the region.

Energy resources—primarily in the form of offshore fields—have recently become a factor in the economies of some Atlantic provinces, catalyzing discussion about their potential to reduce dependency. While we await an assessment of this development, it is clear that the goal is to use oil and gas as a means to reduce unemployment, underemployment, and out-migration.[73] In Newfoundland, with its vast Hibernia field, the objective has also been to ensure that development be controlled by the province rather than by the federal government or by corporations coming into the province with their own agendas. The challenge of oil was to use it to benefit the people of the region.

In many ways, the crisis in the fishery and the restructuring it entails are symptomatic of what is transpiring throughout the Atlantic region as corporatism restructures all forms

RESEARCH CLIP 4.2	Coasts under Stress: The Fishery Crisis

July 1992 is a very important date in Canadian life. On that date, the Atlantic Canada cod fishery was closed by the federal government because of depleted stocks, with the consequence that 40 000 people were put out of work and the survival of dozens of communities was thrown into question. As a result of sheer overfishing—and especially owing to the huge capacity of large factory freezer-trawlers and longliners and to such technological innovations as fish sounders to help locate fish—the biomass, and particularly the reproductive portion, of fish had declined greatly since the early '60s. Because their work was largely seasonal in nature, fishers and fish-factory workers had never had large incomes to begin with; ways of adapting via an informal economy (e.g., building your own home with the help of neighbours and kin) were part of the community sustenance pattern.

While the impact of this closure affected all of the Atlantic provinces,

there is no doubt that Newfoundland experienced the greatest harm, as around 28 000 persons (about 70% of the total) lost their primary means of income. The government instituted a special program known as TAGS (The Atlantic Groundfish Strategy) to provide income support and job-retraining opportunities to cushion the blow. About 72% of those affected had not completed high school and 40% had less than a ninth-grade education, a situation that had severe implications for their prospects of alternative employment. In the end, TAGS was criticized because it merely supported people financially (about 79% of recipients in Newfoundland were heavily dependent on TAGS payments) rather than actually putting them back to work. A significant problem was that the remote location of many of these outport communities, combined with the age and lack of education of those most affected, reduced the options for new forms of employment and made job retraining less appropriate.

What, besides unemployment, have been the effects of the closure of the cod fishery? Of course, the closure has had ripple effects throughout the community. For example, the viability of restaurants and schools has been threatened—particularly the latter, as the out-migration of young people and people of child-bearing age for opportunities elsewhere has meant a higher proportion of older people and a shrinking tax base to sustain community institutions. Those affected by the closure also reported feeling like second-class citizens, often experiencing little empathy from persons living in urban centres. On the other hand, the evidence was overwhelming that despite the trauma, kinship and friendship networks in these communities were very strong and heightened the capacity to absorb the shock. Children did not exhibit maladaptive behaviour and parents did not exhibit the lower self-esteem, mental distress, or weakened social supports typical of unemployment in other places. Attachment to the community and involvement in its activities remained strong.

Despite the continuance of some forms of fishing (such as crab and lobster), there is an increasing realization that even when the cod fishery is reopened, employment opportunities will be severely diminished, which will greatly affect the existence of outport communities. The closure of the Catalina processing plant on the north coast, which once employed 1 100 persons, is a good example of what happens to a community and region when its economic backbone is removed. The long-term implications of this tragedy for Newfoundland society, in terms of rural–urban migration and out-migration from the province, are the threatened existence of communties that have been in existence for hundreds of years, and provide a sombre counterpoint to the new opportunities created by off-shore oil.

While the consequences so far have not been as severe, the depletion of salmon stocks on the Pacific coast in the 1990s is also threatening communities there.

Source: Rosemary E. Ommer, *The Resilient Outport: Ecology, Economy, and Society in Rural Newfoundland* (St. John's: ISER Books, 2002); John C. Kennedy, "At the Crossroads: Newfoundland and Labrador Communities in a Changing International Context," *Canadian Review of Sociology and Anthropology* 34, 3 (1997): 297–317; HRDC Canada, *The Atlantic Groundfish Strategy: Post-TAGS Review Report* (1998); and Dianne Newell and Rosemary E. Ommer, eds., *Fishing Places, Fishing People: Traditions and Issues in Canadian Small-Scale Fisheries* (Toronto: University of Toronto Press, 1999). For a good analysis of the social organization of the Newfoundland inshore fishery, see David Ralph Matthews, *Controlling Common Property: Regulating Canada's East Coast Fishery* (Toronto: University of Toronto Press, 1993).

of primary production.[74] When forests come to be perceived as pulp plantations, the effect on small woodlot operators is great, and the resulting clash of interests affects not only the economy but the social structure of the region. Given that, in the past, the government has provided the mechanisms (e.g., transfer payments) to ensure the stability of the region, it is unclear how the radical downsizing of the state and its revenue streams and the emphasis on market forces will now affect a region in transition.[75] The potential independence of Quebec also represents a threat, in that it would territorially separate the Atlantic region from the rest of Canada on which it is fiscally dependent. For this reason, Atlantic residents have been strong supporters of Confederation in spite of the disadvantages it has brought, and, much like the West, have been frustrated by exclusion from the full benefits of union and national participation.[76]

REGION STUDY III: THE NORTH

For many Canadians who live in the southern extremities of the country, the North may simply refer to the upper regions of their provinces, where rugged adventure (e.g., fishing and hunting) or relaxation may be enjoyed as a getaway from urban life. These provincial northern areas have much in common with the domain north of 60° latitude that does not have provincial status.[77] However, for our immediate purposes, "the North" will refer to that territory north of 60° latitude occupied by the Yukon, the Northwest Territories, and now Nunavut. Images of this area are of tundra, permafrost, short summer nights, ice, and snow.

Since 1961, the population of the Northwest Territories and Nunavut has more than doubled (to 71 000 in 2001), and that of the Yukon has almost doubled (31 000). The population of Canada's smallest province, Prince Edward Island, is greater than the combined populations of both the territories and Nunavut, even though these three territories are more than 6 000 times larger in size. While many of the conditions of life are similar in all three

The Middle North

The Middle North is a vast subarctic belt in the northern part of existing provinces that is sparsely populated, economically unstable, and populated primarily by Aboriginal people. All provinces except the Maritimes have such a "provincial north," and in most cases this territory makes up more than 50% of the province (e.g., Quebec 81%, Newfoundland and Manitoba 74%, Ontario 65%). In being attached to a province, these regions, while similar, have very little sense of a common identity and are overwhelmed by the power of their southern regions. In that sense, these northern regions are internal colonies of the southern population. In territorial size, the provincial norths represent over a third of Canada's land mass.

Southern Canadian governments and corporations pay little attention to this region unless it has natural resources of value to industrial Canada or to global industrial needs. Many Indians and Métis inhabitants live in isolated settlements until their lives are disrupted by resource development. Gold, coal, oil sands, uranium, forestry, and hydroelectric power are the primary engines of economic growth in the region. Development of these resources has a major effect on indigenous peoples; perhaps the most well-known instance has been the James Bay hydroelectric project in northern Quebec, which flooded much of the land important to local Native culture. Natives receive little benefit from these developments, as raw materials are shipped to markets external to the area.

Source: Based on Ken Coates and William Morrison, *The Forgotten North* (Toronto: James Lorimer, 1992). See also Ken Coates and William R. Morrison, eds., *The Historiography of the Provincial Norths* (Thunder Bay: Centre for Northern Studies, Lakehead University, 1996).

territories, one striking difference is that three quarters of the Yukon's population is concentrated in one city, Whitehorse. Yellowknife, which is smaller than Whitehorse, is the major city in the Northwest Territories and contains about 20% of its people; both cities have a significant population of civil servants. Beyond the confines of these cities, particularly in the Northwest Territories and Nunavut, the population is considerably dispersed.

Another significant contrast between the Yukon and the Northwest Territories is that the proportion of Native people in the Northwest Territories is much higher. In the Yukon, Native people are a minority (about 20%), whereas in the Northwest Territories, Native groups—consisting of Indian, Dene, Inuit, and mixed-blood Métis—are a majority. The Inuit form a clear majority in what is known as the eastern Arctic (Nunavut). In the north, particularly in the Yukon, the non-Native population has grown especially rapidly due to in-migration from the south of a transient rotating workforce with different objectives—a pattern that tends to overwhelm the Native population in a variety of ways.[78]

The sparse population and remote location of the North have meant that the region traditionally has been of minor importance to the Canadian economy. Even after the area was claimed as part of Canada, the government maintained a laissez-faire approach to its development, leaving the major initiatives to the fur traders (The Hudson's Bay Company) and the Church (Anglican and Roman Catholic).[79] The vast area and the relatively inhospitable climate meant that both the traditional economy (fishing, hunting, and trapping) and the small settlements of semi-nomadic people were far removed from direct southern Canadian influences.

Southern Canadians have been repeatedly attracted to the North by resources which, though difficult to obtain, offered the promise of quick wealth. Early examples of the activity engendered by this attraction were the Yukon Gold Rush of 1898 and the mining boom around Yellowknife in the 1930s. There was oil in the North as well as gold, and considerable activity was generated by the discovery of oil at Norman Wells in 1921 and on the northern slopes of Alaska in 1968, as well as by the more recent exploration at several land points throughout the territories and offshore in the Beaufort Sea. Other mineral resources which have attracted interest because of their industrial uses are tungsten, silver, lead, and copper.[80]

Much of this resource-based activity has occurred in "boom or bust" cycles typical of a staples economy. What has produced these fluctuations? In the first place, these economic developments have taken place with capital put forward by large southern corporations and have employed a transient southern workforce which moved into the North only for the duration of a project. In the second place, resource extraction has depended on external markets, where gains or slippage in price could either accelerate or entirely close down the extraction process. Problems of transportation and accessibility, as well as high labour costs, meant that operations were faced with high retail prices; meanwhile, drops in the price of resources led to the abandonment of expensive extraction procedures. Thirdly, Native workers, usually hired for temporary or seasonal terms, were poorly integrated into the operation. Not only did the wage economy change expectations among Native workers; it also introduced socio-economic elements that conflicted with the traditional Native economic structure. At the very least, the flurry of activity in the boom phase contrasted greatly with the bleakness of shutdown, and this contributed to instability in Native society. Finally, because most of the wages and profits were taken out of the region, the resource activity had little lasting impact on the region's development—a classic condition of colonialism and underdevelopment.

FIGURE 4.1	Nunavut in the Context of the Canadian North and Its Peoples

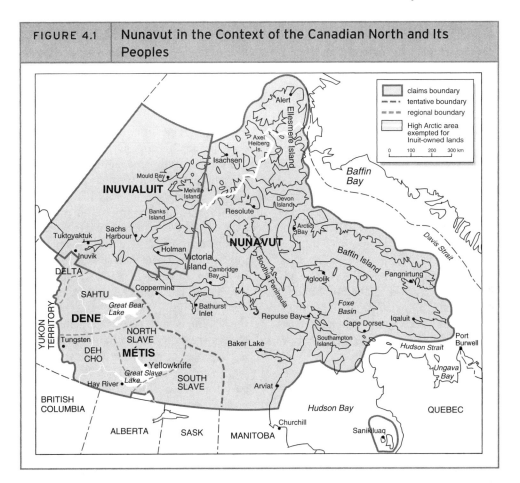

Nunavut: A New Regional Territory, a Distinct Society, a Sense of Nationhood

A new territorial government was created on April 1, 1999, when the old Northwest Territories was divided into east and west, with the eastern two thirds forming a third territorial government, Nunavut. The remaining Northwest Territories in the western Arctic are in the process of their own constitutional discussions.

Nunavut (meaning "Our Land"), a huge geographical area north of the tree-line, is the largest political jurisdiction in Canada. Constituting one fifth of the Canadian land mass at 2 242 000 square kilometres, Nunavut is larger than Mexico or than France, Germany, Great Britain, and Italy combined. Yet its population of 29 000 could almost fit into a typical NHL hockey arena. Residents live in 31 communities, half of which are located north of the Arctic Circle and most of which contain between 500 and 1 500 people. There are no highways in this vast region; it is linked by air travel and sophisticated communications technology.

In contrast to the western Arctic, the eastern Arctic has little resource development. Both areas, however, have high unemployment.

The most striking demographic difference between the eastern and western Arctic is that Nunavut is more ethnically homogeneous. Eighty percent of Nunavut's population is Inuit, and Inuktitut is the mother tongue of 74% of the residents; about 20% speak neither French nor English. Radio broadcasts are available in Inuktitut; there are bilingual signs, a trilingual telephone book, and a bilingual newspaper (*Nunatsiaq News*). In many ways, then, the people of Nunavut are a *distinct society.*

The decision to establish Nunavut was made by plebiscite in 1992 after an agreement was reached between federal and territorial leaders. An important part of the agreement was the settling of land claims, which gave the Inuit sub-surface rights over part of the territory, financial compensation, and participation in the control and management of Crown lands. The establishment of Nunavut thus represents the establishment of a form of self-government for the Inuit.

The remaining area of the Northwest Territories is much more pluralistic. The northwest area is the home of the Inuvialuit, and the southwest region contains five Dene and Métis bands—the Delta (Gwich'in), the Deh Cho, the Sahtu, the North Slave, and the South Slave. With the exception of the Inuvialuit, most of this population lives south of the treeline (essentially a line extending from Churchill to Inuvik.

"Nunavut's most important meaning is that it is a government which reflects the life and life styles, and language, of the people who live along the coasts and by the caribou hunting grounds of our homeland. It is not a government which is trying to make our people act or look or speak like someone down south. It is a government for a largely Inuit community, and in which people can speak, write, work, make important decisions and govern themselves in Inuktitut ... What Nunavut will do is make sure that in Canada with its several provinces and territories, there is one government that is always speaking for the Inuit and making sure that Canada as a country has a large and important Inuit character as part of its national identity."

In some ways, then, Nunavut resembles Quebec, in that in both cases a distinct people with a clear ethnic background and a common language share a territory over which they have considerable control. The paradox is that Nunavut is both a distinct region of Canada and a distinct society or nation in the political-ethnic sense.

Source: Excerpts from the Nunavut Constitutional Forum published in *Information North* (Arctic Institute of North America), 19 (1993): 7, and from "Nunavut" ("Our Land") by Mark O. Dickerson and Karen M. McCullough in the same issue. See also Mark O. Dickerson, *Whose North? Political Change, Political Development, and Self-Government in the Northwest Territories* (Vancouver: UBC Press, 1992); Donald Purich, *The Inuit and Their Land: The Story of Nunavut* (Toronto: James Lorimer, 1992); Cameron W. Stout, "Nunavut: Canada's Newest Territory in 1999," *Canadian Social Trends* 44 (1997): 13–18; and Nunavut Implementation Commission, *Nunavut: Changing the Map of Canada,* 1999.

Prattis and Chartrand applied this internal colonial model to the Inuit in the North and found that there was indeed a disproportionate exclusion of Inuit from the labour force and a systematic underrepresentation of Inuit in the positions of highest rank.[81] In that sense there was a *cultural division of labour*. But through a strong sense of cultural identity (e.g., strong retention of their indigenous language, Inuktitut), the Inuit people strove to reshape the material conditions of their lives in the region.

In any case, whatever development took place in the North was clearly related to southern Canada's industrial needs in the post-World War II era. It should also be noted also that the North represented a strategic political territory for defence purposes in the Cold War between the United States and the Soviet Union.[82] The establishment of a series of radar lines, such as the Dew Line and Pine Tree Chain Line, as well as the construction of the Alaska Highway, bespeak the increasingly frequent southern incursions into a previously unimportant territory—a fact also reflected in recent demonstrations of Arctic sovereignty. In sum, the needs of regions and countries external to the North contributed to the area's increasing importance within Canadian society. This developmental pressure is clearly changing the face of the North—both environmentally and socially.

No other region of Canada is tied as directly to federal control as the North, even though legislative assemblies exist and the people elect representatives to federal parliament.[83] As the territories lack status as provinces, all their natural resources (and the resultant royalties) have been under the control of Ottawa. The federal government appoints a commissioner for each territory. In the case of the Northwest Territories, the commissioner lived in Ottawa until 1967, at which point white civil servants were transferred to Yellowknife to administer the territory. In addition, the federal government exerts political control through the Department of Indian Affairs and Northern Development (DIAND), serves as a major employer, and is also the primary source of funds for health and welfare. Because nurses and teachers, as well as wildlife and resource officers, are all hired by the government, the number of civil servants in the North is three times the national average.[84] Transfer payments, in the form of welfare and unemployment assistance, further illustrate the region's dependency on federal funds and institutions.

Amidst this colonial reality, political awareness has begun to emerge among indigenous peoples, reflecting a desire for more direct control and power over the affairs of the North. Abele has traced the evolution of this changed consciousness by distinguishing three phases in Native–non-Native relations in the North.[85] In the first phase, the Native people maintained their traditional lifestyle but were needed by non-Natives (e.g., traders, police, missionaries) for assistance to survive in the harsh environment. In the second phase (after World War II), the skills of the Native people were in less demand, and non-Natives excluded Natives from the economy and polity being developed. The third phase began in the late 1960s, when the Native people began to demand participation in the shaping of their own region. Perhaps no single event was more symbolic of the new mood of Native Northerners (and belatedly shared by an increasing number of non-Native residents as well) than the Mackenzie Valley Pipeline hearings (Berger Report) held in communities all over the North in the mid-'70s.[86] Southern Canada was being served notice that the North could no longer be considered a passive hinterland in which the environmental and social costs of intrusive development would be ignored. Thus political awareness first began to develop as a reaction to forms of economic development in which the people of the North were allowed to participate only marginally—indeed, often becoming its victims.[87]

Second, the reaction against external intrusion and control led to the formation of new Native organizations to negotiate with outside groups, such as corporations and (in particular) the federal government. Groups such as the Indian Brotherhood of the Northwest Territories, the Métis and Non-Status Indian Association of the Northwest Territories, the Council of Yukon Indians, the Inuit Tapirisat, the Federation of Natives North of Sixty, the Committee for Original Peoples' Entitlement, and the Tungavik Federation of Nunavut were organized in the early 1970s and have effectively represented Native people in negotiation with southern Canadians.

The third expression of this new awareness is focused on the issue of land claims and self-government. When the Dene Declaration was signed at Fort Simpson in 1975, outsiders heard only the Dene's bold assertion that they were a nation. The meaning of nationhood was essentially self-determination; they wanted to control what was happening to their own society rather than being victimized by the actions of others. Real control in this instance did not necessarily mean blocking all development, but controlling what development did occur and the pace at which it took place, and minimizing its negative impacts. Whereas in the mid-'70s the pipeline faced large-scale rejection,[88] by the late '80s Native groups were ready to assess new investment in their region.

Self-government, then, means the exertion of more localized and less bureaucratic federal control in matters ranging from the delivery of health and social services to education, resource ownership, and local taxation.[89] Land claims go far beyond issues of land control or cash compensation; they have to do with the ability of a Native group to retain the viability of its community. For this reason, land-claim agreements and self-government issues have been intertwined. Several claims have already been settled and others have been agreed to in principle.

Many issues still need to be resolved. One is that the federal government has no obligation to deal with the North in the same way that it does other provinces because the units of the North are *territories*, as stipulated in both the Constitution negotiations and the Meech Lake Accord in the 1980s.[90] Another has to do with the need to prepare Native people to be full participants in whatever development does occur, through job training and the reconciliation of hunting and gathering (the traditional economy) with wage labour (the industrial economy) to sustain Native culture.[91] The fact that 75% of the communities with more than 50 inhabitants do not have a consistent economic base only accentuates the dilemma.[92] Be that as it may, Northerners—much like residents of the Western and Atlantic regions—have increasingly come to the conclusion that decisions about resources should benefit their own region first, rather than so obviously treat the region as a hinterland with needs subordinate to those of southern metropoles.[93] It is in this sense that resources, regionalism, and underdevelopment contribute to a complex picture that evokes comparisons with those regions of Canada discussed above.

REGIONALISM REVISITED

While the history, economy, and conditions of social life differ considerably in the regions we have examined, there are certain common aspects. First, in each of these regions, prosperity depends greatly on staple extraction and resource development, whether the resource be grain, coal, fish, fur, oil, or minerals. Second, these primary industries are export-oriented, and little if any secondary industry has developed in the hinterland region. Third, qualitative differences between these regions do not disguise the fact that they support the industrial heartland of Canada. Fourth, each region has its own list of grievances focused on control from outside the region. Fifth, a new class of regional elites and middle-class boosters within each area are seeking greater regional control over development and change. It should not be surprising that regional conflict over the distribution and redistribution of opportunity and control should continue to exist.

In using the term *hinterland* to describe areas as diverse as the North, the Atlantic region, and the West, we must note that there are vast differences within each region. Urban areas are vastly different from remote rural areas, just as northern Ontario may be vastly different from southern Ontario. Furthermore, modern technology and consumerization have reduced many of the differences that might have existed 30 years ago, and there are many ways in which life in these regions is identical to life in core regions. In addition, to speak of Vancouver, Halifax, Calgary, or Fredericton as hinterlands is absurd unless the term is understood in the context of intra-societal relations.

Regionalism, as the politicized articulation of concerns expressed in a territory, will have different manifestations depending on the location, the issue, and the economy. Some forms of regionalism will be short-lived, some will be sustained by enduring cleavages, while others will be deliberately created.[94] Historically, most of the regionalist movements have been based on protest. *Protest regionalism* is a socio-political reaction triggered by erosion of position, and is aimed at either reversing the decline or protecting against further decline.[95] Such slippage was involved in the formation of both the Maritime Rights Movement and the United Farmers Movement in the West. More recently, regionalist activity has been oriented towards the development of new opportunities for growth. *Entrepreneurial* or *expansionist regionalism* reflects the desire to generate or take advantage of new opportunities to benefit a region and its inhabitants. It is not surprising that the high demand for energy has made oil and gas the basis for new hopes and expectations of regional growth and development.

As noted in Chapter Three, the federal government is keenly aware of the issues presented by regionalism. Bickerton has argued that the state has three strategy options when attempting to reconcile divergent structural conditions.[96] One option is *inaction* in the hope that market mechanisms will produce their own self-correction. Another option is a welfare-state strategy of *subsidized protection* (e.g., income supplements) to artificially reduce disparities. A third option is *administrative recommodification,* whereby labour is made more saleable through training or mobility subsidies and industries are rationalized or modernized to be more competitive. The Canadian state has used all of these strategies in combination or at different times. One of the key debates is whether government involvement cushions and supports adaptive processes or whether it interferes with or even retards adaptation and change.[97] It is for this reason that regionalism is far more than a matter of interesting cultural differences; it is at the very heart of structural disparities within Canadian society.

FURTHER EXPLORATION

1. Discuss regional stereotypes thought to be representative of your region. Explain why they exist and assess their accuracy.

2. Are the regional categories discussed in this chapter too large? What sub-regional units exist within these regions? Are they important?

3. Are regional disparities inevitable? Do "have" regions have responsibilities to "have-not" regions when we are all part of the same society? How do you feel about regions that are more or less prosperous than yours?

SELECTED READINGS

Brym, Robert J., ed. *Regionalism in Canada.* Toronto: Irwin, 1988.

Coffey, William J., and Mario Polèse, eds. *Still Living Together: Recent Trends and Future Directions in Canadian Regional Development.* Montreal: Institute for Research on Public Policy, 1987.

Gibbins, Roger, and Sonia Arrison. *Western Visions: Perspectives on the West in Canada.* Peterborough: Broadview, 1995.

Matthews, Ralph. *The Creation of Regional Dependency.* Toronto: University of Toronto Press, 1983.

McRoberts, Kenneth. *Beyond Quebec: Taking Stock of Canada.* Montreal: McGill-Queen's University Press, 1995.

McCrorie, James N., and Margaret L. MacDonald, eds. *The Constitutional Future of the Prairie and Atlantic Regions of Canada.* Regina: Canadian Plains Research Centre, 1992.

Ommer, Rosemary. *Fishing Places and Fishing People: Traditions and Issues in Canadian Small-Scale Fisheries.* Toronto: University of Toronto Press, 1999.

ENDNOTES

1 Harry H. Hiller, "Region as a Social Construction," in Keith Archer and Lisa Young, eds., *Regionalism and Party Politics in Canada* (Toronto: Oxford University Press, 2000).

2 Odum and his colleagues devote specific attention to economic factors, such as regional differences in income, occupation, and other indicators of standard of living. John Shelton Reed, "Sociology and Regional Studies in the United States," *Ethnic and Racial Studies* 3 (1980): 40–51.

3 John Shelton Reed, *One South: An Ethnic Approach to Regional Culture* (Baton Rouge: LSU Press, 1981).

4 Ralph Matthews, "Understanding Regionalism as Effect and Cause," in Dennis Forcese and Stephen Richer, eds., *Social Issues: Sociological Views of Canada*, 2nd ed. (Scarborough: Prentice Hall, 1988), 77–79.

5 This statement is consistent with Matthew's view that regions are not natural but created. Ralph Matthews, *The Creation of Regional Dependency* (Toronto: University of Toronto Press, 1983).

6 T.W. Acheson, "The Maritimes and Empire Canada," in David J. Bercuson, ed., *Canada and the Burden of Unity* (Toronto: Macmillan, 1977), 87–114.

7 Carl Cuneo, "A Class Perspective on Regionalism," in Daniel Glenday, Hubert Guindon, and Allan Turowetz, eds., *Modernization and the Canadian State* (Toronto: Macmillan, 1978), 188.

8 Wallace Clement, "A Political Economy of Regionalism in Canada," in Glenday, Guidon, and Turowetz, *Modernization and the Canadian State*, 100.

9 Kenneth Campbell, "Regional Disparity and Interregional Exchange Imbalance," in Glenday, Guidon, and Turowetz, *Modernization and the Canadian State*, 120. For other evidence of regional disparities, see D.F.G. Sitwell and N.R.M. Seifried, *The Regional Structure of the Canadian Economy* (Toronto: Methuen, 1984); and F.J. Anderson, *Regional Economic Analysis: A Canadian Perspective* (Toronto: HBJ Holt, 1988).

10 Janine Brodie, "The New Political Economy of Regions," in Wallace Clement, ed., *Understanding Canada: Building on the New Canadian Political Economy* (Montreal: McGill-Queen's University Press, 1997), 242.

11 Ibid., 240–61.

12 The study also argued that while economic disparities have lessened between regions since World War II, they are still higher than among US border states. The assumption is that migration is the answer to these regional disparities. Serge Coulombe, report released by the C.D. Howe Institute, *Calgary Herald*, March 10, 1999.

13 For a good review of all of these policies and an attempt to calculate levels of disparity, see Donald J. Savoie, *Regional Economic Development: Canada's Search for Solutions*, 2nd ed. (Toronto: University of Toronto Press, 1992).

14 This explains why the argument that a region is underdeveloped because it lacks entrepreneurs must be qualified by recognition of the power of greater corporate strength. For a discussion of this point, see Ralph Matthews, *The Creation of Regional Dependency* (Toronto: University of Toronto Press, 1983), 46–47.

15 Carl J. Cuneo, "The Class Dimensions of Regionalism," in Lorne Tepperman and James Curtis, eds., *Readings in Sociology: An Introduction* (Toronto: McGraw-Hill Ryerson, 1988), 671–81.

16 James P. Bickerton, *Nova Scotia, Ottawa, and the Politics of Regional Development* (Toronto: University of Toronto Press, 1990), 326–27.

17 See Larry Pratt, "The State and Province-Building: Alberta's Development Strategy," in Leo Panitch, *The Canadian State: Political Economy and Political Power* (Toronto: University of Toronto Press, 1977), 133–62.

18 This is essentially the point of Roger Gibbins, who argued that regionalism might be a much more salient idea to provincial elites than to their electorates. *Regionalism: Territorial Politics in Canada and the United States* (Toronto: Butterworths, 1982), 176.

19 R. Kent Weaver has shown how plurality elections in single-member districts have exaggerated regional differences. "Political Institutions and Conflict Management In Canada," *Annals of the American Academy of Political and Social Science*, 538 (1995): 54–68.

20 Donald J. Savoie, *Governing from the Centre: The Concentration of Power in Canadian Politics* (Toronto: University of Toronto Press, 1999).

21 For discussions of the political basis of regionalism, see Roger Gibbins, *Regionalism: Territorial Politics in Canada and the United States*.

22 Alan C. Cairns, "The Governments and Societies of Canadian Federalism," *Canadian Journal of Political Science* 10 (1977): 707.

23 Larry Pratt, "The State and Province Building: Alberta's Development Strategy," 157.

24 Richard Simeon and Donald E. Blake, "Regional Preferences: Citizens' Views on Public Policy," in David J. Elkins and Richard Simeon, *Small Worlds: Provinces and Parties in Canadian Political Life*, (Toronto: Methuen, 1980), 101–102.

25 Garth Stevenson, "Canadian Regionalism in Continental Perspective," *Journal of Canadian Studies* 15 (1980): 16–28.

26 Martin Lubin, "The Routinization of Cross-Border Interactions: An Overview of NEC/CCP Structures and Activities," in Douglas M. Brown and Earl H. Fry, eds., *States and Provinces in the International Economy* (Berkeley: Institute of Governmental Studies Press, University of California, 1993); and Paul Schell and John Hamer, "Cascadia: The New Binationalism of Western Canada and the U.S. Pacific Northwest," in Robert L. Earle and John D. Wirth, eds., *Identities in North America* (Stanford: Stanford University Press, 1995), 140–56.

27 Kenichi Ohmae develops this idea perhaps to the point of overstatement in referring to this new phenomenon as "region states." "The Rise of the Region State," *Foreign Affairs* 72, 2 (1993): 78–87.

28 Cf. Bell and Tepperman, *The Roots of Disunity: A Look at Canadian Political Culture*, 146.

29 Bernard Bonin and Roger Verreault, "The Multinational Firm and Regional Development," in William J. CoVey and Mario Polès, eds., *Still Living Together* (Montreal: Institute for Research on Public Policy, 1987), 159–202.

30 See, for example, Wallace Clement, *The Challenge of Class Analysis* (Ottawa: Carleton University Press, 1988), chap. 9.

31 Ralph Matthews and J. Campbell Davis, "The Comparative Influence of Region, Status, Class and Ethnicity on Canadian Attitudes and Values," 90–122, and Douglas House, "The Mouse That Roars: New Directions in Canadian Political Economy—The Case of Newfoundland," 162–96, in Robert Brym, ed., *Regionalism in Canada* (Toronto: Irwin, 1986).

32 Richard Simeon and David J. Elkins suggest that unique historical and sociological factors may be important contextual elements in the creation of cultural differences between provinces. "Provincial Political Cultures in Canada," in David J. Elkins and Richard Simeon, eds., *Small Worlds: Provinces and Parties in Canadian Political Life*. Ralph Matthews argued that regionalism is the sum product of economic, social-organizational, and political factors. "The Significance and Explanation of Regional Divisions in Canada: Toward a Canadian Sociology," *Journal of Canadian Studies* 15 (1980): 51.

33 Simeon and Blake, *Regional Preferences: Citizens' Views of Public Policy*, 100.

34 See, for example, Roger Gibbins and Sonia Arrison, *Western Visions: Perspectives on the West in Canada* (Peterborough: Broadview, 1995), 59–69. For an older account, see David J. Elkins, "The Sense of Place," in David J. Elkins and Richard Simeon, eds., *Small Worlds: Provinces and Parties in Canadian Political Life*, 21–23.

35 For an excellent summary discussion of the National Policy and its implications in one volume, see the *Journal of Canadian Studies* 1, 3 (1979).

36 George F.G. Stanley, "The Western Canadian Mystique," in David P. Gagan, ed., *Prairie Perspectives* (Toronto: Holt, Rinehart and Winston, 1970), 6–27.

37 James C. Davies, "Toward a Theory of Revolution," *American Sociological Review* 27 (1962): 5–19.

38 J.F. Conway makes an interesting argument that these movements were essentially a class challenge by the agrarian petty-bourgeoisie for reform of the capitalist system. He suggest that the fact that the Progressives also reached into Ontario reveals that this protest had more of a social-class rather than regional basis. "The Prairie Populist Resistance to the National Policy: Some Reconsiderations," *Journal of Canadian Studies* 14, 3 (1979): 77–91. For an excellent review of the problems of the West in Confederation, see also his *The West: The History of a Region in Confederation* (Toronto: James Lorimer, 1983). Some of the key book-length studies on these movements include W.L. Morton, *The Progressive Party in Canada* (Toronto: University of Toronto Press, 1957); S.M. Lipset, *Agrarian Socialism: The Co-operative Commonwealth Federation in Saskatchewan* (New York: Doubleday, 1968); C.B. Macpherson, *Democracy in Alberta: Social Credit and the Party System* (Toronto: University of Toronto Press, 1953); and John A. Irving, *The Social Credit Movement in Alberta* (Toronto: University of Toronto Press, 1959).

39 Roger Gibbins, *Prairie Politics and Society: Regionalism in Decline* (Toronto: Butterworths, 1980), 167–69.

40 Howard Palmer, ed., *The Settlement of the West* (Calgary: University of Calgary, 1977), as well as the books of C.A. Dawson. For an account of the social organization and evolution of the Prairie community system, see Carle C. Zimmerman and Garry W. Moneo, *The Prairie Community System* (Agricultural Economics Research Council of Canada, 1970).

41 John Stahl, "Prairie Agriculture: A Prognosis," in David P. Gagan, ed., *Prairie Perspectives*, 66.

42 Gibbins argues that the breakdown of the dominant rural agricultural economy has reduced the distinctiveness of the region and brought it into increasing competition with other urban industrial areas of Canada. *Prairie Politics and Society: Regionalism in Decline.*

43 Cf., for example, John Barr and Owen Anderson, eds., *The Unfinished Revolt* (Toronto: McClelland and Stewart, 1971).

44 For an assessment of the actual possibility of such a shift in power, see a symposium entitled "Power Shift West: Myth Or Reality?" in *Canadian Journal of Sociology* 6 (1981): 165–83.

45 For an assessment of the freight-rates issue, cf. David Harvey, *Christmas Turkey or Prairie Vulture? An Economic Analysis of the Crow's Nest Pass Grain Rates* (Montreal: Institute of Research for Public Policy, 1980); and Howard Darling, *The Politics of Freight Rates* (Toronto: McClelland and Stewart, 1980).

46 John Richards and Larry Pratt, *Prairie Capitalism: Power and Influence in the New West* (Toronto: McClelland and Stewart, 1979).

47 Larry Pratt and Garth Stevenson, eds., *Western Separatism: The Myths, Realities and Dangers* (Edmonton: Hurtig, 1981).

48 Andrew Nikiforuk, Sheila Pratt, and Donald Wanagas, eds., *Running on Empty: Alberta after the Boom* (Edmonton: NeWest, 1987).

49 See Trevor Harrison and Gordon Laxer, eds., *The Trojan Horse: Alberta and the Future of Canada* (Toronto: Black Rose, 1996).

50 Gibbins and Arrison, *Western Visions: Perspectives on the West in Canada.*

51 G.A. Rawlyk and Doug Brown, "The Historical Framework of the Maritimes and Confederation," in G.A. Rawlyk, *The Atlantic Provinces and the Problems of Confederation* (St. John's: Breakwater, 1979), 4.

52 E.R. Forbes and D.A. Muise, eds., *The Atlantic Provinces in Confederation* (Toronto: University Of Toronto Press, 1993).

53 Colin D. Howell, "Nova Scotia's Protest Tradition and the Search for a Meaningful Federalism," in David J. Bercuson, ed., *Canada and the Burden of Unity* (Toronto: Macmillan, 1977), 169–91.

54 Ernest R. Forbes, "Misguided Symmetry: The Destruction of Regional Transportation Policy for the Maritimes," in David J. Bercuson, ed., *Canada and the Burden of Unity* (Toronto: Macmillan, 1977), 60–86. It should be pointed out that in response to the recommendations of the Duncan Commission, the federal government passed the *Maritime Freight Rates Act* in 1927 to restore some of the region's previous freight advantages, but these rates lacked the previous rates' flexibility and failed to have the desired result.

55 T.W. Acheson, "The Maritimes and Empire Canada," in David J. Bercuson, ed., *Canada and the Burden of Unity*, 93; and E.R. Forbes, *Challenging the Regional Stereotype: Essays on the 20th Century Maritimes* (Fredericton: Acadiensis Press, 1989), 200–216. Forbes argues that the way Canada was constitutionally set up created a tightly integrated union of central urban dominance that hurt Atlantic Canada, and that the region was not to blame for the effect.

56 Ernest R. Forbes, *The Maritime Rights Movement, 1919–1927: A Study in Canadian Regionalism* (Montreal: McGill-Queen's University Press, 1979).

57 Ernest R. Forbes explores aspects of the common hinterland condition of the Maritimes and the Prairies and discusses the factors that have prevented them from forming a coalition as allies. "Never the Twain Did Meet: Prairie–Maritime Relations 1910–1927," *Canadian Historical Review* 59 (1978): 19–37. For an analysis of the growth and decline of Maritime industry, see T.W. Acheson, David Frank, and James D. Frost, *Industrialization and Underdevelopment in the Maritimes, 1880–1930* (Toronto: Garamond Press, 1985).

58 Rawlyk and Brown estimate that 300 000 people left the region during this period, with three quarters migrating to the United States. "This Historical Framework of the Maritimes and Confederation," in Rawlyk, *The Atlantic Provinces and the Problems of Confederation*, 33.

59 "Canada," in James N. McCrorie and M.L. MacDonald, eds., *The Constitutional Future of the Prairie and Atlantic Regions of Canada* (Regina: CPRC, 1992), 18–36.

60 Gary Burrill and Ian McKay, eds., *People, Resources and Power: Critical Perspectives on Underdevelopment and Primary Industries in the Atlantic Region* (Fredericton: Gorsebrook Research Institute, 1987).

61 Cf. G.A. Rawlyk, "The Historical Framework of Newfoundland and Confederation," in *The Atlantic Provinces and the Problems of Confederation*, 48–81; and James Hiller and Peter Neary, *Newfoundland in the Nineteenth and Twentieth Centuries: Essays in Interpretation* (Toronto: University of Toronto Press, 1980).

62 S.J.R. Noel, *Politics in Newfoundland* (Toronto: University of Toronto Press, 1971).

63 Peter Neary, "Newfoundland's Union with Canada, 1949: Conspiracy or Choice?" in P.A. Buckner and David Frank, eds., *Atlantic Canada after Confederation* (Fredericton: Acadiensis Press, 1985). For an interesting contemporary interpretation expressing sadness at this decision, see Bryn Walsh, *More Than a Poor Majority: The Story of Newfoundland's Confederation with Canada* (St. John's: Breakwater, 1985).

64 Matthews, *The Creation of Regional Dependency*, 57.

65 In 1961, there were 815 communities of fewer than 300 inhabitants in Newfoundland, and the number had fallen to 545 communities in 1971. Ralph Matthews discusses the resettlement program, its objectives, and its consequences in *The Creation of Regional Dependency*, chap. 9. For an interesting study of small communities that resisted resettlement, see his *There's No Better Place than Here: Social Change in Three Newfoundland Communities* (Toronto: Peter Martin, 1976).

66 For an interesting lay expression of the frustrations of Maritime underdevelopment, cf. Paul MacEwan, *Confederation and the Maritimes* (Windsor, N.S.: Lancelot Press, 1976). David Alexander also suggests that Atlantic Canada could have a stronger role in Confederation in his *Atlantic Canada and Confederation* (Toronto: University of Toronto Press, 1983).

67 George Rawlyk, "The Maritimes and the Canadian Community," in Mason Wade, *Regionalism in the Canadian Community 1867–1967* (Toronto: University of Toronto Press, 1969), 102.

68 Robert Finbow, "Atlantic Canada: Forgotten Periphery in an Endangered Confederation," in Kenneth McRoberts, ed., *Beyond Quebec: Taking Stock of Canada* (Montreal: McGill-Queen's University Press, 1995), 61–80.

69 The ACOA 1998 Five Year Report to Parliament 1993–1998 claims that over the duration of the program, Atlantic unemployment has dropped by 2.8%. See also Donald J. Savoie, *Rethinking Canada's Regional Development Policy: An Atlantic Perspective* (Canadian Institute for Research on Regional Development, 1997) for a critique that points out that even though money is poured into the region, nothing much happens because of the Canadian reluctance to make structural changes.

70 Robert J. Brym and R. James Sacouman argue that the capitalist system itself has produced underdevelopment in Atlantic Canada through competition, concentration, and the desire for cheap labour and raw materials. The disparity between large external capitalists and local producers at subsistence and wage-labour levels (e.g., miners and fishers) results in capital drain, a subsistence economy, and chronic unemployment. *Underdevelopment and Social Movements in Atlantic Canada* (Toronto: New Hogtown Press, 1979). For an emphasis on the effect on the region's primary producers, see Gary Burrill and Ian McKay, eds., *People, Resources and Power* (Fredericton: Acadiensis Press, 1987).

71 For an overview of the relationship between dependency and oil as a mechanism for greater independence in Newfoundland, see Harry H. Hiller, "Dependence and Independence: Emergent Nationalism in Newfoundland," *Ethnic and Racial Studies* 19 (1987): 257–75.

72   The distinction between strong and weak staples is made by J.D. House in "Fish Is Fish and Oil Is Oil: The Case for North Sea Comparisons to Atlantic Canada," in his *Fish vs. Oil: Resources and Rural Development in North Atlantic Societies* (St. John's: Institute for Social and Economic Research, 1986), 133–37.

73   J.D. House, *The Challenge of Oil* (St. John's: Institute for Social and Economic Research, 1985). See also the report of the Royal Commission on Employment and Unemployment (of which House was chair), entitled *Building on Our Strengths* (1986).

74   Bryant Fairley, Colin Leys, and James Sacouman, eds., *Restructuring and Resistance: Perspectives from Atlantic Canada* (Toronto: Garamond, 1990).

75   Donald J. Savoie and Ralph Winter, eds., *The Maritime Provinces: Looking to the Future* (Moncton: Canadian Institute for Research on Regional Development, 1993).

76   For this reason, Finbow has said that the region is destined to be someone's periphery, whether that someone be Central Canada, the United States, or whoever. "Atlantic Canada: Forgotten Periphery in an Endangered Confederation?" in McRoberts, *Beyond Quebec*, 77. Forbes has argued that what Atlantic regions want more than anything is to be full participants in an equitable federation. "The 1980's," in Forbes and Muise, eds., *The Atlantic Provinces in Confederation*, 515.

77   Duncan Knowler points out that the North is not an undifferentiated territory but can be divided into regions which include the northern parts of provinces. He identifies 21 remote regions in "Basic Industry in Remote Canadian Regions," *The Northern Review* 2 (1988): 44–66.

78   Kenneth Coates and Judith Powell, *The Modern North: People, Politics and the Rejection of Colonialism* (Toronto: James Lorimer, 1989), 16–19.

79   K.J. Rea, *The Political Economy of the Canadian North* (Toronto: University of Toronto Press, 1968), 345ff.

80   For a good discussion of the role of minerals in the economy of the North, see Rea, *The Political Economy of the Canadian North*, chap. 4.

81   J. Ian Prattis and Jean-Phillippe Chartrand, "The Cultural Division of Labour in the Canadian North: A Statistical Study of the Inuit," *Canadian Review of Sociology and Anthropology* 27 (1990): 49–73.

82   E.J. Dosman, ed., *The Arctic in Question* (Toronto: Oxford University Press, 1976); John Honderich, *Arctic Imperative: Is Canada Losing the North?* (Toronto: University of Toronto Press, 1987); and Shelagh D. Grant, *Sovereignty or Security? Government Policy in the Canadian North* 1936–1950 (Vancouver: University of British Columbia Press, 1988).

83   Mark O. Dickerson, *Whose North? Political Change, Political Development, and Self-Government in the Northwest Territories* (Vancouver: UBC Press, 1992).

84   Gurston Dacks, *A Choice of Futures: Politics in the Canadian North* (Toronto: Methuen, 1981), 18.

85   Frances Abele, *Gathering Strength* (Calgary: Arctic Institute of North America, 1989), vii–viii.

86   Thomas R. Berger, *Northern Frontier; Northern Homeland: The Report of the Mackenzie Valley Pipeline Inquiry,* Vols. 1 and 2 (Ottawa: Minister of Supply and Services, 1977).

87   Robert Page, *Northern Development: The Canadian Dilemma* (Toronto: McClelland and Stewart, 1986).

88   For some opinions on the impact of pipelines on the North, cf. Donald Peacock, *People, Peregrines, and Arctic Pipelines* (Vancouver: J.J. Douglas, 1977); Earle Gray, *Super Pipe: The Arctic Pipeline* (Toronto: Griffin House, 1979); and James Woodford, *The Violated Vision: The Rape of Canada's North* (Toronto: McClelland and Stewart, 1972).

89   Department of Indian and Northern Affairs Canada, Information Sheet No. 3, September 1987. See also Gurston Dacks, ed., *Devolution and Constitutional Development in the Canadian North* (Ottawa: Carleton University Press, 1990).

90 Coates and Powell, *The Modern North*, 76–80.

91 Abele, *Gathering Strength*, and Kenneth Coates, "On the Outside in Their Homeland: Native People and the Evolution of the Yukon Economy," *The Northern Review* 1 (1988): 73–89.

92 Louis-Edmond Hamelin, *Canadian Nordicity* (Montreal: Harvest House, 1979), 220. See also Colin Alexander, *Angry Society* (Yellowknife: Yellowknife Publishing Co., 1976) for the views of a Euro-Canadian Northerner who rejects the concept of no development but prefers that development take place under the auspices of Northerners.

93 Some issues are whether Northerners should be given priority in hiring or training for employment and whether full-time positions should be restricted to Northerners. For a good discussion of all the issues related to Northern control of development, see Robert F. Keith, *Northern Development and Technology Assessment System* (Ottawa: Science Council of Canada Background Study 34, 1976).

94 Peter McCormick, "Regionalism in Canada: Disentangling the Threads," *Journal of Canadian Studies* 24 (1989): 19.

95 The distinction between protest regionalism and expansionist regionalism is made by Raymond Breton, "Regionalism In Canada," in David M. Cameron, ed., *Regionalism and Supranationalism* (Montreal: Institute for Research on Public Policy, 1981), 64–67.

96 James Bickerton, *Nova Scotia, Ottawa, and the Politics of Regional Development*, 313–15.

97 Fred Wien, "Regional Inequality: Explanations and Policy Issues," in James Curtis, Edward Grabb, and Neil Guppy, eds., *Social Inequality in Canada: Patterns, Problems, Policies*, 2nd ed. (Scarborough: Prentice Hall, 1993), 463; and Peter R. Sinclair, "Underdevelopment and Regional Inequality," in B. Singh Bolaria, ed., *Social Issues and Contradictions in Canadian Society* (Toronto: Harcourt Brace, 1995), 396–98.

WEBLINKS

www.acoa.ca

The Atlantic Canada Opportunities Agency (ACOA) is a federal government agency set up to improve the economy of Atlantic communities through the successful development of business and job opportunities.

chapter five

The Issue of Ethnicity

The process of becoming Canadian in outlook has gone far in the Canadian-born children of immigrants. It will go on to completion in their children, or at least their children's children.... At the same time community conflicts and institutional disturbances tend to retard it [assimilation] and render doubtful the seeming advantages of a sudden precipitation of new peoples into a great variety of contacts with those who differ so widely from themselves. It is for this reason that assimilation ... is such a disturbing matter for all concerned.

−Carl A. Dawson, first sociologist in Canada and founder of the only Department of Sociology in Canada for many years (at McGill University), in his classic, *Pioneering in the Prairie Provinces: The Social Side of the Settlement Process* (1940), 38

As seen through European eyes, perhaps the most striking feature of the "New" World, as compared to the "Old" World, was its vast amount of sparsely settled territory. It is this basic fact of relatively small population in an enormous area (in contrast to the crowded Old World), in combination with the expansionist ambitions of European powers, that predestined ethnicity to become a salient issue in the building of Canadian society. First came the arrival of Europeans to lands populated by Native peoples, then the intermingling of European peoples in the new land, and most recently, immigration from new densely populated source-areas, such as Asia and South America. Even after years of residence in Canada, people are still asked about their ethnic origin in the census, and the government policy of multiculturalism ostensibly encourages members of the society to remember, rediscover, or retain their ethnic origins. Ethnicity clearly has been and continues to be a significant element of Canadian society!

Ethnicity is an amalgam of objective factors related to place of birth, citizenship, mother tongue, and customs/traditions which are transmitted as a heritage and characterize the individual.[1] In the Canadian experience, ethnic origin is linked to another nation-state, a fact which provides a "foreign" dimension to the concept. But ethnicity does not only involve objective traits such as language and customs; it also involves a subjective dimension pertaining to how people view themselves, i.e., their ethnic identity. This means that it makes a difference not only whether a person speaks Italian or English or is a citizen of Canada or of Italy, but also whether the identity which that person embraces is Italian, Italian-Canadian, Canadian, or even *Canadien*. Each alternative tells us something important about that person in relation to others in the wider society.

The diversity of contemporary people's responses to questions about the objective and subjective facts of their background makes the analysis of ethnicity both a dynamic and an essential undertaking for the understanding of Canadian society.

ETHNIC ORIGIN AND ETHNIC IDENTITY

As was established in Chapter One, immigration from numerous sources has been an important component of growth in Canadian society. For this reason, the census has always inquired about the ethnic backgrounds of the population through a category known as *ethnic origin*. Before 1981, ethnic origin was established on the basis of paternal ancestry; the 1981 census broadened the parameters to reflect the ethnic or cultural group to which the respondent or respondent's ancestors belonged on first coming to this continent. The 1981 census also gave respondents for the first time the opportunity to indicate multiple origins (though this was not requested) if they chose to do so. As a result of these changes, the data gathered in 1981 and especially in 1986 (when respondents were explicitly requested to specify as many ethnic origins as applied) differ from earlier data. Note that respondents could choose what best represented their ethnic origins (whether the selection was technically accurate may be another matter). Note, also, that it was assumed that the respondent's ethnicity was something *other* than Canadian—at least until the 1991 census. Partly due to a write-in campaign that encouraged people to declare their ethnic origin as "Canadian" in 1991 (3% did so), the proportion of persons declaring a single "Canadian" ethnic origin increased dramatically—to 19% by 1996 and 23% in 2001; this response was most common among those who formerly would have declared themselves of British or French descent.[2]

Figure 5.1 indicates that in 2001 just under two thirds of the population claimed to be of single ethnic origin, and just over one third claimed to be of multiple ethnic origin. Again, remember that this is a self-report, and that a respondent might claim one ethnic origin when two or more might in fact be technically accurate; in that sense, the response might also be a good indicator of a person's *ethnic identity* and not just of ethnic origin. For example, some individuals claiming a "Canadian" ethnic origin might be deliberately ignoring their ethnic heritage, either because it reaches too far back or because they "feel" Canadian. Or someone who claims to be German might be ignoring the fact that his/her ancestors spoke German as a language but actually immigrated from Poland or Austria. So responses to questions of ethnic origin are really open to divergent interpretations.

However, as noted above, the majority of the population claimed to have a single ethnic origin. Figure 5.1 reveals that of that group, the largest single category is composed of the 36% who declare their ethnic origin to be Canadian or *Canadien*. The remaining 64% selected other ethnic categories: 15% percent were British, 6% were French, and 20% were European. These figures might seem surprising, because the British, French, and Western Europeans were formerly the largest component of the Canadian population. However, the fact that these groups have been in Canada the longest might make them the most likely to have switched to a "Canadian" ethnic identity. Indeed a significant percentage of those claiming multiple origins include "Canadian," and many also combine it with British and French ethnic origins. The end result of the fact that many now see themselves as ethnically Canadian, however, is that the well-known French–English duality has been transformed from an *ethnic* duality into a *language* duality (i.e., French and English are

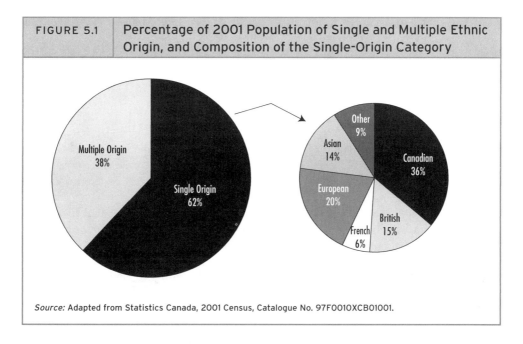

FIGURE 5.1 | **Percentage of 2001 Population of Single and Multiple Ethnic Origin, and Composition of the Single-Origin Category**

Source: Adapted from Statistics Canada, 2001 Census, Catalogue No. 97F0010XCB01001.

considered as languages rather than as ethnic groups). The other significant feature of the change over time is that in Canada today there is a substantial "third force"—a diversity of other groups—moderating the former strength of the two dominant groups. In fact, there are now more Canadians claiming a single ethnic origin that is Asian (14%) and Other (9%) than those claiming British and French combined. Generally, more-recent immigrants are more likely to claim single ethnic origin than are persons whose ancestors have been here for several generations.

What is clear is that census data need to be interpreted carefully, for ethnic origin by itself does not indicate the degree of attachment a person may feel towards his or her ethnic group. Ethnic background or ancestry does not tell us much about the saliency of ethnicity in a society. One study explicitly measuring ethnic identity found that persons declaring an ethnic identity other than Canadian were more likely either to be first- or second-generation immigrants, to live in a geographic territory with a high concentration of persons from the same ethnic background, to have married within their ethnic group, or to have learned a language other than English as children.[3]

So perhaps it is appropriate to ask whether the issue of ethnicity might not be exaggerated in Canadian society. Is it a fleeting phenomenon that will disappear in succeeding generations as more persons, regardless of ethnic descent, are born in Canada? Indeed, has ethnicity already become irrelevant to the majority of Canadians? Or, to put the question differently, why is ethnicity given such importance in any discussion of Canadian society? Has the policy of multiculturalism fooled us into thinking that ethnicity is more important than it really is?

FACTORS SUSTAINING THE IMPORTANCE OF ETHNICITY

There are a number of reasons why ethnicity is far more important in Canadian society than may be readily apparent from the statistical data. The six reasons discussed in this section combine elements of history, government policy, intergroup struggles, and the social psychology of group belonging.

1. The Legacy of Early European Settlement

The initial settlement of the Atlantic region and the St. Lawrence lowlands by the French was challenged first by the Treaty of Utrecht in 1713 and then by the Conquest on the Plains of Abraham in 1759. In both cases, an established and vigorous community of French settlers was taken under direct control by the British. By the time of Confederation it had become clear that while Canada was composed of two founding groups (the French and the English), the English had the upper hand in determining the structure of the new society.

John Porter coined the term *charter group* to refer to the ethnic group that first settles a previously unoccupied territory and subsequently controls which other groups can come in.[4] While it is true that Porter's definition ignored the existence of Native peoples already resident in the territory, the idea that a charter group is itself a foreign people who merely happen to be the first of a diverse stream of immigrants makes the concept a useful one. It must be remembered, however, that French and British charter groups were not of equal strength: the British were the *higher charter group;* the French, the *lower*. Ultimate control over the immigration process resided with the British because the political apparatus was in their hands. One effect of British power over immigration was to enforce upon Native and other ethnic groups an awareness of subordinate status and power. Thus, beginning in the colonial era, a power relationship emerged not only between the two charter groups but between these and all other groups. These ethnic power relationships continue to have an effect on Canadian society.

Several features of Canadian society flow from this legacy. First, the organizational framework of the new society was based on British institutions and traditions—a fact other ethnic groups would not always appreciate. Second, the British allowed francophones to retain some control over events in Quebec, and this is why Confederation is sometimes viewed as a pact between these two founding groups. Clearly the French and English have developed different interpretations of this ethnic power relationship, but it is this very relationship which is at the root of the famed duality of Canadian society. The fact that such a relationship exists was to become an important justification for the argument that Canada ought to have two official languages. In general, the relationship gave the French more or less equal status, and, most importantly, elevated that group above other ethnic groups. While the implications of these ideas are still not clear in the minds of many Canadians, the evolution of the French–English duality and the struggle to arrive at a common understanding of that duality help keep ethnicity an important issue in Canadian society.

A third consequence of this duality is that the division and conflicting loyalties between the two charter groups set a pattern for other groups seeking to retain their own ethnic loyalties. Since the British and French were in conflict themselves, the society had a greater built-in tolerance for the perpetuation of ethnic identities.

2. Territoriality

In Chapter One it was argued that territoriality is necessary to establish a sense of society. When an ethnic group is concentrated in a particular area, it is more likely to maintain its identity as a subgroup of the national society. If members of all ethnic groups were evenly dispersed throughout the country, ethnicity would not be so important; because this is not the case, ethnicity remains a critical variable in Canada.[5]

Perhaps the most important factor sustaining ethnicity as a critical variable in Canadian society is not immigration but the regional concentration of francophones in the province of Quebec. In a manner almost impossible without a sense of territoriality, Quebec francophones have increasingly used the political structure of the province as a vehicle for sustaining their ethnic identity. This geographic factor has two consequences. In the first place, the majority–minority relationship between English and French in Canada as a whole is reversed in the province of Quebec. Quebec anglophones who view themselves as part of the Canadian linguistic majority have felt threatened at finding themselves a declining linguistic minority in that province. Because their concept of territoriality extends to the country as a whole, these anglophones, finding it increasingly difficult to exert power within Quebec, have expected protection from the federal government. In sum, the Quebec government's actions have raised the issue of minority rights within Quebec, sparking national debate about the principles guiding Canadian society.

Second, the vigour with which Quebec has been able to make its ethnic claims has inspired francophone communities in other parts of Canada (e.g., St. Boniface, Manitoba, and northern New Brunswick) to assert their ethnic/linguistic claims. Thus, the territorial concentration of the French community in Quebec, in conjunction with the political actions of the Quebec government, has helped to ensure that ethnicity remains a vital factor within the society. It could also be argued that the federal government's response to this territorial fact helped produce the policy of bilingualism.

Furthermore, other ethnic groups have responded to these territorial precedents by agitating for greater recognition in their territories. For example, Ukrainians in Manitoba, northern Saskatchewan, and Alberta have been somewhat successful in obtaining language support in the school systems there. Francophones in northern New Brunswick were able to obtain their government's support for full provincial bilingualism (a position rejected by all other provinces). Inuit in Nunavut have some school instruction, as well as broadcasting, in their native tongue.

Another form of significant territorial concentration has been the ethnic segregation found in urban areas.[6] This has been particularly important because 94% of all immigrants who arrived in the '90s located in census metropolitan areas, and 73% chose Toronto, Vancouver, or Montreal. Generally speaking, the larger the urban area, the greater the degree of segregation, with Western and Northern Europeans the least segregated, Central and Eastern Europeans (and Italians) somewhat segregated, and Asians and Blacks the most segregated.[7] It is also important to note that visible minorities are not only segregated from Caucasian groups, but also highly segregated from each other. Even when residential segregation is not typical, other mechanisms, such as ethnic associations, keep ethnicity salient to urban residents. Most large Canadian cities have ethnic enclaves in which ethnic retailing and leisure opportunities play a prominent role; "Chinatowns" are probably the most widely recognized example.[8] Given the fact that urban areas are almost exclusively the reception centres for new immigrants, any further immigration will continue to heighten the visibility of ethnicity in these locations, serving as a reminder that ethnic differences are an important feature of the society (see the following section on visible minorities).

3. Immigration Policy

A third reason for the continuing significance of ethnicity in Canada can be found in the waves of immigration which have been so characteristic of the society. At the time of Confederation, the ratio of British to French in the total population was 2:1, and these two ethnic groups made up 90% of the population. Other ethnic groups were small and usually also Northern European. In the succeeding years (particularly in the last decade of the nineteenth century, when the policies of Minister of the Interior Clifford Sifton were in force), Canada's desire to populate the West and fill labour needs led to the immigration of large numbers of other Europeans, including Ukrainians, Germans, and Scandinavians. This wave of immigration lasted until the onset of the Depression. After World War II, immigration from Europe resumed, though it was not until the 1960s that large numbers came from Southern Europe (particularly Italy and Portugal). In the 1970s the sources of migration shifted again, this time to the West Indies and Asia; in the 1980s Central and South America were added.

Pier 21 in Halifax: The "Front Door" to Canada

The peopling of Canada originally took place via ocean transport. Large ships brought people across the Atlantic Ocean from Europe. Because they had deep-water ports, two of the most popular debarkation points were Halifax and Quebec City; Halifax became a particularly strategic entrance point to Canada because it was an important naval base. Once the railroad linked the eastern seaboard to the West Coast, it was convenient to drop passengers off in Halifax, whence they could then be transported across the country by rail to their destinations, mostly in the West.

Pier 21 in Halifax was recently redeveloped as a national historic site to commemorate the massive movement of immigrants from Europe to Canada. The Immigration and Customs shed has been refurbished with interactive and historic exhibits, and an empty old railway passenger car sits right next to the dock, symbolizing the shift of immigrants from one mode of transport to another. Pier 21 at that time was the "front door" to Canada for over one million immigrants, refugees, and war brides (and their children). The exhibit shows the hardships that many immigrants faced on the ocean voyage.

I visited Pier 21 with my mother, and it was a nostalgic moment. My grandfather had assisted many immigrants to come to Canada from Europe after both world wars, and I heard many stories about his trips with these immigrants by train as they travelled across the country. I also found my father's name in the government immigrant-processing list. It said he came to Canada with $25.

Pier 21 was closed as an immigrant-processing centre in 1971, as ocean-going transportation was being replaced by planes. But its closing also represented the end of an era, as immigration patterns shifted from Europe to other global sources of migration. Also of note is the fact that hardly any of the thousands of immigrants who came to Canada through Halifax during this time period (1928–1971) stayed in the region; most moved westward.

Figure 5.2 compares the source countries of immigration to Canada during two five-year periods, 1956–1960 and 1998–2002. The British Isles and Europe were almost the exclusive source regions during the first period. During the second period, immigrants came from a wider range of global sources, especially Asia, although immigration from Africa, the Middle East, and South/Central America became much more pronounced. This

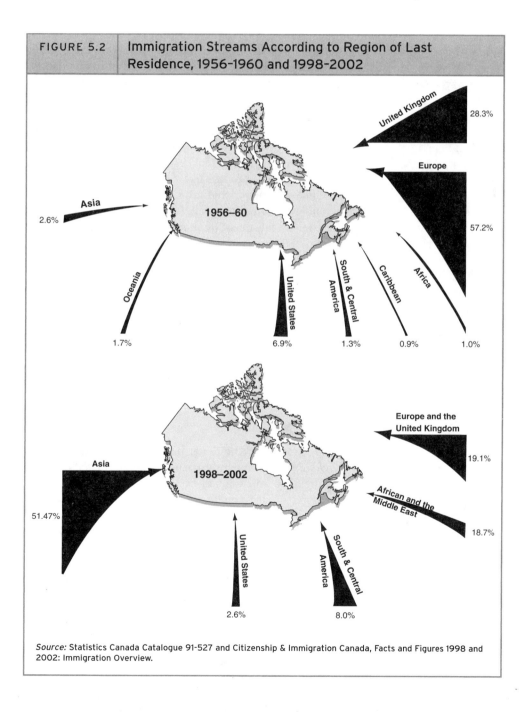

FIGURE 5.2 **Immigration Streams According to Region of Last Residence, 1956–1960 and 1998–2002**

Source: Statistics Canada Catalogue 91-527 and Citizenship & Immigration Canada, Facts and Figures 1998 and 2002: Immigration Overview.

largely non-Caucasian immigration has been called the *fifth force* (following the Indigenous peoples, French, British, and Europeans).[9] This new wave of immigration has raised new questions about integration in cases where religion, cultural practices, and social structures differ from the patterns of mainstream Canadian society—for example, should Sikh RCMP officers should be permitted to wear their turbans?

Immigration to Canada was not random, but rather expressed government policy concerning the suitability of the migrating group. In essence, this meant that immigrants from Great Britain were particularly favoured, with some preference also given to immigrants from other Northern European countries.[10] Other European groups were encouraged to settle less desirable land in the northwest or to fill the need for blue-collar industrial labour. In this way, the British charter group maintained its control over the development of the society. More importantly, however, these repeated waves of immigration reinvigorated ethnic groups already resident in Canada, reminding residents of their own ethnicity.

In 1967, a point system was introduced as a means of evaluating the merits of potential immigrants. This system reduced the *source discrimination* of previous immigration policy.[11] In conjunction with the new *Immigration Act* in 1978, the point system encouraged more migration by non-Europeans, who were less likely to be Caucasian. The complex motives underlying the point system—including Canada's perception of its responsibility for Third World economic and political refugees and its desires for cheap labour (on the one hand) and for capital investment by immigrant entrepreneurs (on the other)—have raised crucial questions about which ethnic groups are preferred in a multicultural society. [12] Residents of the society have been reminded not only of their own ethnicity but of the differences between themselves and the new immigrants.

While Canada has taken in 13.4 million immigrants since 1901, the highest number admitted in any decade since 1931 arrived between 1991 and 2001. During that decade, 2.2 million entered Canada, compared to 1.3 million in the previous decade. Thus, rather than being important only during the initial settlement of the country, immigration is continuing and increasing in importance.[13] Repeated waves of immigration have made ethnicity a livelier issue in Canada than it would be in a society where immigration had ceased or was minimal.

4. In-Group Solidarity

There are two ways of describing ethnic identity. Knowledge or pride about one's ethnic origin is referred to as *symbolic ethnic identity*. But outward expressions of ethnicity, such as speaking a heritage language, belonging to an ethnic organization, or choosing friends or marriage partners from within an ethnic group, are referred to as *behavioural ethnic identity*.[14] Ethnic identity is more easily consolidated when ethnicity is translated into participation in an ethnic organization. In an unfamiliar social world, the individual can find in the minority group an alternative society with more congenial norms, customs, and values.

The importance of ethnic organizations in sustaining ethnic loyalties varies with ethnic group. Raymond Breton coined the term *institutional completeness* to refer to the degree to which ethnic communities provide a structure of organizations providing most of the services their members require.[15] Ethnic periodicals, welfare organizations, medical care, retail outlets, religious institutions, and even sports clubs provide a wide range of the services needed by the ethnic-group member.[16] According to Breton, the more institutionally complete an ethnic group (i.e., the more services available to the group member within the ethnic group), the greater the likelihood that social interaction with the rest of the society will be limited. Breton found relatively high institutional completeness among Greek, German, Hungarian, Italian, Lithuanian, Polish, and Ukrainian groups, and low institutional completeness among Austrian, Belgian, Spanish, and Swedish ethnic groups.

The greater the difference between the ethnic group and the predominant culture in an area, the greater the likelihood that the ethnic group will be more institutionally complete. *Social distance* refers to the fact that cultural differences can distinguish ethnic groups even when different groups are living in close physical proximity. In anglo-Canada, a British immigrant is not nearly as socially distant from the dominant culture as is an Italian or an Asian Indian; hence his/her ethnic group is of less importance to the Briton.

Group solidarity or cohesiveness is related not only to social distance and institutional completeness but to other variables as well. The size of a group in a given location and the tendency to marry within the group (*endogamy*) are also important. Perhaps most significant is retention of the ethnic language; this may be the factor that most clearly distinguishes the group member from the outsider.[17]

Numerous studies have shown that many ethnic groups have developed mechanisms to tie their own people together. We have seen that the English elite developed institutions and mechanisms to maintain its own ethnic superiority. As we shall see, the French have been very successful in ensuring their own relative institutional completeness. In Toronto, where they are the second largest ethnic group, the Italians have grocery stores, newspapers, television shows, churches, social clubs, and social/medical assistance groups, all of which enhance group solidarity.[18] The Jewish community in Canada has likewise established its own institutions (to a large extent centred around the synagogue) to provide assistance to new immigrants and to support Jews and Jewish causes in other countries; these institutions also serve to sustain Jewish identity in Canada.[19] The Greek community in Montreal has approximately 60 organizations serving a variety of this ethnic group's needs.[20] Pakistani Muslims, who previously formed an "incipient" community, have now—as a consequence of the infusion of immigrants in recent years—been able to establish a wide range of structures to accommodate their kinfolk.[21]

To some extent, these ethnic associations may represent transitional institutions which help immigrants adjust to their host society. Ethnic organizations may even go into decline as the first generation of immigrants ages if no fresh wave of immigration arrives from the country of origin (this has happened in the Hungarian community).[22] Nevertheless, in-group solidarity will remain important for some people because of intense ethnic loyalties, or because of perceived social distance between themselves and the dominant ethnic groups in their area. Ethnic organizations, moreover, can contribute to the *politicization of ethnicity*; i.e., the articulation of ethnic group interests to the wider society. Thus we may be made aware of ethnic concerns and differences through organizations whose mandate is the advancement of ethnic interests.

5. Visible Minorities

Throughout this chapter, the concept of ethnicity has been used in a manner which implies that ethnicity includes race. Race and ethnicity are clearly not the same thing, though they may be related. A *racial group* is physically identifiable, while an *ethnic group* is culturally identifiable. It is possible to be of the same race but culturally different (e.g., Caucasians may be either British or French), just as it is possible to be of the same culture

RESEARCH CLIP 5.1	**Toronto: A World in a City**

There is no better illustration of how immigration is changing Canada than what is happening in Toronto. At one time a very British city, Toronto has undergone a massive transformation, becoming what is now probably the most multicultural city in the world. Forty-four percent of Toronto's population is now foreign-born. Other high-immigration cities have lower proportions of foreign-born; for example, Miami (40%), Sydney (31%), Los Angeles (31%), and New York City (24%).

Furthermore, of those arriving in Canada between 1991 and 2001, 43% went to Toronto—a much higher percentage than went to Vancouver (18%) or Montreal (12%). The recency of this transformation is revealed by the fact that 39% of all immigrants in the metropolitan area arrived during that decade; together these new-comers made up 17% of Toronto's population.

Most of the immigrants who came to Toronto prior to 1961 were from Europe; now most come from Asia. Almost 80% of all immigrants who came to Toronto in the last decade belonged to visible minorities. Visible minorities now represent 37% of Toronto's population, up from 25% in 1991, and about the same as the percentage in the Vancouver metropolitan region. About 10% of the city's population is South Asian, 9% is Chinese, 7% is Black, and 3% is Filipino. Put another way: Of all Canada's South Asians, 52% live in metropolitan Toronto, as do 40% of its Chinese, 47% of its Blacks, and 43% of its Filipinos. Markham, Richmond Hill, Mississauga, and Brampton are the suburban municipalities with the highest concentrations of visible-minority populations.

Source: Statistics Canada, The Daily, "Canada's Ethnocultural Portrait: The Changing Mosaic," January 21, 2003. For an excellent discussion of this change, see Paul Anisef and Michael Lanphier, eds., *The World in a City* (Toronto: University of Toronto Press, 2003).

but racially different (e.g., Americans may be either white or Black). Because of the visibility of race, racial differences frequently precipitate a complex of cultural differences. People who are of the same race but of different ethnic backgrounds may have to work harder to sustain their cultural differences when they live together in the same society. For purposes of this discussion, *ethnicity* includes race, and the term will be used to refer to any group whose culture sets it apart. But it is important to understand that race itself is a significant factor in Canada, where Caucasians have been the dominant group.[23] In this context, non-Caucasian groups are referred to as "visible minorities."

Race is a highly visible distinction. It is something that no amount of cultural adaptation can eradicate. Skin colour identifies people to each other, leading to the development of generalizations or *stereotypes* about persons whose skin colour is different. Both *prejudice* (as an attitude) and *discrimination* (as behaviour arising from that attitude) may occur when people associate race with cultural attributes or behavioural traits with which they are unfamiliar and to which they feel superior. Indeed, many groups of non-European (i.e., non-Caucasian) origin have experienced social and job discrimination in Canada.[24]

Non-white immigration to Canada was initially related to the importation (after 1834) of Blacks as slaves, or to the arrival of escaped slaves from the United States to Ontario and Nova Scotia.[25] Through the 1880s, Chinese were brought into British Columbia to work on the Canadian Pacific Railway; some Japanese and East Indians also came to Canada during that period. Each of these Asian groups encountered a generally hostile reaction from most members of the host Caucasian society. A head tax of $10 was imposed on Chinese immigrants in 1884 and gradually raised to $500 by 1904.[26] A Chinese exclusion law banning poor Chinese immigrants was passed in 1923 and not repealed until 1947. Chinese were sometimes denied the right to vote and were excluded from certain occupations, which restricted their employment opportunities to the running of laundries and restaurants. Japanese immigrants faced many of the same restrictions, but were tolerated because they too provided cheap labour.[27] After the Japanese attack on Pearl Harbor during World War II, Japanese people in Canada were interned in remote camps, and many lost all they had. Through the years, federal policy has always been basically racist; non-white immigration was discouraged. It was not until after World War II and even later, when the point system was established as the basis for immigrant selection, that the more obvious forms of *institutional discrimination* were reduced.

Institutional racism refers to systematic and legal social practices that are rationalized by the belief in the superiority or preferability of one group over another.[28] The right to exclude certain groups because of their physical characteristics, to deny them the vote, to relegate them to low-paid work or pay them according to a differential pay-scale have all been part of Canada's past. But even if the legal mechanisms that support such overt racism are removed, discrimination can still exist. In fact, while the old discrimination was based on skin colour and appearance, the new discrimination allows racism to operate more covertly by *denying* the relevance of race and attempting to apply universal standards.[29] Henry and others have proposed the term *democratic racism* to refer to the coexistence of two competing sets of values: democratic principles of justice and equality versus negative attitudes/behaviours towards minority groups and the differential treatment of those groups.[30] Thus, Canadian values of fairness and openness do not always match up with our actual behaviour; in consequence, immigrants from non-traditional source countries may find themselves at a competitive disadvantage because of their race.[31]

It could be argued that significant improvements have occurred in intergroup relations over the past 40 years. And yet, racial controversy in both its cultural and economic dimensions (see Chapter Three on ethnic stratification) has taken on new importance. Tolerance and appreciation of differences may represent ideals that many people have difficulty putting into practice. While Nova Scotia Blacks and British Columbia Chinese and Japanese have a long history as visible minorities in Canada,[32] they have more recently been joined by immigrants from the West Indies, Haiti, Vietnam, Hong Kong, Taiwan, China, India, and many other countries. Each of these immigrant groups brings with it a cultural and racial identity. For example, Blacks from Haiti bring with them their French language, while Blacks from the West Indies typically use English and their culture reflects many years of British cultural influence. Rather than finding cohesion with others of their racial group, these visible minorities maintain important cultural/ethnic differences. *The Employment Equity Act* defines *visible minorities* as all persons who are non-Caucasian in race or non-white in colour (but excludes Aboriginal people, whom we will discuss later in the chapter).

Thus, visible minorities—and the Caucasian response to them—also contribute to the centrality of ethnicity as an issue in Canadian society. Visible minorities represent about

13.4% of the Canadian population—up considerably from 4.7% in 1981, largely as the result of immigration. During the 1990s, 73% of all immigrants belonged to visible minorities, although about one third of all members of visible minorities were born in Canada (the group most likely to be Canadian-born was of Japanese origin). Figure 5.3 indicates that in 2001 the Chinese, at 25%, were the largest visible-minority group; they were closely followed by South Asians at 23%, then Blacks at 17%. Together these three groups make up about two thirds of all Canada's visible minorities. Current global demographic pressures suggest that 100 years from now, Canadian society will have a very different ethnic and racial character than it does now—just as it has been transformed by demographic pressures over the last 100 years.

6. Unresolved Aboriginal Issues

As the original peoples of the Canadian territory were swept aside by European settlement, Europeans assumed that domination and assimilation would eventually remove "the Indian problem." But if French Canadians have defied all odds and retained their language and culture on an anglophone continent, it is much more remarkable that Native groups, lacking similar institutional supports, have embarked on a rediscovery of their own group identity. The assimilationist objectives of Euro-Canadians in relation to Aboriginal peoples have been both a failure and an international embarrassment. High unemployment, low incomes, and poor housing among Native people, in combination with anger, alienation, and even self-destructive behaviour, have intensified Aboriginality as a public issue in Canadian society.[33]

| FIGURE 5.3 | Visible Minority Population in Canada by Group, 2001 |

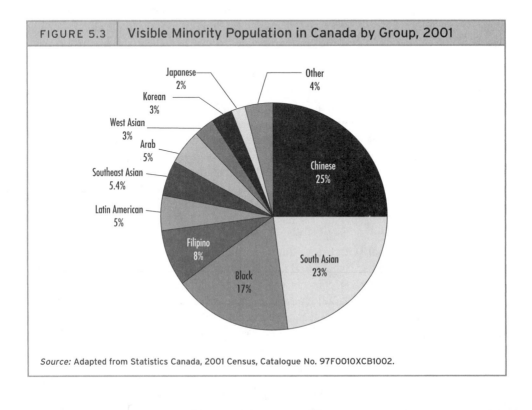

Source: Adapted from Statistics Canada, 2001 Census, Catalogue No. 97F0010XCB1002.

Visible-Minority Neighbourhoods

Territoriality is an important factor in raising the profile of ethnicity and race. The number of visible-minority neighborhoods (i.e., neighbourhoods where visible minorities make up over 30% of the population) has grown dramatically. In 1981, there were only 6 such neighbourhoods in Canada; by 1991 there were 77, and by 2001 there were 254. Toronto had over half (135) of these neighbourhoods, and Vancouver had 44% (111). Montreal only had 8 such neighborhoods. Sixty percent of these neighbourhoods were Chinese, and one third were South Asian.

Source: Feng Hou and Garnett Picot, "Visible Minority Neighbourhoods in Toronto, Montreal, and Vancouver," *Canadian Social Trends* 72 (2004). Statistics Canada Catalogue 11-008.

As a reaction against dependency and domination, Native groups have attempted to secure more direct control over their destiny and to reverse the downward spiral of cultural confusion. Along with a new collective consciousness, a new Aboriginal leadership has arisen that has begun to confront established elites and oppressive conditions; this has led to a new level of negotiations between Aboriginal peoples and the state to redefine their place in Canadian society. Rejecting, just as French Canadians have, the notion that they are "just another ethnic group," First Nations perceive themselves as the original peoples and founding nations of this territory.

First Nations are now in a process of *decolonialization.* Having been dehumanized by colonization, Aboriginal people (as post-colonialists) are attempting to reverse the negative effects they have incurred. This shift in stance from quiescent subordination to activist negotiation as "nations within"[34] amplifies the issue of ethnic relations in Canadian society. We will return to this topic in more detail later in the chapter.

The discussion of the preceding six factors is not meant to be exhaustive but rather to suggest why ethnicity has been a vital issue in Canadian society and will continue to be so for some time to come. The structure and substance of ethnic diversity have changed over time, and new generations of Canadian-born children will develop different feelings about their ethnic background and new ways to express it. Nevertheless, the continuation of immigration, in conjunction with government policies encouraging the maintenance of ethnic traditions and identities, has supported ethnicity as an important underlying variable in the population. At the very least, ongoing negotiation with Canada's First Peoples, and between the French and English charter groups, politicizes ethnicity as a major factor in Canadian society and reminds others of their own ethnic origins.

THE MOST DOMINANT FORMS OF GROUP CONFLICT

The fact that a wide variety of ethnic backgrounds are represented in a society is of greater importance if ethnicity is a significant basis for group formation among members of the society. Furthermore, the mere presence of minority groups does not in itself mean that ethnic conflict will ensue. A minority group may accept its subordinate status quite passively unless resistance is sparked by two factors: a feeling of deprivation and a sense of group awareness.

Differing Perspectives

Structural Functionalism

Racial and ethnic differences accentuate the fact that society is a kaleidoscopic mix of diverse groups that must be "managed" or accommodated to ensure its effective functioning. Rather than emphasizing how race and ethnicity are divisive, efforts must be made to help racial and ethnic groups feel more comfortable within Canadian society (e.g., by policies such as multiculturalism) and to explore ways of breaking down barriers (e.g., by providing language training, skills development, or entrepreneurship programs to facilitate adaptation). When minorities organize themselves to challenge their marginalized position, efforts must be made to address their concerns so that society can be stabilized. Recent arrivals into the country should expect to start at the bottom and work their way to the position they deserve by their own efforts. If that outcome is not achieved in their own lifetimes, at least some persons from the next generation should benefit from an open society.

Conflict

Dominant groups use racial and ethnic differences as ways to sustain their own position of power and privilege. Members of some groups may gain acceptance over time if they are able to acculturate to the dominant group, but other groups almost seem to be permanently disadvantaged. Even upon entering Canada some new immigrants enjoy more privileges than others, who may experience various forms of discrimination because of their place of origin or skin colour. Visible minorities in particular may constantly struggle with prejudice and be unable to find full acceptance into the society. Partially as a defence mechanism and also to provide mutual support, racial and ethnic groups may form solidarities to challenge the status quo. In any case, racial and ethnic differences often serve as mobilizing factors in the face of power differentials that sustain division in society.

Symbolic Interactionism

Race and ethnicity are an essential part of the personal identity of all people—whether they are aware of it or not. Each individual learns of his/her racial or ethnic identity through a process of negotiation and interaction with others in the society. In some cases, this identity becomes very public, through the individual's identification with customs, language, and other aspects of culture; in others, it is highly private and hidden. The way in which personal identities are related to familial groups, reference groups, and ultimately to the dominant group in society (which strives to create a society-wide collective identity) tells us a lot about how subgroups are related to and interact with the national society.

Relative deprivation is the disadvantage a group feels upon comparing its own status or opportunities with those of another group. For example, upon beginning to compare their status with that of the English (especially in the 1960s), the French began to resent their subordinate status, and conflict became more explicit. *Group awareness* is the consciousness of kind or of unity felt by persons who share similar characteristics. For example, when Canadian Native people, who were for many years just a loose aggregation of dispersed bands, began to develop a sense of group awareness in relation to the more dominant group, a collective sense of power developed. Thus as an ethnic group becomes more conscious of itself as a comparatively disadvantaged group and takes the next step to transform that situation, the likelihood of ethnic-group conflict increases.

The two most visible and unresolved ethnic-group conflicts in Canadian society are the French–English conflict and the Aboriginal–non-Aboriginal conflict; these dominate the public agenda. We will discuss each in turn.

QUEBEC AND FRENCH-ENGLISH RELATIONS

A phrase that is typically used to describe Canadian society is "two solitudes" or "two nations warring within one bosom." The reality of two ethnic groups with different ideas about the shape of Canadian coexistence has been maintained to a large extent by considerable territorial segregation. Nowhere is this clearer than in the comparison of the two provinces in Canada with the largest populations: Ontario and Quebec. In Ontario, persons of British ethnic origin are the largest single ethnic group and persons of French descent are a minority; in Quebec, on the other hand, the overwhelming majority of the population is of French descent and a small minority of English descent. Quebec is also 83% Catholic, whereas Ontario is only 35% Catholic. When it comes to the language most frequently used at home, 82% of Ontarians use English and 3% use French; in Quebec, however, 83% use French and 10% use English. These figures illustrate why these two neighbouring provinces represent such different conceptions of society. Evidence presented in Chapter One suggests that these differences also make Quebec unique in relation to other provinces.

The Evolution of Quebec Society

In contrast to many of the early settlements in the United States, which were populated by people wanting to break ties with the Old Country, the early French settlements were populated not by dissenters but by people who wanted to *retain* ties to France through church, state, and commerce. Initially, therefore, the key persons in these settlements were administrators, missionaries, traders, and explorers. Monière has argued that even after the conquest of the French by the British in 1759, there was a vitality to the francophone community that was only suppressed by the defeat of the Patriots in the 1837–38 Rebellion.[35] This rebellion represented Quebec francophones' first movement towards independence.

What did the British conquest imply for Quebec society? First of all, it caused resentments and antagonisms towards the British that were sometimes submerged, but never obliterated. Conquest, along with all that it came to symbolize, has been referred to as a *primordial event* because it left an indelible mark on the French-Canadian people, producing a minority complex which they have struggled to overcome.[36] The second effect of the conquest was the *social decapitation* of Quebec. The previous French leadership, which returned to France, was replaced by British leadership, particularly in political administration and in mercantile commercialism. Thus, a pattern of anglophone control was established which also produced resentment. The third effect was related to the French community's mission to preserve their language and culture on the continent (what has been called "*the beacon of light*" theme); in order to do so, the French community insulated itself against alien British influence by organizing the agricultural *habitant* family around the small-town parish. Parish priests emerged as the leaders of this society, buttressing French identity by promoting both Catholicism and the French language in the midst of anglophone Protestantism and the English language. The ideology that emerged from this blend of church and state, the primacy of agriculture and rejection of industrialization, and the belief in the moral mission of French Canadians in North America is known as *ultramontanism*.

The British were content not to interfere with French culture, because British ambitions for Canada revolved primarily around economic development. In exchange for their subordination to British political and economic control, the French were allowed control over their own culture, which was focused at that time on parish and school life. The *Quebec Act* of 1774 restored French civil law and placed education under the control of the Catholic church. Quebec's will to survive as a French cultural entity led to *agrarian isolationism,* which was reflected by defensive and conservative Quebec governments. Led by doctrinally conservative priests (many of whom had fled France in disagreement with the liberalizing effects of the French Revolution) and supported by an extremely high fertility rate, the French-Canadian community succeeded in preserving its cohesiveness and strength.[37] In fact, the community grew to the point of overpopulation, which caused great numbers of francophones to migrate to the New England states to seek the employment opportunities that industrialization had created there.[38]

Anglophone dominance went largely unquestioned as long as Quebec remained rural and agrarian. By the middle decades of the twentieth century, however, significant changes had occurred. These included greater urbanization and the growth of an emergent industrial complex centred around textiles. Cheap hydroelectric power and capitalist demand for natural resources contributed to a significant movement away from agriculture as the material basis of the population. Accompanying these changes was a decline in the birth rate, along with a desire for an education oriented towards active participation in the technological society. In sum, increasing urbanization, secularization (i.e., in the cities, the church was no longer the centre of community life), and industrialization brought the French community in more direct contact with the anglophone elite and capitalist structures.[39] This contact became the source of a sense of group awareness, and a sense of relative deprivation emerged among francophone Quebecers.

The defeat of the provincial Union Nationale party in 1960 by the Liberals is usually viewed as symbolic of a changing world view in Quebec. This change became known as the *Quiet Revolution.* Underlying the Quiet Revolution were urbanization and industrialization, which had two class-related effects. The first was the growth of a industrial working class, who developed a critical view of anglophone capitalist exploitation.[40] The second was the growth of a new middle class of white-collar workers in the public sector (and to some extent also in the private sector), who saw their ambitions for upward social mobility blocked by anglophone dominance and control.[41] Learning English and discarding French accents were typically viewed as measures necessary for success in the anglophone system; such changes, however, could not alter the fact that anglophones were both the owners of capital and the real decision-makers in Quebec. As a result of this entrenched anglophone dominance, francophone Quebecers sought changes in French–English relations and a restructuring of traditional Quebec society.

The first thrust of the Quiet Revolution was devoted to *rattrapage* ("catching up") in order to bring Quebec into the stream of modern Western economic development. The provincial Ministry of Education, created in 1964, replaced church-controlled education

Quebec: The Velocity of Demographic Social Change

The socio-political and demographic changes which have occurred in Quebec are not only fascinating but tell a significant story with enormous implications for the future.

The research of Caldwell and Fournier has shown that the 1960s were a significant turning point for Quebec—in fact, the province set a global record in the industrialized world for rapid change from a high to a low birth rate. In the late 1950s Quebec still had one of the highest fertility rates among industrialized societies, but by the 1980s the fertility rate had dropped to the bottom, close to that of the Scandinavian countries. In 1954 the birth rate was 31.0 per thousand; by 1984 it had dropped to 13.4 per thousand. The birth rate fell to below the replacement level in 1970; thereafter, despite some increase attributable to births to baby boomers (known as the "baby boom echo"), the it declined further. Furthermore, after 1986 the older age-structure of the female population reduced the possibility of increased births.

The second trend of note is the decline in nuptiality. In 1987, Caldwell and Fournier predicted that Quebec was approaching a scenario in which only half of the population would marry and between one quarter and one half of that number divorce, which would further depress the fertility rate. The third trend is the aging of the population as the result of the low fertility rate. By the year 2001, they predicted, almost half of the Quebec population could be over 50 years of age.

What has exacerbated these trends even further is the single most impor-tant factor in the decline of Quebec's growth rate—negative net migration. First, there was a heavy outflow of Quebec residents to other parts of Canada during the '60s and '70s. While some of these out-migrants were francophone, the vast majority were anglophone. This outflow reached its peak during the 1976–1981 era of Parti Québécois rule. Second, the flow of in-migrants from other parts of Canada, as well as international migration, had diminished considerably. By the 1980s French-speaking immigrants from Haiti and Vietnam represented the largest group of new residents (though their numbers were not large). In any case, by the '80s Quebec had become a much more stable francophone society, but with the new demographic problem of shrinking population-growth.

Caldwell and Fournier pointed out that Quebec is not unique in its declining growth rate, but that the extremely rapid and dramatic change has enormous consequences for the future viability of the province. Quebec has not only lost its one-third proportion of the Canadian population, but, according to the researchers, restricted economic expansion and blocked opportunities will result if the growth rate does not improve. While strengthening the boundaries of the francophone linguistic community has enhanced cultural survival, the province cannot ignore the dramatic changes in values and social behaviour that will determine how the society will survive.

Source: Gary Caldwell and Daniel Fournier, "The Quebec Question: A Matter of Population," *Canadian Journal of Sociology* 12 (1987): 16-41.

with a new emphasis on technological and industrial skills, such as engineering and accounting. One result of this change was that university enrollment grew at an unprecedented rate. As a means of fostering economic development, financial aid was given to francophone-owned enterprises, such as the steel corporation SIDBEC. In addition, in an effort to create employment opportunities within the francophone milieu of an important Quebec resource-industry, Hydro-Québec was nationalized in 1962. By these and other means the Quebec government sought not only to encourage Quebec participation in industrial development but also to strengthen francophone control over Quebec's destiny. These measures were adopted with the aim of establishing the Québécois as *maîtres chez nous* ("masters in our own house"). Just as the existing structure of society had excluded francophones from control, so Québécois now sought to challenge the English establishment, to remove the barriers restricting their own opportunities, and to create a new structure of society using a provincial-state apparatus in which their control was clear.[42]

Many of the processes identified with the Quiet Revolution actually began before 1960 and continued on into the 1970s. But in 1970 an event occurred that shattered the stillness of the so-called "quiet" revolution. On October 16, Prime Minister Trudeau invoked the *War Measures Act* in response to the kidnapping of Quebec cabinet minister Pierre Laporte and British High Commissioner James Cross by the terrorist Front de Libération du Québec (FLQ). This event, known as the *October Crisis,* came to symbolize the escalation of the need for change in Quebec and demonstrated the depth of nationalist feeling at the extreme. That was also the year of the much-publicized cavalcade of nine Brinks trucks from Montreal to Toronto, which demonstrated anglo-Canadians' fear of Quebec nationalism. It was also the year in which the avowedly separatist Parti Québécois made political advances by taking about a third of the votes in the provincial election.

During the 1970s the process of *l'épanouissement* ("flowering") continued in Quebec, with heavy reliance on the provincial government as a mechanism of change.[43] During this decade, measures were taken which affected not only the economy but also the culture, with language the dominant issue. Ironically, immigration had made Quebec much more ethnically pluralistic than it had been before—particularly since the declining birth rate made immigration more important. By 1971 only 10.8% of immigrant children were attending French schools.[44] The fact that Quebec was being drawn more tightly into the North American economy also threatened the distinctiveness of the Quebec community. The French language, then, became the mechanism for integrating the Quebec population, regardless of background, and for reinforcing the province's boundaries. Whereas French had once been the language of a particular ethnic group, it was now to become the language of the people of Quebec, regardless of ethnic descent.

Although the separatist Parti Québécois made strong decisions when elected in 1976, its approach to sovereignty was one of *gradualism* ("étapisme"). Bill 101, the Charter of the French Language in Quebec, was passed in 1977, but support for the increased mandatory use of French had been building for some time. French was no longer to be just the language of the shop floor but was to be used by management in all communications throughout both the public and private sectors. To prove their compliance, businesses were required to obtain a *francization certificate.* Immigrant children were to be educated in French. The status of French was to be elevated by ensuring that French lexicons would be available for every application, from computer usage to automobile repair. Flying in the face of the Canadian government's official policy of bilingualism, the government of Quebec made French the official language of Quebec. Whether all of these regulations were enforceable or not may be another matter, but Quebec did take on a clearly French public character.

The Quebec government also became more proactive in other areas. Quebec immigration officers were placed in federal foreign-immigration offices to encourage immigration compatible with the province's cultural goals. The province also began to participate in the francophone commonwealth of nations. A Department of Cultural Affairs was created to strengthen Quebec culture in the face of anglo-Americanization. All of this activity had the effect of strengthening the French character of the province of Quebec, a process symbolized by the transformation of its residents' identity from "French Canadian" to "Québécois."[45]

With a goal of *sovereignty association*—political independence accompanied by economic association (including a common currency) with the rest of Canada—the Quebec government issued in 1979 its White Paper entitled *Quebec–Canada: A New Deal.*[46] This document paved the way for the promised referendum on Quebec independence. Held on May 20, 1980, with an 85.6% voter turnout, the referendum was defeated although 40% voted in favour of independence. The precise meaning of sovereignty association was sufficiently ambiguous, and the supporters of this objective were sufficiently numerous, to allow the results to be interpreted in various ways.[47] It is significant that the separatist position of the Parti Québécois was rejected in the 1980 referendum but the party advocating it was re-elected in 1981. However, when the Parti Québécois was defeated in 1985, the new Liberal government pursued many of the Québécois nationalist themes, though without the threat of independence (until the Meech Lake issue heated up in 1990). In any case, it was widely believed that the independence movement was far from dead.

In sum, since 1960 the Quebec state has abandoned its traditional position of defensive nationalism, adopting instead a philosophy of advocacy and intervention on behalf of its constituent French majority. The provincial government became a means of collective advancement, and frequently its policies challenged the federal government. Refusal to sign the new federal constitution (1982) symbolized Quebec's fusion of historical and contemporary group consciousness.[48]

Herein lies the dilemma of Quebec society within Canadian society. The federal policy of two official languages (bilingualism) was in large measure an attempt to appease Quebec in particular and francophones throughout Canada in general. By redesigning Canada to more clearly include francophones, it was hoped that the two founding partners of Confederation might accept each other in a new way and that the historical anglophone domination of francophones would be forgotten. However, instead of embracing bilingualism, Quebec has increasingly supported greater unilingualism, challenging federal policy.

Quebec's refusal to sign the new Constitution in 1982 was precisely over the issue of its ability to control its own future as a society. Embarrassed at having a Constitution not ratified by the province containing one quarter of Canada's people, Prime Minister Mulroney sought and obtained the support of Quebec (and of the other provinces) for what is known as the Meech Lake Accord, signed on April 30, 1987.[49] The thrust of the accord was the decentralization of more power and authority to provincial governments in matters such as immigration and the selection of Senate members. For Quebec, however, what was perhaps the agreement's most significant feature—and the most controversial for some of the other provinces—was the recognition of Quebec as a "distinct" society. This phrase implied that in significant ways Quebec was different from the rest of Canada, although it

The Royal Commission on Bilingualism and Biculturalism

The social changes occurring in Quebec in the 1960s challenged anglophone dominance, which had relegated francophones to inferior positions in the work world, postulated English unilingualism in federal government institutions, and expected the disappearance of the French language and culture. A cultural awakening was underway, French traditions were being defended, and the spectre of Quebec separatism was being raised. The federal government was sensitive to these changes and appointed a Royal Commission to explore the concept of Canada as a bilingual and bicultural society.

The Report of the RCBB fundamentally restructured Canadian culture. One of the key results was the *Official Languages Act,* passed in 1969, which made both French and English official languages in Canada. This Act attempted to give both languages equal status, whether on product labels, on airline-flight announcements, or in the federal civil service.

The Commission distinguished between *individual bilingualism* (command of both languages) and *institutional* or *state bilingualism* (the provision of services in both languages in principal public and private institutions) and opted for the latter. At the same time, education in both English and French was to be available throughout the country. Language training was to be made available to the federal civil service in particular, so that both language groups would be qualified for management positions and the Canadian public could be served in both official languages.

The establishment of the equality of both languages in order to make Canada "an equal partnership between the two founding races" still generates debate. But perhaps the most unexpected outcome was the response of those who were neither French nor English—the so-called "third force" of persons of other ethnic origins. Pressure from this plurality of ethnic groups (particularly in the West), who also sought recognition and acceptance, led to the deletion of the word "biculturalism" and its replacement with "bilingualism within a multicultural framework," and eventually to the policy of multiculturalism.

Further Reading

The multi-volume Report of the Commission is a valuable, if cumbersome, piece to read. A one-volume abridged edition by Hugh R. Innis, *Bilingualism and Biculturalism* (Toronto: McClelland and Stewart, 1973) presents the highlights of the original report.

was unclear what implications this recognition had for the rest of Canada or for Quebec.[50] What some viewed as a explicit recognition of an existing fact, others viewed as the conferring on Quebec of a special status that threatened Canadian unity, while still others viewed the acknowledgement as merely another step towards Quebec independence. For these reasons, the "distinct society" clause in the Meech Lake agreement became a critical issue for all Canadians.

Indicators of Quebec as a Distinct Society

1. Over 80% of the population have French as a mother tongue and continue to use it as a home language. Language is a symbolic marker of a distinct collectivity.

2. The term "Québécois" reflects an intimate relationship between culture and personal identity (i.e., who I am and how I relate to others).

3. Quebec is the only province in Canada that has several times elected a government whose explicit platform has been the removal of that province from the existing Canadian federation.

4. Quebec has had many distinct institutions, such as a dual confessional public school system, the *caisses populaires* (alternatives to national banks), and CEGEPS (public colleges).

5. Quebec understands itself as distinct as a totality (not just as the random sum of its parts); this understanding initially embraced primarily francophone Quebecers but now attempts to embrace all residents of the province.

6. Quebec has a distinct sense of history and nationhood that began before the Conquest and is reflected in the phrase *Je me souviens* ("I remember"), printed on automobile licence plates.

7. The provincial state has been empowered to intervene in and regulate the society in order to promote the collective identity.

Further Reading: Marcel Fournier, Michael Rosenberg, and Deena White, eds., *Quebec Society: Critical Issues* (Scarborough, ON: Prentice Hall, 1997)—particularly the Introduction and Chapter 4 by Greg Neilsen, "Culture and the Politics of Being Québécois: Identity and Communication."

The 1987 *Meech Lake Accord* was initially an agreement made by the ten provincial premiers and the federal government after protracted bargaining behind closed doors. Each premier was to obtain ratification from his provincial legislature within three years. The problem was that during that interim period some provinces changed governments, and the new leadership did not necessarily feel bound by the commitment to the original agreement. This was particularly the case with Manitoba and Newfoundland, where the strongest opposition to the Accord was expressed. Despite feverish last-minute negotiations, Newfoundland failed to even put the Accord to a vote, and Manitoba was unable to put the accord to a vote because unanimous consent could not be obtained for the suspension of normal legislative procedures to consider this issue. In consequence, the Meech Lake Accord died on June 23, 1990.

The failure of Meech Lake is generally thought to have precipitated another national crisis. Not only was Quebec still not part of the constitutional process, but the province claimed that the failure to recognize its unique status was tantamount to rejection by the rest of Canada. Premier Bourassa then announced that Quebec would not return to the bargaining table, would deal only with the federal government and not the provinces in on-going matters, and would activate a commission to explore alternatives for the province's future. Ironically, it was the refusal of the only Native member of the Manitoba legislature,

Elijah Harper, to provide consent—on the grounds that Native peoples had been totally ignored in the constitutional process and that they too were a distinct society—that held up final ratification in that province. Thus, instead of serving as a mechanism of unity, Meech Lake fostered discord and new uncertainty.

Another attempt to bring Quebec in under acceptable constitutional arrangements was made in 1992, in what is known as the *Charlottetown Accord.*[51] This agreement had many of the same features as the Meech Lake Accord. In particular, it acknowledged that Quebec was a distinct society, guaranteed Quebec 25% of the seats in the House of Commons, and accepted the principle of *asymmetrical federalism* (in other words, that Quebec was a special case and not just the same as other provinces). Yet in the months between the agreement and the national referendum held to ratify it on October 26, 1992, support for the Accord unravelled as a result of challenges from both former Prime Minister Trudeau and the Reform Party, and even as a result of Prime Minister Mulroney's own declining popularity. Even in Quebec support faltered. The uncertainty of the meaning and consequences of the distinct society idea, along with the opposing attitudes of francophones ("it does not go far enough") and anglophones ("it goes too far"), clearly played a major role in under-

Renegotiating Quebec's Place in Canadian Society: A Chronology

Perhaps the key feature of efforts to establish a renewed Canadian polity has been the search for some way to acknowledge the uniqueness of Quebec as a distinct society. The chronology of the major events is as follows:

Constitution Act 1982

The federal government, in what is known in Quebec as "the night of the long knives" (in reference to a meeting to discuss compromise to which they were not invited), proceeded to adopt a new Canadian Constitution without the support of Quebec.

Meech Lake Accord

Signed in 1987, but failed to win the approval of all provinces in 1990

Charlottetown Agreement

Rejected in a national referendum held October 26, 1992.
Results: 55% No – 45% Yes

National Elections in 1993 and 1997

The consequences of the failure to resolve Quebec's place within Canadian society were the formation of the sovereigntist Bloc Québécois, which elected members to the Canadian Parliament in 1993 (ironically becoming the official opposition party), and the provincial election of the Parti Québécois in 1994 with a clear agenda of sovereignty. In the West, the Reform Party, which wanted to block Quebec's claim for special status, arose in the 1993 election and became the official opposition in 1997, stepping into the place of the Bloc Québécois. These two elections clearly divided the country along regional lines. The Liberal party won the election primarily because it took most of the seats in Ontario, Canada's most populous province.

mining the agreement. In the end, the referendum was defeated 55% "No" to 45% "Yes." Opposition was strongest in the West and in Quebec, and support was strongest in the Atlantic provinces, except for Nova Scotia (51% No). Ontario accepted the agreement but only barely, with a 51% margin. In any case, establishing a clear place for Quebec within Canadian society remains unfinished business.

Amidst frustration at the inability to achieve a reconciliation, a feeling emerged among some francophones (and even some anglophones) that the time for compromise and negotiation was over and it was time for Quebec to decide once and for all.[52] The 1995 Quebec referendum provided the opportunity for Quebec to do so, and yet its exceedingly close vote resolved nothing. In fact, support for sovereignty was 10% greater than it had been in the first referendum in 1980, and another referendum in the near future appears likely. Perhaps the key factor in a significant last-minute increase in "Yes" support was the shift in the campaign strategy from an insistence on "sovereignty" to the idea of "sovereignty partnership," which emphasized the negotiation and retention of links with Canada.[53] The Canadian government, however, took the issue of the legality of Quebec's potential unilateral declaration of independence to the Supreme Court, which in 1998 ruled that—providing a "clear" referendum question produced a "clear" result—independence could not be declared unilaterally but must be negotiated by both sides in good faith. In 2000 the government of Canada passed the *Clarity Act,* which set out the the protocols, both procedural ("was the referendum question clear?") and substantive ("was the majority adequate?"), for a valid referendum on the secession question. Thus negotiation and change continue to be elusive ideals in the effort to preserve the Canadian entity.[54]

Understanding Quebec Nationalism

In many developing societies, modernization has meant the blurring of cultural distinctions as foreign influences have led to massive changes within the traditional society. Somewhat paradoxically, Quebec has experienced both social change and economic development at the same time as the sharpening of cultural distinctions. Instead of yielding to the pressures of anglo-conformity, Quebec has accentuated its cultural uniqueness. What underlying forces have made this development possible? How can we understand this surge of nationalist spirit? While this is a very complex matter which resists simple explanations, five interpretations can be offered.

The most obvious explanation is the *historical resistance to colonialism*, which was heightened by the more direct contact with anglophones that resulted from industrialization and urbanization. Industrialization only accentuated the issue of anglophone control (whether Canadian or American) and provoked a collective spirit of resistance to that control, most strongly expressed as Quebec's desire for complete independence. While this explanation does not explain who led the resistance, the implication is that only when anglophones and francophones came into *competition* with each other through urbanization (in contrast to francophones' previous isolationism) did reaction to colonialism became more heated.[55]

The second and third explanations suggest that the new spirit developed because specific social groups sought to destroy Quebec's double class structure—the francophone world on the one hand and the anglophone world on the other. One explanation points to the role of the *francophone bourgeoisie,* whose economic interests were well served by the ideology of the Quiet Revolution and sovereignty association. A stronger state which

The 1995 Referendum: A National Crisis

October 30, 1995

"Do you agree that Quebec should become sovereign after having made a formal offer to Canada for a new economic and political partnership, within the scope of the Bill respecting the future of Quebec and of the agreement signed on June 12, 1995?"

Results: No   50.6%
                  Yes   49.4%

Turnout: 94% of 4.8 million eligible voters

Spoiled ballots: 86 000 (more than the margin of difference between the two sides)

The Campaign in National Context

This referendum precipitated the greatest crisis in Canadian history, as the possibility of an independent Quebec and a fractured Canada was driven home to many Canadians who had previously conceived of Quebec nationalism as a minority dream. In the last two weeks of the campaign, as the momentum shifted under the leadership of the charismatic Lucien Bouchard, many Canadians began to panic and a great outpouring of emotion supporting a united Canada was expressed. On the Friday before the referendum, a rally in Montreal attracted 100 000 people from all over the country, pleading with Quebecers to stay in Canada. Throughout the weekend, rallies were held in other parts of Canada, prayer vigils were organized, telephone companies offered free phone-calls to Quebec, airlines lowered their fares to Montreal, and children wrote letters imploring Quebec to keep Canada united. The campaign prompted the most fervent and spontaneous expression of Canadian nationalism in history.

The Meaning of the Results

Questions have been raised about the variant meanings of the terms "sovereignty" and "partnership" and about the complexity of the referendum question. Polls indicated that some Quebecers expected a sovereign Quebec to still remain part of Canada and to continue to send representatives to Ottawa. The meaning of a "Yes" vote is therefore ambiguous. Was it primarily an expression of ethnic pride, a mandate for a strong negotiating position, or a clear declaration of independence?

The Internal Division of Quebec Society

While 90% of anglophones and allophones (persons of non-English/non-French mother-tongue) voted "No," francophones themselves were divided on the issue, even though approximately 60% voted "Yes." Many rural areas were especially supportive of the "Yes" side, while in Montreal both the francophone east end and anglophone/allophone west end supported the "No" side. The "Yes" side was also not as strong as expected in Quebec City, though it did have the majority. The intensity of feeling on both sides within the province, compounded by linguistic/ethnic and rural–urban divisions, amplified the uncertainties of the future.

Just days prior to the referendum, the Cree and Inuit of northern Quebec held their own referendums on Quebec sovereignty as a way of declaring their own position, which was one of near-unanimous opposition. Aboriginal people threatened to withdraw their territory (added to the province's borders in 1898) in the event of independence; for Quebec, this would have meant the loss of natural resources and the gigantic James Bay hydroelectric project. This action marked the beginning of *partitionism*, expressed by some anglophone/allophone groups as well: the argument that a particular region had the right to stay in Canada and reject any decision to secede.

Outside Quebec, the federal government shifted from Plan A (which sought reconciliation as a means to preserving unity) to Plan B (which sought to specify the precise terms (including legality and costs) under which Canada would allow separation to occur (a type of "tough love" scenario). As a gesture of appeasement, the Canadian government also immediately passed a resolution (not the same as a Constitutional amendment) recognizing Quebec as a distinct society.

protected francophones from alien influences meant the strengthening of Quebec's francophone business class, and the new spirit was congenial because it challenged the competing Canadian bourgeoisie.[56] Gagnon and Montcalm have argued that francophone entrepreneurs have risen to new prominence in Quebec because of that province's growing economic peripheralization in the continental economy (which still has not been reversed).[57] In any case, it is widely recognized that the francophone business class have been the clear winners in the Quiet Revolution.

Quebec nationalism served the interests not only of the francophone elite but also of the new middle class of young, university-educated, upwardly mobile francophones who were angered by obstacles to mobility within Quebec. Thus, the *rise of the new middle class* provides a third explanation for the new Quebec spirit.[58] Confident of their own abilities and frustrated by the barriers and control encountered in anglophone corporations, these francophones found government, government corporations, and government agencies to be growth industries in the economic development of Quebec. During the 1960s, the number of civil servants mushroomed from 32 000 to 70 000.[59] Here these ambitious young people could not only find employment but also exert policy control. Thus the new middle class strongly supported and participated in provincial state intervention. Indeed, research has shown that Quebecers embracing the new "Québécois" identity were likely to be younger and possess higher levels of education than those preferring the old French-Canadian label.[60] It has been pointed out that "intellectuals" (e.g., scientists, scholars, teachers), as part of this middle class, play a role through their written and oral presentations in the dissemination of new ways of thinking about Quebec.[61]

The fourth and fifth explanations suggest that Quebec has undergone too-rapid social change. The swiftness of social change, which involved the destruction of the old order, produced uncertainty; in the face of this uncertainty,some people sought to reassert traditional values, while others had new ideas about the direction in which things should move. Rather than deal with internal disagreement, one solution to confusion was to *direct internal aggression against outsiders.*[62] The need to unite against external threat provided the basis for much collective action which would not have been possible in other circumstances. Fifth, the changes within Quebec also reflected an *intense desire to forge a new identity.*[63] The movement for greater self-determination was meaningful to Quebecers who sought a new image, a new self-concept, and a new and more modern collective identity. Coleman notes that the replacement of the old values with North American materialist values produced an identity crisis and sense of loss in Quebec which was translated into an active search for a distinctive culture.[64] Finding their new image in the designation "Québécois," many strove to forge a new identity by uniting ethnicity and polity in an assertion of nationalist sentiment.

Evaluating Forty Years of Change

There is no question that Quebec has indeed undergone massive change and that its provincial government has taken significant steps to change the province since 1960. We are now in a position to begin to evaluate these initiatives in terms of their results.[65]

One of the major indicators of change has been a shift in identity among the Quebec population. In 1970, about ten years after the Quiet Revolution had begun, 44% of the Quebec population identified themselves as French-Canadian and 34% as Canadian; only 21% thought of themselves as Québécois. By 1990, the percentage identifying themselves as French-Canadian had dropped from 44% to 28% and the percentage viewing themselves as Canadian had dropped even more significantly, from 34% to 9%. In contrast, the percentage choosing the relatively new and more nationalistic identification "Québécois" had increased from 21% to 59%.

Furthermore, in the 1960s support for Quebec independence was usually at less than 10%, though it increased through the 1970s to a peak of 24% in 1980. After the loss of the referendum in 1980, support for independence decreased to 15% in 1985 but then showed spectacular growth, hovering around 40% from 1989 to 1992, with a high of 56% in 1990 after Meech Lake died. By the late '90s, studies were showing that the greatest support for independence came from employed people aged 18–54 who had been socialized politically since the Quiet Revolution. Older people and those who were not working and were more dependent on the state were least likely to support independence. The most volatile contingent was those members of the 18–54 age group who felt alienated or adversely affected by Quebec government policies and voted against sovereignty as a protest. For these reasons, it was concluded that the possibility of rebounding support for separatism should not be ruled out.[66] The area in which change is most obvious is language. French has clearly become the language of Quebec. Many anglophones have left Quebec and those who have stayed cannot ignore the French environment around them. While there are exceptions, French is the language of the workplace and of the schools (an exception is made for anglophones who had been educated in English in Quebec; these are allowed to have their children educated in English). This is not to imply that English has disappeared from French culture. Indeed, 30% of the time that Quebecers spend watching television is spent watching English programming.[67] However, the linguistic hierarchy or economic inequality that formerly existed between English and French in Quebec has been considerably reduced if not reversed. For example, 32% of Montreal's highest-paid workers in 1961 were unilingual anglophones, compared to only 7.8% in 1985.[68] One half to two thirds of all Montreal's anglophones are now bilingual. Marc Levine's interesting book *The Reconquest of Montreal* has traced how Montreal, once an English city with many French inhabitants, has been transformed into a French city with English as a second language; he has also shown how the language of schooling has been central to this transformation.[69] Montreal has always been the primary meeting-ground between French and English, but the French language and culture have now become dominant rather than subordinate.

Montreal's place within Canadian society has also changed. Although Montreal and Toronto were once paired as premiere centres of commerce for all of Canada, Toronto has now become the hub on Canada's east–west axis, as well as the access point for American capital and doorway to American markets. Montreal, epitomizing Quebec's feelings in general, is oriented towards the United States much more than towards Toronto and English Canada.[70] Ironically, Montreal's linkage to the northeastern states has contributed to the economic weakening of Quebec as the American economy has developed in a westwardly direction and the northeastern region declined in importance. In other words, the continentalization of the Canadian economy elevated Toronto in importance while contributing to the economic marginalization of Montreal and Quebec.[71] Consequently, the rivalry between Ontario and Quebec is based not just on ethnic differences but on economic disparities (e.g., consider Quebec's higher unemployment rates). Gagnon and Montcalm have argued that the growing economic peripheralization of Quebec in the continental economy was not caused by the emergence of Quebec nationalism but preceded it. In fact, they argue that the use of the state as a mechanism of intervention was an attempt to take control of an economy that had already begun to decline.

It is also useful to examine what effect state interventionism has had on the Quebec economy. Again it is clear that there have been important shifts towards francophone ownership and control in certain sectors, such as food and beverages, printing and publishing, metal fabrication, and mineral products. Small- and medium-sized businesses are increasingly controlled by francophones. Quebec Crown corporations are still important to the economy and are key symbols of national pride. There are major pools of francophone capital in Quebec, such as Groupe Desjardins and a Caisse de dépôt; moreover, the commercial activities of major Quebec companies, such as Provigo, Bombardier, and Power Corporation, even reach beyond Quebec's borders. This is not to ignore the American or English-Canadian economic presence but to state that Québécois have made major strides in controlling their own economy.

Virtually all analysts agree that by the mid-1980s, movement began away from state capitalism and state intervention in the economy towards free-market principles. The public-sector middle class that had embraced the Quiet Revolution now feels increasingly squeezed by neo-liberal principles and downsizing. As Quebec becomes more entrepreneurial and is increasingly captivated by free-market principles, its economy becomes more international; in this sense, free trade also contributes to *de-Canadianization* (i.e., a move away from dependency on Canadian markets). Thus, the old economic ties that bound Quebec into the Canadian economy are slowly being weakened, though clearly not severed.

What is clear is that debate about the nationalist project and Quebecers' relationship to each other, the rest of Canada, the continent, and the world have not ceased. A new perspective, sometimes known as *revisionist thinking*, has rejected the old survivalist ideology that held Quebec's uniqueness to have been a matter of its having been inferior and backward. According to the new perspective, Quebec went through processes of modernization and urbanization similar to those which took place elsewhere in Canada (if not elsewhere in the world). Quebec has always been the site of the convergence of many cultures, and the influences of France, Great Britain, Rome, and the United States have made Quebec a much more international place than is often assumed. Furthermore, the migration of other ethnic groups into Quebec—even since the Quiet Revolution—has created an awareness among Quebecers that the concept of a distinct people with a singular history needs to be modified to accommodate pluralistic realities (i.e., the presence of Aboriginal people, Italians, Haitians, etc.) in the building of a territorial nationalism. In that sense, Quebec has become more of a *region-state,* differing from other provinces in that it has a higher international profile, a strong cohesive relationship between political leaders and local stakeholders, and a model of social integration in which it is different from and yet part of the central state. While Quebec nationalism is still fed by the traumatic memory of the past, there is also a sense in which a new form of activism or political voluntarism contributes to new efforts to define the meaning of what it is to be a Quebecer.[72]

Language and Group Survival

Nationalist feeling in Quebec is primarily energized by the conviction that francophone cultural survival is a critical issue.[73] The maintenance of linguistic distinctiveness, moreover, has become pivotal to cultural survival. Immigration posed a threat to francophones because most immigrants learned English and became part of the anglophone majority, upsetting the earlier balance of power both in the country as a whole and in Quebec. Bill 101, the Charter of the French Language, made French the official language of the province of Quebec in 1977. The goal of this Bill was to ensure not only that French would be the language of business but that the children of immigrants would be educated in French.[74] There were elaborate regulations to ensure that all of this happened. When the legality of such exclusivity in a bilingual country was challenged in the Supreme Court, Quebec Premier Bourassa introduced Bill 178, invoking the *notwithstanding clause* of the Charter of Rights to override the Court's decision and ensure the universal presence of French in the province. The *indoor–outdoor solution* was to make French-only signage mandatory on the outside of stores but to allow some English signage inside.

Francophones Outside Quebec With some exceptions, francophones outside Quebec were dispersed throughout anglophone communities and therefore found it difficult to maintain their mother tongue. Because francophone migrants to English Canada were concerned more with adaptation and adjustment to their new environment than with cultural survival, they became *invisible minorities.*[75] Furthermore, over the generations, children of francophones found it virtually impossible to maintain their mother tongue, becoming *francogènes* (people who do not speak French but have some degree of attachment to the French culture of their ancestry). The French language was much more likely to survive where residential segregation supported a reasonable amount of institutional completeness and, above all, schooling in French.[76] Areas such as St. Boniface, Manitoba, and rural areas adjacent to the Quebec borders in New Brunswick (the only officially bilingual province in Canada) and Ontario continue to contain French-speaking communities. More recently, we have learned that francophone minorities can demonstrate vitality without a territorial basis, in what are called *l'espaces francophones* (francophone spaces) in niches such as schools, churches, and community organizations.[77] Generally, however, the greater the distance from Quebec, the greater the extent of language loss.[78]

Anglophones in Quebec The initial focus of our discussion of language and group survival was the survival of francophones outside Quebec. More recently, however, Bill 101 and Bill 178 have raised the question of the survival of anglophones inside Quebec. When

RESEARCH CLIP 5.2	How Do Francophones Survive in Anglophone Canada?

The conventional wisdom has been that French-speaking persons face enormous assimilationist pressures in anglophone regions of Canada. In fact, it is assumed that long-term francophone survival is well-nigh impossible. Yet francophone communities do exist. One study of 85 francophone adults in the city of Calgary (where 10 000 francophones reside almost invisibly) produced some striking results.

Francophones in Calgary were not a homogeneous ethnic group but were of diverse backgrounds and origins, tracing their heritage not only to Quebec but to Europe, North Africa, and South Asia. They possessed a wide range of values, beliefs, and practices, and certainly were not territorially concentrated. Despite their ethnic differences, what they shared was a mother tongue (French) or a commitment to preserve their French-language capability.

Most of the francophones were bilingual but made a deliberate choice to use French, for their own enjoyment, to develop or maintain linguistic competence, or to help sustain the francophone community. Since their professional and service activities were normally conducted in English, the use of French became associated with leisure (defined as non-obligatory daily-living activity, not just recreation). This meant that these franco-phones might deliberately speak French at home to children or at social gatherings, read French books, buy French greeting cards, or patronize commercial establishments where French was spoken (e.g., stores, professional services, restaurants).

The key contribution of the study was the identification of what is called a "francophonie" in the city of Calgary. A *francophonie* is a loose network of French-speaking persons in a community, having a set of organizations and interpersonal ties but no territorial boundaries. It is a symbolic community, which serves as a reference group for francophones who choose to retain their language skills and provides them with the resources to do so. The francophonie consists of persons who deliberately pursue a lifestyle that makes the preservation and transmission of French possible. But it is not just the existence of formal organizations (e.g., French-language churches and schools) that is important to the francophonie, but the informal interactions outside work or school that sustain the community in a minimally coalescing fashion.

Source: Robert A. Stebbins, *The Franco-Calgarians: French Language, Leisure, and Linguistic Lifestyle in an Anglophone City* (Toronto: University of Toronto Press, 1994). See also René Guindon and Pierre Poulin, *Francophones in Canada: A Community of Interests* (Ottawa: Heritage Canada, 1996).

French became the official language of Quebec and English lost its official status, the anglophone community felt its own existence threatened. The initial militant reaction of anglophones exacerbated the antagonism already felt by francophones towards them, and seemed to strengthen Quebec nationalist objectives.[79] Bill 101, in particular, employed language as an economic and political tool in such a way as to *transform ethnic national-ism into territorial nationalism.*[80] In other words, the unifying element of the entire popu-lation was now to be the common French language, regardless of other differences. The heightening of the Québécois identity placed all Quebec anglophones in a dilemma which accentuated their minority-group status.

The massive concentration of Quebec anglophones (75%) in the metropolitan Montreal area and in some rural settlements in the Eastern Townships and Ottawa Valley, along with the fact that only one in three of these anglophones were likely to be bilingual, suggests that the anglophone population maintained its identity through close ties with English North America (e.g., Ontario and New York).[81] Quebec anglophones have in recent years felt overwhelmed by the changes happening around them, and the anglophone com-munity has been severely weakened by large-scale out-migration. Anglophone minorities have increasingly been subject to the same pressures as francophone minorities have known in the rest of Canada.[82]

Bilingualism

The federal policy of *bilingualism* was meant to reaffirm to francophones, in Quebec and elsewhere, that they were not second-class citizens.[83] As founding partners of Confederation, the francophones were to possess the same rights and privileges as anglo-phones. The policy declared the federal government's commitment to making its serv-ices accessible to both anglophones and francophones throughout Canada. The new nationalist spirit in Quebec spilled over to francophone groups elsewhere in Canada, emboldening them to demand their rights to bilingual service (particularly in education). At the same time, however, the tightening of the boundaries of nation and state (as expressed in the new Québécois identity) created distance between francophones inside and outside Quebec. In the end, as Guindon expresses it, the policy of bilingualism became politically irrelevant to Quebec and a political irritation to anglophones outside Quebec.[84] Many anglophones viewed bilingualism as a threat and became defensive about their own language. Others found it difficult to accept a policy of federal bilin-gualism so long as the government of Quebec maintained a contradictory policy of French unilingualism in that province.

The emerging pattern of French–English relations seems to support the idea, proposed by Richard Joy, that two languages of unequal strength cannot coexist in intimate contact. According to Joy's *bilingual belt thesis*, linguistic segregation in Canada is proceeding in such a way that linguistic minorities are disappearing.[85] Just as French is being over-whelmed as a living language outside Quebec, so English is being overwhelmed by the strength of French within Quebec; Bill 101, for example, is just another in a series of developments that have made anglophones less comfortable in Quebec. The bilingual belt, where French and English coexist, can only be found in a narrow strip along the Quebec border, including the Eastern Townships of Quebec, the Ottawa Valley, Northern Ontario, and the City of Montreal. The effect of Bill 101, moreover, may actually have been to shrink this bilingual belt; since Joy's initial study, there has been evidence that in every region the majority linguistic group has been growing while linguistic minorities are shrinking. As a result, duality is being replaced by *linguistic polarization.*[86] In sum, in spite of the existence of linguistic minorities, Canada seems to have moved towards *territorial unilingualism,* with bilingual federal institutions at the core.[87]

In the type of bilingualism described above, each language has its own territory of operation, and unity and common ground are found in federal institutions (*institutional bilingualism*). Yet the ideal implied in the work of the Royal Commission on Bilingualism and Biculturalism and in the actions of the federal government since that time is that individual Canadians ought to know both languages (*individual bilingualism*). As we noted in Chapter One, francophones are more likely to be bilingual. In fact, 43.4% of francophones are bilingual, in contrast to only 9% of anglophones.[88] Within Quebec, about two thirds of all anglophones are bilingual, compared to only about one third of francophones (though that number continues to rise). But in the rest of Canada, over 85% of francophones are bilingual, compared to only 7% of anglophones.

Since programs to teach the "other" language to adults are not highly successful, second-language education for children has been promoted quite strongly throughout the school system. About 9% of Canadian children participate in French immersion, with a high of about 21% in New Brunswick, 16% in Prince Edward Island, 8% in Manitoba, and 9% in Ontario; rates in the Western provinces and Newfoundland are lower than the national average at around 5%.[89]

Somewhat less demanding are the French second-language programs that are available in about 80% of the public schools outside Quebec. Whereas 17.7% of Canadian teenagers (aged 15–19) considered themselves bilingual in 1981, that percentage increased to 24.4% in 1996. These bilingual rates were highest in New Brunswick (49%) and Quebec (42%), but were mainly between 10% and 20% in the rest of the country.[90] Outside Quebec, anglophones aged 15–19 were more likely to be bilingual than the general anglophone population, but five years later (at the ages of 20–24) there was a slippage of three percentage points; this suggests that young anglophones lose their bilingual ability over time. Interestingly, second-language French education is stronger at the elementary than at the secondary school level, where it falls off dramatically. While it is noteworthy that familiarization with the "other" official language is taking place, it is likely that many children are picking up only a rudimentary knowledge of the language, which is not to be interpreted as functional or working bilingualism.[91] The extent to which knowledge of the country's "other" language is necessary for functioning within the society will clearly be a matter of continuing debate.

Developments in Quebec since 1960 have clearly affected the nature of Canadian society and have restructured French–English relations. These relationships coexist in dynamic tension, and many aspects have yet to be resolved. In recent years, however, another restructuring of ethnic relations has occurred among Canada's Aboriginal peoples, and it is upon this restructuring that we will now focus our attention. With the Aboriginal peoples, as with francophones, there are longstanding unresolved issues and a case to be made for a historically validated, unique, or special position within Canadian society.

ABORIGINAL–NON-ABORIGINAL RELATIONS

Who Are the Indigenous Peoples?

At the time Europeans arrived in Canada, 55 separate Aboriginal nations shared the territory (see Figure 5.4).[92] Native peoples first had contact with Europeans through dealings with explorers, traders, and trappers, who needed the assistance of Native people in the new land. The immigration of increasing numbers of Europeans who adopted agriculture

FIGURE 5.4	Indigenous Peoples in Canada

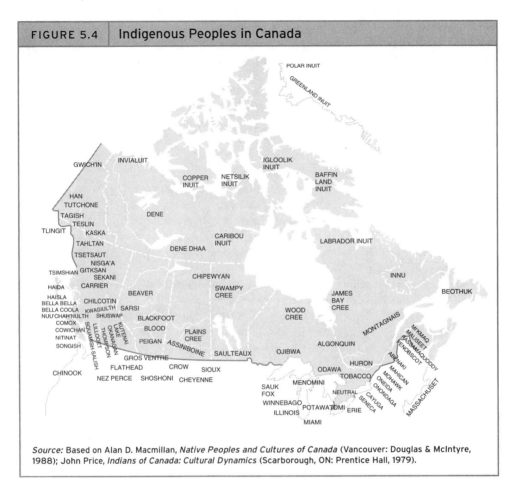

Source: Based on Alan D. Macmillan, *Native Peoples and Cultures of Canada* (Vancouver: Douglas & McIntyre, 1988); John Price, *Indians of Canada: Cultural Dynamics* (Scarborough, ON: Prentice Hall, 1979).

as a livelihood, however, posed problems to the Native way of life owing to differences in attitudes towards land ownership, commercial use of plants, and domestication of animals. With their superior technology (such as railroads) and sheer numbers, white people used brute force or the threat of force, in addition to the treaty process, to remove Native people from the path of European settlement. In this way, Euro-Canadian domination of Native peoples in Canada began.[93]

Denied self-government, removed from most of their land and livelihood, and partially transformed by European culture, Aboriginal peoples took on the character of a classic colonized minority.[94] Not only was their own social structure significantly eroded, but their place within Canadian society caused them to become perpetually disadvantaged. With the somewhat contradictory objectives of "protecting" and "civilizing" Aboriginal peoples, white colonists ultimately marginalized the Native people, dismantling their societal structures while restricting their participation in the dominant society.[95]

The *Indian Act* of 1876 essentially made Native people wards of the federal government, placing them on tracts of land called *reserves*. More importantly, the Act defined explicitly who was to be given the *legal status of "Indian."* This definition divided Aboriginal people into those with treaty status and those who fell into other categories, such as *non-status Indian* and *Métis*. Until recently, only persons whose fathers had treaty status—regardless of their mothers' status—were legally considered status Indians and thus eligible to receive whatever benefits accrued from that status.[96] The offspring of the frequent marriages or informal sexual associations between whites and Indian women formed a marginal group of Aboriginal people. It was not until 1985, through Bill C-31 in accordance with the Charter of Rights, that the Indian Act was amended to eliminate sexual discrimination. Many who had lost their Indian status began to apply for reinstatement as legal Indians, and by 1996 about 104 000 persons (about one fifth of all registered Indians) had been reinstated.[97] As long as government defined who was an Indian on the basis of arbitrary legal formulae rather than social, cultural, or self-definitions, the Native community was divided by invidious distinctions.

Aboriginal People in Canada

There are many ways of counting Aboriginal people, and the numbers vary depending on the criteria used. The Department of Indian Affairs has a strict definition of "Indian" because of the legal implications of Indian status. However, Aboriginal people in general have been enumerated in two ways: using ancestry and using identity. The broader definition includes persons who self-declare their *ancestry* as Aboriginal and/or who are of partly Aboriginal origin. The ancestry question in the 2001 census revealed that about 1.3 million persons (4.9% of the Canadian population) reported Aboriginal ancestry; over half of these were of mixed ancestry. However, an *identity* question was also included to determine whether respondents explicitly defined themselves as either North American Indian, Métis, or Inuit. According to this method of enumeration, about one million people (3.3% of Canada's population) are Aboriginal. Sixty-two percent of the Aboriginal population are North American Indian, 30% are Métis, and 5% are Inuit. This tighter definition of Aboriginal is the one we will use.

In general, birth rates and death rates are higher among Aboriginal people than among non-Aboriginal people, though the gap seems to be narrowing. Nationally, there has been a decline in the ability of Aboriginal people to speak an Aboriginal language (from 29% to 24% in the five years from 1996 to 2001). Cree and Ojibway are among the languages

Some Aboriginal Population Comparisons

Canadian comparisons:

Median age: Aboriginals – 24.7 years   Non-Aboriginals – 37.7 years

Percentage of children
under 14:   Aboriginals – 33.3%   Non-Aboriginals –19%

International Comparisons:

percentage in national populations:

Canada – 3.3%   New Zealand –14%   Australia – 2.2%   United States –1.5%

Source: Statistics Canada Catalogue 96F0030XIE2001007

that have declined in use, but use of Dene and Montagnais-Naskapi has increased. It is very important to understand that sweeping generalizations about Aboriginal people are seldom correct and that there is considerable variation within this group, just as there is in any population.

Figure 5.5 shows that in 2001 the Aboriginal population was largely concentrated in the provinces from Ontario westward, with Ontario (19.3%) and British Columbia (17.4%) having the largest share of Canada's Aboriginal population. Perhaps somewhat surpris-

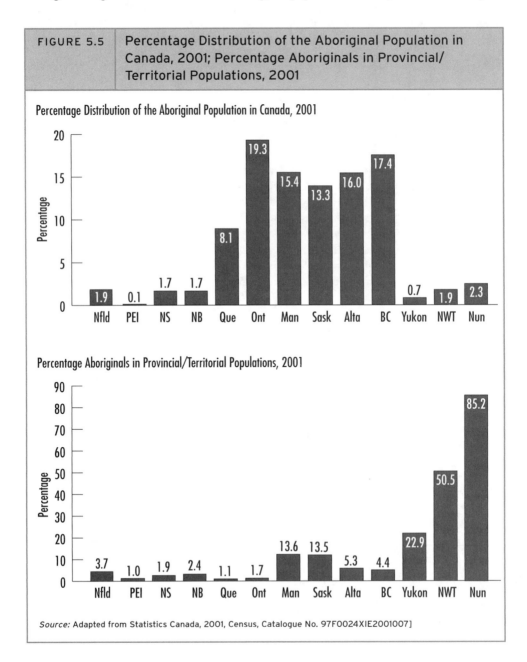

| FIGURE 5.5 | Percentage Distribution of the Aboriginal Population in Canada, 2001; Percentage Aboriginals in Provincial/Territorial Populations, 2001 |

Source: Adapted from Statistics Canada, 2001, Census, Catalogue No. 97F0024XIE2001007]

ingly, the territories to the north had a very small share of the national Aboriginal population. On the other hand, when Aboriginal people were considered as a percentage of provincial/territorial populations, these same territories had the largest proportions of Aboriginal population, with Nunavut at 85.2%, the Northwest Territories at 50.5%, and the Yukon at 22.9%. Among the provinces, Manitoba and Saskatchewan stood out has having the highest proportions of Aboriginal people (around 14%). Despite the fact that Ontario had the largest percentage of Canada's Aboriginal people, the province's non-Aboriginal population was overwhelmingly larger: Aboriginal people made up only 1.7% of the provincial population. The population patterns among North American Indian and Métis are similar to those described above. It is only Inuit who are specifically concentrated in Nunavut, with a significant presence in Quebec and Newfoundland as well.

North American Indians

It is estimated that in the 1600s there were approximately 250 000 Native people in what is now Canada. As a result of epidemics, poor health, and combat, this number fell to about 102 000 by 1867. There are approximately 623 000 registered Indians in Canada today; in 1961, there were only 192 000. This dramatic increase is partly attributable to changes to the *Indian Act* in 1985 (Bill C-31), as well as to a high birth rate. Twenty-two percent of the Indian population live in Ontario, 22% live in British Columbia, and 14%–15% live in each of the three western-interior provinces.

Less than half of Canada's North American Indians live on reserves. Twenty-four percent live in census metropolitan areas, some live on reserves near urban centres, but many registered Indians live at some distance from urban centres or in more remote locations. There are approximately 2 720 reserves across Canada; these vary considerably in size. The basic political structure among Indians is the *band*; there are 614 bands in Canada, with an average size of about 500 persons.[98]

Métis

Persons with partial Indian ancestry are called *Métis,* although the term was formerly used only to describe children of French–Indian unions. Again, as a result of the Charter of Rights, Métis—particularly those who live in or come from Métis settlements, such as those in Northern Alberta—are taking on the character of a distinct group. The 2001 census lists more than 292 000 Métis in Canada (a 43% increase in five years), most of whom reside in the northern parts of the three western-interior provinces. Traditionally, the Métis were Catholic and French-speaking.[99] There is now also a significant mixed-blood community that is urban, dispersed throughout in the country, and of more varied descent.

When the Métis realized that western lands were being transferred from the jurisdiction of fur-trading companies to the Canadian government with no recognition of their rights, they formed a provisional government which attempted to negotiate a new accord with Canada. In 1885 the Métis, led by Louis Riel, staged a rebellion. The rebellion ended with the defeat of the Métis, and Riel was found guilty of treason and hanged.[100] Most Métis today subsist on marginal farmland with high levels of dependency and unemployment. Their history of maltreatment has recently inspired the Métis to protest anew for the redress of their grievances.

Inuit

The smallest distinct group of Native people are the *Inuit*. There are about 45 000 Inuit in Canada. In spite of their small numbers, the Inuit population is not dying out.[101] A birth rate twice as high as that of the Canadian population as a whole and substantial decreases in infant mortality have produced a growth rate substantially above the Canadian growth rate. One half of all Inuit live in Nunavut; most live in small communities of 600–800 people, such as Pangnirtung, Igloolik, Baker Lake, and Tuktoyaktuk. (See Chapter 4 for additional discussion of the Métis and Inuit).

If the Inuit as a people are thriving, their culture and economy are not surviving nearly as well. About two thirds of Inuit have Inuktitut as their mother tongue and speak Inuktitut at home.[102] The more remote the community, the more likely the Inuit are to retain their mother tongue; consequently, Inuktitut remains a significant medium of communication, particularly in the eastern Arctic.[103] On the other hand, more than two thirds of the Inuit now know English, and the trend is towards greater use of English, especially among the young, who are exposed to southern-style education. As the traditional economy has become more marginal and exposure to southern culture (e.g., magazines, television) has increased as a result of a shift from nomadic life to settlement in permanent communities, the Inuit have been struggling to maintain their identity. The creation of Nunavut as a new, largely Inuit-controlled territory has played a key role in strengthening group consciousness and supporting the retention of the traditional language.

These three groups—status/non-status North American Indians, Métis, and Inuit—constitute the Indigenous peoples of Canada. Together with other Aboriginal peoples living within nation-states throughout the globe, they form what has been called the *fourth world*.[104] However, a more contemporary term is *Indigenous peoples;* in speaking of North American Indians, the appropriate term is *First Nations*.

The State and First Nations

From the point of view of the state, the primary objective of federal policy was to remove Aboriginal people as impediments to economic and political development. The spread of capitalist agriculture required the separation of Native people from their land and the transformation of that land into private property.[105] The treaties, then, were a way for Europeans to consolidate their control while securing the cooperation of the Aboriginal people. So while the reserve represented protection, it also gave Europeans the opportunity to wean Native people from their past life and prepare them for eventual assimilation. Federal policies through the years have been built on these premises, but without the consent or participation of Native people. Epitomizing the federal position was the *Indian Act of 1876*, frequently described as "a total institution" because it paternalistically attempted to structure all aspects of Native life. Even with good intentions, federal policy essentially controlled and disempowered Aboriginal people. A key instrument of forced assimilation was the residential school, designed to erase the Aboriginal identity.[106] Racist attitudes and stereotypes intensified the marginalization of Aboriginal people. In sum, the traditional society had been demolished but there was nothing to replace it, since Euro-Canadian culture was alien and repressive to most Aboriginal people. The federal strategy of segregation and guardianship (with the goal of absorption) was not merely ineffective; it was meeting with increased resistance.

The government's first attempt at a solution was the *White Paper* of 1969. This paper proposed terminating Native special status by repealing the *Indian Act*, abolishing the Department of Indian Affairs and Northern Development (DIAND), and eliminating reserves. The *White Paper* was met with strong opposition on the grounds that repealing the *Indian Act* would be the ultimate assimilation technique: Native people would have no special status at all. In light of the objections, the White Paper was withdrawn. Since then, federal policy has moved towards greater support of Aboriginal peoples' autonomy and control over their own destiny.

In 1966, the Hawthorn Report advanced the concept of "citizens plus," acknowledging that Native people are citizens like everyone else but have special historic rights as well.[107] This concept was in sharp contrast to earlier practices, which embodied the notion that Aboriginal people held special rights while denying them other basic rights (e.g., the right to vote or the opportunity to obtain loans [because reserve property was not acceptable as collateral]). However, a major step forward, and indicative of the changed mood on the federal scene, was the *constitutional recognition* given to Aboriginal people and treaty rights in the *Constitution Act, 1982*. This document was also important for the fact that it acknowledged Métis as a distinct Aboriginal people for the first time. Another major advance was the 1983 Penner Committee Report, which recommended that Indian government be a distinct order of government within Canadian federalism, and that the structure and form of this government should be determined by Native people themselves.

In an effort to transform the federal government's "caretaker" role to a more respectful relationship,[108] Native people and political leaders have thus increasingly turned to the concept of self-determination.[109] *Self-determination* means that Aboriginals must have some type of *political mechanism* that will allow them to be accountable to their own people and to make decisions on matters that affect them. In order to be effective, it requires a *specific division of powers* between the levels of Canadian government and Aboriginal government. It requires Aboriginal *control over group membership, fiscal policy, and land*.[110] The settlement of *land claims* has become the central issue for many Native people because it establishes the basis whereby their communities can move away from dependency and foster economic development. Land claims thus go beyond lump-sum payments from the government; they are fundamental to issues of social policy and service delivery (e.g., health care), the establishment of a more effective justice system (e.g., policing and sentencing), and the creation of mechanisms to strengthen economic development.

The land-claims issue is frequently controversial because natural resources make Native lands desirable for capitalist expansion; as a result, governments find themselves caught between corporate and native interests. Capitalist growth also indirectly threatens Native territory. For example, the James Bay Project and several other northern hydroelectric projects proposed by provincial governments, as well as the Mackenzie Valley Pipeline, are enormously disruptive to Native cultures and economies.[111]

In many ways, the White Paper helped to crystallize Aboriginal solidarity for the first time. It was the catalyst for the 1970 *Red Paper*, spearheaded by Harold Cardinal of the Indian Association of Alberta. While Aboriginal groups were scattered all over Canada in small numbers with no unifying mechanism, the perception of external threat helped to build a sense of *pan-Indianism*, which emphasized commonalities of the Native experience rather than traditional differences.[112] Furthermore, the need to find a common voice in order to address the federal government as a unified interest group led to increased political activity. National lobbying organizations include the Assembly of First Nations, the

Native Council of Canada, the Métis National Council, and the Inuit Tapirisat of Canada. Other organizations exist at provincial levels, such as the Union of Ontario Indians and the Indian Association of Alberta. Realizing the value of having Natives represent themselves and their own interests, the federal government agreed in 1970 to provide funding for these organizations in order to ensure that Native leadership would have adequate opportunity to defend and advocate their point of view. However, disagreements within Native organizations about strategies and objectives sometimes lead to splits or defections.

Political lobbying on matters of self-government, economic development, land-claims settlement, and self-determination kept Native issues high on the national agenda after 1982, until the Quebec constitutional crisis took a higher priority. There was a clear sense that Native issues were no longer to be viewed as "their" problem but were a responsibility of all Canadians.[113] But one of the greatest insults that Canadian Aboriginal people experienced in the contemporary era was to be virtually left out of the Meech Lake Accord. As we have seen, it was a Native member of Parliament from Manitoba, Elijah Harper, who played a key role in its defeat. However, the Charlottetown Accord had much greater input from Aboriginal people and acknowledged the right of Native people to self-government. Even though the Accord was defeated in 1992, the Royal Commission on Aboriginal Peoples had already been established in 1991 in direct response to the Oka Crisis of 1990.

The *Royal Commission on Aboriginal Peoples* accepted the argument that in addition to the *Constitution Act, 1982*, a historic document existed that enshrined Native special rights. That document was the *Royal Proclamation of 1763,* which is now being referred to as the "Magna Carta of Aboriginal rights."[114] In that document, the British government agreed to protect Aboriginal peoples and acknowledged them as nations (hence independent entities) connected to the Crown by treaty and alliance. Moreover, it stated that the Aboriginal peoples were not to be disturbed in their possession of unceded lands. In other words, lands over which no treaties had been signed were deemed to be Native lands. Thus, the *Royal Proclamation* is a basis for the argument that land claims and self-government have historic support which somehow was obscured over the years.

In order for a reorganization of Aboriginal–non-Aboriginal relations to take place, Aboriginal peoples must experience *decolonization,* both in the way that they are treated and in the way that they think of themselves. In order to facilitate this, the Royal Commission accepted the principle that Native rights are *inherent* (i.e., existent as a per-

---

Revising the Dualistic Conception of Canadian Society

"The distinct society perpetuates a myth. Canada was not born when the English and French cultures joined. It was born when the treaties were signed with the First Nations. We allowed people from Europe to come here and settle peacefully."

Georges Erasmus, 1990

"We are the founding nations of Canada and we will not allow the lie of two founding nations (English and French) to continue."

Ovide Mercredi, 1991

Source: Maclean's, July 2, 1990, and The Globe and Mail, August 27, 1991. Cited in Augie Fleras and Jean Leonard Elliott, The Nations Within (Toronto: Oxford University Press, 1992), 23 and 69.

Oka: A Major Turning Point

Just as the violent action by the FLQ in Quebec produced the 1970 October Crisis, which attracted national and international attention to a cause which desperately needed resolution for Québécois, so the Oka crisis in 1990 represented both a protest against Aboriginal subjugation and a positive affirmation of Aboriginal sovereignty.

Oka is a small village 40 kilometres west of Montreal. Since March of 1990, Mohawk warriors had been protesting the extension of a municipal golf course on land which they considered to be their own. There is no reserve at Oka but there is land held by the federal government. Originally used as a mission by the Sulpician religious order (as granted by the King of France in 1717), the land was occupied by the Mohawks and had been the subject of an ownership dispute for a long time. What was at issue was who owned this land (did European settlement pre-date Mohawk settlement?) and what its precise boundaries were.

On July 11, 1990, the Sureté du Québec raided the Kanesetake Mohawks' four-month-old blockade of a road to this disputed land, and in the ensuing confusion an officer was killed. At the nearby Mercier Bridge, which served thousands of suburban commuters to Montreal each day, the Mohawks of Kahnawake established a sympathy blockade that became the site of considerable public protest and demonstrations. Thousands of Canadian troops were later brought in for what became a 78-day armed standoff. The Mohawks surrendered on September 26, but they had succeeded in drawing public attention to the frustration and impatience felt by Native people across the country over the government's failure to resolve Native issues. In solidarity, other Native groups across Canada staged blockades, and the Canadian public and government realized that new initiatives and negotiations were required. Towards that end, the federal government announced in 1991 the formation of the Royal Commission on Aboriginal Peoples.

Ironically, the form of militant protest that took place at Oka also revealed divergent views within the Native community. The Mohawk Warriors who staged the blockade considered themselves traditionalists and rejected the decisions of the band council, which they perceived as an adaptation to the Euro-Caucasian world. While the appropriateness of militancy was debatable, the importance of the standoff in consciousness-raising about Native issues was indisputable.

Further Reading: Robert M. Campbell and Leslie A. Pal, *The Real Worlds of Politics*, 2nd ed. (Peterborough: Broadview, 1991), chap. 4. See also Gerald R. Alfred, *Heeding the Voices of Our Ancestors: Kahnawake Mohawk Politics and the Rise of Native Nationalism* (Toronto: Oxford University Press, 1995).

manent attribute of the Native people, rather than conferred upon them by a beneficent federal government), *circumscribed* (i.e., applicable to distinct areas of responsibility under First Nations' jurisdiction), and *sovereign* (i.e., supreme over areas under Native control). It was thought that once these principles were clearly accepted, progress could be made in determining the meaning and extent of self-government. (Note in the boxed insert on the following page that the Royal Commission speaks of self-government "within the context of Canadian citizenship.")

The matter of the precise means whereby self-government is to be achieved is a complex and difficult one. Measures which are either being considered or already being implemented include separate Aboriginal seats in Parliament and provincial legislatures, tribal justice programs, community municipality control, various economic development programs (including urban reserves), and the transfer of expenditure controls from government agencies to band councils.[115] There are many ways in which Aboriginal peoples are now being empowered through the settlement of land claims (e.g., the Nisga'a treaty), the establishment of Aboriginal investments and business (e.g., the First Nations Bank), cultural revival (e.g., the National Aboriginal Achievement Awards), and some new administrative and constitutional powers.[116] On the other hand, disempowerment is perpetuated by systemic discrimination, racism, internal difficulties, comparative poverty, low education levels, and poor health (as measured by the United Nations Human Development Index). While there is much to be done, it is clear that new efforts are being made to transform the previous, unsuccessful patterns of Canada's relations with First Nations.

National surveys of public opinion give us some indication of attitudes towards Aboriginal people.[117] While these surveys reveal a low level of knowledge about Aboriginal issues and a strong reluctance to grant Aboriginals special status, they also somewhat paradoxically reveal strong support for Native self-government and the settlement of land claims. In other words, there is substantial acceptance of the idea of Native self-determination. Yet, after about 20 years of measuring public opinion, surveys are finding that support for Aboriginal peoples has slipped somewhat and that debilitating stereotypes still prevail. The protest strategies used by Aboriginal peoples, although effective as a negotiating device, may have led to weaker support from the general public (often thanks to the nature of media coverage).[118] Evidence suggests that prejudice is likely to be dormant until activated by direct conflict, and Native protest has often heightened such conflict. Research has also found economic conservatism to be the most important predictor of respondent attitudes. Since settlement of land claims involves financial compensation, and in recent years there has been an ideological shift towards curtailing government expenditures, the economic underpinnings or practical side of the Canadian public's desire to see justice done for the Native people may be more elusive. In the interim, selected forms of self-government are being instituted on a limited basis; in 2000 one new treaty was signed with the Nisga'a in northwestern British Columbia, allowing for land ownership by the tribe and considerable self-government in local laws, health, and education.[119]

THE MEANING OF MULTICULTURALISM

Much of the dynamic of Canadian society has its origin in ethnic differences among the population. From the response of non-English/non-French Canadians to the Royal Commission on Bilingualism and Biculturalism, it became clear that the government could no longer prudently ignore the wide range of other ethnic groups represented in the country. Consequently, in 1971 the federal government declared a policy of bilingualism within a multicultural framework, and in 1988 the *Multiculturalism Act* established the right of Canadians to identify with a cultural heritage. The official status given to ethnic differences has raised considerable debate about its precise significance and purpose.[120]

The Royal Commission on Aboriginal Peoples

The Royal Commission on Aboriginal Peoples was appointed by the federal government in 1991 and presented a five-volume report in 1996. While its recommendations are potentially as influential and groundbreaking for Native issues as the Royal Commission on Bilingualism and Biculturalism was for French–English relations, there is little evidence so far that the government intends to implement many of the recommendations—largely because they often involve new costs. However, what the Report does do is propose a new relationship between Aboriginals and non-Aboriginals, and it is hoped that the new attitude it embodies will shape and inform future decision-making. The 470 recommendations are too numerous to deal with here, but a sampling is listed:

"If one theme dominates our recommendations, it is that Aboriginal peoples must have room to exercise their autonomy and structure their own solutions. The pattern of debilitating and discriminatory paternalism that has characterized federal policy for the past 150 years must end. Aboriginal people cannot flourish if they are treated like wards, incapable of controlling their own destiny.

"We advocate recognition of Aboriginal nations within Canada as political entities through which Aboriginal people can express their distinctive identity within the context of their Canadian citizenship . . .

"At the heart of our recommendations is recognition that Aboriginal peoples are people, that they form collectivities of unique character, and that they have a right of governmental autonomy." (Vol. 5, p. 1)

Recommendations regarding suicide prevention and criminal justice were given greatest priority. Among the other proposals were the preparation of a new Royal Proclamation outlining the principles of Aboriginal–federal government relations, the creation of an Aboriginal Parliament or House of First Peoples (without law-making power but with an advisory role to the House of Commons and Senate), the creation of a new federal Department of Aboriginal Relations, the establishment of an Aboriginal Peoples' International University, the creation of an Aboriginal Languages Foundation and Aboriginal Arts Council, the provision of programs for economic development and training, and the improvement of housing and the provision of incentives for home ownership both on and off reserves

Further Information: In addition to the publications of the RCAP, there is also a CD-ROM entitled *For Seven Generations: An Information Legacy of the Royal Commission on Aboriginal Peoples.*

As a policy promoting tolerance and diversity, multiculturalism was to represent the opposite of *assimilation,* for to assimilate is to lose those characteristics which differentiate a group from the surrounding culture. In reality, however, instead of promoting cultural retention, the multicultural policy has predominantly produced *anglo-conformity*; i.e., a situation in which ethnic groups feel pressured to conform to the anglo majority. While anglo-conformity may have been Canada's objective in the past, multiculturalism, at least ostensibly, was intended to represent a new approach.

Multiculturalism was also thought to contrast with *amalgamation*, a process in which each ethnic group contributes to the nation's culture but loses its identity as the people of a state find a totally new identity. At one time, the *melting pot thesis* held that Canada contrasted with the United States in that the latter was a "melting pot" in which constituent ethnic groups amalgamated, while Canada was a pluralist society. *Pluralism* occurs where cultural differences coexist in an atmosphere of mutual toleration; this Clairmont and Wiens have called "The Canadian Way."[121] However, in a recent study of ethnic relations in Canada and the United States, it was discovered that whatever differences in tone may exist, the realities of pressure towards conformity are really very similar in both countries, and similar levels of discrimination exist in matters such as employment and housing (see Chapter Six).[122]

Since many of the early immigrants to Canada settled in rural areas, they were able to retain some of their ethnic identity. It must be recognized, however, that (at least until World War II) there were very strong pressures on ethnic groups to Canadianize, and discrimination against non–Anglo-Saxons was strong. This reflected *nativism*—opposition towards any new group that poses a threat, real or imagined, to Canadian life as understood by the dominant group.[123] The greater prosperity of the post-war years caused a relaxation of interethnic attitudes. Later on, the backlash against the Bilingualism and Biculturalism Commission by non-charter ethnic groups, and the model of a proud ethnic identity established by Quebec francophones, both contributed to recognition of the need to more fully appreciate the role of ethnic cultures in Canadian society as a whole.

The policy of multiculturalism seems to imply that people are encouraged to maintain their own ethnic cultures in Canada. In reality, that scenario is virtually impossible. Not only will these cultures be modified through the process of relocation, but they will also be difficult to sustain at all. With the exception of Quebec francophones, who have their own school system, media supports, and regulations controlling economic and cultural environment, ethnic groups in Canada are bombarded with cultural influences emanating from the anglophone media, schools, and working world. Ethnic cultures experience enormous struggles in trying to maintain their languages beyond the first generation.[124] Can a complete culture survive without full institutional supports and a language which sustains it? How is it possible to have two official languages and a plurality of cultures all with equal value?

In the first place, not all cultures are of "equal" value in Canada, except in the ideal sense. In reality, pressures towards either anglo-conformity or franco-conformity are still strong. In the second place, the fostering of certain aspects of culture should not be confused with the preservation of a complete culture. In the third place, it could be that the aim of multiculturalism is psychological: to give people confidence in their own identity and to create a "respect for others and a willingness to share ideas, attitudes, and assumptions."[125]

The preservation of ethnic folk dances, cuisine, and other arts is not equivalent to the preservation of culture. It has been argued that these cultural fragments give minorities the illusion of preserving their ethnic identity, while at the same time ensuring anglo-conformity.[126] The *critical approach to multiculturalism* understands it as a strategy of containment that sustains the hegemony of the dominant cultural group rather than ensuring access and equity for all members of the society. While the *liberal-pluralist view of multiculturalism* stresses tolerance and quaintness ("saris, samosas, and steel-bands"), the critical approach understands multiculturalism as a way to defuse "resistance, rebellion, and rejection."[127]

Multiculturalism as the preservation of select cultural artifacts with more nostalgic value than importance in everyday life is referred to as *symbolic ethnicity* or *partialized* or *fragmented ethnicity*.[128] While some segments of an individual's life (e.g., occupation) may be de-ethnicized, other aspects (e.g., kinship and friendship) may retain links to ethnic heritage even as the person participates fully in the mainstream of Canadian society. It has also been argued that technological culture seems to heighten the need for identity and that later generations may become involved in "ethnic rediscoveries," selecting a few items from their cultural heritage and preserving them in their private lives.[129] Weinfeld describes this pattern as *affective ethnicity*—a warm but superficial way of giving ethnic distinctiveness to individual identity in a society dominated by conformity and convention.[130]

The shift to new source-countries of immigration, and especially the immigration of visible minorities, has helped to bring about a shift in multiculturalism policy. The old cultural-retention approach has been replaced by a new emphasis on race relations and the elimination of ethnocentrism and discrimination through greater sensitivity and education.[131] Critics, however, have argued that multiculturalism represents a type of image-framing by elites, which seeks to give the impression of intergroup harmony while denying the problems of race, minimized as ethnic differences.[132] In Quebec, the federal policy of multiculturalism is viewed as a threat because its assumption that all cultures are of equal value challenges that province's efforts to strengthen francophone culture. Therefore, the

---

REAL PEOPLE 5 — The Meaning of Ethnicity

Two Cameo Snapshots

One: "I love my open-air jeep. I love to feel the wind around me. I have a flag hanging from the rear-view mirror and it is the Croatian flag. Me, I was born here. But my parents were born in Croatia. They love Canada but their heart is still in Croatia and I have been brought up with that culture and identity. They identify with Croatian people and cheer for the homeland, and in a way, I am into it too. We are not Croatian-Canadian but Croatian and Canadian—I think there is a difference."

Two: "I grew up in Vancouver. Our Oma (Grandma) lived with us so the rule of the household was that we speak German when in the house. So I am fluent in German and English. But like many Canadian kids, I also learned some French in school and when I became an adult, I moved to Quebec City to learn more French. I loved that place. And I decided to stay there. I married a guy there and now we have children. I wanted to pass on my native tongue to my children so German is the language of our home. My husband knew no German and spoke primarily French but he has learned some German. So German is the language at home and French is the language at school, and somewhere in between we fit English in. When people hear us talking German in the stores, it is amazing how many people reach out to us."

Question to Consider:

What does this mixture of ethnic identity and language-use mean for people who have a single idea of what Canadian society is?

Assessing the Opposition to Multiculturalism

In recent years, the policy of multiculturalism has come under attack on the grounds that it does not encourage immigrants to think of themselves as Canadians, that it exaggerates differences that serve as the basis for antagonism and resentments, and that it alienates people from the mainstream of society rather than promoting integration.

Kymlicka argues that the evidence suggests exactly the opposite. Immigrants have a high rate of naturalization (i.e., the taking-out of Canadian citizenship), and immigrants from the new source-countries have the highest rates of naturalization, whereas immigrants from the United Kingdom have the lowest. In other words, the greater the cultural gap for new immigrants, the more likely they are to declare their allegiance to the Canadian state. Ethnic groups have also participated in existing national political parties rather than creating their own political vehicles. Immigrants are also heavily committed to learning one of the official languages, and rates of intermarriage outside of each ethnic group is increasing. In comparison to ethnic groups in the United States, Canada's ethnic groups demonstrate higher rates of naturalization and political participation and lower rates of residential segregation. In short, there is little evidence that the policy of multiculturalism promotes ethnic separation.

According to Kymlicka, opposition to multiculturalism is also sustained by the fear that the policy has no limits (i.e., that there are no boundaries to our acceptance of cultural differences). But he counters such concerns by pointing out that a more powerful protection supersedes multicultural policy: Canada will not tolerate anything that threatens individual rights and equal opportunity as defined by the Charter of Rights and Freedoms. He also notes that the government spends much more on measures to promote immigrants' integration (e.g., language training, job training, child education) than it does on aspects of ethnic culture that divide.

So why, then, have anti-multicultural feelings emerged? Kymlicka feels that these feelings are due to our inability to resolve the longstanding conflicts of the nations within, in particular the Québécois and First Nations. This failure has reduced our confidence in our ability to deal with ethno-cultural relations; in consequence, immigrants and multiculturalism have become the scapegoats for fears and frustrations arising from our inability to obtain internal national reconciliation.

To ponder:

Why do you think some people oppose or fear multiculturalism?

Source: Will Kymlicka, "The Theory and Practice of Canadian Multiculturalism," *Breakfast on the Hill* 1998, hssfc.ca. See also his *Finding Our Way: Rethinking Ethnocultural Relations in Canada* (Oxford: Oxford University Press, 1998). For an example of a critique of multiculturalism, see Neil Bissoondath, *Selling Illusions: The Cult of Multiculturalism in Canada* (Toronto: Penguin, 1994).

Quebec program is known as *interculturalism* and emphasizes intercultural understanding rather than intercultural equality.[133]

Perhaps the best way to understand multiculturalism is not in terms of programs or policies but of ideology. Multiculturalism is an ideology because it is *prescriptive*, i.e., it holds out ideals about the way things should be. Because ideologies constantly shift and change, our views of multiculturalism and what it means will also change. When multiculturalism was first proposed, it was almost a kind of motherhood issue, which made everyone feel good and to which no one could object. Its focus on celebrating differences generated considerable debate.[134]

The issues of multiculturalism and immigration were often confused because multiculturalism seemed to call into question the society's capacity to absorb new immigrants. Second, the persistent threat of Quebec separation, in combination with the in-migration of new visible minorities, has tried the patience of anglophone nativists who want to get on with building a strong Canadian identity. To them, multiculturalism is "mosaic madness," "visionless coexistence," and "an inadequate national dream."[135] Backlash reactions against pluralism can also be found in the United States and Europe; these reactions can be related to the erosion of older conceptions of these societies. The danger is that rejection of multiculturalism's openness and tolerance can stem from racism and intolerance, which breed new anxieties and injustices.[136] For this reason, the meaning of multiculturalism has now shifted to constructive engagement between groups to foster the building of a more inclusive citizenry of all Canadians.

It is interesting that in recent years the federal government has emphasized the need to promote the self-sufficiency and integration of immigrants rather than the aim of supporting their multicultural attributes.[137] In the end, however, the multiculturalism debate is itself an acknowledgment of the fact that Canadian society is changing and that new ways must be found to accommodate all residents in the process of nation building. In recognition of the remarkable resilience of ethnicity, multiculturalism is now being looked at in terms of *social incorporation;* according to this concept, an ethnic group can still retain its identity while being included and part of the wider society.[138] The policy of multiculturalism is at the heart of an internal struggle over control of the symbolic order of Canadian society in which the status of ethnic groups and the perceptions of what Canadian society should be is contested.[139]

FURTHER EXPLORATION

1. Some groups, such as the Québécois and Native people, have requested "special" status rather than "equal" status. Why have they done so and what are the implications? Are they "distinct societies"?

2. Why do some people want to "shed" their ethnicity while other people eagerly maintain it? Why do people several generations removed from immigration want to rediscover their ethnic background?

3. In Canada, there is frequent reference to "the French problem" or "the Native problem." Why might it instead be called "the English problem" or "the white problem"?

4. What type of bilingualism predominates in your area? Why is bilingualism a good policy? Why is bilingualism problematic?

SELECTED READINGS

Driedger, Leo, *Race and Ethnicity: Finding Identities and Equalities.* Toronto: Oxford, 2003.

Fleras, Augie, and Jean Leonard Elliott. *Unequal Relations: An Introduction to Race, Ethnic, and Aboriginal Dynamics in Canada. 2nd ed.* Scarborough, Ont.: Prentice Hall, 1996.

Fournier, Marcel, Michael Rosenberg, and Deena White, eds. *Quebec Society: Critical Issues.* Scarborough, Ont.: Prentice Hall, 1997.

Frideres, James S., and Rene R. Gadacz. *Aboriginal Peoples in Canada.* 7th ed. Toronto: Prentice Hall, 2005.

Gagnon, Alain G., ed. *Quebec: State and Society*, 3rd ed. Peterborough: Broadview, 2004.

Isajiw, Wsevolod W., *Understanding Diversity: Ethnicity and Race in the Canadian Context.* Toronto: Thompson, 1999.

Kalbach, Madeline A., and Warren E. Kalbach, eds. *Perspectives on Ethnicity in Canada.* Toronto: Harcourt Brace, 2000.

Li, Peter S. *Race and Ethnic Relations in Canada*, 2nd ed. Toronto: Oxford, 1999.

———. *Destination Canada: Immigration Debates and Issues.* Toronto: Oxford University Press, 2003.

Ponting, J. Rick, ed. *First Nations in Canada: Perspectives on Opportunity, Empowerment, and Self-Determination.* Toronto: McGraw-Hill Ryerson, 1997.

Reitz, Jeffrey. *Warmth of the Welcome: The Social Causes of Economic Success for Immigrants in Different Nations and Cities.* Boulder: Westview Press, 1998.

ENDNOTES

1 This paragraph alludes to the subjective and objective aspects of ethnicity which, in their complexity, make the concept of ethnicity very difficult to define simply. For a discussion of the issues involved, Cf. Wsevolod W. Isajiw, "Definitions of Ethnicity," *Ethnicity* 1 (1974): 111–24.

2 Ravi Pendakur and Fernando Mata, "Patterns of Ethnic Identification and the 'Canadian' Response," *Canadian Ethnic Studies* 30, 2 (1998):125–37.

3 Frances E. Aboud, "Ethnic Self-Identity," in Robert C. Gardner and Rudolf Kalin, eds., *A Canadian Social Psychology of Ethnic Relations* (Toronto: Methuen, 1981), 43–44.

4 John Porter, *The Vertical Mosaic*, 60.

5 Leo Driedger, *The Ethnic Factor: Identity in Diversity* (Toronto: McGraw-Hill Ryerson, 1989), chap. 4.

6 See Edward N. Herberg, *Ethnic Groups in Canada: Adaptations and Transitions* (Scarborough: Nelson, 1989), chap. 6; Leo Driedger, *Multi-Ethnic Canada: Identities and Inequalities* (Toronto: Oxford, 1996), chap. 9. For an interesting account of an urban ethnic community, see Grace Anderson, *Networks of Contact: The Portuguese in Toronto* (Waterloo: Wilfrid Laurier University Press, 1974). See also Statistics Canada, Canada's Ethnocultural Portrait, *The Daily*, September 20, 2003.

7 T.R. Balakrishnan and Sephen Gyimah, "Spatial Residential Patterns of Selected Ethnic Groups: Significance and Policy Implications," *Canadian Ethnic Studies* 35, 1 (2003):113-134.

8 See, for example, Kay J. Anderson, *Vancouver's Chinatown: Racial Discourse in Canada* (Montreal: McGill-Queen's University Press, 1991) and David C. Lai, *Chinatowns: Towns Within Cities in Canada* (Vancouver: UBC Press, 1988).

9 Patricia E. Roy, "The Fifth Force: Multiculturalism and the English Canadian Identity," *Annals of the American Academy of Political and Social Science* 538 (1995):199–209.

10 For a good review of the history of Canada's immigration policy, see Elliot L. Tepper, "Immigration Policy and Multiculturalism," in J.W. Berry and J.A. Laponce, eds., *Ethnicity and Culture in Canada: The Research Landscape* (Toronto: University of Toronto Press, 1994), 95–123. See also Donald A. Avery, *Reluctant Host: Canada's Response to Immigrant Workers 1896–1994* (Toronto: McClelland and Stewart, 1995).

11 Anthony H. Richmond, "Canadian Immigration: Recent Developments and Future Prospects," in Leo Driedger, ed., *The Canadian Ethnic Mosaic*, 105–23; and Alan B. Simmons, "New Wave Immigrants: Origins and Characteristics," in Shiva S. Halli, Frank Trovato, and Leo Driedger, eds., *Ethnic Demography: Canadian Immigrant, Racial and Cultural Variations* (Ottawa: Carleton University Press, 1990), 141–59.

12 Peter S. Li, *The Making of Post-War Canada* (Toronto: Oxford University Press, 1996), chap. 6.

13 Statistics Canada, The Daily, January 21, 2003. For a review of Canadian immigration policy, particularly since World War II, see Freda Hawkins, *Canada and Immigration: Public Policy and Public Concern*, 2nd ed. (Montreal: McGill-Queen's University Press, 1988).

14 Rudolf Kalin and J.W. Berry, "Ethnic and Multicultural Attitudes," in Berry and Laponce, *Ethnicity and Culture in Canada*, 293–321.

15 Raymond Breton, "Institutional Completeness of Ethnic Communities and the Personal Relations of Immigrants," *American Journal of Sociology* 70 (1964): 193–205.

16 Tina O. Walter, Barbara Brown, and Edward Grabb, "Ethnic Identity and Sports Participation: A Comparative Analysis of West Indian and Italian Soccer Clubs in Metropolitan Toronto," *Canadian Ethnic Studies* 23, 1 (1991): 85–96; Daphne N. Winland, "The Role of Religious Affiliation in Refugee Resettlement: The Case of the Hmong," *Canadian Ethnic Studies* 24, 1 (1992): 96–119; and Joanne Van Dijk, "Ethnic Persistence among Dutch-Canadian Catholics and Calvinists," *Canadian Ethnic Studies* 30, 2 (1998): 23–49.

17 Jeffrey G. Reitz, "Language and Ethnic Community Survival," in Rita M. Bienvenue and Jay E. Goldstein, eds., *Ethnicity and Ethnic Relations in Canada*, 2nd ed. (Toronto: Butterworths, 1985), 105–23.

18 Clifford J. Jansen, "Community Organization of Italians in Toronto" in Leo Driedger, ed., *The Canadian Ethnic Mosaic*, 310–26.

19 William Shaffir, "Jewish Immigration to Canada," in Jean Leonard Elliott, ed., *Two Nations, Many Cultures: Ethnic Groups in Canada* (Scarborough: Prentice Hall, 1979), 280–89.

20 Efie Gavaki, "Urban Villagers: The Greek Community in Montreal," in Jean Leonard Elliott, ed., *Two Nations, Many Cultures,* 123–47.

21 Regula B. Qureshi and Saleem M.M. Qureshi, "Pakistani Canada: The Making of a Muslim Community," in Earle H. Waugh et al., eds., *The Muslim Community in North America* (Edmonton: University of Alberta Press, 1983), 127–48.

22 Steven T. DeZepetnek, "A History of the Hungarian Cultural Society of Edmonton, 1946–1986," *Canadian Ethnic Studies* 25, 2 (1993): 100–117.

23 The relationship between ethnicity, power, and race is discussed in Veronica Strong-Boag, Sherrill Grace, Avigail Eisenberg, and Joan Anderson, eds., *Painting the Maple Leaf: Essays on Race, Gender, and the Construction of Canada* (Vancouver: UBC Press, 1998).

24 Vic Satzewich, "The Political Economy of Race and Ethnicity," in Peter S. Li, ed., *Race and Ethnic Relations in Canada*, 2nd ed. (Toronto: Oxford University Press, 1999), chap. 11. See also Vic

Satzewich, ed., *Racism and Social Inequality in Canada* (Toronto: Thompson, 1998); and B. Singh Bolaria and Peter S. Li, *Racial Oppression in Canada*, 2nd ed. (Toronto: Garamond, 1988).

25 For a short history of non-white immigration into Canada, see Subhas Ramcharan, *Racism: Nonwhites in Canada* (Toronto: Butterworths, 1982), 12–18.

26 For excellent discussions of the evolution of attitudes towards Chinese, see the Special Issue of *Canadian Ethnic Studies* 19 (1987) entitled "Coping with Racism: The Chinese Experience in Canada"; and Peter S. Li, *The Chinese in Canada*, 2nd ed. (Toronto: Oxford University Press, 1998).

27 For a review of the Japanese experience in Canada, see Thomas Berger, "The Banished Japanese Canadians," in Leo Driedger, ed., *Ethnic Canada: Identities and Inequalities* (Toronto: Copp Clark Pittman, 1987), 374–94; and Audrey Kobayashi, "The Japanese-Canadian Redress Settlement and its Implications for Race Relations," *Canadian Ethnic Studies* 24, 1 (1992): 1–19.

28 Peter S. Li, *The Chinese in Canada*, 37.

29 E. D. Nelson and Augie Fleras, *Social Problems in Canada* (Scarborough: Prentice Hall, 1995), 256–58.

30 Frances Henry, Carol Tator, Winston Mattis, and Tim Rees, *The Colour of Democracy: Racism in Canadian Society* (Toronto: Harcourt Brace, 1995).

31 James Stafford has pointed out that in the past, immigrants from non-traditional source-countries hoping to gain admittance to Canada needed higher levels of education to compensate for their skin colour, but recent immigrants from these countries have lower levels of education. "The Impact of the New Immigration Policy on Racism in Canada," in Vic Satzewich, ed., *Deconstructing a Nation: Immigration, Multiculturalism, and Racism in 90's Canada* (Halifax: Fernwood, 1992), 69–91.

32 See Donald H. Clairmont and Dennis W. Magill, *Africville: The Life and Death of a Canadian Black Community* (Toronto: McClelland and Stewart, 1974); Frances Henry, *Forgotten Canadians: The Blacks of Nova Scotia* (Don Mills: Longman, 1973); Morris Davis and Joseph F. Krauter, *The Other Canadians: Profiles of Six Minorities* (Toronto: Methuen, 1978); also Peter S. Li and B. Singh Bolaria, eds., *Racial Minorities in Multicultural Canada* (Toronto: Garamond Press, 1983).

33 Pauline Comeau and Aldo Santin, *The First Canadians: A Profile of Canada's Native People Today* (Toronto: James Lorimer, 1990).

34 Augie Fleras and Jean Leonard Elliott, *The Nations Within: Aboriginal–State Relations in Canada, the United States, and New Zealand* (Toronto: Oxford University Press, 1992).

35 Denis Monière, *Ideologies in Quebec: The Historical Development* (Toronto: University of Toronto Press, 1981), 288. See also Francois-Pierre Gingras and Neil Nevitte, "The Evolution of Quebec Nationalism," in Alain G. Gagnon, ed., *Quebec: State and Society* (Toronto: Methuen, 1984), 3–4.

36 The three concepts developed here (*primordial event*, *social decapitation*, and *beacon of light*) can be found in numerous places, but one good reference is Richard Jones, *Community in Crisis: French-Canadian Nationalism in Perspective* (Toronto: McClelland and Stewart, 1972).

37 Kenneth McRoberts and Dale Posgate, *Quebec: Social Change and Political Crisis*, rev. ed. (Toronto: McClelland and Stewart, 1980), 30.

38 For an interesting study of French-Canadian life in the New England states, see Gerard J. Brault, *The French Canadian Heritage in New England* (Montreal: McGill-Queen's University Press, 1986).

39 For a review of the social changes occurring in Quebec and their implications, see Raymond Breton, "The Socio-Political Dynamics of the October Events," in Dale C. Thomson, ed., *Quebec Society and Politics: Views from the Inside* (Toronto: McClelland and Stewart, 1973), 213–38; and William D. Coleman, *The Independence Movement in Quebec 1945–1980* (Toronto: University of Toronto Press, 1984).

40 Sheilagh Hodgins Milner and Henry Milner, *The Decolonization of Quebec* (Toronto: McClelland and Stewart, 1973), chap. 10.

41 For the classic statement on this phenomenon, see Hubert Guindon, "Social Unrest, Social Class and Quebec's Bureaucratic Revolution," *Queen's Quarterly* 7 (1964): 150–62.

42 Raymond Murphy, "Teachers and the Evolving Structural Context of Economic and Political Attitudes in Quebec Society," *Canadian Review of Sociology and Anthropology* 18 (1981): 157–82.

43 For a good discussion of the role of the state in the new Quebec, see Henry Milner, *Politics in the New Quebec* (Toronto: McClelland and Stewart, 1978), chap. 3.

44 William D. Coleman, *The Independence Movement in Quebec 1945–1980* (Toronto: University of Toronto Press, 1984), 148.

45 In their study of the use of the designation "Québécois" in Quebec, Donald M. Taylor and Ronald J. Sigal point out that anglophones in that province reject that label and the political and cultural values it signifies. "Defining Québécois: The Role of Ethnic Heritage, Language, and Political Orientation," in Bienvenue and Goldstein, *Ethnicity and Ethnic Relations in Canada*, 125–37.

46 McRoberts and Posgate, *Quebec: Social Change and Political Crisis*, chap. 10 presents a good discussion on the meanings and objectives of sovereignty association and the strategies involved.

47 For one view, see Reginald Whitaker, "The Quebec Cauldron: A Recent Account," in Gagnon, *Quebec: State and Society*, 88–91.

48 Stanley B. Ryerson, "Disputed Claims: Quebec/Canada" in Gagnon, *Quebec: State and Society*, 59–67.

49 There are numerous discussions on the Meech Lake Accord available. See, for example, Robert M. Campbell and Leslie A. Pal, *The Real Worlds of Canadian Politics* (Peterborough: Broadview Press, 1989), chap. 5; Michael D. Behiels, ed., *The Meech Lake Primer: Conflicting Views of the 1987 Constitutional Accord* (Ottawa: University of Ottawa Press, 1989); and Bryan Schwartz, *Fathoming Meech Lake* (Winnipeg: University of Manitoba Legal Research Institute, 1987).

50 Raymond Breton points out that Meech Lake recognizes Quebec as a society but views the rest of Canada as a population. "The Concepts of Distinct Society and Identity in the Meech Lake Accord," in K.E. Swinton and C.J. Rogerson, eds., *Competing Constitutional Visions: The Meech Lake Accord* (Toronto: Carswell, 1988), 3–10.

51 For a good chronological discussion of issues and events of the Charlottetown Accord, see Chapter 3 of Robert M. Campbell and Leslie A. Pal, *The Real Worlds of Canadian Politics*, 3rd ed. (Peterborough: Broadview, 1994). In terms of the Accord's implications for the results of the 1993 federal election, which resulted in significant societal division, see Chapter 5.

52 John Conway, *Debts to Pay*, 1–9; Pierre Bourgault, *Now or Never!: Manifesto for an Independent Quebec* (Toronto: Key Porter, 1991); David E. Smith, Peter MacKinnon, John C. Courtney, eds., *After Meech Lake: Lessons for the Future* (Saskatoon: Fifth House, 1991); Patrick Monahan and Ken McRoberts, *The Charlottetown Accord, the Referendum, and the Future of Canada* (Toronto: University of Toronto Press, 1993).

53 Guy Lachapelle, "The 1995 Quebec Referendum: How the Sovereignty Partnership Proposal Turned the Campaign Around," *Quebec Studies* 24 (1997): 180–96.

54 Kenneth McRoberts and Patrick Monahan, eds., *The Charlottetown Accord, the Referendum, and the Future of Canada* (Toronto: University of Toronto Press, 1993); John E. Trent, Robert Young, and Guy Lachapelle, eds., *Quebec–Canada: What Is the Path Ahead?* (Ottawa: University of Ottawa Press, 1996); Simon Rosenblum and Peter Findlay, eds., *Debating Canada's Future: Views from the Left* (Toronto: James Lorimer, 1991).

55 An exploration of the competition hypothesis in relation to the restructuring of Quebec by francophones and of its current manifestations in perceptions of inequality in Quebec is presented in an analysis by Leslie Laczko, *Pluralism and Inequality in Quebec* (Toronto: University of Toronto Press, 1995).

56 Pierre Fournier, *The Quebec Establishment*, 2nd rev. ed. (Montreal: Black Rose, 1976), 204–205.

57 Alain G. Gagnon and Mary Beth Montcalm, *Quebec: Beyond the Quiet Revolution* (Scarborough, Ont.: Nelson, 1990).

58 Marc Renaud, "Quebec New Middle Class in Search of Social Hegemony," in Gagnon, ed., *Quebec: State and Society*, 150–95, and Hubert Guindon, *Quebec Society: Tradition, Modernity, and Nationhood* (Toronto: University of Toronto Press, 1988), 27–37.

59 Gagnon and Montcalm, *Quebec: Beyond the Quiet Revolution*, 46.

60 Bernard Blishen, "Perceptions of National Identity," *Canadian Review of Sociology and Anthropology* 15 (1978): 129–32.

61 In this regard, a Quebec sociologist, Fernand Dumont, has played a key role in popularizing a new vision of Quebec. He speaks of the pre-1960 period of Quebec as the *winter of survival* —a period of hibernation that now must be left behind as Québécois builds a new society, in dialogue with anglo-Canadians but independent from them. See his *Genèse de la société québécoise* (Montreal: Boréal, 1993).

62 Daniel W. Rossides, *Society as a Fundamental Process: An Introduction to Sociology* (Toronto: McGraw-Hill, 1968).

63 Dale Thomson, "Language, Identity, and the Nationalist Impulse: Quebec," A*nnals of the American Academy of Political and Social Science* 538 (1995): 69–82.

64 Coleman, *The Independence Movement in Quebec*, 131, 181–82.

65 The best single comprehensive source that monitors these changes is Simon Langlois et al, *Recent Social Trends in Quebec 1960–1990* (Montreal: McGill-Queen's University Press, 1992). For a French-language assessment in terms of Quebec–Canada relations, see a special issue of *Recherches Sociographiques* 30, 2–3:1998 entitled *Quebec et Canada: Deux references conflictuelles*.

66 Gilles Gagné and Simon Langlois, "Is Separatism Dead? Not Quite Yet,*" Policy Options* (June 2000): 29-45

67 Pierre Fournier, *A Meech Lake Post-Mortem? Is Quebec Sovereignty Inevitable?* (Montreal: McGill-Queen's University Press, 1991), 87. Fournier argues that individual bilingualism will continue in Quebec but with a priority given to French.

68 Guy Lachapelle, Gérald Bernier, Daniel Salée, and Luc Bernier, *The Quebec Democracy: Structures, Processes, and Policies* (Toronto: McGraw-Hill Ryerson, 1993), 345.

69 Marc V. Levine, *The Reconquest of Montreal: Language Change and Social Policy in a Bilingual City* (Philadelphia: Temple University Press, 1990).

70 Robert Chodos and Eric Hamovitch have discussed the pro-Americanism of Quebec nationalism and point out how Quebec is thoroughly North American rather than French European. *Quebec and the American Dream* (Toronto: Between the Lines, 1991).

71 Economic continentalization and the shift to free-market principles in Quebec are discussed in a number of places. For example, see Alain G. Gagnon and Mary Beth Montcalm, *Quebec: Beyond the Quiet Revolution*; and Guy Lachapelle, Gérald Bernier, Daniel Salée; and Luc Bernier, *The Quebec Democracy: Structures, Processes, and Policies*. These authors also discuss the rise of francophone economic power.

72 These ideas are prominent in Alain G. Gagnon, ed., *Quebec: State and Society*, 3rd ed. (Peterborough: Broadview, 2004). See particularly the chapter by Turgeon. See also Michel Seymour, "An Inclusive Nation That Does Not Deny Its Origins," and 146–54 in Michel Venne, ed., *Vive Quebec! New Thinking and New Approaches to the Quebec Nation* (Toronto: James Lorimer, 2001).

73 Robert M. Gill, "Language Policy, Culture and Identity: The Case of Quebec," in André Lapierre, Patricia Smart, and Pierre Savard, *Language, Culture and Values in Canada at the Dawn of the 21st*

Century (Ottawa: Carleton University Press, International Council for Canadian Studies, 1996), 99–114.

74 See Fournier, Rosenberg, and White, *Quebec Society: Critical Issues*, Chapter 3, "The Breaking Point: Language in Quebec Society (Christopher McAll), and Chapter 5, "Immigration and Ethnic Relations in Quebec: Pluralism in the Making" (Greg Neilson).

75 The concept of invisible ethnic minorities and its application to francophones in Toronto is developed in Thomas R. Maxwell, "The Invisible French: The French in Metropolitan Toronto," in Elliott, *Two Nations, Many Cultures*, 114–22. The insecurities felt by francophone groups in an English environment are described in Sheila McLeod Arnopoulos, *Voices from French Ontario* (Montreal: McGill-Queen's University Press, 1982). The role of intermarriage in the anglicization of French minorities is discussed in Charles Castonguay, "Intermarriage and Language Shift in Canada, 1971 and 1976," *Canadian Journal of Sociology* 7 (1982): 263–77. The concept of *francogènes* is discussed in Richard J. Joy, *Canada's Official Languages: The Progress of Bilingualism* (Toronto: University of Toronto Press, 1992), 63.

76 Robert Stebbins, *The French Enigma: Survival and Development in Canada's Francophone Societies* (Calgary: Detselig Enterprises Ltd., 2000). See also Richard Wilbur, *The Rise of French New Brunswick* (Halifax: Formac, 1989).

77 Michael O'Keefe, *Francophone Minorities: Assimilation and Community Vitality* ([n.p.] Heritage Canada, 1998).

78 Ronald Wardhaugh, *Language and Nationhood: The Canadian Experience* (Vancouver: New Star, 1983), 107.

79 Sheila McLeod Arnopoulos and Dominique Clift, *The English Fact in Quebec* (Montreal: McGill-Queen's University Press, 1980), 125.

80 Raymond Breton, "The Production and Allocation of Symbolic Resources: An Analysis of the Linguistic and Ethnocultural Fields in Canada," *Canadian Review of Sociology and Anthropology* 21 (1984): 123–44.

81 Gary Caldwell and Eric Waddell, *The English of Quebec: From Majority to Minority Status* (Quebec: Institut québécois de recherche sur la culture, 1982), 27–71.

82 For an interesting comparison of an anglophone community in Quebec and a francophone community in Prince Edward Island in more peripheral locations where each was disadvantaged, see Maurice Beaudin, René Boudreau, and George De Benedetti, *The Socio-economic Vitality of Official-Language Communities*, Heritage Canada Catalogue No. CH3-2/2-1996E.

83 For a thorough and readable review of languages and language policies in Canada and its regional variations, see John Edwards, ed., *Language in Canada* (Cambridge: Cambridge University Press, 1998).

84 Hubert Guindon, "The Modernization of Quebec and the Legitimacy of the Canadian State," *Canadian Review of Sociology and Anthropology* 15 (1978): 227–45.

85 Richard Joy, *Languages in Conflict: The Canadian Experience* (Toronto: McClelland and Stewart, 1972).

86 Jean Dumas, Report of the Demographic Situation 1987, Statistics Canada Catalogue 91-209E, 115; and Joy's updated study *Canada's Official Languages: The Progress of Bilingualism.*

87 For a good review of this trend, see Roderic P. Beaujot, "The Decline of Official Language Minorities in Quebec and English Canada," *Canadian Journal of Sociology* 7 (1982): 367–89.

88 Statistics Canada, *The Daily*, "Profile of Languages in Canada," December 10, 2002.

89 Official Languages 2002-2003 Annual Report, Heritage Canada.

90 Stacy Churchill, *Official Languages in Canada: Changing the Language Landscape*, Heritage Canada Catalogue CA3-2-7/1998, Table 4.

91 Ronald Wardhaugh, *Language and Nationhood*, 54–55. For a discussion of issues in official-language education in schools, see Heritage Canada, *The Canadian Experience in the Teaching of Official Languages*, Catalogue No. S53-33/1996E.

92 Olive Patricia Dickason, *Canada's First Nations: A History of Founding Peoples from Earliest Times* (Toronto: McClelland and Stewart, 1992).

93 Victor Valentine distinguishes between the "accommodation" between Native people and whites typical of the pre-Confederation period and the "domination" typical of the post-Confederation era. "Native Peoples and Canadian Society: A Profile of Issues and Trends," in R. Breton, J.G. Reitz, and V.F. Valentine, *Cultural Boundaries and the Cohesion of Canada* (Montreal: Institute for Research on Public Policy, 1980), 71–78.

94 Rita M. Bienvenue, "Colonial Status: The Case of Canadian Indians," in Bienvenue and Goldstein, *Ethnicity and Ethnic Relations in Canada*, 2nd ed., 199–214.

95 Harley Dickinson and Terry Wotherspoon, "From Assimilation to Self-Government," in Vic Satzewitch, ed., *Deconstructing a Nation*, 405–21.

96 Sally M. Weaver, "The Status of Indian Women," in Jean L. Elliot, *Two Nations: Many Cultures,* 2nd ed., 56–79.

97 J. Rick Ponting, "The Socio-Demographic Picture," in his *First Nations in Canada: Perspectives on Opportunity, Empowerment, and Self-Determination* (Toronto: McGraw-Hill Ryerson, 1997), 69.

98 James S. Frideres and Rene R. Gadacz, *Native Peoples in Canada,* 7th ed. (Scarborough, Ont.: Prentice Hall, 2005), chap. 3.

99 D. Bruce Sealey and Antoine S. Lussier, *The Métis: Canada's Forgotten People* (Winnipeg: Pemmican Publications, 1975); and also their *The Other Natives: The-Les Métis* (Winnipeg: Manitoba Métis Federation Press, 1978).

100 G.F.G. Stanley, *The Birth of Western Canada: A History of the Riel Rebellion* (Toronto: University of Toronto Press, 1978).

101 Norbert Robitaille and Robert Choiniere, *An Overview of Demographic and Socio-economic Conditions of the Inuit in Canada* (Ottawa: Indian and Northern Affairs Canada, 1985).

102 Statistics Canada, *The Daily*, January 13, 1998.

103 Jean-Philippe Chartrand, "Survival and Adaptation of the Inuit Ethnic Identity: The Importance of Inuktitut," in Bruce Alden Cox, ed., *Native People Native Lands* (Ottawa: Carleton University Press, 1988), chap. 18. See also James S. Frideres, *Aboriginal Peoples in Canada*, chap. 12.

104 George Manuel and Michael Posluns, *The Fourth World: An Indian Reality* (New York: Free Press, 1974).

105 The relationship between Native policy and the needs of capitalism is discussed in Terry Wotherspoon and Vic Satzewich, *First Nations: Race, Class, and Gender Relations* (Regina: Canadian Plains Research Center, 2000).

106 Bernard Schissel and Terry Wotherspoon, *The Legacy of School for Aboriginal People: Education, Oppression, and Emancipation* (Toronto: Oxford University Press, 2003).

107 H.B. Hawthorn, *A Survey of Contemporary Indians of Canada* (Ottawa: Indian Affairs Branch, 1966–67).

108 For a good discussion of the transitions which DIAND has made and the problems of a bureaucratic administration, see J. Rick Ponting, "Relations Between Bands and the Department of Indian Affairs: A Case of Internal Colonialism?" in J.R. Ponting, ed., *Arduous Journey: Canadian Indians and Decolonization* (Toronto: McClelland and Stewart, 1986), chap. 3. The issue of how the federal government attempts to "administer" Indian Affairs is also discussed in J. Rick Ponting and Roger Gibbins, *Out of Irrelevance: A Socio-political Introduction to Indian Affairs in Canada* (Toronto: Butterworths, 1980); and in Leroy Little Bear, Menno Boldt, and J. Anthony Long, eds., *Pathways*

to Self-Determination: Canadian Indians and the Canadian State (Toronto: University of Toronto Press, 1984). See also Noel Dyck, *What Is the Indian 'Problem'? Tutelage and Resistance in Canadian Indian Administration* (St. John's: Institute of Social and Economic Research, 1991).

109 For a discussion of the issue of Native rights and self-determination, see John Bird, Lorraine Land, and Murray Macadam, eds., *Nation to Nation: Aboriginal Sovereignty and the Future of Canada* (Toronto: Irwin, 2002); and Frank Cassidy, ed., *Aboriginal Self-Determination* (Toronto: Institute for Research on Public Policy, 1991); John H. Hylton, ed., *Aboriginal Self-Government in Canada* (Saskatoon: Purich, 1999).

110 These points are made by Roger Gibbins and J. Rick Ponting, "An Assessment of the Probable Impact of Aboriginal Self-Government in Canada," in Alan Cairns and Cynthia Williams, eds., *The Politics of Gender, Ethnicity and Language in Canada* (Toronto: University of Toronto Press, 1986), 177–78.

111 Bruce Alden Cox, "Changing Perceptions of Industrial Development in the North," in his *Native People Native Lands*, chap. 16.

112 James S. Frideres, *Aboriginal Peoples in Canada*, chap. 8.

113 James B. Waldram, "Canada's 'Indian Problem' and the Indians' 'Canada Problem,'" in Les Samuelson, ed., *Power and Resistance: Critical Thinking about Canadian Social Issues* (Halifax: Fernwood, 1994), 53–70; and David C. Hawkes, ed., *Aboriginal Peoples and Government Responsibility: Exploring Federal and Provincial Roles* (Ottawa: Carleton University Press, 1988).

114 Royal Commission on Aboriginal Peoples, *The Right of Aboriginal Self-Government: A Commentary*. Ottawa, February 13, 1992. For a different approach to the Royal Proclamation of 1763, see Menno Boldt, *Surviving as Indians: The Challenge of Self-Government* (Toronto: University of Toronto Press, 1993), chap. 1.

115 A good source dealing with initiatives in economic development is Royal Commission on Aboriginal Peoples, *Sharing the Harvest: The Road to Self-Reliance*, Ottawa, 1993. See also John Loxley and Fred Wien, "Urban Aboriginal Economic Development," in David Newhouse and Evelyn Peters, eds., *Not Strangers in These Parts: Urban Aboriginal Peoples* (Ottawa: Policy Research Initiative, 2003), 217–42.

116 The notions of empowerment and disempowerment are discussed in J. Rick Ponting, "An Overview of First Nations' Empowerment and Disempowerment," *First Nations in Canada,* chap. 5. See also Dan Beavon and Martin Cooke, "An Application of the United Nations Human Development Index to Registered Indians in Canada," in Jerry P. White, Paul S. Maxim, and Dan Beavon, *Aboriginal Conditions* (Vancouver: UBC Press, 2003), 201–221.

117 All of the national opinion surveys are reviewed in J. Rick Ponting and Jerilynn Kiely, "Disempowerment: Justice, Racism, and Public Opinion," in Ponting, *First Nations in Canada,* 174–85.

118 James S. Frideres found that media coverage of the Royal Commission on Aboriginal Peoples was quite weak and did not raise Aboriginal–non-Aboriginal relations to a higher level of public awareness. However, he argues that the Royal Commission did capture the imagination of Aboriginal peoples as a vital opportunity to bring about change. "The Royal Commission on Aboriginal Peoples: The Route to Self-Government?" *Canadian Journal of Native Studies* 16, 20 (1996): 247–66.

119 See Karen Lochead, "Whose Land Is It Anyway? The Long Road to the Nisga'a Treaty," in Robert M. Campbell, Leslie A. Pal, and Michael Howlett, *The Real Worlds of Canadian Politics*, 4th ed. (Peterborough: Broadview, 2004), 334–67.

120 For a good overview of the multiculturalism policy, its diverse meanings and political purposes, see Peter Li, "The Multiculturalism Debate," in Peter S. Li, ed., *Race and Ethnic Relations in Canada*, 2nd ed., 148–77.

121 D.H. Clairmont and F.C. Wien, "Race Relations in Canada," in Jay E. Goldstein and Rita Bienvenue, eds., *Ethnicity and Ethnic Relations in Canada* (Toronto: Butterworths, 1980), 313–15.

122 Jeffrey G. Reitz and Raymond Breton, *The Illusion of Difference: Realities of Ethnicity in Canada and the United States* (Toronto: C.D. Howe Institute, 1994).

123 Howard Palmer, *Patterns of Prejudice: A History of Nativism in Alberta* (Toronto: McClelland and Stewart, 1982).

124 Jeffrey G. Reitz, *The Survival of Ethnic Groups* (Toronto: McGraw-Hill Ryerson, 1980), and Morton Weinfeld, "Ethnic Assimilation and the Retention of Ethnic Cultures," in Berry and Laponce, *Ethnicity and Culture in Canada*, 238–66.

125 Jean Burnet, "Multiculturalism 10 Years Later," in Jean L. Elliott, ed., *Two Nations: Many Cultures*, 2nd ed., 239.

126 David R. Hughes and Evelyn Kallen, *The Anatomy of Racism: Canadian Dimensions* (Montreal: Harvest House, 1974), 190–91.

127 Frances Henry and Carol Tator, "State Policy and Practices as Racialized Discourse: Multiculturalism, the Charter, and Employment Equity," in Peter Li, *Race and Ethnic Relations in Canada*, 2nd ed., 95–98.

128 Lance W. Roberts and Rodney A. Clifton, "Explaining the Ideology of Canadian Multiculturalism," *Canadian Public Policy* 8 (1982): 88–94; and Raymond Breton, "The Structure of Relationships Between Ethnic Collectivities," in Driedger, ed., *The Canadian Ethnic Mosaic*, 60–61.

129 Wsevolod W. Isajiw, "Olga in Wonderland: Ethnicity in a Technological Society," in Dreidger, ed., *The Canadian Ethnic Mosaic*, 29–39.

130 Morton Weinfeld, "Myth and Reality in the Canadian Mosaic: Affective Ethnicity," in Bienvenue and Goldstein, *Ethnicity and Ethnic Relations in Canada*, 65–86.

131 Laverne Lewycky, "Multiculturalism in the 1990's and Into the 21st Century," in Vic Satzewich, ed., *Deconstructing a Nation: Immigration, Multiculturalism, and Racism in 90's Canada*, 372–75; Yvonne Hebert, "Citizenship Education: Towards a Pedagogy of Social Participation and Identity Formation," *Canadian Ethnic Studies* 29, 2 (1997): 82–96.

132 Sheila M. Croucher, "Constructing the Image of Ethnic Harmony in Toronto, Canada: The Politics of Problem Definition and Non-definition," *Urban Affairs Review* 32 (1997): 319–47.

133 Danielle Juteau, "The Sociology of Ethno-National Relations in Quebec," in Vic Satzewich, ed., *Deconstructing a Nation*, 323–41.

134 For an analysis of criticisms of multiculturalism, see Yasmeen Abu-Laban and Daiva Stasiulis, "Ethnic Pluralism Under Siege: Popular and Partisan Opposition to Multiculturalism," *Canadian Public Policy* 18 (1992): 365–86; and Augie Fleras and Jean Leonard Elliott, *Multiculturalism in Canada: The Challenge of Diversity* (Scarborough, ON: Nelson, 1992), 131–44. See also Augie Fleras and Jean Lock Kunz, *Media and Minorities: Representing Diversity in a Multicultural Canada* (Toronto: Thompson, 2001), chap. 1.

135 Reginald W. Bibby, *Mosaic Madness: The Poverty and Potential of Life in Canada* (Toronto: Stoddart, 1990), 104.

136 Vic Satzewich, "Race Relations or Racism: Unravelling the New Race Discourse in Canada," in Les Samuelson, ed., *Power and Resistance: Critical Thinking about Canadian Social Issues*, 39–51.

137 Yasmeen Abu-Laban, "Welcome/STAY OUT: The Contradiction of Canadian Integration and Immigration Policies at the Millennium," *Canadian Ethnic Studies* 30, 3 (1998): 190–211. For a critique of an immigration policy that stresses entrance requirements more than adaptive strategies, see Lorne Foster, *Turnstile Immigration: Social Order and Social Justice in Canada* (Toronto: Thompson, 1998).

138 The concept of social incorporation is meant to provide an alternative to assumptions about inevitable assimilation that allows for ethnic vitality. Wsevolod W. Isajiw, "On the Concept and Theory of Social Incorporation," in W.W. Isajiw, ed., *Multiculturalism in North America and Europe* (Toronto: Canadian Scholars Press, 1997), 79–102.

139 Raymond Breton, "Intergroup Competition in the Symbolic Construction of Canadian Society," in Peter S. Li, *Race and Ethnic Relations in Canada*, 2nd ed., 291–310.

WEBLINKS

www.crr.ca

The Canadian Race Relations Foundation's Web site provides visitors with documentation of racism in Canada as well as links to other relevant sites.

www.magenta.nl

The Crosspoint Anti-Racism home page is one of the Internet's biggest links in the field of human rights, anti-racism, refugees, etc.

www.afn.ca

The Assembly of First Nations is a First Nations institution that brings together government leaders to devise common strategies on collective issues, and to present the views of various First Nations in such areas as Aboriginal and treaty rights, environment, economic development, education, housing, health, social services, and land claims.

chapter six

The Question of Uniqueness

In addition to the things which could be done anywhere to add to the knowledge of human societies, what are the features of Canadian life to which the "more-so" principle might apply–those things which are highlighted somewhat in Canadian life, and from which one might learn something more about some aspect of human society than one would elsewhere.
—Everett C. Hughes, an American analyst of Quebec's social change (1940s), suggesting a distinctive thrust for Canadian researchers

As you read through this book, you may think that Canadian society is surely unique. This perception is particularly common among those who are caught up in Canada's societal problems and are trying to resolve them as though they had never occurred anywhere before. The object of this chapter is to show that Canada's situation is not as uncommon as we might think, and to allow us to learn more about Canadian society by comparing it with other societies. Such comparisons are important because the fact that each society is unique can lead us to assume that the society under review has few parallels elsewhere. A comparative analysis helps us to see that there are other societies with similar problems for which various solutions have been found. It is also important for those studying Canadian society from the outside to see linkages to other societies with which they may be more familiar. In sum, a comparative approach enables us to place a society in a global context, sharpening our ability to identify differences and similarities. This not only broadens our horizons but also enables us to understand the dynamics of Canadian society in a new way.

This chapter does not attempt to exhaustively detail the many ways in which Canadian society contrasts with other societies; in fact, some of the contrasts will remain implicit or weakly developed because of space limitations. Yet it is possible to identify some of the characteristic features of Canadian society, to look for parallels in other societies, and to sketch something of their significance and meaning in that social context.

We have already seen how Canada's land surface, settlement history, population distribution, and regional differences have produced a society with its own character. We have also noted how the variables of social class, ethnicity, language, religion, and occupation add a dynamic to these formative features. What have been the experiences of other societies in which similar factors have been present? How unique is Canadian society? In this chapter, we will develop comparisons by focusing on distinctive Canadian features of demographic distribution, value differences, immigration, ethnic regionalism, and language. While we could examine societies which are strikingly different from Canadian society (e.g., Brazil, India), most of our comparisons will be drawn from societies which have a level of development similar to Canada's and to which comparisons are frequently made. Those societies include the United States, Australia, the United Kingdom, and selected European countries.

DISTINCTIVE CANADIAN FEATURES

Large Area and Small Population

> **DISTINCTIVE CANADIAN FEATURE:**
> **Large land surface and relatively small population**
>
> *Comparison: Global*

Russia has the largest land surface of any country in the world. Canada is second largest in territorial size, though it is only slightly larger than China and the United States and a bit larger still than Brazil and Australia, the world's next largest countries (see Table 6.1). Brazil is approximately 85% the size of Canada, and Australia about 75% the size.

Population size, however, tells us a different story. China's population is the largest by far, followed by the population of India. While Canada has one of the largest land surfaces in the world, its population is comparatively very small. The industrialized countries of France, Germany, and the United Kingdom each have more than double Canada's population in territorial areas half Canada's size or less. Mexico has almost three times Canada's population in a territory only one fifth as large. Japan has less than 4% of the territory Canada has, but a population almost five times as large. India's population is 34 times larger than Canada's, even though its territory is only one third the size.

The best measure of these national differences is *population density per square kilometre*. Canada has the most in common with Australia, where a smaller population and smaller land size yields a density similar to Canada's. The former Soviet Union, Brazil, Argentina, and New Zealand also have rather low densities despite large land surfaces, reflecting the fact that significant portions of these countries' territory are also uninhabited owing to inhospitable climate or terrain. There are many countries whose population densities are high even though they are not large in territory or population (e.g., United Kingdom, Japan, Philippines, Germany).

Canada is one of few countries with a large land surface and a low population density. In this, Canada most closely resembles Australia, which has one of the world's larger territories (though smaller than Canada's) and a population about three fifths the size. China and the United States are close to Canada in total land area, but their population densities

TABLE 6.1	Population Size, Land Area, and Density for Selected Countries, 2001		
Country	Population (000)	Surface Area (km²)	Density (person/ km²)
Canada	30 007	9 970 610	3
Russia	145 537	17 075 400	8
China	1 242 612	9 596 961	128
United States	281 421	9 629 091	30
Brazil	169 799	8 514 047	20
Australia	18 972	7 741 220	3
India	1 027 015	3 287 263	314
Argentina	36 223	2 780 400	13
Greenland	49	2 175 600	0
Mexico	97 483	1 958 201	52
Iran	60 055	1 648 195	39
Nigeria	88 992	923 768	129
France	58 520	551 500	107
Germany	77 782	357 022	231
United Kingdom	58 789	242 900	246
Korea	46 136	99 538	476
Philippines	76 504	300 000	260
Japan	126 925	377 873	336
New Zealand	3 820	270 534	12

Source: Compiled from United Nations Demographic Yearbook, 2001, Table 3, pp. 54-64.]

are much higher. Canada is clearly somewhat distinctive in terms of both its land size and population density.

Unevenly Distributed Population

DISTINCTIVE CANADIAN FEATURE:
Uneven distribution of the population

Comparison: Australia

Few countries have evenly dispersed populations. Such factors as mountains and forests, cities and jobs combine to either repel or attract population. What is unique in Canada's case is that much of this vast country's relatively small population is highly concentrated in a single area, the Golden Triangle, with much of the remaining population huddled at the country's southern extremities. In this, too, Canada can be compared with Australia.

Figure 6.1 reveals that the population of Australia is unevenly dispersed throughout its territory. Just as Canada's Golden Triangle (in southern Ontario and southern Quebec) is where population concentration is the highest, so Australia has its own zone of high population concentration in its southeast corner, south of a line from Adelaide to Sydney. Approximately two thirds of Australia's total population live in this relatively small geographic area. The remaining population concentrations are found along the east and southwest coasts, with only a small scattered population in inland locations.

One of the consequences of this uneven population distribution is that about 60% of Australia's total population is found in two states, Victoria and New South Wales (compare with Ontario and Quebec, whose percentage of Canada's total population is very similar). Victoria and New South Wales also contain the country's two largest cities, namely Sydney (at 4.2 million people) and Melbourne (at 3.5 million).[1] The surpassingly large size of these two cities, which are home to about 40% of Australia's population, invites their comparison with Canada's primate cities of Toronto and Montreal. Brisbane (population 1.7 million) and Perth (1.4 million) are the two newly expanding cities, while Adelaide (1.1 million) is somewhat more like Winnipeg, both in its more central location and in the fact that it is not growing as fast as the above-named metropolises. All of these cities are also the capitals of their states and the primary destinations for rural–urban and international migrants.

Uneven population distribution means that the states with large urban metropolitan populations while be dominant, while those with smaller urban centres and large uninhabited spaces will have less power. Indeed, political and economic power is concentrated in the southeastern states (i.e., New South Wales and Victoria), to the chagrin of Queenslanders (nicknamed "banana benders") and Western Australians (nicknamed "sandgropers").

Among Western Australians, the fact that vast uninhabited territory separates their population centres from the southeastern states—Australia's industrial heartland—has led to a nagging belief that this imbalance is ultimately responsible for their state's arrested development and hinterland position. Just as Western Canada had its own protest movements in the '20s and '30s, so too did Western Australia.[2] However, in Western Australia the regional rebellion culminated in a 1933 vote to secede from Australia. Although the vote was 2:1 in favour of secession, it was never actually carried out. Given the persistence of perceptions of the state's lack of power within Australian federalism, it was not surprising that protest and even secession-threats arose again in the mid-'70s when the federal government attempted to centralize its control of natural resources, which Western Australia had in abundance.

In sum, demographic imbalances and geographic features have combined with other factors to produce a continuing sense of marginality, alienation, and powerlessness in Western Australia. Western Australia's situation is directly comparable to that of Western Canada, cut off from Canada's industrial heartland by the Canadian Shield. While the historical details differ, the structure and dynamics of regional relations within Australian and Canadian society are very similar. Population imbalances, while not the cause of regional conflicts, serve to intensify those conflicts within each society.

Canada has no parallel to the ACT (Australian Capital Territory), which includes the urban centre of Canberra in a small territory similar to the District of Columbia, which contains the capital city of Washington in the United States. On the other hand, Tasmania, with its lower level of metropolitan urbanization, is somewhat like Canada's Atlantic provinces, having low employment diversity and opportunity. The weakly populated Northern Territory (1% of the country's population), with its large numbers of Aboriginal people and large tracts of uninhabitable land, also bears some resemblance to the

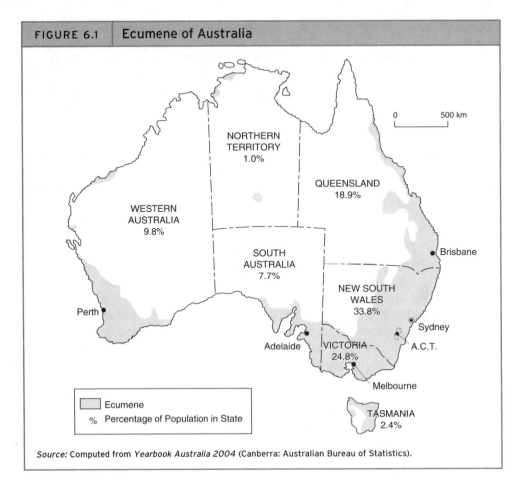

FIGURE 6.1   Ecumene of Australia

Source: Computed from *Yearbook Australia 2004* (Canberra: Australian Bureau of Statistics).

Northwest Territories of Canada, aside from the fact of opposite climates—hot desert in Australia and cold tundra in Canada.

In much (but not all) of its territory, Canada has a problem with poor soil or poor growing conditions resulting from the cold climate. In Australia aridity is a problem in some locations, and a tropical rainy climate in others. Consequently, just as most of the population of Canada has gravitated to the southern extremities of the country where the climate is more moderate, so the population of Australia clusters along the more temperate south and east coasts. Large portions of the land in both countries are virtually uninhabited. These vast hinterlands have been valued for their resources, which are exported to urban centres or to other countries. As a result, the economies of these regions are dependent on the vagaries of the market. Many of the metropolis–hinterland relationships which are developing in Australia have their parallels in Canada.[3]

By way of further contrast, it is interesting to note that the higher levels of economic development in Canada and Australia result in much less of a cleavage between rural and urban peoples (with the possible exception of the Native or Aboriginal populations) than is found in a country like Brazil.[4] In that country there is great disparity between the more modern affluent sector and the primarily rural poor majority (although there are urban poor as well). The technology gap between the traditional society and the more modern sector produces deeper cleavages in Brazil because it means that large portions of the population are excluded from participation in economic growth.

Although, as we will see later, there are other reasons to compare Australia with Canada, the uneven distribution of population over a large and relatively uninhabited territory is fundamental to the similarity between the two societies.

Dominance of One Region

DISTINCTIVE CANADIAN FEATURE:
The continued consolidation of dominance in Central Canada (especially Ontario)

Comparison: The United States

We have already seen how the southeast of Australia plays a dominant urban-economic role in that country, much like the Golden Triangle in Canada. Now we will look to the United States for illustration of a change from the dominance of one region (namely the the Northeast) to a significant regional dispersal of power.

The arrival of Europeans on North America's eastern coast meant that the natural internal movement of population on the continent would be from east to west. By the end of World War II, a pattern was clearly established that resulted in the largest population concentrations being located in the Northeastern states and extending up into Ontario and Quebec. As the centre of industrialization, the New England states had attracted both immigrants and internal migrants to their growing cities. Other industrial cities in the North, such as Detroit, Cleveland, and Chicago, attracted white rural populations that had been pushed off the land by the mechanization of agriculture, and Southern Black people who were beginning to seek employment opportunities in Northern cities. Toronto and Montreal experienced the same kind of growth from rural–urban population shifts (with the exception of Black migration from the South).

While the dynamics of industrial growth meant that internal migration was clearly in the direction of the Northern cities in the United States, a gradual movement of population to the West Coast (cities such as Seattle, San Francisco, and Los Angeles) was also occurring. The geographic centre of the population had been steadily moving westward—from Maryland in 1790, to Indiana by 1900, to Illinois in 1960, and still further westward to well past St. Louis, Missouri, by 2000.[5] Most of this shift was due to an internal redistribution of the population rather than to an influx of new residents. By the 1970s it became clear that the Northeastern region was losing its growth dynamic; its share of the national population declined from 26% in 1950 to 19% by 1997. Even the Midwest's share declined from 29% in 1960 to 23% in 1997. On the other hand, the Western region's share of the population had increased from 13% to 22%, and the South's grew from 31% to 35% over the same period.[6] With the exception of New York, which always experiences large numerical increases because of its large population, the highest increases were in the states of California, Texas, and Florida. The population seemed to be moving from areas of high density, such as the Northeast (315 persons per square mile), to areas of low density, such as the West (31 persons per square mile).

Canada has seen a similar long-term pattern of movement westward, particularly to British Columbia and more recently to Alberta. It might also be argued that Canadians have been caught up in the general continental population-shift to the American South and Southwest, whether as temporary or semi-permanent migrants. What makes Canada different, however, is that the redistribution of population within the country has not as yet had any significant effect on the redistribution of power. Exceptions to this statement might be the shift away from the earlier-industrialized Atlantic region towards Central Canada (noted in Chapter Four), and the growth of Alberta and British Columbia, particularly in recent years. However, southern Ontario, with an already substantial population at the beginning of the 1980s, was the single most important growth point in Canada in that decade, and in the '90s Ontario remained consistently strong in spite of what was occurring in the far West. Thus Canada has been unlike the United States; movement away from "old" centres of industrial strength has only meant a decrease in Quebec's relative strength and a greater concentration of strength in Ontario.

California: "The Promised Land"

The California of the last two decades is markedly different from the California of the 1960s, when most of its in-migration came from the US Midwest (and some from the Eastern seaboard). Now California has become the nation's port of entry for global immigration.

In the 24-year period from 1971 to 1995, immigration flows into the United States have exceeded the 18 million immigrants admitted in the great migration of 1900–1924. Whereas Europe was the dominant source-area during that earlier period, Asia and Latin America are now the source of over 80% of all immigrants, including many illegal migrants.

Until the last two decades, California grew primarily through internal migration, but in the last decade alone, more than 30 countries have sent 10 000 or more immigrants each year to California. California receives three times as many immigrants as New York, the next-most popular destination. More than one fifth of all foreign-born residents in the whole United States live in California. The Latin American population make up over half of all foreign-born in the state. Non-Hispanic whites are expected to be a minority in the state around the turn of the century. This change has been relatively sudden; in 1960, California was 90% non-Hispanic white.

Immigrants move to big cities where there are existing immigrant communities. Over 40% of all immigrants to California settle in Los Angeles, and another 20% in the Bay area. About one third of the California population speak a language other than English at home; about one quarter of California's students have limited English proficiency.

This very different ethnic and racial mix raises major questions about assimilation and about whether California is a mirror for major changes that the United States as a whole will have to face. While some celebrate this diversity, others fear a balkanization of society into enclaves as a result of inequalities and social tensions.

Source: William A.V. Clark, *The California Cauldron* (New York: Guilford Press, 1998). See also A. Portes and R. Rumbaut, *Immigrant America: A Portrait* (Berkeley: University of California Press, 1996).

One explanation of the redistribution of population in the United States is that it is a symptom of the redistribution of economic and political power in that country.[7] It is argued that the Southern Rim (the area south of a line drawn from the Carolinas to California) has challenged the dominance of the Eastern economic establishment through agribusiness, the defence industry, advanced technology, oil and gas production, real estate, construction, tourism, and leisure. Consequently, many cities have experienced remarkable growth. The population of Houston, for example, increased from a paltry 385 000 residents in 1945 to 2.7 million in 1980, and this story has been repeated in many other Southern Rim cities, such as Ft. Lauderdale, Austin, and Phoenix. Instead of relying on secondary manufacturing industries such as were the mainstay of the Northeast, Southern Rim communities encouraged tertiary service industries (e.g., electronics) and quaternary leisure-related industries. These initiatives provided new employment opportunities in the Southern Rim and reduced the economic strength of the Northeast. Some have argued that notwithstanding the developments in the American South, this power shift has been exaggerated. [8] The truth, though, is that the South has penetrated the political and economic mainstream in a manner which has changed the nature of regional relationships.

In Canada, despite the slow redistribution of the population westward, there is only minor evidence of any significant shift in power. The rapid growth of Edmonton and Calgary in the 1970s actually reversed itself in the early 1980s, as their growth was tied directly to the exploitation of oil and gas. Alberta's efforts at greater industrial diversification (e.g., the establishment of an electronics industry) had only marginal success in the 1980s but increasing success in the 1990s. Since 1996, Alberta's population and economy experienced particularly strong growth; Calgary often pointed to the fact that it now had the second highest concentration of head offices in Canada. Yet those head offices were concentrated in only one industry—energy, and there was little evidence of other shifts of power to that province. In British Columbia, despite the fact that a coastal climate and favourable location, making it the gateway to the Pacific Rim, have increased Vancouver's importance for international trade, the province's economy is still highly dependent on resources.[9] In sum, if in the United States there have been some important shifts of both population and technology away from the Northeast (or in competition with it), there seems little evidence that any substantial shift of power has occurred in Canada. In fact, southern Ontario in particular appears to have consolidated its position as the centre of economic power.

While the United States has experienced a redistribution of its economic activity to new urban nodes, Canada has had only limited success in doing so. With the comparative decline of Montreal,[10] Toronto and southern Ontario have become even more of a population magnet.

Continental Differences

DISTINCTIVE CANADIAN FEATURE:
Explaining continental differences

Comparison: The United States

Canada shares with the United States the experience of being a colonial outpost of European empires. Louis Hartz's *fragment theory* suggests that these new societies were founded as fragments of European culture and ideology.[11] In his view, contemporary differences between New World societies can be traced at least partially to the sponsoring societies. While many European societies featured a multiplicity of divergent ideologies (e.g., conservatism, liberalism, socialism), the societies of the New World tended to be constructed on only one aspect or fragment of the European political culture. Therefore, Hartz argued, the society of New France (French Canada) was established as a fragment of conservative feudal French society while English-America was much more a liberal bourgeois fragment of England.

On the one hand, this kind of analysis implies that English Canada and the United States should be very similar. McRae has argued that the conservative French fragment became entrenched with the British conquest in 1759, when the entrepreneurial spirit was removed from Quebec and the Catholic Church took over the guardianship of traditional values and social life.[12] On the other hand, the American War of Independence in 1776 demonstrated the failure of the liberal English fragment to claim the entire continent. However, neither Quebec nor what is now English Canada supported the American rebellion, and this rejection of the independence movement reasserted Old World loyalties and ideologies in Canada, establishing the basis for essential differences between Canadian and American society.

Canadian-American Differences For Canada, perhaps the most significant consequence of the rejection of the American independence movement was the migration of the Loyalists from the United States. The *United Empire Loyalists* were persons who wanted

---

REAL PEOPLE 6

Canadian-American Differences

Banff, Alberta. A summer tourist.

"Hey, these Canadian Rockies are cool. I'm from Colorado and I thought Rockies were Rockies, but the jagged peaks they have up here make the Rockies so much more impressive.

Can't figure it out though. Enjoyed the scenery on the drive up here and Canada seems just like the States, you know, the people, McDonalds and all that. The only thing that bugs me is that they were trying to make me change my money—you know that coloured paper you have up here. I went into one store today and one owner said he just wouldn't take my US money. He said he was proud to be Canadian and that I should get my money changed. Obviously he does not know how business works 'cause he was throwing away a sale.

Then he told me that he had been visiting in San Diego and they sure didn't take Canadian money. They even gave him a hard time with Canadian-dollar traveller's cheques. So he vowed that he would never take US money in Canada. But you know, we're just up here for a few days so it hardly pays to go through all that hassle.

I like Canada because it is just like the United States. But it is also different and I can't say what it is or why. Maybe it's just the different money. I don't know."

Question to Consider:

Why are people surprised that Canada and the United States are so similar and yet perplexed because they are different?

to retain British ties. It is estimated that between 30 000 and 60 000 Loyalists arrived in Canada around the time of the American rebellion; prior to this, Canada had only about 15 000 anglophone residents in all.[13] In many ways, English Canada emerged as a direct consequence of the American Revolution.

Bell and Tepperman have argued that the irony of the Loyalists' position was that while rejecting American republicanism, they remained deeply affected by their American experience. Loyalists were "anti-American Yankees" who created a "myth" about being British, embracing a "peculiar form of coat-tails imperialism."[14] Caught between the societal worlds of the United States and Britain, Canada took up the struggle of retaining British traditions while creating national distinctiveness in a North American environment. The context in which this took place, however, is critical. The American Revolution and the War of 1812 (in which British forces blocked attempts by American invading forces to end British colonial rule on the continent) both served as *formative events* in the delineation of basic differences between the two societies.

If the United States was born of revolution, Canada was born of *counter-revolution.* Revolution had meant breaking ties with the mother country, as the United States did with Britain; counter-revolution meant preserving those ties. The effect of this difference between the two societies has manifested itself in two major areas: settlement of the frontiers and the formation of basic values.

The *frontier comparisons* have been made by S.D. Clark.[15] Clark felt that both societies had the common experience of settling a series of frontiers in the pursuit of staples. While the frontier societies of both countries may have shared characteristic features of rugged individualism and non-traditional behaviour, the Canadian frontiers were more stable and less disorganized because of the order created by traditional and organized authority. The structures of traditional authority included a military police force (the North West Mounted Police), a privileged upper class, a large commercial organization (The Hudson's Bay Company), and representatives of the church (Anglican and Catholic), who provided greater social stability as outposts-of-empire controls. The heroes of American frontier settlement, on the other hand, were individualists who confronted disorder because the symbols of law and order did not precede settlement. People like Davey Crockett, Daniel Boone, and the appointed or elected sheriff are not part of Canadian history because the institutions of empire were established in advance of settlement and created different traditions and expectations. Thus Canadian frontiers reflected empire controls rather than independence and experimentation, and these controls provided a very different foundation for Canadian society.

The argument about differences in basic *values* has been made by S.M. Lipset, who concluded that Canada's counter-revolutionary tradition has made its society much more conservative and traditional than American society.[16] According to his thesis, which contrasts the two societies using four dichotomous variables, Canada is more elitist, ascriptive, particularist, and collectivity-oriented, whereas the United States is more egalitarian, achievement-oriented, universalist, and self-oriented. The ideology of the United States is replete with egalitarian themes—free enterprise, individualism, and upward mobility through personal achievement reign supreme. In comparison, Lipset argued, Canada has tended to follow the British pattern of values based on an aristocratic background of privilege and a more hardened class structure.

What evidence did Lipset use to build his case? Gathering evidence that lower levels of educational attainment were a good indicator of lesser opportunity, he noted that in Canada there was less equality of opportunity through the educational system. He asserted that Canada's greater acceptance of government participation in the economy indicated that it was more collectivist than the United States, which staunchly defended individualistic free-enterprise ideas. Government involvement in Canadian broadcasting and transportation, for example, and the traditional strength of the Roman Catholic and Anglican churches were viewed as part of a general pattern of the reinforcement of traditional community values and the suppression of excesses of individualism. Noting the greater respect for law and order in Canada, as evidenced by a lower ratio of policemen and lawyers to population, Lipset maintained that Canada had a more stable traditional order. In contrast, higher crime and divorce rates in the United States indicated less respect for traditional order.

Lipset's thesis has generated considerable controversy and debate.[17] In the first place, Lipset depended on data from the 1950s, and Canada has undergone considerable changes since that time, particularly in education and in the growth of divorce and crime rates. Secondly, it is questionable whether any of the data he used really identify dominant societal values. For example, a case can be made that Canada is more, rather than less, egalitarian than the United States. Greater racial inequalities in America and the greater gap between rich and poor serve to support this case. In fact, Canada's British working-class heritage puts greater value on equality of living standards and income than on competitive achievement. Third, Canada has produced numerous reform movements, which have brought about innovations in medical care, creative third-party politics, and institutional change. Such social-democratic innovations have been tolerated to a much greater extent in Canada than in the United States.

Lipset's Revision Given recent developments such as free trade (which has linked the economies of the two countries more clearly) and the Charter of Rights (which, in its emphasis on individual rights, arguably makes Canada more like the United States), Lipset has returned to the question of what differentiates Canadian and American societies. He sees convergence and change on a variety of dimensions.[18] For example, the United States has become much more involved in state-supported welfare (reflecting collectivism); moreover, affirmative-action programs have addressed the plight of disadvantaged groups (group orientation, ascription). In Canada, access to higher education has improved (achievement orientation) and crime has increased (individualism).

Yet Lipset argues that the *historical events* upon which the two societies were founded—namely, acceptance or rejection of the American Revolution—established *values* and predispositions which have an ongoing effect because they became the basic *organizing principles* of the society. So even though Canada and the United States resemble each other more than any other society resembles either of them, value differences exist; although they are a long way from where they started, the two societies (like trains on parallel railway tracks) are still separated. Lipset concludes that Canada is more class-aware, elitist, law-abiding, statist, and group-oriented, whereas the United States "tends" in the opposite direction as a result of its primary emphasis on individualism. In evidence, he offers the facts that in the United States the welfare-support network is one of the weakest in the industrialized world, no real socialist or social-democratic party exists, a relatively small percentage of the labour force is unionized, and judges and sheriffs are popularly elected.

Lipset's "interpretive essay" is intriguing and provocative. He has clearly made an effort to incorporate the changes which have taken place in both Canada and the United States since the 1950s. In some ways, his subtle air of American superiority or "exceptionalism" (his more recent term) is not quite as obvious because it is no longer possible to speak of Canada as a less-developed nation. Yet his explanation of why differences between the two societies exist is less convincing. Can everything be blamed on a single formative event without reducing the discussion to absurdity? Can values be attributed to an entire nation as though all people embraced them, and are those values not perhaps ideals more than real features of the society? What structural explanations can be proposed for Canadian–American differences?

Lipset concludes by observing that while Canada once differentiated itself from American society with right-wing criticisms (i.e., that the US was too "vulgar," "materialistic," "individualistic"), it now does so with a left-wing critique (Canada is "less elitist," "more egalitarian," more "anti-imperialist").[19] Yet we have already seen that recent developments related to globalization suggest that Canadian concern about differentiation may be decreasing. Value differences that may have existed in the past may not continue to exist. In fact, Nevitte's study concluded that since the 1980s Canada has sustained an extraordinary shift in values in the same direction as values are shifting in other industrialized countries.[20] The sustained prosperity experienced by these countries has led to new post-materialist values; deference to authority and confidence in government and other institutions are waning. In this value shift, Canada does not follow the United States; it is even leading the way. Moreover, the increased adoption of free-market principles and declining government intervention have reduced barriers that formerly helped to sustain value differences.[21]

A New Perspective: The Deep-Structures Approach Reacting to Hartz and McRae's founding-fragment approach and Lipset's revolutionary-origins approach, Grabb and Curtis have recently proposed what they call the *deep-structures* approach. They argue that both Canada and the United States have similar core values or deep, structured principles of individual freedom (liberty), equality before the law (legal equality), rule of the people (popular sovereignty), and the right to be different (pluralism), which are rooted in their similar origins as colonies of Britain. Thus, it is not the Revolutionary War that is important but the fact that both societies are rooted in the language, values, and institutions of a common British heritage. Observed differences between the two societies are primarily the result of different cultures in Quebec and the American South.

Grabb and Curtis propose that the United States and Canada should be viewed not as two societies but as four regional subsocieties: Quebec, with its origins in hierarchical conservativism, is different from English Canada, while the American South, with its history of slavery and particularism, produced a culture different from that of the American North. In fact, the four subsocieties can be placed on a continuum, with Quebec at one end, the American South at the other, and English Canada and the American North in the middle. Quebec, while it retains a strong societal identity through collective nationalism and a distinct language, experienced a rebellion against its conservatism and has now become the most liberal society. The American South has retained a strong moral and religious conservatism, as revealed by very strong religiosity scores and high levels of patriotism and trust in government. Attitudes towards crime and moral issues (e.g., gay rights) are the most lenient in Quebec but strict in the American South. Support for labour unions, government spending, and political activism is also much stronger in Quebec than in the South. When the two regional societies of English Canada and the American North are considered separately from their respective countries, their similarity becomes apparent. Thus, comparisons that do not take these two unique subsocieties into consideration produce a misleading picture of national differences.

RESEARCH CLIP 6.1	Comparing Canada and the United States: The Four Societies

Differences between Canada and the United States are often magnified because they do not take into account the fact that Quebec is different from English Canada and the American South is different from the American North. When these four societies are considered separately, it is clear that Quebec tends to be at one end of the continuum and the American South at the other. Here are some comparisons.

Crime Rates

Crime rates are often said to be higher in the United States. This is partially true because rates of violent crime, particularly homicide, are higher in the United States. Nevertheless, homicide is both a rare and a declining phenomenon in both societies. When non-violent crimes (e.g., assault, burglary, vehicle theft) are considered, the rates of the two countries are rather similar and sometimes even slightly higher in Canada. The United States has more police officers than Canada, a fact which may contribute to more crime reports; it also has more big cities where such crime is likely to be reported, but both societies have a "culture of lawfulness." The big difference, though, emerges when we compare Quebec and the American South. The American South has more violent and non-violent crime and Quebec has the lowest rates of all kinds of crime.

Economic Inequality

Income inequality is greater in the United States than in Canada, although the differences are not large. It is at the extreme ends of the income scale that the differences are notable. The top 1% of earners in the United States possess 35% of the wealth, whereas the top 1% in Canada hold 25%. Poverty rates in the United States are higher; the biggest contrast, once again, is found between the American South and Quebec. Quebec has the highest unionization rate, much more government intervention, and much less income inequality. The American South, on the other hand, has the lowest rate of unionization, the lowest levels of government support for health, education, and welfare, and the greatest amount of income inequality.

Religion and Morality

Americans are more active in religious participation and hold more conservative moral views. But in large part differences between the two countries can be accounted for by differences between Quebec and the American South. In Quebec, affiliation rates with the Catholic Church are high but participation level is low; people are much more open to varied lifestyles and liberal attitudes. In contrast, the mostly Protestant American South has high levels of participation and much more conservative views of morality and social values.

Conclusion:

Generally, the American North and English Canada are much closer to each other on these indicators, and it is the disparities between Quebec and the American South which magnify the differences between the two countries.

Source: Edward Grabb and James Curtis, *Regions Apart: The Four Societies of Canada and the United States* (Toronto: Oxford University Press, 2005).

RESEARCH CLIP 6.2	Comparing the American "Melting Pot" with the Canadian "Mosaic"

The dominant metaphors used to describe ethnic diversity in the United States and Canada suggest that Canada is more tolerant of diversity whereas the United States works towards assimilation and the erasing of ethnic differences. Do these metaphors accurately reflect reality or are they myths?

This question is important because multiculturalism is official federal policy in Canada; no such policy exists in the United States. Furthermore, the proportion of foreign-born is twice as large in Canada as in the United States, despite the fact that immigration into both societies has been heavy. In the United States, the dominant issue has been the incorporation of racial minorities, particularly Blacks, into the mainstream; in Canada, the dominant issue has been the accommodation of anglophones and francophones.

What is the evidence of societal differences?

1. There is insufficient evidence to prove that Canada values and encourages cultural diversity more than the United States, and certainly insufficient evidence strong enough to support the implication of the metaphors. For example, only 20% of Americans think of the United States as a melting pot, and in reality more Americans (47%) than Canadians (34%) cherish the ideal of cultural retention.

2. The multiculturalism discourse in Canada implies a higher degree of tolerance of diversity; in reality, however, attitudes towards immigration in both Canada and the United States suggest both a tolerance for diversity *and* a bias towards assimilation.

3. In the United States, assimilation is viewed as a dominant ideology, while the assertion of a minority culture is viewed as an individualist anti-establishment position. Such individualism is more highly valued in American ideology. In Canada, multiculturalism is an establishment idea most highly favoured by those of British origin but highly opposed by the largest minority group (the French), who see multiculturalism as a threat to their own group's position.

4. There is no evidence of less discrimination in Canada; indeed, blatant marginalization is prevalent in both countries. However, racial minorities make up a greater proportion of America's poor.

5. While there is evidence that interest in ethnicity wanes by the third generation, ceasing to be a dominant factor in shaping behaviour, the fact that Canada has a higher proportion of first- and second-generation immigrants makes ethnicity a more salient issue in Canada at this time than in the United States.

Source: Jeffrey G. Reitz and Raymond Breton, *The Illusion of Difference: Realities of Ethnicity in Canada and the United States* (Toronto: C.D. Howe Institute, 1994).

In some ways, Quebec and the American South have pulled English Canada and the American North away from each other, but over time the two latter regions are still more similar than different. Grabb and Curtis conclude that extreme events and short-term trends notwithstanding, it is a myth that Canada and the United States are all that different. As expressed in the values and behaviours of their citizens, the differences are not all that significant when the subsocieties of Quebec and the American South are considered separately. Grabb and Curtis point to value convergence, rooted in a common origin that continues to make the two societies more alike than different.

For most Canadians, comparisons with the United States are a part of everyday life, as residents grapple with the obvious similarities yet remarkable (and subtle) differences between the two societies. While the counter-revolutionary thesis is helpful in articulating these differences, it is clear that the issue of differences in values is exceedingly complex and resists simple generalizations. It is also difficult to assess how shifts in economic values are influencing social and political values and to determine whether the resultant value convergence may inevitably efface other national differences. In fact, another recent study argues yet again that value convergence between the two countries is a myth; Americans, the study found, see themselves as lone warriors under seige to whom dominance is essential, whereas Canadians value compromise and harmony.[22]

Immigration and Native-White Relations

DISTINCTIVE CANADIAN FEATURE:
Patterns of immigration and Native–White relations

Comparison: Australia

Canada and Australia were both originally British colonies, and both countries have remained members of the British Commonwealth. Just as Canada came into being as a nation by an Act of the British Parliament in 1867, so Australia was created by the *Commonwealth of Australia Constitution Act,* passed in 1900. British sponsorship has affected many aspects of Australian life, just as it has affected many aspects of life in Canada. Australia, however, has been most profoundly influenced by the fact that it was primarily settled and exclusively controlled by people from the British Isles.

The British did not have to compete against other European powers or settlers for control of Australia, as they had to do in Canada against the French. In Australia there was also no legacy of armed rebellion against British influences, such as occurred in the United States, with considerable impact on Canadian society. What all three countries had in common was a dispersed Native population, whose culture and members were deeply affected by invading colonists hoping to start a new life in the New World.[23] Australia's population of approximately 300 000 Aborigines was severely reduced as the result of their maltreatment by British settlers.

White settlement began in Australia in 1788 through the presence of the British military and the shipment to Australia of unwanted British convicts. Sheer distance from Europe and the popularity of North America as a destination for immigration reduced the attractiveness of Australia to European immigrants. The first major influx of free settlers was associated with the gold rush in the mid-nineteenth century; about one million persons entered Australia between 1852 and 1861. Between 1850 and 1900, 40% of the total population-growth was due to immigration from Great Britain and Ireland. Some migration also took place from Northern Europe, but by World War II Australia was still 90% British.[24] Non-Europeans had been excluded from the country by the 1901 *Immigration Restriction Act;* which immigrant groups were deemed acceptable was related to perceptions of how easily they could be assimilated into Australian society. This much more explicit immigration-policy ensured even greater ethnic uniformity in Australia than there was in North America.

The population of Australia during the World War II was about six million people. Over the next 30 years, an extremely rapid pace of growth increased the population by eight million.[25] Much of this growth was due to a high rate of immigration, actively promoted by the government through travel-assistance packages offered to British (in particular) and European migrants who agreed to stay in Australia for a minimum of two years. Another source of the growth was European refugees admitted under the sponsorship of the International Refugee Organization. The goal of a migrant intake of about 1% per year was established in response to a minor industrial revolution that occurred during this period in Australia's major cities, creating a large demand for labour. World War II had also brought home the awareness that the country's sparse population would provide little security in the event of a foreign invasion, and an alarming decline in the birth rate suggested that this problem demanded attention. The phrase "populate or perish" reflected the urgency with which Australia viewed the necessity of immigration in the immediate post-war era. Though this urgency for settlement came somewhat later than it did in Canada, it is interesting to compare Australia's concern for national security with Canada's concern to claim the West from possible American penetration by populating it with immigrants.

Perhaps the most significant thing about the post-war immigration policy was that the search for settlers moved beyond the British Isles to Southern and Eastern European countries.[26] In 1947, fully 97.9% of the population was born in Australia, the United Kingdom, Ireland, or New Zealand; Italians were the next-largest group, at 0.4%. Between 1947 and 1974, only 40% of the large number of new arrivals came from the British Isles, and only 10% came from Northern Europe (primarily from Holland and Germany).[27] Much larger contingents came from Southern European countries (e.g., Italy, Greece, and Cyprus) and Eastern European countries (particularly Yugoslavia). Asian and African countries have been new sources of immigration to Australia (as has been the case in Canada). So whereas 78% of the settlers in 1925 were British nationals, that number dropped to 13% in 1995. Furthermore, the proportion of foreign-born Australians from the United Kingdom and Ireland dropped from 79% in 1901 to 29% in 1997.[28] Into the 1990s, the proportion of European-born was declining and the proportion of Asian-born increasing. In 1972, there was virtually no immigration to Australia from Vietnam and Hong Kong, for example. But by 1997, China, Hong Kong, Vietnam, and the Philippines were among the six largest source-countries for new immigrants. Because of Australia's proximity to Asia in the context of regionalizing and globalizing trends, it is expected that Australia's high rate of foreign-born (22%, compared to 18% in Canada and 11% in the U.S.) will mean that Asian immigration will play a more prominent role in the future.[29]

The relatively recent infusion of these non-British groups into Australia is important for several reasons. First, immigrants compose about 24% of the Australian population; the fact that over one half of them come from non-English speaking countries and more than one third still regularly use a language other than English suggests that they may have a significant cultural influence on the second (i.e., Australian-born) generation.[30] In fact, when immigrants and their second generation are combined, they make up about one third of the national population.

The second reason this immigration is thought to be significant is that most of these migrants have settled in urban locations where they have been able to establish viable ethnic communities (as has been the case in Canada). For example, by the 1970s, 25% of Sydney's population was foreign-born; when their Australian-born children were included in the calculation, they made up 38% of the population.[31] Whereas pre–World War II immigrants went largely to rural areas, the post-war immigration located in the largest cities, particularly Sydney, Melbourne, and Adelaide. Consequently, Melbourne has the third-largest Greek population in the world, behind Athens and Salonika. Southern and Eastern Europeans are most likely to reside in the ethnic enclaves of the inner city; migrants from Holland and the British Isles are much less likely to be residentially concentrated. Moreover, chain migration usually strengthens these enclaves, as immigrants sponsor friends and relatives from the homeland.

Perhaps the most critical reason immigration remains a significant issue in Australian society has to do with the sense of Nordic superiority of the British-oriented majority, who have also developed a strong Australian nationalism.[32] Foreigners were historically disliked and were expected to assimilate (as the label attached to immigrants, "New Australians," indicates). The primary purpose of the "Good Neighbour" movement, established in 1950, was to condition Australians to accept immigrants and to assist them to learn English and assimilate as quickly as possible.[33] Such a policy was needed because immigrants, as a result of their social and economic disadvantages and heightened urban visibility, had come to be viewed negatively; their underemployment and the inability of their children to speak English in the schools were seen as symptomatic of the immigrant "problem." However, the growing viability of their ethnic enclaves and their increasing ability to articulate their group needs eventually changed immigrant groups into ethnic pressure groups. By the 1970s the *White Australia policy* was changed to a multicultural model similar to

Replacement Migration: A New Reason for Immigration

Replacement migration refers to the international migration that would be required to offset population decline caused by low fertility, reduction in the working-age population, and the overall aging of the population. For example, it is projected that the population of Japan could actually decline from 127 million to 105 million by 2050, and that the average age could increase by eight years, from 41 to 49. A similar phenomenon is projected for all industrial-

ized countries. The import of this trend is that that the working-age population will be less able to support the rest of the population. So when fertility declines past replacement levels, as it already has in Canada, more and more immigration is needed. Another option might be to increase the age of retirement to 75.

Source: United Nations Population Division, Replacement Migration: Is It a Solution to Declining and Aging Populations? (New York, 2001).

A Referendum in Australia in 1999

In 1999, a referendum was held in Australia over whether the country should remove the Queen as symbolic head of state and become a republic. While polls showed strong support for an Australian head of state, the referendum failed (55% to 45%), probably because what was proposed was having a president appointed (by the prime minister and government) rather than elected. It is expected that the drive to remove the British monarchy from its constitutional position will continue—though not without fierce debate.

While the idea of removing the monarch as symbolic head of the Canadian state arises from time to time,

it has not received strong support. Two possible explanations are that the monarchy is an important factor in differentiating Canada from the United States, and that Canada is too preoccupied with more critical issues, such as Quebec and Aboriginal self-government.

It is also interesting that the same Australian referendum included a second section which proposed changing the preamble to the constitution to recognize the historical role and place of Aboriginal people. Even though this proposal was largely symbolic and had little substance, it failed 60%–40%. It is clear that Australia struggles with many of the same issues as Canada.

Canada's.[34] In a complete reversal of the earlier approach, the policy of assimilation was replaced by one of ethnic pluralism, implying a new approach to ethnic relations.

Had immigrants of diverse origins not settled the Canadian West and had there not been a concentration of persons of French descent in Quebec, Canadian society would probably have been more similar to Australian society. While British settlers, as the dominant charter group in both countries, propagated British traditions, the multi-ethnic nature of the West and the French–English duality at the foundation of Canadian society attenuated those traditions considerably. In fact, Canada's post-war shift to an official multicultural policy was a direct response to the strong demands of francophones in Quebec and European ethnic groups in the West rather than the reflection of a new perspective on ethnic tolerance by the British charter group. Since World War II, immigration patterns in Australia and Canada have been rather similar, although Dutch, Yugoslavian, Maltese, and Greek immigration have been more prominent in Australia than in Canada. In establishing its own multiculturalism policy, Australia borrowed heavily from the Canadian experience (minus the bilingualism).

Another significant comparison pertains to the permanence of immigrants' settlement in the New Land. In Chapter One it was pointed out that until World War II, immigration into Canada had been somewhat counterbalanced by emigration; in such cases, immigrants usually used Canada as a stepping stone to eventual settlement in the United States. Australia had no strongly industrialized neighbour, but lost a significant proportion of its population through *return migration*—usually to the land of origin. In the past, immigrants from the British Isles and Northern Europe have had the highest rates of departure from Australia, usually estimated at about 20%.[35] Australia's two-year residency requirement for assisted immigrants made it difficult to know how many had intended to remain in Australia in the first place and how many viewed their stay as merely a foreign-travel experience. Return migration also took place in Canada, but it is doubtful whether much stepping-stone migration occurred from Australia. Historically, then, population loss through emigration has been a problem common to both societies, but the reasons for it have been different.

The proportion of Aboriginal people in Australia is similar to that of Native people in Canadian society; each group represents approximately 2%–3% of the population. In Canada, Native people are a distinguishable brown-skinned racial group, in much the same way that Aborigines, as a black-skinned people, are distinguishable from the white Euro-Australians. Initial contact with whites led to severe reduction in the Aboriginal population, though recent growth has resulted in an Aboriginal population of about 372 000, a large portion of whom live in the southern urban areas.[36] The largest Aboriginal populations are in New South Wales and Queensland, but just as Canada's Northern territories contain a larger share of the Native population than the provinces, so Australia's Northern Territory contains the highest percentage of Aborigines (27%).

Australia's Indigenous peoples suffered a fate similar to that of North American Indians. They were placed on Aboriginal Protectorates or reserves, though without the same legal foundation as in Canada. There have also been similar difficulties in ascertaining Aboriginal status, although Australia has been more willing to accept social and self-definitions rather than hereditary ones.[37] The Aboriginal dilemma of being caught between a desire to maintain their traditional way of life and the need to adapt to white economic goals and urban life has also led to considerable poverty and unemployment.

Comparing Indigenous Peoples in New Zealand

In all parts of the "new world," Indigenous peoples have had to deal with the intrusion of European powers and their settlers. The typical pattern of domination, reaction to resistance, paternalism, and attempts at assimilation represented policy for many years. While Canada, Australia, and New Zealand followed similar patterns in that regard, New Zealand does exhibit important differences.

The Treaty of Waitanga was signed in 1840 as an agreement between the British Crown and the Maori people to stem the conflicts that might be part of the settlement process. It provided for Maori self-government in exchange for the chiefs' ceding of their land, and gave the Maori all the rights of British subjects. As a result, the Maori were recognized as full citizens over 100 years before such rights were extended to Aboriginal peoples in Australia or Canada.

Maori children usually stayed in their own community and were raised by their extended families rather than being separated from their kin to be sent away to residential schools, as in Canada and Australia. While cultural conflict and tensions periodically erupted, the Aboriginal experience in New Zealand was generally less rigid and less harsh.

Source: Based on Andrew Armitage, *Comparing the Policy of Aboriginal Assimilation: Australia, Canada, and New Zealand* (Vancouver: UBC Press, 1995).

In 1967, Aborigines were made a federal rather than state responsibility, and an Office for Aboriginal Affairs was established. Used primarily as a vehicle for negotiations, a white-inspired National Aboriginal Consultative Council sought to unite dispersed local tribes or clans into a single body to coordinate Aboriginal programs and to act in an advisory capacity to the government.[38] While the granting of self-determination to Aborigines remains particularly controversial in some states, the granting of land rights has proceeded apace, with great ramifications in the outback regions where mining and other forms of resource extraction take place. Thus, though the contexts are different, the history and plight of the Indigenous peoples of both Australia and Canada appear rather similar.

ETHNIC REGIONALISM: AN INTRODUCTION

It is generally recognized that in Canada, two different conditions have produced regional political movements. One condition is *uneven economic development and disparities* which cause regional animosities or hostilities between geographic segments of the society. Examples of movements caused by this condition include the Western agrarian movements and the Maritime Rights movement. The second condition is *ethnic solidarity;* the most obvious example of a region in which this prevails is Quebec. In this province a national consciousness quite distinct from that of English Canada evolved from the francophone majority's own heritage and traditions. While the economic and ethnic aspects of regionalism might appear to be two different matters, the evidence suggests that regionalist ethnic movements are most effective when an economic grievance mobilizes their constituents; conversely, regional movements with economic/political objectives are much more likely to be compelling when they have an ethnic basis. Thus, from the national point of view, a regional ethnic group is merely a minority, while from the regional point of view, it is a majority in its own territory and ought to possess the right to self-determination. It is from the dynamic tension between regional and federal objectives that societal conflict emerges.

Because industrialization and modernization are usually thought to negatively affect traditional culture, it has been assumed that ethnic minorities will eventually lose their historical distinctiveness and be drawn into the dominant social system of the majority. If this were true, we might expect Quebecers to have experienced considerable erosion of their linguistic and cultural uniqueness as they have been drawn increasingly into the anglo world. Yet surprisingly, the post-war period has seen a resurgence rather than a decline of ethnic identity in Quebec. What is noteworthy about this fact is that it has many parallels in other countries where regional ethnic majorities have challenged the power and policies of the federal state.[39]

A popular regionalist movement arising among an ethnically different majority in a given territory is frequently referred to as *a nationalist movement*. When a nationalist movement agitates not to improve its position within the established political entity (though that may be the preferred goal preferred of some) but to establish its own political entity, it is considered an *independence movement*. One of the moot questions in this situation is precisely how much independence is desired; sometimes more regional control (known as *devolution*) is acceptable.[40] When an ethnic difference exists, as in the case of Quebec, internal debate is waged over how much separateness from the central state, or cooperation with it, should prevail. Needless to say, opinions

FIGURE 6.2	European Countries/Regions with Features Relevant to Canadian Society

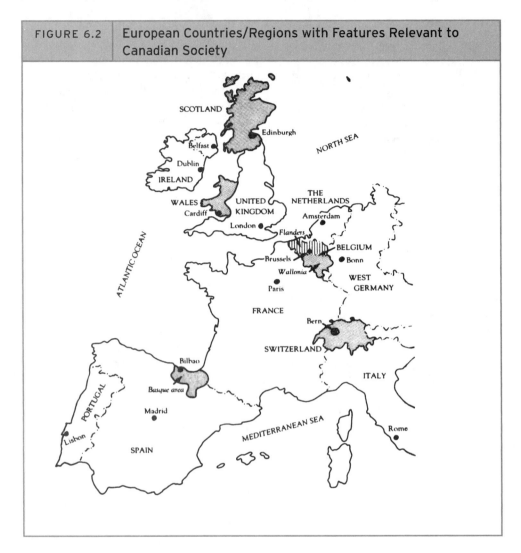

within the territory will vary greatly. In order to illustrate three different types of regional responses, we will examine the cases of Scotland, Wales, and the Basque region of Spain.

Two interpretive perspectives have been proposed to explain how and why ethnicity is mobilized by a regional movement: reactive ethnicity and ethnic competition.[41] *Reactive ethnicity* suggests that ethnic solidarity emerges when a disadvantaged group rebels against a dominant authority of another ethnic group. In this case, ethnicity almost becomes synonymous with class consciousness because inequality intensifies ethnic consciousness. *Ethnic competition* refers to new-found ethnic solidarity that arises when groups that were formerly separate must compete for the same occupations, rewards, and resources. Cultural distinctiveness is mobilized to ensure that the group obtains its share of the opportunities produced by changed conditions. Rather than view these perspectives as in conflict with each other, we may find elements of both to be appropriate to our discussion.

Economic Marginality, Ethnicity, and Autonomy

DISTINCTIVE CANADIAN FEATURE:
Against significant odds, Quebec culture and francophone identity
have survived over many years and are now thriving in an unprecedented
way despite anglophone dominance in Canada. As a result, the reaction
against central government control increases the call for more autonomy.

Comparison: Scotland

Scotland is not a separate country, but is part of the United Kingdom as a result of the 1707 *Act of Union* with England. Scotland was not conquered by England; it agreed to the Union so that Scottish industry would gain access to the British Empire. Many Scots were astounded at this decision at the time, but the potential economic benefits were reasonably convincing. In consequence, throughout the nineteenth century—a time when other nation-states were forming in Europe—there was little expression of Scottish nationalist feeling, as the link with England ensured a strong local economy.[42] Scotland then existed as a region within the United Kingdom (Great Britain), with no barriers to the movement of people, capital, or goods. Until very recent developments, Scotland did not have its own government, electing representatives to the British Parliament, which makes social and economic policies that are applied to the entire United Kingdom.

In spite of being part of the United Kingdom and experiencing pervasive English influences, certain aspects of Scottish civil society were preserved through social institutions and traditions. For some, the Gaelic language was an important part of Scottish culture, but it is now spoken by less than 2% of the population. Scotland did retain aspects of its own legal system; as well, there was a distinct religious difference: England's established church was the Church of England (Anglican), whereas the Church of Scotland was Presbyterian. In addition, centuries of past conflict and competition with England had engendered a wealth of folktales and a pantheon of national heroes and martyrs which also helped sustain an ethnic identity. These traditions, which embodied a sense of history and past national greatness, were also taught in the schools. It is significant that although these cultural factors were always present, an articulated and growing sense of ethnic difference intensified only as Scottish people became aware of being marginal to the centre of British power. This awareness of being a marginal, ethnically homogeneous region provided a framework for interpreting economic decline. After World War I, and again after World War II, unemployment began to grow in Scotland. The more enterprising members of the entrepreneurial class were increasingly enticed to the centres of English finance and industry. In fact, out-migration of Scots to opportunities in England meant a perpetual drain of manpower, brainpower, and even capital. Scots became increasingly sensitive to their peripheral status, both within the British Isles and in Europe. Scotland had not always had this marginal position; in the nineteenth century, it was one of the first parts of Britain to industrialize.[43] However, as the coal, iron, and textile industries went into decline, unemployment began to grow, particularly in the Glasgow industrial region. Investment in new industries, such as electronics, provided some opportunities for middle-class workers but did not help those displaced by the deterioration of the older industries. As a result of these changes, the Scottish economy became more of a branch-plant economy owned largely by "outsiders" such as the English, Germans, or Americans, and the sense of external control and marginality increased.[44]

It might be said that when economic conditions have been good, there has been little feeling of marginality and little need to politicize ethnic differences. Nevertheless, Scotland's remoteness from the centre of economic and political control in southeast England, along with its lingering sense of ethnic difference, have led to repeated calls for some decentralization away from London. Scottish complaints about poor treatment and a distant government led to the establishment in 1885 of a Scottish Office in Edinburgh, staffed by a government minister with full cabinet status. Yet animosities lingered, and in 1928 the Scots National League and the Scottish Home Rule Association united to form the National Party of Scotland. After several breakaway movements and subsequent mergers, the Scottish National Party (SNP) was founded in 1934. Throughout the 1950s and 1960s the movement grew through petitions and electioneering, but only in the 1970s did the SNP begin to see more electoral success. Since 1970 the SNP has never polled less than 10% of the popular vote in general elections, reaching as high as 30% in 1974.

If deteriorating economic conditions were behind the agitation for greater regional control and Scottish independence, it was the discovery of oil in the North Sea off Scotland's coast that provided the catalyst and new confidence to challenge existing structural arrangements. The SNP put emphasized broad cultural issues less than economic grievances, and the discovery of oil sparked Scottish expectations of rising power within the UK and regionally based leverage against economic decline. At the same time, it increased Britain's determination both to maintain control over oil production in Scotland and to respond to apparent public agitation there. After considerable discussion and debate, particularly through the work of a Royal Commission, the British Parliament allowed a referendum to take place in Scotland in 1979 to determine support for self-government (i.e., a separate Scottish parliament to effect more local control). The referendum was won by the "Yes" side, 52% to 48%, and yet was lost because the British Parliament had decreed that only a "Yes" vote by 40% of the total population would constitute victory. Only 64% of the population voted, meaning that people who voted "Yes" only represented 33% of eligible voters. This break from normal voting procedure inspired considerable conflict in itself, and both "Yes" and "No" votes were subject to a variety of interpretations. Many considered the results inconclusive and both sides argued that they had won.[45]

Since this first referendum, the issue of self-government and independence has continued to be an important item on the Scottish agenda.[46] Particularly during the years of the Thatcher government, Scots felt that the UK had become dominated by London-area interests that marginalized them.[47] As a result, the Scots shifted their votes to parties that were more sensitive to regional needs (particularly Labour) and that advocated devolution of control to local society. Support for some kind of devolution has been widespread in Scotland and crosses party and social class lines; the debate focuses on how it should be operationalized. The SNP continues to work for outright independence, but the Labour government under Tony Blair has also supported greater local autonomy. In 1997, a referendum was held in Scotland that reflected clear support for devolution. Three quarters (74%) of those voting agreed that there should be a Scottish Parliament (note that this is not the same as independence, although there are those who see it as another step in that direction), and a slightly lesser number (64%) agreed that a Scottish Parliament should have taxing power. In 1999, the first elections were held for the new Scottish Parliament. No party won a majority; even though Labour won the most seats, the SNP was a strong second. The irony of this result, of course, was that Labour was arguing for more independence for Scotland *within* the United Kingdom, while the SNP advocated a more clear-cut independence.

FIGURE 6.3	Responses to Independence Movements in the United Kingdom

Scotland		Wales	
1707	Gave up independence in *Act of Union*	1536	Gave up independence in *Act of Union*
1979	Referendum obtained majority (52% Yes) but was defeated on technical rules		Referendum defeated (80% No)
1997	Referendum passed to establish a Scottish Parliament (74%) and to give it taxation power (64%)		Referendum passed to establish a National Assembly for Wales (50.3%)
1999	Elections for Scottish Parliament		Elections for National Assembly

▼

▼

Powers
Can pass laws in areas such as education, health care, transportation, culture
Can vary taxation by 3%

Powers
No taxation or legislative powers
Allocates government funds supplied to Wales

Some have argued that Scottish nationalism is primarily a response to Scotland's marginality and dependency within the United Kingdom and the global capitalist system. McCrone, however, has argued that Scotland's incorporation into greater Britain was always incomplete because Scotland's elite negotiated some degree of institutional autonomy that has survived.[48] The Church of Scotland was not replaced by the Church of England, Scottish university traditions have always made higher education far more accessible, the legal system has its own distinctive features, Scotland has retained its own national sport teams (e.g., football and rugby), an independent voice in trade unionism has supported home rule, and international capital (not just English capital) has a growing presence in Scotland. All of this has meant that Scotland has expanded its purview beyond the UK and that a distinctive civil society has not only been sustained but has grown stronger in recent years. No longer is Scottish nationalism fixated on the past and on old myths and traditions; it is now focused on the present and future and seeks to carve out a new niche, more independent of the central British state, in the changing global system.

A useful comparison may be made between Scotland and various regions of Canada: Quebec, because both are ethnically distinct societies, and the Western and Atlantic regions, because both share feelings of geographic remoteness and economic marginality. It is noteworthy that in both Canada and Scotland it is oil that has helped kindle conflict and arouse regional sentiment. However, neither the West nor the Atlantic region possesses an ethnic heritage that could serve as a cohesive factor in external conflict. In Quebec, however, as in Scotland, culture and ethnicity have increasingly been marshalled in the political battle for more autonomy. Ethnic survival has been an enduring theme in both places, along with the demand for greater independence from the central state. The major difference between the two is that Quebec has always had its own provincial parliament, which it has increasingly used to promote its local objectives and which even provides a potential vehicle for independence. In contrast, Scotland until recently lacked any localized government; now that it has its own political vehicle, we can expect even greater nationalist assertiveness. On the other hand, there seems to be considerable evidence that in both places the new nationalism is becoming less ethnocentric; there is growing recognition that a globalizing world requires different hierarchies of identities, in which new partnerships rather than restrictive barriers are the dominant themes.

Perhaps of most importance is the fact that the European Union provided a new anchor for the Scottish economy, in many ways loosening its ties to the British economy. Scotland no longer feels like a junior partner in the British Empire; only the older people have a lingering British identity, while the young only feel British insofar as their passports identify them as such. The population's sense of Scottish identity is tied not to the old attributes of privilege and class but to education and openness. Scottish nationalism has thus served to support globalization. In this sense, McCrone argues that in not being totally independent, Scotland demonstrates the declining relevance of nation-states in a globalizing world.[49]

Scotland has less than one tenth the population of the United Kingdom; like Canada in relation to the United States, it is keenly aware of the more populous country's dominance. Quebec's position in relation to Canada is similar, and both Quebec and Scotland seek to alter old dependency relationships with governments in London and Ottawa. Unlike French in Quebec, Scotland's distinctive language has waned significantly in usage. McCrone notes the remarkable fact that even though Scotland lost its political identity 300 years ago, seven out of ten residents now give priority to their Scottish, rather than British, identity. If anything, identification with regional political structures has increased rather than decreased. Both Scotland and Quebec clearly evince a reaction against a dominant authority acting from without (reactive ethnicity), while simultaneously demonstrating a new outward-looking orientation (rather than the old inward-looking nationalism) and a desire to embrace the new opportunities brought by globalism (ethnic competition).

Ethnic Nationalism

DISTINCTIVE CANADIAN FEATURE:
As Quebec nationalism has grown, anglophones and allophones have felt less at home in Quebec and significant numbers have left the province, with the result that there has been less resistance to nationalist sentiment in Quebec.

Comparison: Wales

Wales was an autonomous state until the *Act of Union* in 1536 incorporated it into the English state. As long as the Welsh people remained rural and traditional, British rule, though resisted in some quarters, meant little to Welsh language and culture. With the onset of the Industrial Revolution in the nineteenth century, however, Wales began to undergo considerable change. By 1900, the population of Wales had increased fivefold, and by 1911 two thirds of the population was urban.[50] Urbanization and industrialization, along with Wales's comparative geographical proximity to the British industrial complex and its political integration into British national parties, reduced the sense of marginality in Wales as compared with Scotland.[51] The fact that Lloyd George, a leader of the Young Wales Movement in the late nineteenth century, became British Prime Minister symbolized this fact.

In spite of having a distinct national language (Welsh), the population of Wales became increasingly anglicized. The immigration of British people into the industrial centres of South Wales reduced the usage of the Welsh language there, and the use of Welsh became restricted to the more rural areas of Northwest Wales. On the other hand, road signs and official documents are in Welsh and English, and Welsh-language television is available. If Wales, as Hechter has argued, was an internal colony for British capitalist development, it must also be recognized that Wales became a secondary centre of industry (iron and steel) rather than an undeveloped region.[52] For this reason, independence issues of a cultural nature have not had strong appeal to the working class, which has been more concerned about economic issues.

The Welsh nationalist movement, Plaid Cymru, was founded in 1925 but has had little impact on Welsh politics. Its base has traditionally been in Northwest Wales and it has taken a gradualist nationalist approach, focusing on cultural matters such as language. While the creation of vital Welsh institutions, such as the University of Wales, the Welsh Department of Education, and the Church of Wales, had the potential to support language as a source of ethnic differentiation, the fact that the Welsh middle class was integrated into British structures removed one of the common foundations of a nationalist movement.

A referendum, similar to the one held in Scotland, was held in Wales in 1979 on whether to establish a Welsh national assembly. Amidst economic insecurities, the proposal was defeated by a 4-to-1 margin. Advance polls had indicated that a majority of persons of Welsh descent wanted a Welsh parliament; however, the large number of non-Welsh residents who had migrated to Wales overwhelmed the Welsh nationalists in the vote. Indicators suggested that English-speaking Welsh voters (i.e., residents of Wales who could not speak Welsh) were fearful that the nationalists would insist on Welsh being spoken in an independent Wales, which would put them at a distinct disadvantage.[53] In other words, the English-speaking majority was reluctant to support the nationalists, who formed only a 20% linguistic minority.

In Wales, regionalist/nationalist feeling is essentially cultural and not economic, as Wales (particularly Southeast Wales) is economically integrated into the British economy. Whereas 90% of the residents of Scotland are born-Scots and conscious of their Scottish identity, the same cannot be said of Wales, where an influx of migrants from England has taken place.[54] Cultural regionalism/nationalism has thus been confined to a minority of the population found in the rural northern areas. This example illustrates how residents of a former nation-state (Wales) can hold a dual identity (i.e., British and Welsh) in an almost regional rather than nationalist manner. The integration of South Wales (at least) into the British economy and the influx of persons from England into Wales have dissolved the potency of nationalist appeals.

In 1997, a second referendum was held in Wales, parallel to the referendum in Scotland and consonant with the British Labour government's support of further devolution. With a 50% turnout, 50.3% answered "Yes" to the question of whether there should be a Welsh Assembly, and the National Assembly for Wales was established in 1999. The fact that the number of "Yes" votes was barely enough to support such an initiative suggests both that there was strong nationalist feeling and that many voters were either opposed or apathetic. The major difference between the Scottish Parliament and the Welsh Assembly is that the latter has no legislative or taxation powers and its primary purpose is to disburse government funds allocated to Wales. Thus we see that devolution has meant different things to different UK constituencies. Voting in favour of the Welsh Assembly had much weaker nationalist implications; consequently, it was harder for opposition to it to gel. In some ways, this constitutional change was primarily a moderate variant of the status quo, but with important symbolic significance.

In Wales, there has been considerable intermingling of English and Welsh people, and the Welsh economy has been intimately tied to a strong British economy. In Canada, in contrast, francophones and anglophones are becoming increasingly territorially separate, particularly as the result of out-migration from Quebec and language-assimilation pressures both within and outside the province. While Quebec's economy has been intimately tied to the Canadian economy, its strong linkages to the United States have produced a stronger sense of confidence in its economic survival outside of Canada. The UK has demonstrated willingness to allow different patterns of devolution, whereas Canadians are divided on anything that suggests special status for particular regions or social groups.

Regionalized Control

DISTINCTIVE CANADIAN FEATURE:
Quebec has sought more regionalized control and a sense of autonomy, but nationalist movements often divide the population, creating considerable concern over the economic welfare of the region.

Comparison: The Basque Region of Spain

In the northeast corner of Spain, on approximately 3% of the country's land surface, live 1.5 million Basques. The Cantabrian mountains serve almost as a barrier between this region and the rest of Spain, and the coastal location of the most significant Basque population promotes more of an international frame of reference than an inward link to Spain. Here shipyards, steel mills, and manufacturing provide the highest average per-capita income of any region of Spain, which as a country has the highest unemployment rate in the European Union. Spain itself is made up of several linguistic/cultural groups, including the Castilians, Galicians, Andalusians, Catalans, and the Basques.

The Basques occupy an area between France and the rest of Spain; for this reason, early Spanish monarchies sought the cooperation of the Basques in border defence. In an effort to secure their loyalty, they agreed to allow the Basque provinces to retain their own legal system, which provided a substantial measure of self-governance. Part of the legacy of these concessions was the concept of *collective nobility*, the automatic granting of noble rank to any person of Basque parentage. While this entitlement meant little in actuality, it provided a heritage of uniqueness which later came to serve as part of the rationale for greater autonomy.

Basque uniqueness is also related to language and lineage. The Basque language, Euskera, is unrelated to any Indo-European language. The Basque people also have the highest incidence of Rh-negative blood factor of any population in the world—a biological reflection of closed social groupings.[55] When these two factors are considered in combination with geographic location and noble status, the Basques' strong perception of themselves as unique is understandable. On the other hand, only one in four Basques uses Euskera and most are fluent in Spanish.

Considerable self-governance was allowed by the Spanish monarchs until the nineteenth century, when attempts were made to override local autonomy. The Spanish goal of greater centralization threatened the Basque community, and a Basque nationalist movement emerged in the 1890s. The Basque language was a primary focus of government attack; in the period following the Spanish Civil War (1937) it became illegal to use Euskera in public or in the media or to teach it in schools. By the late 1960s, Euskera was allowed back into the schools, and the new constitution of 1978 made regional languages co-official with Spanish. But all of this did not occur without considerable agitation from the Basque nationalist movement, which by this time had renamed their land Euzkadi.

The industrial opportunities available in Basque cities, in conjunction with a tax system that discouraged agriculture, meant that the Basque population became more urban. These same opportunities also attracted non-Basques to cities like Bilbao. Currently only 65% of the population of the Basque provinces is indigenous. This decline is chiefly attributable to the 20 000 to 30 000 people per year who have migrated into the region since the 1950s.[56] As a consequence of this immigration, the use of Euskera has declined, and traditional Basque family life has been in a state of upheaval. Anxious to maintain their economic position, the Basque bourgeoisie frequently compromised their ethnicity in order to build economic bridges to other countries or to other regions of Spain. It was precisely this greater intermingling, however, that the working and middle classes perceived as a threat to Basque identity. Intense feelings of frustration led to the formation of an organization called Basque Homeland and Freedom (ETA), which engaged in revolutionary insurgent activities, including kidnapping and assassination. A more moderate Basque Nationalist Party is also active.

Enduring feelings of persecution by the Spanish government and of a compelling but threatened ethnic identity were further exacerbated by regional grievances of inequality. Basques felt that high taxation was not being justified by government spending or provision of services in the Basque region and that this uneven distribution was the result of Spanish discrimination against the Basques. When the Spanish government offered a referendum to the Basque region in 1979, proposing greater autonomy in matters of language, taxation, and the judiciary, it was overwhelmingly accepted, although about 50% of the Basque population abstained from the vote.[57] The first elections to the Basque parliament were held in 1980, and Basque nationalists have gained control over all key institutions.

Just as the Basques argue that they are an ethnic people with a distinct and unique heritage, so francophone Quebecers assert that they have a distinct "peoplehood," with a long history firmly rooted in the Conquest. As a result, increased central-government control has represented a threat to both groups. What may make the Basque region unique, however, is that its concern for self-determination is also related to its having been the richest region in Spain—a position that aspiring Basques were particularly zealous to safeguard, and which, as we will see, began to erode. It is essentially a similar group of aspiring francophones which has been effective in mobilizing Quebec pro-sovereignty sentiment, although Quebec's comparative economic position has not been as strong.

The industrial strength of the Basque region in the '60s and '70s made it a significant magnet for employment-seeking migrants from other parts of Spain. In a sense, the economic success of the Basque area has been responsible for its problems. In-migrants dilute the region's Basque identity and threaten its language. The region's economic success also meant that central-government tax revenues were likely to be diverted to more needy parts of Spain (of course, the question of which area has the most pressing needs is itself controversial). The Basques thus feared that central-government control of economic and language policies could weaken the Basque region both economically and culturally. Indeed, in the years since the Basques obtained home rule, an economic crisis has occurred in the region, unemployment has increased, and the legitimacy of the Spanish state continues to be under question.[58] Violence involving the ETA, which receives its support from the most vulnerable parts of the population, has led to several hundred deaths. The internal battles between "Basques" and "non-Basques" (i.e., people with Basque heritage and identity but not supportive of a Basque nation), as well as the repressive actions of the Spanish police, add to a volatile situation and are used by both sides to justify more concerted action.[59] The election in 1996 of a right-wing Spanish government committed to a strong Spanish state renewed the animosities and tensions.

Basques, like the Québécois, want more control over their own territory in order to preserve the ethnic identity of the region.[60] Yet internal divisions between Basques and non-Basques, and a less-healthy economy, have created tensions and power struggles that are difficult to resolve, along with new gulfs between radicals and moderates. Two points emerge here with relevance to Quebec. One is that a healthy economy with low unemployment is an important objective in a nationalist movement, and its absence can trigger all kinds of new tensions. The second is that deteriorating conditions can easily polarize nationalist movements between moderates and radicals, and can either weaken the nationalist movement or rouse it to more concerted action. It should also be pointed out that devolution to more local autonomy in 1980 has not resolved the matter for all time either.

POLITIES WITH MORE THAN ONE OFFICIAL LANGUAGE: AN INTRODUCTION

If you want to create some controversy in a group of Canadians, there is no faster way to do it than to bring up the issue of bilingualism. Everyone has an opinion about bilingualism and everyone also has stories or anecdotes to tell from everyday life to justify their position. Whether what sets them off is hearing a bilingual version of "O Canada," hearing two sets of pre-flight instructions on an airplane, or seeing a simultaneous translation of a document or instructional sign, Canadians still react to bilingualism because it is foreign to the unilingual manner in which most people live their lives.[61]

It is frequently assumed that most countries operate with a single dominant universal language. Many Canadians are aware that the United States has taken in many immigrant peoples who utilize numerous languages, but note that English is still the primary language of communication. What is perhaps less well-known is that the large influx of Spanish-speaking peoples into the southern United States in recent years has created a real battle in some areas (e.g., California and Florida) over whether two languages, English and Spanish, should be endorsed.[62] The national English-speaking majority has so far successfully argued that unilingualism should be the American norm. The facts of Canadian history and polity, however, are somewhat different, though there is a tendency for people to assume that unilingualism ought to be the normal pattern in Canada as well.

But if unilingualism is the norm in many countries, are there countries where more than one language is officially recognized, or does Canada stand alone on this issue? The existence of regional linguistic enclaves is one thing, but the formal recognition of more than one language is another. Have other countries officially recognized the equal dominance of more than one language within their society as a whole? If so, what has been their experience?

The purpose of this section is to introduce two countries which officially sanction more than one language. These countries are Belgium and Switzerland.

Linguistic Plurality

DISTINCTIVE CANADIAN FEATURE:
The federal policy of bilingualism sought to reorganize Canadian society by declaring that government services would be universally available in two official languages, but also subtly implied that Canadians throughout the country ought to work towards becoming bilingual.

Comparison: Switzerland

Switzerland had its beginnings as a loose alliance of Alpine-valley communities banding together to defend themselves against challenges to their independence. The idea of a voluntary federation of political communities led in 1848 to a constitution which established political neutrality and the idea of one foreign policy, one citizenship, and a customs union. On the other hand, matters of education and culture were left totally in the hands of local jurisdictions called *cantons*.[63] No attempt was to be made to secure national political unity on the basis of descent or language; rather, it was to be based on local allegiance, which was to be paid directly to the canton.

The *principle of cantonal autonomy* is directly related to Switzerland's ethnic diversity, which varies with locality. About 74% of the population of Switzerland speak German, 20% French, 4% Italian, and less than 1% Romansch.[64] Consequently, Switzerland has 23 cantons, of which 14 are German, 4 French, 1 Italian, 3 bilingual, and 1 trilingual. Ninety-five percent of German Swiss live in German regions, 86% of French Swiss live in French regions, and 85% of Italian Swiss live in Italian regions, reflecting considerable cantonal homogeneity.[65] A 1996 referendum approved semi-official status for Romansch, meaning that government services, but not all government documents, would be made available in that language

Each canton is entitled to preserve its own language, and all immigrants must learn the language used in that canton. Language boundaries are guaranteed and cannot be changed, although when conflict emerges, a canton may be split (as happened when the new canton of Jura was established from a part of the canton of Berne).[66] The split was accepted because it separated the French Catholic community (Jura) from the German Protestant one (Berne), removing the basis for much internal conflict. The recent interest in adding English-language courses to school programs has provoked considerable debate, as some fear that the introduction of an additional language may violate linguistic purity. Each canton writes its laws and documents in its own language and forms its own military units as part of the Swiss army. The primary unit of group identity is thus the canton, not ethnicity or language group, although language becomes the marker of the canton. Political decentralization and local autonomy remove the frustrations minorities normally feel in a highly centralized state.

Switzerland is frequently perceived as a model of linguistic harmony because, despite of the unequal strength of its linguistic groups, the territorial sub-units known as cantons ensure more localized control. While this most basic structural element is critical to Switzerland's success, other factors also come into play.[67] These include the following:

1. The Swiss view cultural diversity and the (mandatory) learning of a second language as positive features of their society. The socialization of children from a young age inculcates this attitude, which is also supported by the fact that the three language groups are dominant in the surrounding European community.

2. The Constitution rejects the concept of minority status, embodying strict equality instead. The Constitution gives Switzerland three "official" languages and four "national" languages. The federal civil service is linguistically proportionate. As a result of these federal policies, linguistic groups tend to overestimate the strength of other language groups (e.g., even though French is technically a minority language, it has high prestige), with the consequence that no group suffers from a minority complex. The existing pluralingual cantons serve as bridges between the language groups, even though linguistic territoriality exists within the cantons as well. Wherever possible, more-than-proportionate representation is the norm.

3. Cantons are sovereign in linguistic matters, meaning that each canton has the right to protect its own linguistic character against both external forces and in-migrants, who are obligated to adjust to cantonal language practices. Federal authorities must deal with each canton in its own language.

4. Language divisions are cross-cut by other divisions, such as political affiliation, religion, social class, and rural–urban differences, making it hard to mobilize one language group against the other. For example, approximately one half of all French are Catholic and one half are Protestant. Language is only one of many social divisions, which are decentralized through cantonal control.

5. Economic disparities between cantons are small. In fact, disparities within cantons are greater than those between cantons. Wherever disparities have arisen, the federal government has responded with programs for regional economic development. Appeasement of all disadvantaged groups through fiscal support is a dominant objective of the federal government and political elites.

Canadian federal policy has clearly rejected the idea of linguistic territoriality, though the concept of a "distinct society" suggests pressure in that direction. Bilingualism as a national policy has sought, not entirely successfully, to make both languages available throughout the country and to protect each official-language group when it is a minority in a particular region. Federally initiated language and cultural policies have been favoured over local autonomy and control. Inter-regional economic disparities and competition have further exacerbated the politicization of language groups. In Canada—particularly in Quebec—provincial and national loyalties are considered to be in conflict, whereas in Switzerland, strong cantonal and federal identities and loyalties are considered compatible. Recently, pressures have arisen in Switzerland to make English the second language that children must study from the age of 7 or 8; in 2004, Zurich was the first to adopt such a policy. By potentially undermining knowledge of other European languages, this policy may add a totally new dimension to language realities in the country.

Canadian society follows a very different principle of social organization than Swiss society. The federal objective has been to create a more highly integrated society and a centralized bilingualism policy rather than to encourage and support more regional control of language use. Switzerland provides a significant model of decentralized control and tolerance achieved through the principle of linguistic territoriality, which has produced surprising stability.

Two Unequal Language Groups

DISTINCTIVE CANADIAN FEATURE:
Conceived as a way to accord francophones their full place in the fabric of Canadian society, bilingualism became a legislated ideal that ignored the realities of increasing territorial unilingualism.

Comparison: Belgium

The country of Belgium had its genesis in the Belgian Revolution of 1830. The northern half of the country, an area known as Flanders, was populated by persons of Dutch origin who spoke Flemish, while those of French descent populated the southern section in an area called Wallonia. At the time of Belgium's creation, Wallonia was the stronger section, and partly because of the influence exerted by France, French became the official national language of the new country. French also was the language of the cultured upper class, therefore becoming the language of secondary education and upward mobility throughout Belgium.

By the latter half of the nineteenth century, a significant change had begun in the balance of power between these two regions.[68] A higher birth rate led to sizeable population increases in Flanders, and a Flemish national consciousness emerged. The Flemings, desiring to use their language in the courts, public administration, and schools, challenged the exclusiveness of the French language. Regional bilingualism was first initiated in Flanders, and by 1898 Flemish became an official language of the country along with French.

The emergent Flemish consciousness also evoked a Wallonian consciousness.[69] The apparent concessions to the Flemish, along with the comparative weakening of the Wallonian position (two thirds of the total population was now Flemish), made control of the large city of Brussels critical. Flemings who moved to Brussels were becoming bilingual, whereas Wallonians remained unilingual; yet there were still clear differences between bilingual Flemings and the French-speaking Walloons. The Flemish middle classes preferred language policies which ensured the survival of Dutch, yet were also aware that urbanization meant greater use of French.

By World War II, Belgium essentially consisted of two unilingual areas: Flanders (Flemish or Dutch) and Wallonia (French). Flemings were conscious of the fact that Brussels was already considerably French and that this French dominance was increasing. Conflict became particularly intense as the urban population moved into the predominantly Flemish suburbs. The Constitution adopted in 1970 proposed a solution that would see Belgium divided into three administrative units: Flanders, where Dutch would be used; Wallonia, where French would be used; and Brussels, where there was to be parity between the two groups with some regional unilingualism in the suburbs.[70] At the federal level, a parity principle was to prevail so that the cabinet would comprise an equal number from both linguistic groups. The Dutch agreed to parity in the cabinet in exchange for parity in Brussels, where they were a minority. The language of instruction in schools was to be the language of the area, although residents of Brussels could make a free choice. Parity was also to be sought in the civil service, in which the Dutch were underrepresented. Two cultural councils were to be established to ensure the cultural survival of both ethnic groups.

Thus, a rather sharply defined linguistic frontier exists across Belgium in an east–west direction, dividing the Flemish dialects and Dutch to the north from the Walloon dialects and French to the south. This language boundary does not correspond to any political barrier, and trade and commerce proceed freely across the two language regions. Although the French language historically had the upper hand, a renaissance in Flemish socio-political life over the last hundred years has transformed the old relationship between the two linguistic groups. The result has been decades of conflict and negotiation, in which Brussels, as the major Belgian city—a predominantly francophone capital in Flemish territory—has been the centre of inter-group tension. Consequently, inter-group sympathy ratings are much lower in Belgium than in Switzerland.[71]

The Flemings (56%) now outnumber the Walloons (32%). An additional 10% of the population is bilingual, and the small remainder is German.[72] Even though the country is linguistically divided, most of Belgium's residents are Catholic. The regional imbalance continues, although the modern industries are now in Flanders and the declining industries in Wallonia. In 1993, Belgium was officially transformed from a unitary state to a federation of linguistic communities with three self-governing regions (Dutch-speaking Flanders, French-speaking Wallonia, and bilingual Brussels), each with directly elected assemblies. Only defence, foreign relations, and monetary policy have remained federal domains; this has meant that the size of the federal government has been reduced considerably.

Whereas Switzerland has been a model of political stability within a decentralized system, Belgium, like Canada, has experienced much more upheaval and realignment, (although in Canada these have taken place over a much shorter period). Both Belgium and Canada have had a uniform, centralized language policy that they attempted to impose on the entire country. However, the changing position of Belgium's two groups has meant a long process of negotiation and transition, eventually leading to a policy that does not so much reorganize the society linguistically as acknowledge and accept regional linguistic differences. In Canada, at least at the federal level, there has been considerable resistance to such an approach, in spite of the realities.

Rather than move to a national policy of bilingualism as Canada has done, Belgium has moved to *territorial unilingualism* and has established mechanisms to institutionalize *parity* and the survival of both groups. Territorial unlingualism and parity have done much to relieve the tendency to see ethnic interaction in terms of "losers" and "winners." Although the Canadian bilingualism policy also represented an attempt to minimize the perception of losers and winners, it has been less successful because it failed to anticipate the tendency towards greater territorial unilingualism. The size difference between the two charter demographic groups has also made the concept of parity less palatable in Canada. The increasing integration of the North American economy through free-trade agreements raises questions about the survival of an autonomous and sovereign Canadian society (see Chapter Two). While the creation of regional trading-blocs is currently a global phenomenon, it is unclear whether economic integration must necessarily result in some form of political, social, or cultural integration.

Removal of Trade Barriers

> **DISTINCTIVE CANADIAN FEATURE:**
> **Long-standing barriers between Canada and the United States have been at least partially removed by trade agreement, integrating the two societies in a new way but with uncertain consequences for the future.**
>
> *Comparison: The European Union*

The changes occurring in Europe as a result of the creation of the European Community (EC), now known as the European Union (EU), provide an interesting counterpoint to the Canadian experience. In many ways, the EU began as an experiment in economic collaboration, but has moved more and more towards a type of political integration. Whereas nation-states usually guard their sovereignty, the voluntary sharing of sovereignty as exemplified by the European Union is unprecedented in modern history—particularly in light of the fact that not long ago many of these countries were bitter enemies.

The first half of the twentieth century was a time of much turmoil for Europe, as hostilities between nation-states broke out and world wars resulted in massive destruction. These events, followed by the Cold War between the Soviet bloc and Western capitalist democracies, led to a period of rebuilding in which European countries made a mutual commitment to prevent such continental devastation from ever occurring again.[73] In 1951, the two great industrial powers of Western Europe, Germany and France (which had been so often been at war with each other),[74] became the leaders in establishing the European Coal and Steel Community, which also included Belgium, Italy, Netherlands, and Luxembourg. The idea was to harness coal and steel—the two key ingredients of a strong industrial economy—in the cause of peace and economic collaboration. These six countries broke new ground again in 1957 when they signed the Treaty of Rome, forming the European Economic Community. Over the following years, efforts were made to create a customs union or a common market which would remove internal barriers to trade among member countries while establishing a common external barrier to other countries.

In 1973, Denmark, Ireland, and the United Kingdom joined the EC, followed by Greece in 1981 and Portugal and Spain in 1986 (see Figure 6.4). The apparent economic success of the EC, and the dynamic created by new and continuing initiatives in the last couple of decades, has meant that every nation in Europe has wrestled with the thought of joinging the EC—however, even EC member countries have had second thoughts (e.g., Denmark) or have become ambivalent partners (e.g., United Kingdom). In 1995, Austria, Finland, and Sweden joined, but Norway declined. The collapse of the Eastern bloc has produced new interest in economic collaboration on the part of Eastern European countries; ten new countries joined the EU in 2004, effectively ending the European split between the free- and Communist worlds. Turkey has also become a candidate, although its location on the margins of Europe raises questions about where Europe actually ends. The European Union now comprises 25 countries and 454 million people. Clearly this economic community is becoming *broader;* a vital question, however, is to what extent its influence should become *deeper,* reaching into matters of politics, culture, and well-being—because the goal is not merely free trade but a real form of internal cohesion.[75]

Two things are remarkable about this evolving entity. One is that the EC is indeed moving towards *full economic integration,* as represented by the 1992 Maastricht Treaty, which

| FIGURE 6.4 | The European Union: Member Countries, Year Joined, and Percentage of EU Population (Before Enlargement in 2004) |

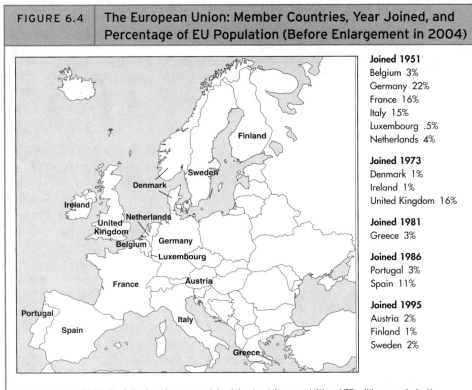

Joined 1951
Belgium 3%
Germany 22%
France 16%
Italy 15%
Luxembourg .5%
Netherlands 4%

Joined 1973
Denmark 1%
Ireland 1%
United Kingdom 16%

Joined 1981
Greece 3%

Joined 1986
Portugal 3%
Spain 11%

Joined 1995
Austria 2%
Finland 1%
Sweden 2%

Note: On May 1, 2004, the following 10 new countries joined, adding an additional 75 million people to the European Union: Cyprus, Czech Republic, Estonia, Hungary, Latvia, Lithuania, Malta, Poland, Slovakia, and Slovenia. In order to qualify for admittance, countries had to (a) be stable democracies, (b) have functioning market economies that could withstand the pressures of competitive market forces, and (c) agree to adhere to the EU's laws and economic terms and to embrace the monetary union. Because incomes in many of these countries were only 40% as high as in older parts of the EU, financial assistance was provided to launch the new economies.

Further Reading: Eurostat, Social Portrait of Europe, 1998, p. 29, and Youri Devuyst, *The European Union at the Crossroads* (Brussels, 2003).

Source: Compiled from *Eurostat, Social Portrait of Europe*, 1998, p. 29

created the European Union (EU) to replace the EC: Not only was there to be free movement of goods and services, but capital and labour could move without restriction anywhere within the entity. In 1995, passport controls were removed between France, Germany, Spain, Portugal, Belgium, Luxembourg, and the Netherlands. Perhaps the most dramatic step, and certainly the one that most clearly affected people's everyday lives, was the establishment in 1999 of a new unit of currency called the *euro*. The EU is also under increasing pressure to protect its worldwide interests by developing its own foreign policy, and a Common Foreign and Security Policy is in effect.[76] Thus while the EU is certainly not a superpower in terms of military might, it is certainly a power in terms of economic strength, and has developed more and more of the organizational apparatus to make it so.

Second is that the EU has developed its own *supranational institutions*, including a civil service and policy-initiation/implementation body called the European Commission, a directly elected European Parliament (which is assuming more powers in such areas as budgets and treaties), a powerful Council of Ministers (consisting of cabinet ministers from representative states), a European Council (consisting of heads of state), and a European Court of Justice to administer the legislation of the community. In some important ways, then, the EU is already a type of supranational state.[77] It even has its own tax base through the *value added tax* (VAT). However, in other ways it is still dependent on the voluntary participation of member states—and some do opt out of things like the monetary union. As power and authority is given or assumed by the EU and its headquarters in Brussels, the role of the member state changes, but not without controversy and concern among some Europeans with strong national identities.

The creation of the EU is still very much in process. Its member states have a "semi-sovereign"[78] position, retaining some key political powers. The working languages of the Commission are English and French, but all EU publications are printed in the languages of the member states. Some states, such as the United Kingdom, have maintained a more independent position, while others are highly committed to the EU. In general, however, the EU has been a creation of political elites rather than of populist action. The EU's lack of systematic accountability to the popular will (because of the relative weakness of the European Parliament) has led to what is called the *democratic deficit*[79] of the EU. In that sense, while the EU has its own internal dynamic, it is still a product of its member nations. But the level of integration already achieved is indeed remarkable, with future plans promising even more integration.[80]

Is the EU a paradigm for NAFTA? Will integration of the kind experienced in Europe occur in North America? While this is very much a question for the future, it can be stated quite unequivocally that NAFTA features none of the supranational institutions which the EU has created. And while the idea of a monetary union with the United States has often been raised, there is no immediate prospect of the unique Canadian currency being replaced. Furthermore, as Figure 6.4 indicates, while there is some disparity in population size and GDP among EU members, it is not of the magnitude of that found in North America, where the United States is a *regional hegemon.*[81] In Europe, Germany's power is somewhat counterbalanced by that of France, and the EU also contains a plurality of smaller nations. But in North America there is enormous asymmetry between the United

Economic Integration in South America: Mercosur

Although Argentina and Brazil had established economic ties earlier, in 1991 these two countries, plus Paraguay and Uruguay, established a new cooperative alliance known as *Mercosur.* In 1994, the beginnings of an institutional structure were created (with a transitional phase extending to 2006) whereby old barriers would be broken down and new relationships developed. Chile and Bolivia joined in 1996, and a "political Mercosur" was established in 1998. In 2003, a Committee of Permanent Representatives and a Dispute Settlement Court were created. Mercosur is another illustration of how regionally based alliances and integration have become almost a global phenomenon.

Source: Francisco Dominguez and Marcos Guedes de Oliveira, eds., *Mercosur: Between Integration and Democracy* (Oxford, 2003).

States and all other countries, especially those in Latin America which have also expressed interest in forming new economic arrangements.

So far, then, NAFTA is considerably different from the EU. It creates a free-trade area rather than a customs union or common market.[82] NAFTA emphasizes trade of goods and services, with only limited interest in labour mobility. It does not create new institutions with autonomy or authority over governments. A common currency is not in the immediate plans and has only recently been proposed. And yet, the North American experience may ultimately not be significantly different from the European one. Integration into the hegemon may occur more subtly but nevertheless be no less real. The American dollar, for example, may already indirectly serve as the common currency. And just as the EU discovered that a relationship that was originally established to facilitate economic flows has cultural effects,[83] so too is Canada very aware that matters of economy and culture cannot be separated. *Formal integration* refers to a government's deliberate facilitation of interaction with other societies by means of rules and regulations.[84] *Informal integration* refers to the spontaneous, non-state-promoted increase of such interaction through market forces, technology, and communication. It is this dual process of formal and informal integration that causes political boundaries to lose their significance and become primarily symbolic—with uncertain consequences for the future.

UNIQUENESS RE-EXAMINED

In spite of the brevity of some of these comparisons, it is clear that many other societies struggle with issues similar to those identified in Canadian society. More lengthy analyses are needed to explain the factors that produce the different effects and that result in alternative solutions.

One thing that this comparative study has highlighted is the way in which power is used to either accommodate or deny minority interests, whether in marginal regions or weakly populated areas, among poorer people, or in terms of minority language and cultures. The basic democratic principle of majority rule can legitimate policies that may create considerable societal tensions when minorities, feeling marginalized and powerless, become vocal and strident. While political states may be somewhat reluctant to support the devolution of their powers, decentralization may represent a better way to accommodate local interests. A society in which power is shared or distributed between groups rather than centrally controlled by a majority is known as a *consociational* form of society.[85] Because Canada is not unique in its struggles with regional and ethnic interests and uneven economic development, it may learn much by examining the experience of other societies.

FURTHER EXPLORATION

1. How can Canada learn from the experience of other societies? Discuss and illustrate with examples.

2. Why do people outside of North America frequently visualize Canadian society and American society as essentially the same? List some of the reasons why this assumption is true or not true and elaborate on them.

3. Compare the current federal policy on bilingualism with the principle of linguistic territoriality. Which is a better solution for Canada?

4. What do you think the consequences of free trade might be? Watch for articles in your newspaper on developments in the European Union and compare these with what is unfolding in North America.

SELECTED READINGS

Burridge, Kate, Lois Foster, and Gerry Turcotte, eds. *Canada–Australia: Towards a Second Century of Partnership.* Ottawa: International Council for Canadian Studies, Carleton University Press, 1997.

Close, Paul. *Citizenship, Europe and Change.* London: Macmillan, 1995.

Grabb, Edward, and James Curtis. *Regions Apart: The Four Societies of Canada and the United States.* Toronto: Oxford University Press, 2005.

Isajiw, Wsevolod. W., ed. *Multiculturalism in North America and Europe.* Toronto: Canadian Scholars Press, 1997.

Lipset, S.M. *Continental Divide: The Values and Institutions of the United States and Canada.* New York: Routledge, 1990.

McCrone, David. *Understanding Scotland: The Sociology of a Nation.* London: Routledge, 2001

Thomas, David, ed. *Canada and the United States: Differences That Count.* Peterborough: Broadview, 1993.

ENDNOTES

1 *Australia Yearbook 2004* (Canberra: Australian Bureau of Statistics, 1998), 91.

2 Further discussion of Western Australia can be found in my "Secession in Western Australia: A Continuing Phenomenon?" *Australian Quarterly* 59 (1987): 222–33; and "Western Separatism in Australia and Canada: The Regional Ideology Thesis," *Australian–Canadian Studies* 5 (1987): 39–54.

3 L.S. Bourne and M.I. Logan, "Changing Urbanization Patterns at the Margin: The Examples of Australia and Canada," in Brian J.L. Berry, ed., *Urbanization and Counter-Urbanization* (Beverly Hills: Sage, 1976), 116–18.

4 Elisa Maria Reis and Simon Schwartzman, "Spatial Dislocation and Social Identity in Brazil," *International Social Science Journal* 30 (1978): 98–115.

5 Statistical Abstract of The United States, 2003, (Washington D.C.: Bureau of Census, 1998), 20.

6 Statistical Abstract of The United States, 1984, 10 and 12; and 1998, Table 29.

7 Kirkpatrick Sale, *Power Shift: The Rise of the Southern Rim and Its Challenge to the Eastern Establishment* (New York: Random House, 1975).

8 Robert B. Cohen, "Multinational Corporations, International Finance, and the Sunbelt," in David C. Perry and Alfred J. Watkins, eds., *The Rise of the Sunbelt Cities* (Beverly Hills: Sage, 1977), 211–26.

9 Thomas A. Hutton, *The Transformation of Canada's Pacific Metropolis: A Study of Vancouver* (Montreal: Institute for Research on Public Policy, 1998).

10 Benjamin Higgins, *The Rise and Fall of Montreal?* (Moncton: Canadian Institute for Research on Regional Development, 1986).

11 Louis Hartz, ed., *The Founding of New Societies* (New York: Harcourt, Brace and World, 1964), chap. 1. For a critique of Hartz, see Gad Horowitz, "Conservativism, Liberalism, and Socialism in Canada: An Interpretation," *Canadian Journal of Economics and Political Science* 32 (1966): 143–50.

12 Kenneth McRae, "The Structure of Canadian History," in Hartz, *The Founding of New Societies.* See also his "Louis Hartz's Concept of the Fragment Society and its Applications to Canada," *Études canadiennes* 5 (1978): 17–30.

13 David Bell and Lorne Tepperman, *The Roots of Disunity* (Toronto: McClelland and Stewart, 1979), 45.

14 Bell and Tepperman, *The Roots of Disunity*, 76 and 79.

15 See in particular "The Social Development of Canada and the American Continental System," *Culture* 5 (1944): 132–43; and "Canada and Her Great Neighbour," *Canadian Review of Sociology and Anthropology* 1 (1964): 193–201.

16 *Revolution and Counter-Revolution: Change and Persistence in Social Structures,* rev. ed. (Garden City: Doubleday, 1971); and "Canada and the United States: A Comparative View," *Canadian Review of Sociology and Anthropology* 1 (1964): 173–85. For a broadening of the comparison to Britain and Australia, see his "The Value Patterns of Democracy: A Case Study in Comparative Analysis," *American Sociological Review* 28 (1963): 515–31. A recent restatement of Lipset's argument can be found in "Canada and the United States: The Cultural Dimension," in Charles F. Doran and John H. Sigler, eds., *Canada and the United States* (Englewood Cliffs: Prentice Hall, 1985).

17 See, for example, Tom Truman, "A Critique of Seymour M. Lipset's Article," *Canadian Journal of Political Science* 4 (1971): 513–25; Irving Louis Horowitz, "The Hemispheric Connection: A Critique and Corrective to the Entrepreneurial Thesis of Development with Special Emphasis on the Canadian Case," *Queen's Quarterly* 80 (1973): 336–37; Craig Crawford and James Curtis, "English Canada–American Differences in Value Orientations: Survey Comparisons Bearing on Lipset's Thesis," *Studies in Comparative International Development*, 1979; and Bell and Tepperman, *The Roots of Disunity*, 24–32. For a good review of these critiques, see Robert J. Brym, *From Culture to Power: The Sociology of English Canada* (Toronto: Oxford University Press, 1989), 29–32.

18 Seymour Martin Lipset, *Continental Divide: The Values and Institutions of the United States and Canada* (New York: Routledge, 1990). Published first in 1989 by the C.D. Howe Institute and the National Planning Association.

19 Lipset, *Continental Divide,* cha12.

20 Neil Nevitte, *The Decline of Deference* (Peterborough: Broadview, 1996)

21 Gordon Laxer, "Constitutional Crises and Continentalism: Twin Threats to Canada's Continued Existence," *Canadian Journal of Sociology* 17, 2 (1992):199–222.

22 Michael Adams, *Fire and Ice: The United States, Canada and the Myth of Converging Values* (Toronto: Penguin, 2003).

23 Pierre L. Van Den Berghe, "Australia, Canada, and the United States: Ethnic Melting Pots or Plural Societies?" *Australia and New Zealand Journal of Sociology* 19 (1983): 238–52.

24 See Charles A. Price, "The Immigrants," in A.F. Davies, S. Encel, and M.J. Berry, eds., *Australian Society: A Sociological Introduction* (Melbourne: Longman Cheshire, 1977), 331–55; and Dennis Laurence Cuddy, *The Yanks Are Coming: American Immigration to Australia* (San Francisco: R and E Research Associates, 1977), 4–5. For an analysis explicitly comparing the immigration policies of Canada and Australia, see Freda Hawkins, *Critical Years in Immigration: Canada and Australia Compared* (Montreal: McGill-Queen's University Press, 1989).

25 M.L. Kovacs and A.J. Cropley, *Immigrants and Society: Alienation and Assimilation* (Sydney: McGraw-Hill, 1975).

26 First Report of the National Population Inquiry, *Population and Australia: A Demographic Analysis and Projection*, vol. 1 (Canberra: Government of Australia, 1975), 99.

27 Australian Council on Population and Ethnic Affairs, *Multiculturalism for All Australians* (Canberra, 1982), 33–34. Statistics in this section are also from *Australia Yearbook 1988*, 263–64.

28 *Australia Yearbook* 1998, 159 and 170.

29 Christine Inglis, "Globalisation and the Impact of Asian Migration on Australia and Canada," in Kate Burridge, Lois Foster, and Gerry Turcotte, eds., *Canada–Australia: Towards a Second Century of Partnership* (Ottawa: International Council for Canadian Studies, Carleton University Press, 1997), 45–75. See also Statistics Canada, *The Daily*, January 21, 2003.

30 *Multiculturalism for All Australians*, 1. The emphasis on second-generation effects of immigration is repeatedly found in the Australian literature whereas it is mentioned much less in the Canadian literature. This may reflect the greater concern about assimilation in Australian society.

31 I.H. Burnley, "Geographic–Demographic Perspectives on the Ecology of Ethnic Groups in Australian Cities," in Charles A. Price and Jean I. Martin, eds., *Australian Immigration: A Bibliography and Digest*, Part I (Canberra: Australia National University, 1976), 124–49.

32 Kovacs and Cropley, *Immigrants and Society: Alienation and Assimilation,* chap. 4

33 Jean I. Martin, *The Migrant Presence: Australian Responses 1947–1977* (Sydney: George Allen and Unwin, 1978).

34 See Malcolm Alexander, "Globalisation and Civil Society: Multiculturalism, Citizenship, and Nationalism in Australia and Canada," 125–137, and Lois Foster and Paul Bartrop, "The Roots of Multiculturalism in Australia and Canada," in Burridge, Foster, and Turcotte, eds., *Canada–Australia: Towards a Second Century of Partnership,* 267–286; Freda Hawkins, "Multiculturalism in Two Countries: The Canadian and Australian Experience," *Journal of Canadian Studies* 17 (1982): 64–80; and Anthony H. Richmond and G. Rao, "Recent Developments in Immigration to Canada and Australia: A Comparative Analysis," *International Journal of Comparative Sociology* 17 (1976): 183–205.

35 Jean I. Martin, *The Migrant Presence: Australian Responses 1947–1977*, 30–31; and *Population and Australia: A Demographic Analysis and Projection*, 124. The difficulty of determining immigrants' intentions on arrival and on departure makes obtaining precise figures a problem. However, emigration is clearly recognized as a significant matter in Australia.

36 Rita Bienvenue, "Comparative Colonial Systems: The Case of Canadian Indians and Australian Aborigines," *Australian–Canadian Studies* 1 (1983): 30–43. Donald Edgar, *Introduction to Australian Society: A Sociological Perspective* (Sydney: Prentice Hall, 1980), 297. *Australia Yearbook 1998*, 154.

37 Bradford W. Morse, *Aboriginal Self-Government in Australia and Canada* (Kingston: Queen's University Institute of Intergovernmental Relations, 1984).

38 Colin Taz, "Aborigines: Political Options and Strategies," in R.M. Berndt, ed., *Aborigines and Change* (Canberra: Australian Institute of Aboriginal Studies, 1977), 384–401.

39 For a brief comparison, see Mary Beth Montcalm, "Quebec Separatism in Comparative Perspective," in Alain G. Gagnon, ed., *Quebec: State and Society* (Toronto: Methuen, 1984), 45–58; and Peter A. Gourevitch, "Quebec Separatism in Comparative Perspective," in Elliot J. Feldman and Neil Nevitte, eds., *The Future of North America* (Cambridge: Center for International Affairs, 1979), 238–52. See also Edward Tiryakian, "Quebec, Wales, and Scotland: Three Nations in Search of a State," *International Journal of Comparative Sociology* 21 (1982): 1–13.

40 Mark O. Rousseau and Raphael Zariski, *Regionalism and Regional Devolution in Comparative Perspective* (New York: Praeger, 1987).

41 For a discussion of these two perspectives, see Charles C. Ragin, "Ethnic Political Mobilization: The Welsh Case," *American Sociological Review* 44 (1979): 619–35; and Francois Nielsen, "The Flemish Movement in Belgium After World War II: A Dynamic Analysis," *American Sociological Review* 45 (1980): 76–94.

42 Tom Nairn, *The Breakup of Britain* (London: NLB, 1977), 105–106.

43 Jack Brand, "The Rise and Fall of Scottish Nationalism," in Charles R. Foster, ed., *Nations Without a State* (New York: Praeger, 1980), 33ff.

44 Milton J. Esman, "Scottish Nationalism, North Sea Oil, and the British Response," in M.J. Esman, ed., *Ethnic Conflict in the Western World* (Ithaca: Cornell University Press, 1977), 256–58.

45 John Bochel, David Denver, and Alan Macartney, eds., *The Referendum Experience: Scotland 1979* (Aberdeen: Aberdeen University Press, 1981).

46 For example, see the document by Owen Dudley Edwards, ed., *A Claim of Right for Scotland* (Edinburgh: Polygon, 1989).

47 John Foster, "Nationality, Social Change and Class: Transformations of National Identity in Scotland," in David McCrone, Stephen Kendrick, and Pat Straw, *The Making of Scotland: Nation, Culture, and Social Change* (Edinburgh: Edinburgh University Press, 1989), 31–52.

48 Jack Brand takes the view that ethnicity is not as important to the Scottish movement as is the depressed region's hope to find relief from economic marginality. But he does show how Scottish folk songs serve as a mobilization device among young voters; *The National Movement in Scotland* (London: Routledge and Kegan Paul, 1978). Other approaches that use a world systems or class-based approach include Michael Hechter, *Internal Colonialism* (London: Routledge and Kegan Paul, 1975); and Tom Nairn, *The Breakup of Britain*. For a different emphasis (on which much of the following discussion is based), see David McCrone, *Understanding Scotland: The Sociology of a Nation,* 2nd ed. (London: Routledge, 2001); and Michael Keating, *Nations Against the State* (London: Macmillan, 1996).

49 David McCrone, *Understanding Scotland: The Sociology of a Nation* (London: Routledge, 2001).

50 John Osmond, "Wales in the 1980's," in Charles R. Foster, ed., *Nations Without a State*, 45.

51 Ray Corrado, "The Welsh as a Nonstate Nation," in Judy S. Bertelsen, ed., *Nonstate Nations in International Politics* (New York: Praeger, 1977), chap. 6.

52 Tom Nairn, *The Breakup of Britain*, and Michael Hechter, *Internal Colonialism: The Celtic Fringe in British National Development* (Berkeley: University of California Press, 1975).

53 Walker Connor, "The Political Significance of Ethnonationalism Within Western Europe," in Abdul Said and Luiz R. Simmons, *Ethnicity in an International Context* (New Brunswick, NJ: Transaction, 1976), 117; and Osmond, 62.

54 H.M. Drucker and Gordon Brown, *The Politics of Nationalism and Devolution* (London: Longmans, 1980).

55 Davydd J. Greenwood, "Continuity in Change: Spanish Basque Ethnicity as a Historical Process," in Milton J. Esman, ed., *Ethnic Conflict in the Western World*, 84–87; and Pedro G. Blasco, "Modern Nationalism in Old Nations as a Consequence of Earlier State Building: The Case of Basque-Spain," in Wendell Bell and Walter E. Freeman, eds., *Ethnicity and Nation Building: Comparative, International, and Historical Perspectives* (Beverly Hills, Sage, 1974).

56 Robert P. Clark, "Euzkadi: Basque Nationalism in Spain Since the Civil War," in Charles R. Foster, ed., *Nations Without a State*, 77.

57 The number who voted for regional autonomy was 832 000; only 47 000 voted against it. International affairs, trade, defence, and currency were still to be federal matters. Ibid., 75–100.

58 Maria Heighberg, *The Making of the Basque Nation* (Cambridge: Cambridge University Press, 1989), 227–30.

59 Thomas C. Davies, "Patterns of Identity: Basques and the Basque Nation," *Nationalism and Ethnic Politics* 3, 1 (1997): 61–88.

60 Stanley G. Payne, "Nationalism, Regionalism and Micro-Nationalism in Spain," *Journal of Contemporary History* 26 (1991): 479–91.

61 Ronald Wardhaugh, *Language and Nationhood: The Canadian Experience*, 26.

62 Regarding the referendum in California, see E. Erlich, "Should English-Only Be the Law of the Land?" *Business Week*, Nov. 10, 1986; and "Language War in Florida," *Newsweek,* June 30, 1986. See also William A.V. Clark, *The California Cauldron* (New York: Guilford, 1998).

63 E.K. Francis, *Interethnic Relations* (New York: Elsevier, 1976), 104.

64 Carol Schmid, "Comparative Intergroup Relations and Social Incorporation in Two Multilingual Societies: Canada and Switzerland," in W.W. Isajiw, ed., *Multiculturalism in North America and Europe* (Toronto: Canadian Scholars Press, 1997), 484.

65 Kenneth D. McRae, *Conflict and Compromise in Multilingual Societies: Switzerland* (Waterloo: Wilfrid Laurier University Press, 1983), 55.

66 Kurt Mayer, "Ethnic Tensions in Switzerland: The Jura Conflict," in Charles R. Foster, ed., *Nations Without a State*, 189–208.

67 These points are found in McRae, *Conflict and Compromise in Multilingual Societies: Switzerland*; and in Schmid, "Comparative Intergroup Relations and Social Incorporation in Two Multilingual Societies: Canada and Switzerland." It is important not to overstress the unity aspect, because the 1992 vote on joining the European Union split the two largest linguistic groups; there was strong French support but mostly German opposition, which, because of the latter group's size, carried the vote (see Schmid, "Comparative Group Relations," 484).

68 Jaroslov Krejci and Vitezslav Velimsky, *Ethnic and Political Nations in Europe* (London: Croom Helm, 1981), 103–104.

69 Reginal DeSchryver, "The Belgian Revolution and the Emergence of Belgium's Biculturalism," in Arend Lijphart, ed., *Conflict and Coexistence in Belgium* (Berkeley: Institute of International Studies, 1980), 13–33.

70 Aristide R. Zolberg, "Splitting the Difference: Federalization Without Federalism in Belgium," in Milton J. Esman, ed., *Ethnic Conflict in the Western World*, 103–142.

71 Kenneth D. McRae, *Conflict and Compromise in Multilingual Societies: Belgium* (Waterloo: Wilfrid Laurier University Press, 1986), 109.

72 *The Political Handbook of the World* 1998, 84–88.

73 The peace incentives that stand behind European economic cooperation are a strong theme in all accounts of the EU. For example, see Desmond Dinan, *Ever Closer Union? An Introduction to the European Community*. (Boulder: Lynn Rienner, 1994). For a good overview of the issues in European integration, see Brigid Laffan, *Integration and Cooperation in Europe*, (New York: Routledge, 1992).

74 James Laxer discusses France and Germany's historic enmity, which he calls a major "fault-line" whence the strongest desires for European cooperation were expressed. *Inventing Europe: The Rise of a New World Power* (Toronto: Lester, 1991), 16.

75 "Widening" and "deepening" are two critical and debatable concepts within the European Union.

76 Christopher Piening, *Global Europe: The European Union in World Affairs* (Boulder: Lynn Rienner, 1997).

77 Gretchen M. Macmillan, "Managing Convergence in the European Union," in Donald Barry, ed., *Toward a North American Community? Canada, the United States, and Mexico* (Boulder: Westview, 1995), 229–40.

78   Gretchen M. Macmillan, "The European Community: Is It a Supra-National State in the Making?" in Stephen J. Randall and Roger Gibbins, eds., *Federalism and the New World Order* (Calgary: University of Calgary Press, 1994), 233.

79   Peter H. Smith, "Decision Rules and Governance," in Peter H. Smith, ed., *The Challenge of Integration: Europe and the Americas* (New Brunswick, N.J.: Transaction, 1993), 366.

80   There is considerable discussion about whether the European Union spells the death of individual European states; most see that outcome as unlikely. See, for example, Alan Milward, *The European Rescue of the Nation-State* (London: Routledge, 1992); Michael Mann, "Nation-States in Europe and Other Continents: Diversifying, Developing, Not Dying," *Daedalus* 122 (1993); "Has Globalization Ended the Rise of the Nation-State?" *Review of International Political Economy* 4 (1997); and David McCrone, *The Sociology of Nationalism* (London: Routledge, 1998), chap. 9. A good discussion of the shift away from nationally bounded societies is found in Chris Rumford, *The European Union: A Political Sociology* (Oxford: Blackwell, 2002).

81   Cf. Peter H. Smith, "Decision Rules and Governance," 377–79.

82   Edelgard Mahant and Xavier DeVanssay, "The Origins of Customs Unions and Free Trade Areas," 181–210; and Brigitte Lévy, "The European Union and NAFTA: Two Regional Economic Blocs in a Complex Globalized and Interdependent International Economy," *Journal of Economic Integration*, 17, 2–3 (1994): 211–33.

83   Bruno de Witte, "Cultural Linkages," in William Wallace, ed., *The Dynamics of European Integration* (London: Pinter, 1990), 192–210.

84   William Wallace, "Introduction," in *The Dynamics of European Integration*, 9.

85   The distinction between majoritarian and consociational societies was made by Arend J. Lijphart in his preface to *Conflict and Coexistence in Belgium*.

WEBLINKS

www.un.org/Depts/unsd/sd_social.htm

Visit this section of the United Nations Statistics homepage to view demographic and social statistics from around the world.

chapter seven

The Question of Identity

The Canadian social scientist cannot take the existence of this society for granted. There is nothing about the society that can be fully understood except in relation to how the society developed, how its very survival as a society, flanked as it was by the powerful republic to the south, remained problematic . . .

Canadian nationhood was attained, not by the making of different people into one, or by the strengthening of forces of consensus, but by fostering the differences between people within the nation and thereby securing the differences between Canadian people and American.

—S.D. Clark, the dean of Canadian sociology, whose career began in the 1930s

The comparative analysis conducted in the previous chapter is very important because it reveals to us that Canada is not the only society fraught with internal conflict and pressures towards change. The image of nation-states as harmonious families where all are united in the pursuit of common objectives is seldom borne out in reality. It is important to recognize this because many Canadians lose patience with the constant negotiations, debate, and uncertainties that pervade national life—as though Canadian society were some kind of outlier in the world of nation-states.

The enormous amount of energy put into seeking consensus and the resolution of divisions, both long-standing and emergent, has made negotiation and constitutional reform almost a national preoccupation. This fact has given rise to a plethora of pessimistic characterizations—such as "perpetual crisis," "anguished introspection," "inconclusive attempts at self-definition," "world champions of insecurity," "ceaseless self-psychoanalysis"—applied to Canada and Canadians. Uncertainty has turned into a national neurosis, reflected in the self-deprecating question "why does a Canadian cross the road?" While the chicken may have done so to get to the other side, the Canadian, in the relentless pursuit of acceptable compromise, does so "to get to the middle." Keith Spicer sums up the situation by saying that "Canada's identity is its identity crisis."[1]

While most Canadians feel no sense of imminent threat to their society and leave most of this debate to politicians, most are indeed aware that Canada is in the midst of significant transitions, the end result of which is still unclear. The material presented in the earlier chapters attempted to "unpack" the constituent elements of the Canadian society, laying bare the regional, class, and ethnic cleavages which are the basis for social conflict. This analysis may have shattered the romantic images of the nationalists or patriots who, out of love for their country, are only too willing to overlook the trouble spots. Yet too many recent events remind us that societies are fragile negotiated entities, always "in the making." People who think of Canadian society in terms of what it was 50 or even 20 years ago may be truly disconcerted by the changes they see around them. In this chapter, we will see that it is not only the constituent groups within a society that change; so too do our conceptions of the good society. Indeed, developments such as free trade, Quebec separatism, and Aboriginal self-determination, are constantly expanding our minds to consider new structural forms for Canadian society. In this chapter we will examine the competing elements of Canadian identity that must be reckoned with in the search for common ground and explore alternative ways of looking at society. This kind of thinking will be necessary as we face the transitions of the contemporary Canada.

ISSUES IN ASSESSING THE CANADIAN IDENTITY

Analyzing a Societal Identity

It is the commonalities of shared territory (in spite of its size) and polity (in spite of its inequities) that make this country's residents Canadian. To the extent that borders are real, they demarcate territory in which *people transform simple space into places where they live and share relationships with others inhabiting that space*. A societal identity emerges as people engage in this type of *place-making*.[2] Out of collective interactions among people who share the symbol "Canadian," a national identity is constructed.

A *societal identity* is the sum of the sentiments, cultural attributes, and structural arrangements people share; it gives them a feeling of belonging together. While individuals and groups *create* and contribute to that identity, they can also *internalize* the national identity into their self-definition. A societal identity, then, has a *collective* as well as an *individual* dimension. For this reason, it is possible to speak both of Canada's residents collectively creating and constructing a national society and of individual members accepting that collective identity as something personally meaningful.

Flowing from the key idea that national societies are social constructions is a corollary: Societies are not fixed entities but are *constantly changing* and *in process* owing to the existence of *competing visions* represented by *conflicting groups*. Rather than understand societies as fixed, immutable, and resistant to change, we must recognize that (at least in contemporary Canada) there are constant pressures, often difficult and painful, towards the development of new structures and formulations. For example, there are pressures to change the Senate, which was created as an arm of government, from an appointed to an elected body; resistance to such change, however, promotes considerable conflict. The definition of Quebec as a distinct society is another new idea which reveals the pressure for change but has provoked resistance and conflict. On the other hand, the policy of bilingualism, at one time a new idea, became policy in spite of resistance. So we do not just accept or internalize things as they are; we seek new and better ways to do things, continuously responding to change and thereby modifying the nature of societies.

A third aspect involved in analyzing a societal identity is distinguishing a society and its interests from others. One study found that members of Canadian society became most

I Am Canadian: Constructing a Unique Identity?

I work in the Toronto office of a United States-based multinational corporation that bought the company from a British firm. Today I helped negotiate a contract by e-mail with someone I have never seen nor spoken to. I drove home in my Japanese car and on the way bought a panini loaf from an Italian bakery.

My husband works for a Canadian accounting firm that does the books for a manufacturer that exports around the world but requires lots of currency transfers in US funds. On the way home, he picked up the children in his German Bug (which they love) and (in the middle of our winter) gave them a fresh peach from Chile as a snack.

For supper we had New Zealand lamb, California lettuce and tomatoes, French cheese, South African grapes, and Spanish wine. Then we watched the TV special on the Three Tenors from Europe.

As I nestled in my bed that night, I was so happy to be Canadian.

aware of their national identity through travel outside the country and interaction with foreigners.[3] It has been argued that the only time that Canadians wave the flag is when they are on vacation in Europe and do not want to be mistaken for Americans. It could also be argued that state negotiations with other societies make Canadians more aware of their national interests. For example, the turbot dispute with Spain in 1995 and the armed stand-off with Spanish fishing vessels in international waters off Newfoundland not only made a public global statement about Canadian concerns about fish conservation but also defended the interests of Atlantic-coast fishers. The point is that a national identity can crystallize as a result of *external relationships;* as a consequence of external dialogue, a society may become more aware of its internal relationships and of the concerns its people share.

There is also a fourth aspect to a national identity. According to a *descriptive* understanding of national identity, a distinctive identity simply emerges from things as they are. For example, no society has quite the same relationship between anglophones and francophones as Canada does, and for better or for worse, that helps give Canadian society its identity. But another understanding is far more *prescriptive*, offering a vision and ideals of what Canadian society *should be*. It can be argued that a descriptive focus (i.e., a focus on *what is*) is more likely to emphasize identity problems, whereas a prescriptive focus— dreaming and working towards a new and better Canadian society—shifts the emphasis from propping up the current fragmented identity to consolidating a new societal identity. However, as we shall see, there may be considerable disagreement among opposing groups about what *ought* to be.

CONTRADICTIONS IN THE ANALYSIS OF CANADIAN SOCIETY

There are five key contradictions or tensions at the heart of debates about the nature and character of Canadian society.

1. Homogeneity vs. Heterogeneity

Should our goal be the development of a society where everyone has similar traits and similar loyalties, or can we tolerate diversity? If the latter, how much diversity should be encouraged? What impact does the answer to this question have on immigration policy? On language policy? Does multiculturalism, which promotes a plurality of ethnic identities, detract from a single Canadian identity? Should "Canadian" be defined in a uniform way or should differences be tolerated, encouraged, and even fiscally supported?

2. Insularity vs. Openness

In order to develop a national consciousness, to what extent should our national borders be sealed from foreign influence? Should members of the society be discouraged from reading foreign magazines, watching foreign television, investing in foreign countries, or listening to recordings of foreign musicians? While liberty to pursue these activities may be central to our conception of individual freedom, should the government attempt to encourage national development by using its powers to minimize foreign influence? The question is, How does one determine the degree of insularity necessary to encourage national development? How much openness to other societies is necessary to prevent ethnocentrism and to encourage creativity, new ideas, and new social forms?

3. Legitimacy vs. Illegitimacy

Legitimacy has to do with being recognized as lawful and proper. In general, members of Canadian society accept the rule of their democratically elected governments as legitimate and worthy of support. Yet challenges to national authority and objectives have repeatedly been made by those who have alternate conceptions of what the society should be like, who question the right of the central state and its agencies to make decisions for them, or who feel that majority rule oppresses minorities.

When Quebec rejected the Supreme Court's decision regarding Bill 101, it was challenging the legitimacy of the Canadian state to interfere with this aspect of Quebec life. After the 1980 federal election, the West questioned the legitimacy of federal policies promoted by a government with poor representation from that region. The election to Parliament of many Bloc Québécois members in 1993 also created an ironic situation in which a separatist party seeking independence from Canada formed the official opposition, with all of the rights and privileges associated with that status. Other challenges to the legitimacy of the central state have arisen over Native rights, resource ownership, and even metrication.

In Canada, the cental state's actions have recurrently been accused of illegitimacy on the grounds that they represent specialized interests (e.g., of the Golden Triangle or of corporate capitalists). Should minority interest groups or hinterland interest groups be specially accommodated? How can the state wield power in the national interest when the national interest is defined in terms of a narrow interest group? Whose interests are legitimate and who is to decide whose interests are illegitimate or less legitimate?

4. Centralization vs. Decentralization

Some argue that in order to build a strong Canadian society, a strong central government is needed to establish policies promoting societal uniformity and homogeneity; only through such strong social control, they claim, can fragmentation of the society be prevented. From this point of view, the Meech Lake Accord and the Charlottetown Agreement were seen as unacceptable, because they strengthened the provinces by decentralizing too much authority, emasculating the federal government of its nation-building role. Do regional or local identities strengthen the national identity or compete with and distract from it? To what extent can certain groups be considered "distinct societies" or have self-government and still remain part of Canadian society? How much decentralization and regional variation can be tolerated without making a mockery of the idea of a national society?

5. Equality vs. Inequality

Inequalities are a feature of all societies; the question is, how much inequality should be tolerated—especially if it is argued that the structure of the society fosters and deepens inequalities? Should one region of a society care whether another region is disadvantaged? Does a prosperous region have a responsibility to a disadvantaged one? If so, how should inequalities be addressed? Do equalization grants really help, or do they merely perpetuate inequities? And what about language, employment, and gender inequities? To what extent must existing inequities be removed in order to foster a greater sense of personal or group identification with the national society?

These tensions remain major issues in Canadian society; they are never resolved but evoke a variety of sometimes contradictory responses. These responses, however, become "made-in-Canada" solutions to unique Canadian problems. For example, the particular form of bilingualism found in Canada represents a particular solution to a unique Canadian problem. It can be argued that the Canadian identity is the product of struggles to cope with the tensions and conflicts that emerge within the society. In that sense, the Canadian identity is not a once-and-for-all, carved-in-stone complex of traits, but an evolving entity.

While in one sense societal conflict may be problematic, it may also be viewed as a struggle in which conflicting parties participate together to find unique compromises which may reshape Canadian society. This was the perspective taken in the 1970s by the federal government-appointed Task Force on Canadian Unity, which tried to reinterpret diversity as a *national resource* rather than a societal problem.[4] Diversity was to be encouraged rather than submerged, but with the goal of harmonious coexistence. However, merely giving a positive spin to Canada's dilemmas does not remove them or lead to quick solutions.

The most important nation-defining tensions preoccupying Canadians have to do with the French–English clash over different conceptions of society, the contradictions between the federal centre and the regions, and the differentiation of Canadian society from American society.[5] There are other tensions or contradictions (e.g., between First Nations and Euro-Canadians), but the struggle around these key contending realities is at the heart of the evolution and development of national identity in Canada.

Conceptualizing the Contradictions: Two Perspectives From an analytical point of view, there are two basic approaches to assessing Canadian identity: the pan-Canadian or unitary approach and the segmentalist approach.[6] The *pan-Canadian* or *unitary approach* contends that society is made up of *individuals* who find their collective identity in belonging to the national society. This perspective devalues regional or ethnic loyalties and characteristics (e.g., speaking a non-official language at home), stressing wider allegiance to the national society. In stressing the individualistic basis of society, this approach accentuates the role of the Canadian state in promoting the necessary feeling of belonging.

The *segmentalist approach* focuses on groups or communities, founded upon regional, racial, linguistic, occupational, or cultural similarities. The segmentalist considers *group commitments* (rather than individuals) the building blocks of Canadian society, and does not aim to dissolve these groups even when they compete with allegiance to the larger society. Anglophones, particularly in Ontario, tend to prefer the pan-Canadian approach to societal unity; francophones, Aboriginal people, and some residents of hinterland regions with other group ties are more likely to prefer the segmentalist approach.

It is important to understand the distinction between the pan-Canadian (unitary) and segmentalist approaches at the outset. Although they represent different models of society with different outcomes, both are valid models of society. You may be biased towards one or the other depending on what you think Canadian society should be like, but be aware that there are those who can make a strong case for the opposing model.

There was a time when it was thought that the pan-Canadian view would eventually win out. It was thought that as immigrants were assimilated, as the continental crush of the dominant English language overwhelmed Quebec francophones, and as hinterland regions were integrated more closely into the national economy, commitment to the national society would become primary. Yet ethnic associations remain vital, Quebec uniqueness remains strong, First Nations' commitment to self-determination is growing, and regional loyalties and grievances foster community attachments. For some Canadians at least, commitment to the national society remains diluted, a fact that supports a more segmentalized society. Clearly, most of the key issues in Canadian society can be understood in terms of this unitary–segmentalist debate.

FACTORS IN IDENTITY FORMATION

Although national identity is not immutable and unchanging nor even evolving towards a fixed form, and although there are many different versions of what it means to be a Canadian,[7] it is important to identify the central features of the evolving Canadian identity. Six features will be discussed.

1. Responding to the Colonialist Legacy

British sponsorship of Canadian society has produced a legacy of British influence, including the parliamentary system and British law. Images of British royalty continue to appear on Canadian coins, and children are still taught "God Save The Queen" in schools (although use of this anthem is declining). The position of Governor General (the monarchy's representative in the government) was filled by a Canadian for the first time in 1952, with the appointment of Vincent Massey. Even though British sponsorship has weakened considerably (first through the creation of the British Commonwealth of Nations and more recently through Britain's shift away from her former colonies and towards the European Union), a special relationship with the mother country still prevails. Members of the royal family still make regular visits to Canada, and thousands flock to see them.

Canadians are by no means in agreement on the role of the monarchy in contemporary Canadian society. Obviously, persons of British descent are more likely to have positive feelings about ties to the monarchy, while those of other ethnic backgrounds are more likely to prefer a more independent rather than sponsored identity. It was not until 1947 that Canadian citizens were differentiated from British subjects, so British ties were real for many Canadians until after World War II. Perhaps the strongest negative response to the colonialist heritage has come from the Québécois, who see the symbols of the monarchy as reminders of their defeat by the British and their position as a subordinate minority. Consequently, while the colonial legacy is part of Canada's "roots," it is far from a source of pride and unity for all Canadian residents, and in fact may divide more than it unites.

In one sense, Canada sustained her unique identity through the years as a result of her alliance with Britain.[8] On the other hand, Britain's relationship with Canada can be viewed as an essentially maternalistic one which has overshadowed Canada's own expressions of independence. No issue could better symbolize Canada's concern about this dependent condition than the repatriation of the Constitution. The fact that the *British North America Act of 1867*, an Act of the British Parliament, was for many years Canada's only Constitution served as a reminder that Canadian society had never created a charter for its own existence. To francophones, it was also a galling and persistent reminder of British dominance and French colonial defeat. Consequently, the proclamation of the new *Constitution Act, 1982* on April 17, 1982, with its own amending formula and a Charter of Rights and Freedoms, had the potential to signify the dawn of a new independent existence for Canada. There was, however, no great outpouring of nationalist sentiment and little

---

REAL PEOPLE 7	Questioning the Taken for Granted

Every morning before school, 9-year-old Stephen dutifully practised for his Wednesday piano lesson. This week his teacher gave him a new song to practise and Stephen picked his way through the melody. It sounded strangely familiar.

"That's it!" Stephen exclaimed. "'God Save The Queen.' We sing that song at school assemblies."

Mom was in the kitchen and had vaguely overhead Stephen's discovery over the noise of his brother yelling about what clothes to wear.

"Hey, Mom," inquired Stephen. "Is the Queen the queen of the whole world?"

"No Steve, she's the Queen of England."

There was a pause as he plunked out a few more notes.

"Hey, Mom, England is another country, isn't it?"

"Yes, dear," his mother assured him.

"We're on a different continent than England, right, Mom?"

"Yes, you're right."

A few more notes came from the piano.

"Then how come we sing 'OUR noble Queen?'"

"It's always been that way, Steve. Now get ready for school."

Questions to Consider

Do you think symbols of the monarchy should be more or less important in Canadian society? What are the advantages or disadvantages of their use?

public enthusiasm; perhaps more importantly, Quebec did not sign the accord.[9] Thus the document that was to be the cornerstone for the new sense of society lacked the ratification of one of that society's most significant segments.

The adoption of the new Canadian Constitution was not a moment of great celebration in Canada; it was a painful process that revealed once again some of the basic underlying struggles within the society.[10] Yet the Constitution's role in the creation of a societal identity has been, and will continue to be, pivotal. That is why Quebec's absence from the signing was so lamentable and why the constitutional revisionism represented by the Meech Lake Accord and the Charlottetown Agreement was a sign of hope (but a hope which was eventually dashed). On the other hand, Canada's continuing constitutional struggles represent Canadians' search for mechanisms with which to shape their own society and move even farther away from their colonial legacy.

Even though the colonial legacy continues in a largely symbolic form, it reasserts old ties that some feel belong in the past and should not be part of the new era of independence.[11] Canada's colonial heritage is still a vestigial part of its identity, and the maintenance of symbolic ties seems to be a comfortable way of remaining linked to the society's roots while building symbols of independent identity.[12] So far, there has been no public discussion of cutting those ties entirely (as there has in Australia)—although that course of action is clearly implicit in Quebec nationalism.

2. Proximity to the United States

The fact that Canada was created to be a North American political entity distinct from the United States is central to understanding the formation and evolution of Canadian society. In many ways, the pursuit of expanded markets and territory created Canada's political structures. The Canadian state then became the primary instrument of regulation and development for an autonomous national entity. Canada was deliberately created to be a separate and distinct unit from the United States.[13]

As we saw in Chapter Two, sharing a continent with a larger, more powerful society has always made distinctiveness a problem. During some periods, such as the '60s and '70s, it seemed that the more Canadian society came to resemble American society, the greater its efforts to differentiate itself. One analyst has described the amalgam of feelings between the two societies as being composed of attraction, rejection, and ambivalence.[14] Canadians feel at home in the United States, to which they travel in great numbers, and Americans struggle to explain subtle differences between the two societies that go beyond Canada's metric signposts.

The amount of interaction between the two societies is indeed considerable. In recent years there have been significant shifts in travel patterns as a result of the Canadian dollar's devaluation relative to the American dollar and the effects of September 11, 2001. Whereas in the past more Canadians visited the United States than vice versa (66 million Canadians travelled to the United States in 1993), that number dropped to 35 million in 2002.[15] In the same year, more Americans took trips to Canada (40.9 million, up from 32 million in 1993). Canadians tended to stay longer in the United States (average length of stay 7.7 nights) than Americans stayed in Canada (4.0 nights); this tendency primarily reflects the annual Canadian "snowbird" migration to warmer climates in the winter months. But what is particularly remarkable are the number of same-day trips (mostly by automobile) across the border. The majority of trips by Canadians to the United States are of this kind, which suggests that intermingling is part of a daily lifestyle. Small American border communities such as Bellingham, Washington; Grand Forks, North Dakota; and Plattsburg, New York, are all commercially overbuilt for their size because they are service large Canadian cities (Vancouver, Winnipeg, Montreal). In 2002, even though the exchange rate was highly unfavourable, 21.6 million Canadians made trips to the United States, leaving and returning on the same day (down from a high of 60.2 million trips in 1991). Seventy-six percent of all trips to the United States were for non-business reasons (i.e., for pleasure or to visit friends and relatives), as were 79% of American visits. The extent of the intermingling of Canadian and American people is revealed by the fact that 88% of Canadian residents returning from international destinations were returning from the United States; 91% of all international visits to Canada in 2002 were made by American residents.

Many factors foster the integration of Canadian and American societies, but perhaps none is more pervasive than television and popular culture. Canadians watch a large number of American television programs, which are broadcast on Canadian stations as well as on cable networks and satellites. American programming accounts for almost two thirds of all television watched by Canadians.[16]

John Meisel, former chairman of the Canadian Radio-television and Telecommunications Commission, has noted that Canadians feel they have a right to access American programming.[17] One factor working against efforts to promote Canadian programming is that the majority of Canadians, because of their proximity to border stations, were able to receive US signals even before cable was available. Another problem is

Language and National Identity?

Which spelling is Canadian: "color" or "colour"? "neighbor" or "neighbour"? "centre" or "center"? The "-or" ending is usually identified as American and the "-our" as British.

Some people find the British spelling preferable because it helps Canada maintain a separate identity from the United States. Others argue that use of a different spelling is impractical and even a non-issue, since most Canadian newspapers, for example, use American spellings. Furthermore, such use leads to inconsistencies; we spell "favour" and "odour" with "-our," but not, for example, "horror" and "tremor."

Socio-linguists point out that both spellings have been part of Canadian usage since before Confederation. Also, there are regional differences in the predominance of one spelling over the other. Both spellings appear to be tolerated within Canadian schools. But there is some evidence that Canadians are increasingly using a consistent British spelling of certain words, such as "centre." Which spelling is right? Does it matter?

Questions to Consider

Why do some people feel so strongly about this issue? Is it important for a society to have its own distinctive spellings? What does language usage tell us about our culture? What are the typical spellings in your region?

that American networks can amortize their programming costs over a vast domestic market, then sell their programs to foreign networks for 3%–6% of cost. Canadian producers, who cannot compete at these costs, readily purchase US shows as a way to balance their budgets. Meisel also identifies a *mass–elite dichotomy* as a third problem. The better-educated, high-income groups are more interested in indigenous programming, while American programming has more of a popular following. Rather than making access to American networks more difficult, the government's approach has been to license cable companies and add a tax to help finance Canadian programming. But the point is that Canadians have ready access to both American interpretations of the news and most aspects of American popular culture.

While there is much that propels Canadian society into the American orbit, the lesson of history is certainly that Canada's existence has been predicated on differentiating itself from American society. In fact, Richard Gwyn has noted that Canadian survival has depended on being "not-American."[18] Gwyn claims that while Canadians have become as fully North American as Americans, they have become a distinct kind of North American. What Gwyn is arguing is that although Canadian and American societies are integrated in specific ways, Canada is still a different society primarily because it has a different political culture.

The presence in Canada of various forms of *anti-Americanism* (from mild to overtly hostile), counteracting other trends which pull the two societies together, should not be surprising.[19] Doran and Sewell have argued that anti-Americanism reflects dynamics in the perceiving nation as much as characteristics of the nation being perceived. They go so far as to assert that anti-Americanism is an important element in the cohesion of Canadian society, and "if the United States did not exist, Ottawa would have to invent it."[20] While Canadians may lament the fact that most Americans are apathetic or ignore Canada, in a curious sort of way, the United States is very important to Canadian identity.

Another effect of American proximity is to cause Canadians to compare the Canadian "identity" with the apparent feeling of national unity and sense of destiny that exist in the United States. In the United States, the American War of Independence and ensuing events created a pantheon of national heroes, momentous historic documents, and a charter of ideals. It has often been argued that the Canadian identity has been diffuse because Canadian society has lacked this kind of revolutionary origin.[21] While a national mythology may help differentiate a society and engender patriotic feelings, it may be wrong to assume that societies lacking such origins or the heightened collective feelings resulting therefrom are impoverished. In sum, members of Canadian society are frequently affected by the ideals or expressions of national unity and societal identity they observe in American society.[22]

There is no doubt that Canada's integration with/resistance to the American presence is an important piece in the Canadian identity puzzle. However, free trade and the current climate of neo-liberalism are removing some of the historical barriers of differentiation. The Canadian state no longer appears to be as willing to support resistance to integration or to provide the instruments to do so. The shift in government policy away from public interventionism and towards letting market mechanisms prevail means that historical instruments of national culture, such as the Canadian Broadcasting Corporation, have been subjected to major fiscal cutbacks. Furthermore, the flow of capital across borders is no longer subject to the same scrutiny. In general, Canada's abandonment of independent economic strategy has contributed to greater and greater continental convergence.[23]

9/11 and the Issue of Canadian Sovereignty

On September 11, 2001, 3000 people died as the result of terrorist attacks on the World Trade Center in New York, the Pentagon in Washington, D.C., and a plane crash in Pennsylvania. Among the dead were 25 Canadians. While this highly organized attack took place on American soil, it has had a significant impact on Canada.

The feel-good part of this horrific event was the way that Canadians rallied to provide for the 250 aircraft which were diverted and landed in Canada after the attack, with their 44 000 bewildered and frightened passengers. No place in Canada was affected more strongly than Newfoundland and Labrador, where approximately 13 000 airline passengers were stranded. At the airport at Gander, 38 unexpected aircraft landed, and 6 500 passengers were accommodated in the surrounding communities for a number of days. The hospitality that was demonstrated has been described as a "love story" in Canadian–American relations, as stranded passengers were provided with food, shelter, and simple things like toothpaste as their luggage was confiscated and searched.

But there is another side to this event that affects Canada in another way. Most Americans interpret 9/11 as a direct attack against them collectively; this is reflected in the way the anniversary of the event is commemorated each year, with the replay of footage of planes crashing into buildings and collapsing towers. In that sense, 9/11 has been a defining event for American society, and the world has been reconfigured into "supporters" and "enemies." Canada may have always been the biggest ally of the US and is certainly its largest trading partner, but Canada did not endorse America's subsequent invasion of Iraq and therefore became suspect. The calamity of 9/11 made Americans especially vigilant about their security, and the border to the north immediately became an issue ("a launching pad for terrorists"); criticisms were launched about Canadian immigration policy, military preparedness, and fiscal and foreign policy. Seeking to establish a defence perimeter around their country, Americans attempted to influence Canadian decision-making much more directly, also initiating collaborative approaches to enhancing border-crossing security (e.g., the so-called smart cards).

For Canadians, 9/11 is a significant illustration of the dilemma Canada faces: attempting to retain sovereignty over its own policies, yet caught up in economic forces of continental integration while living next-door to the world's superpower.

References: Jim DeFede, *The Day the World Came to Town: 9/11 in Gander, Newfoundland* (New York: Regan Books, 2002); David Carment, Fen Osler Hampson, and Norman Hillmer, *Canada Among Nations 2003: Coping with the American Colossus* (Oxford: Oxford University Press, 2003); Kent Roach, *September 11: Consequences for Canada* (Montreal: McGill-Queen's University Press, 2003); Yasmeen Abu-Laban and Christina Gasbriel, "Security, Immigration, and Post-September 11 Canada," in J. Brodie and L Trimble, eds., *Re-Inventing Canada* (Toronto: Prentice Hall, 2003).

Although at this point it is hard to know where all this will lead, it is clear that continental integration is proceeding incrementally. One interesting study of television viewing-habits shows that even though Canadians overwhelmingly prefer American programming for entertainment and relaxation, they normally choose Canadian news-programming for coverage that reflects their essential political identity.[24] Congressional politics may be irrelevant to most Canadians, who prefer to hear from their own decision makers; however, it may well be that the values embodied in American TV dramas and sitcoms represent just as pervasive, if unconscious, an influence on Canadians.[25] If differentiation from the United States is crucial to Canadian identity, then decreasing interest in such differentiation in the face of continentalism could make the political identification "Canadian" nothing more than a regional distinction. Continental integration clearly tends to undermine Canadian political integration, although it has been argued that free trade is not so much the cause of this process as the culmination of a longstanding trend.[26]

3. Internal Cleavages

The internal cleavages within Canadian society are another crucial factor in national identity. Pierre Berton noted that Canada's persistent ethnic and regional loyalties "hold us together as a distinctive people even as they tear us apart—a typical Canadian contradiction."[27] Language, ethnicity, and region are critical variables; it is also appropriate to add gender to this list.

Language is not only the vehicle of a person's expression of identity, but places the language-user into a larger group. A common language can build bridges between dissimilar people, just as language differences can create barriers. The notion of two official languages can be viewed as a keystone of national identity, but it can also be considered a "mythical unity" of two language groups, as only a small majority of Canadians have bilingual capacity or conduct their life in a bilingual format.[28] In fact, the French and English languages have become increasingly territorialized as official-language minorities have declined in size outside their respective regions.[29] Furthermore, the existence of two different-language broadcasting networks, for example, implies far more than the use of two different languages: It signifies two different presentations of the news (and even of what is considered newsworthy), targeted at two different groups.

Language can also be related to ethnic culture. Francophone Quebec is clearly articulating a new identity. One observer has likened Quebec to an orphan suffering from a trauma of infancy, claiming that the fact of the province's origin in separation from the mother country (France) implanted in Québécois the fear of a tragic destiny.[30] So if anglo-Canada perceives Canadian society as stronger because of the British sponsorship from which it can now become more independent, franco-Canada has had to deal with the lack of any sponsorship whatsoever. Two different agendas have resulted from these historical origins, creating the distinctive "two solitudes." While Quebec has developed its historical sense of nationhood more or less independently, anglophone Canada's British heritage has been diluted by decades of immigration from diverse sources, a fact that makes nation-building a more contemporary issue.[31] For this reason, anglophone Canadians desperately want to include francophones in the nation-building process, whereas Quebec vacillates between giving priority to its own objectives and participating in the Canadian entity.

It is clear that the spectre of Quebec's separation from Canada, kept alive through repeated threats and divisive referendums, has taken its toll on perceptions of nation-building.[32] In fact, the Quebec question has now become the most critical internal factor, leading many analysts to begin to imagine the consequences and reality of a Canada without Quebec. At some moments, this conflict appears to be pulling the national society apart,

A Typology for Understanding Internal Cleavages

A *multination state* results when previously self-governing, territorially concentrated cultures are involuntarily incorporated into a larger state. As national minorities, these cultures wish to remain distinct societies alongside the dominant culture, and demand various forms of self-government or autonomy to ensure their survival.

A *polyethnic state* arises when immigrants seek to be fully accepted as members of the society in spite of their differences. They seek modifications of the dominant society in order to accommodate their own identities.

Canadian society is both multinational and polyethnic. The French and Aboriginal communities were involuntarily incorporated into Canada by the British, and at various points have sought ways to renegotiate their own autonomy as national minorities within the broader society—for example, by being recognized as a distinct society (Quebec's goal in the Charlettown Accord) or by attaining self-government (the quest of Aboriginal peoples). National minorities usually feel allegiance to the larger state only insofar as the larger state recognizes and respects their distinct existence.

Canadian society is polyethnic because of its high rates of immigration. The old Anglo-conformity model has been replaced by a pluralistic multicultural model. However, the expression of ethnic subcultures' distinctiveness is largely confined to family life and voluntary associations; these groups are expected to participate in the dominant language(s) and public institutions.

Question to Consider

In what ways do these two concepts of Canadian society clash?

Source: Based on Will Kymlicka, *Multicultural Citizenship* (Oxford: Oxford University Press, 1995), Chapter 2.

but at other times compromise, negotiation, and creativity have enabled us to perceive the possibility of a revised yet distinctive Canadian character emerging from the turmoil.

Regional inequities have also thwarted Canadian unity. Uneven economic development has occasioned regional dissatisfaction; provincial governments have sometimes taken up the cause, pitting the sub-units of the national society against one another or against the federal government, thus arousing further animosities.[33]

Some consider ethno-linguistic and regional cultures an entirely negative phenomenon because they see them as implying a weak and fragmented national identity. Such a view, of course, is based on a unitary rather than segmentalist conception of society. While it is true that a regional or ethnic identity may be in competition with a national identity, the two are not necessarily incompatible and may be held simultaneously.[34] In other words, an identity as a Prince Edward Islander, a farmer of Scottish origin, or even a Maritimer does not necessarily exclude the broader and more distant Canadian identity. Even a Québécois identity may coexist with an identification in some significant sense with other Canadians.[35] A considerable range exists in terms of what level of the society people feel primary allegiance to—local, regional, or national. There are strong indications that notwithstanding the diversity of reactions, some attachment to the national society is felt by most of its members. In other words, the national society is, at least in some important ways, part of every resident's frame of reference.

There is also another element in societal identity which has historically been overlooked because of the dominant position held by men. In many cases, our understanding of the role women have played in Canadian life must be revised because gender bias has obscured the contribution of women.[36] In contemporary Canada, the feminist movement has not only challenged male conceptions of the dynamics of Canadian society but has also played a key role in urging women to play a different role than they have in the past.

4. National Debate of Social Issues

Many issues that emerge within Canadian society create new alignments and debate. In the background of all of these debates is the question of what kind of society Canadian society should be. While at times such debates seem to tear the society apart, making us aware of what divides us, they also play a role in stimulating the formation of a distinct societal identity.

One such category of issues pertains to the environment—including pollution, acid rain, resource depletion, and nuclear armaments. Another has to do with matters such as gender equality, capital punishment, and abortion. The Vietnam War was a hot-button issue in the '60s, and the Iraq war became a critical focus of national debate in the new millenium. Free trade has been an issue with implications far beyond the exchange of goods, and public indebtedness and deficit reduction have also generated debate about what Canadians want their society to be like. Immigration policy has been another controversial topic; an emerging vision of a different kind of society has challenged older conceptions of what Canadian society should be like.

Robin Matthews has argued that at the heart of the Canadian identity is the dialectic between *communitarianism* and *competitive individualism*.[37] On the one hand, Canadians

---

A Fragile Social Fabric?

Every society has a social infrastructure or *social fabric* that defines what people can expect from their society and what their society can expect from them. This can be called a societal *covenant*. The problem is that our market culture promotes individual rather than collective goals, eroding the social covenant. In a national study, 90% of respondents said that "there are too many people preoccupied with what they can get out of the system rather than what they can contribute to the common good," and 75% said that "too many people will sacrifice their principles in order to get ahead economically." The study concluded that the value Canadians place upon collective well-being may even supersede our preoccupation with material well-being. How do most Canadians resolve the dilemma of personal rights versus obligation to society? Is a shift in values emerging, away from rights and towards obligations?

Source: Raymond Breton, Norbert J. Hartmann, Jos L. Lennards, and Paul Reed, *A Fragile Social Fabric? Fairness, Trust, and Commitment in Canada.* (Montreal: McGill-Queen's University Press, 2004).

recognize the sanctity and freedom of the individual, while on the other they emphasize the values of community, social well-being, and universal justice. Historically, this dialectic has led to a blend of public and private enterprise, a series of social safety nets (ranging from medicare to regional equalization), and concern for the disadvantaged in the community. The fact that these distinguishing features of Canadian society are currently under threat suggests an erosion of the basic values that have characterized Canadians over the last 40-plus years.

All of these controversies expose members of a society to a diversity of opinions and attune them to the need to develop national policies. The media play a particularly important role in these debates.[38] Resulting federal policies usually reflect both compromise between interest groups in the society and the differential power of those groups. These policies thus represent uniquely Canadian resolutions to problems that may not be unique to Canada but are resolved differently elsewhere.

5. The Evolution of Symbols of Societal Unity

Public symbols are important: They help create the boundaries and coherence of a society as a people, rather than as a collection of individuals. However, which symbols will prevail and whose interests will they represent? Competition over the specification of the *symbolic order* occurs over issues such as defining-words (e.g., "distinct society," "founding peoples"), language use (bilingualism, monolingualism, "non-official languages"), public policies (immigration, multiculturalism), objects (flags, monuments), special holidays (Canada Day, St-Jean-Baptiste Day), and constitutional issues ("self-government," decentralization, or agreements such as the Charlottetown Accord).

For many years, Canada's identity as a political entity was shaped by its position as a *sponsored society*. The symbols of societal unity were those of the mother country, such as the Union Jack (used as Canada's flag) and "God Save The Queen" (sung as an anthem at public gatherings). The fact that these symbols, to French-Canadians, were irritating reminders of colonial defeat by the British made them divisive rather than unifying. It has only been since 1980 that "O Canada" has had official status as the national anthem, although it had been in use for many years. Perhaps even more significant is the fact that the anthem's bilingual version is not widely used. Another important symbol, the Maple Leaf flag, was only adopted in 1965.[39] Thus, as measured by the above-mentioned symbols, a national rather than a sponsored identity has only crystallized in recent years. Vestiges of the old symbol-system persist (such as the monarchy symbols on Canadian currency), but the transformation of some aspects of the symbolic order is in process.

What happens, however, if societal symbols are alienating to some segments of a society, or if changes to existing symbols create so much conflict that people feel alienated from their own society?[40] Francophones have been historically unhappy with British symbols, but many of the changes to the symbol system designed to make francophones more comfortable have alienated anglophones, causing them to feel estranged from their own national society. Language, of course, is the most powerful symbol: Just as the English language was alienating to francophones, so has the new status of French been alienating to anglophones—to say nothing of the effect on Quebec anglophones of the mandated use of French in that province. In a similar manner, the shift from the Imperial system to the metric system and the devaluation of British symbols in public ceremony have broken continuity with the past in favour of transformation to a new collective identity. In the long run, these changes in the symbolic order may be significant in the production of a new societal identity; however, they sometimes occasion new conflicts within the national society.

The Struggle over Societal Symbols: The Constitution

In many ways, a constitution is a blueprint for a society. It not only establishes the society's *instrumental order* (i.e., its institutional arrangements—including a structure of government, a division of powers, and a judicial system), but it also defines the set of ideals and principles on which the society is based (the *symbolic order*). These principles will govern the basic components of the social order—from the status of individuals to that of specific groups, as well as their relation to one another. For example, to declare English the country's official language and to make the Constitution only available in English is to make a clear statement about what other language groups can expect. On the other hand, to define both French and English as official languages is to make a different statement, namely, that both language-groups have equal status (this still leaves out people who speak other languages, however). The declaration of two official languages in the Constitution establishes a basic principle or ideal which is to guide legislation and judicial rulings.

Whose ideals will be represented in the symbolic order? What is, is not, or should be in the Constitution and how it should be interpreted are important issues because of the document's symbolic significance. The Constitution articulates what Canadian society should be like, and that is why debate over the Constitution is so heated: People disagree fiercely over the contents of the Constitution because they have opposing visions of what Canadian society should be like. Furthermore, the Constitution may be interpreted as symbolically allocating status to particular groups; this perception may create conflict, as certain groups feel left out or seek to change their position.

In Chapter Five, we observed that the Canadian Constitution continues to be a problematic symbol rather than an integrating one. Quebec wants constitutional recognition as a *distinct society* on the basis of the fact that they *are* a distinct society. From this perspective, the distinct-society clause can be viewed as merely an explicit recognition of what already exists, the affirmation of a cultural reality that it is absurd to deny. But to others the distinct-society clause suggests special status rather than equality and represents nothing more than an inadmissible claim for special powers. The "distinct-society" clause, then, has become *symbolic of an ongoing battle* between competing factions over the role of Quebec within Canadian society. Putting two little words in the Constitution may seem innocent enough, were it not that those two words have symbolic meaning about the nature of Canadian society. The fact that people interpret "distinct society" in a variety of ways only makes the dilemma more complicated.

Further Reading: Raymond Breton, *Why Meech Failed: Lessons for Canadian Constitution-making* (Toronto: C.D. Howe Institute, 1992); and Kenneth McRoberts, *Misconceiving Canada: The Struggle for National Unity* (Toronto: Oxford, 1997).

The Backpack Maple Leaf

While they often struggle with their national identity at home, Canadians who travel abroad proudly carry the Maple Leaf (usually in miniature) on their backpacks as they move about in countries all over the world. At first the Maple Leaf was a way to distinguish themselves from Americans in the '60s and '70s; now it has become a symbol that works to open doors, establish friendships, and even obtain special treatment. This is because Canadians are often highly regarded elsewhere in the world and are seen as non-threatening.

Most of the world travels incognito, but Canadians wear the flag almost as part of their uniform whenever they travel overseas. Sometimes even non-Canadians are seen sporting the flag.

Question to consider
What does this tell us about the power and meaning of a symbol?

In fact, as societal change accelerates and creates even more ambiguities, dispute over societal symbols intensifies. The control of symbols has become an important indicator of societal control; thus key symbols, such as language or immigration/multiculturalism policies, represent important struggles over the future of the society as a collectivity. Controversy over societal symbols often reflects *status anxiety* among groups who feel that they are losing power or who want to gain power in transforming the symbol system. Breton has argued that the constitutional process failed because too many different groups were using the occasion to engage in socio-political bargaining over the societal symbols important to them.[41] It could be said that Canadian society is currently in the throes of a radical symbolic transformation; where it will lead is still unclear. A national identity crisis may be partly the result of a lag between the melting-down of the old symbolic order and the emergence of a new one.[42]

6. Globalization

It almost seems trite to say that we live in a shrinking world. No one could have anticipated how the World Wide Web has changed how we do things, or how satellites and other communication/transportation improvements make it impossible for any political state to exist as an island. As we have seen, Canadian society has always been linked to other countries (first France, then England, and then the United States), but now the range of internationalization is much broader, and contacts are often mediated by international bodies and trade agreements. Whereas anti-Americanism was once part of a form of defensive nationalism that helped sustain Canadian identity, globalization now minimizes that "spine" of societal difference.[43] The free flow of products, culture, and ideas makes it more difficult to establish and sustain a distinct societal identity. In the past, Canadian identity was also sustained by state enterprises which we now have seen eroded or privatized, and distinctive public policies such as bilingualism and multiculturalism are under pressure.

Not all analysts see the impact of globalization in the same way. Rather than assuming that globalization necessarily means integration, Watson argues that governments still have

The New Transnational Migrant

In the past, immigrants were thought of as "uprooted" and "transplanted," struggling to adjust and resettle in the new society. The understanding was that the "old world" had been left behind and adjustment to the "new world" required a reconstruction of ethnic identity. Originally we thought that immigrants turned their backs on the old ethnicity and eventually became assimilated.

This view is increasingly becoming outdated, thanks to a globalized world of telecommunications and travel that allows immigrants to retain ties with their country of origin and with people who have left their homeland and settled elsewhere. Homelands serve as symbolic anchors to emgrants who travel back and forth, often dwelling for alternate periods in the community of origin and the new country. These people may engage in business across borders, morally and financially support activities and movements back home, and hold positions in networks and organizations that span political boundaries. Transnational migrants often have multiple identities, which may be anchored in the homeland but may also include immigrant communities of similar descent elsewhere. The Internet plays a particularly important role in supporting these links. Moreover,

transnational immigrants may not have any intention of staying at the new destination for the rest of their lives; therefore, their relationship to the host society is tentative at best. This tenuous commitment may be reflected in the holding of citizenship in both the country of origin and the destination, or in plans to return to the country of origin on retirement or after the accumulaton of sums of money.

Transnational immigrants may leave money back home or continue to own businesses there. They may own real estate in the country of origin or even in a third country where they may also have money. Transnational capital flows back and forth between countries. People may hold Canadian citizenship and vote here but may also vote in another country; in other words, they may play a role in the political activities of two or more countries. They may also be caught up in debates about political events "back home"; this often occurs among Jews, Arabs, Muslims, and Croatians resident in Canada.

Source: Based on Daphne N. Winland, "Our Home and Native Land? Canadian Ethnic Scholarship and the Challenge of Transnationalism," *Canadian Review of Sociology and Anthropology* 35 (1998): 555–577; Vic Satzewich and Lloyd Wong, eds., *Negotiating Borders and Belonging: Transnational Identities and Practices in Canada* (Vancouver: UBC Press, 2005).

some degree of freedom and that trade between states does not mean cultural harmonization.[44] In fact, because the impact is not as negative as presumed, he encourages Canadians to choose greater economic integration with a yet smaller role for government. Others would argue that government must be the backbone of societal survival, otherwise free-market forces will eventually obliterate cultural distinctions. Calhoun, for example, noting that the world is too large to be one state, asserts that independent states can become movements of democratic power that counteract other globalizing forces.[45] Whatever its outcome, globalization is changing people's thinking about the importance of the nation-state and the role it should play in a world with porous borders. While its full impact is yet to be felt, globalization does undermine a single rigid national identity and potentially encourages the formation of multiple and flexible identities.[46]

Each of these six factors makes an important contribution to the articulation of a societal identity. Society is dynamic rather than static; the evidence we have examined suggests that the old sponsored society is undergoing large-scale changes that are clearly producing a very different societal shape and tone. It is not that Canadian society once had an identity and lost it, nor that it never had an identity and is searching for it, but that the shape and structure of that identity is changing over time.

NEGOTIATING A SOCIETAL IDENTITY

The Concept of Nationalism

Intense feeling about primary allegiance to the national society and its well-being is known as *nationalism*. Much like other words that end in "ism" (such as *communism* or *capitalism*), nationalism implies a set of beliefs, convictions, and a world view pertaining to the defence and advocacy of the society contained within a political jurisdiction. It is possible to be a resident of a nation-state yet not be nationalistic. Nationalism emerges out of strong feelings about the collectivity as a whole (rather than as individuals) and the belief that the welfare of the group, as determined by established parameters, must be a first principle in any action within the society.

A Canadian nationalist is someone who assesses the virtue of any action by its impact on the residents of Canada as a collectivity. While one person may enjoy going to a concert, judge the music or musicians on their own merits, and leave it at that, a nationalist will ask whether the concert helps Canadians develop their own unique musical style. Similarly, the nationalist will ask whether schools are promoting knowledge and love of country, or whether corporations are using their organizations to strengthen the Canadian economy and provide opportunities for Canadians. A Quebec nationalist or Dene nationalist will ask the same kinds of questions with reference to their group. What is important to note is that some people always think in terms of this wider group, while other people never do. Perhaps the most typical stance is midway between these two extremes, as other concerns (e.g., personal gain, lifestyle preference, or personal priorities) frequently displace nationalistic concerns.

One of the biggest dilemmas with nationalism is that different definitions of what constitutes the national group may exist within the same country. To a segmentalist, nationhood may be circumscribed within a sub-territory or an ethnic group.[47] This view may challenge or at least compete with the pan-Canadian view, which sees Canada's entire population as constituting a national society. Furthermore, not everyone agrees that loyalty to the nation-state should be a priority; some may opt for an individualistic or local-group approach to life in society. Consequently, nationalist sentiment is highly variable over time; it may be widespread for a short period, or it may be adopted by interest groups who find it intriguing or advantageous.

For the majority of the population, identification with the nation-state is but one of a chain of identities (e.g., family, ethnicity, religion) they hold. The mere experience of exposure to the news, and even to the weather map, sensitizes persons to the national context in which they live; this leads to the assumption that a minimal level of national consciousness must exist in all residents. Particular events (e.g., the Canada–Russia hockey series, Olympic competitions, national elections, disasters or wars, travel abroad) may also heighten one's consciousness of being part of a national fabric. A strongly positive sentiment or attitude towards one's country is known as *patriotism*. As love for one's country or nation-state, patriotism is not as demanding or commanding as nationalism, which submerges other commitments in allegiance to the collective entity.

According to the strongest version of nationalism, individuals should subordinate all other interests and loyalties to the nation-state. This type of "full-blown nationalism" lends itself particularly well to socialist societies or to societies with a strong central government.[48] A more moderate nationalism believes in the right to societal self-determination; the state is expected to support a flexible program of actions and policies to maintain and preserve the independence and integrity of the society as a whole. Obviously, opinions will differ as to how flexible a national society can afford to be. Any looser conception of the nation-state (e.g., that the state is only a framework for cultural and economic activities) suggests a more federated society such as Switzerland, where only minimal societal cohesion prevails.

Patriotism or love of country is an age-old phenomenon. Most people have always identified with, and been loyal to, their place of birth or of residence. History demonstrates that people have always been conscious of the group to which they belonged, and com-

---

REAL PEOPLE	A Canadian with a Turban

"I was born in Canada, but I wear a turban. Do you have any idea how strong you have to be to do that?

My mother and grandmother brought me up with Sikh values, and lots of children that I played with had similar values. But in high school it hit me. On the one hand, there were all kinds of pressures to conform to the dominant youth culture. On the other hand, that same culture emphasized a strong sense of self that encouraged people to be different. Some of my buddies and I found the kind of countercultural support we needed in the Black American culture of rap music. We tried to be tough physically at the same time that we worked hard to be on the honour roll in order to assert our supremacy.

Wearing a turban sort of satisfied our desire to stand out and be different.

When I got to university, I didn't need that way of thinking anymore but I still felt trapped between the Khalsa appearance, as represented by unshaven hair, and the norms of the dominant culture. Many young Sikhs no longer wear turbans because it is not required. But I still wear a turban because for me it is a symbol of something sacred. Wearing a turban develops the characteristics of grace and humility which I think are personal virtues."

Note: For a good discussion of the problems of Sikh adaptation to Canada, especially in the third generation, see Kamala Elizabeth Nayar, *The Sikh Diaspora in Vancouver* (Toronto: University of Toronto Press, 2004)

mitment to the group has always been valued; however, the idea of loyalty not just to a geographic locale or a social group but to a political state is a more recent phenomenon. *Loyalty to the state* was first clearly articulated during the French Revolution in the latter half of the eighteenth century.[49] In post-revolutionary France, the state attempted to create a society out of all people living within the borders of the state, regardless of sub-group allegiances. A single language and culture was imposed on all regions of the country, breaking down barriers and aiding the creation of a single nation and sense of nationhood. An ideal was thus established of a national society; other forms of group identity were to be subsumed under a single united identity focused on the state.

The principle that the *state serves as the basis of society*, establishing its boundaries and blending its people into a nationality, came to be accepted as a foundation of world order. Nationality has become a part of personal identity, much like gender or skin colour, and has become much more significant than earlier types of socio-political organization. Until recently, its legitimacy had hardly been questioned, though instances of ethnic groups creating their own states by breaking away from existing states repeatedly emerge around the globe. So, in contrast to "states creating nations" (i.e., states attempting to blend all residents into a single nationality), there is also the possibility of "nations creating states" (i.e., people who share an ethnic commonality creating a new state).[50] The former Soviet Union and Yugoslavia are but two illustrations of the shifting boundaries between state and nation.

Alternative Explanations of Canadian Nationalism

At the time of Confederation in 1867, there was little sense of a Canadian nationality. Many residents of Canada had little conception of a society of the nation-state because of

---

How Important Is Citizenship?

In some counties, such as Germany and Japan, citizenship is very hard to obtain. Countries such as Australia, the United States, and Canada are much more open in terms of allowing people to apply for citizenship.

Despite globalization and a shrinking world, citizenship still is an important means of classifying people:

- It is a means of categorizing individuals in a global context and giving them an identity.
- It implies loyalty and commitment to a state which in turn defines and protects individual rights and responsibilities.

- Historically, treason or betrayal of one's citizenship has been considered a most heinous crime.
- Everyone must have a citizenship. To be stateless (as are refugees) is a pitiable and unacceptable condition.
- Citizenship is both a legal and an emotional matter.
- People are often asked to be prepared to die for their state.

Source: Based on Desmond Morton, "Divided Loyalties? Divided Countries?" 50-63; and William Kaplan, "Who Belongs? Changing Concepts of Citizenship and Nationality," in William Kaplan, ed., *Belonging: The Meaning and Future of Canadian Citizenship* (Montreal: McGill-Queen's University Press, 1993), 245-64.

intense local attachments, warm sentiments towards the mother country, identification with a foreign place of origin, or even ambivalence towards this new political creation known as Canada. Confederation was based on the idea that a strong central government would be needed to establish a national society, but considerable latitude was given for the expression of regional uniqueness (e.g., the church-based school system in Quebec). The "Canada First" movement of the 1870s was a short-lived campaign to forge a nationalism based on British culture.[51] In other words, a major issue for the new country was the development of some basis for unity. To the dominant group, which wanted to disseminate its ideas about what the new society should be like, nationalism became a useful tool for ethnic assimilation. This goal was viewed with particular suspicion by Quebec francophones, who had a different sense of nationality.

Conflict theories of nationalism point out that it is not so much the *content* of nationalism that is important as *who its advocates are*. From this perspective, nationalism reflects power relationships. Nationalism is seen as an ideology used in the interests of particular groups within a collectivity. Dominant groups use nationalism to promote their objectives, though minority groups can also use their own brand of nationalism to challenge the dominant group; thus, nationalism is related to domination.[52]

One type of domination has an external or foreign orientation. Powerful nations impose their will on weaker collectivities; nationalism can be a reaction to this external control. Concern about American domination is a major impetus to nationalist feeling and action in Canada, and it is for this reason that there is a strong relationship between nationalism and anti-Americanism.[53] But domination can also have an internal basis. Members of one ethnic or territorial group may resist pan-Canadian nationalism because it thwarts their own collective interests, and may counter that nationalism with their own nationalism (e.g., Quebec nationalism). In another example: Quebec francophones have been trying to build a political community that would transcend ethno-cultural differences, yet some minorities have rejected that objective because of *ressentiment* about being excluded from power and have used victimhood as a strategy for minority empowerment.[54] In sum, the conflict perspective points out that nationalism is an ideology used by groups in a struggle for power.

Another perspective within conflict theory suggests that nationalism is related to the class structure. The issue is not just one of domination by another group but of domination by a group representing specific class interests, which embraces nationalism because it is supportive of their class position. For example, as representatives of the capitalist class, the Canadian Manufacturing Association was historically ardently nationalist, implying that good citizens should buy "Canadian" manufactured goods whatever the price.[55] In short, nationalism was good for business. But it has also been argued that nationalism can be an ideology congenial to the middle class. Just as the new Quebec middle class became ardent Quebec nationalists, so the new middle class of young well-educated anglophones in the rest of Canada became Canadian nationalists in the 1960s and 1970s when their own interests and careers were in question.[56] Thus we see that support for a new societal identity and for commitment to a nationalist position can be explained by locating such ideals within the class structure in order to identify their sources and primary proponents.

While nationalism may be explained by focusing on which specific groups become its advocates, nationalism may also have a broad-based origin. *Integration theories* point out that nationalisms are part of larger social processes, such as urbanization and industrialization, that break down traditional group loyalties and draw people into larger collectivities.[57] In fact, it has been argued that nationalism is a response to the modern society, which requires more centralization and a single form of communication. Nationalism is the glue that binds people together in order to create a more homogeneous culture and increase competitiveness in the world economy.[58] Nationalism has also been linked to secularization (i.e., the decline of traditional religious attachments); the state may become the new object of loyalty and devotion in what is almost a form of surrogate religion. In other words, nationalism is viewed as a natural bonding process that produces shared meanings and symbols and evolves over time, facilitating greater unity within a political entity.

It is undoubtedly true that the industrialization of Canada and the concomitant social and cultural changes have contributed to a growing nationalist spirit. As population shifted to Central Canada (particularly Ontario) because of burgeoning industry, as new technologies brought East and West closer together, and as the increasingly urban population became better-educated, old attachments and ethnocentrisms slowly began breaking down.[59] Many people celebrate this trend because national unity and national pride represent important ideals to them; the nation-state (i.e., pan-Canadianism) has become an important part of their personal identity, and the fact that a successful artist, athlete, or corporation is "Canadian" is important to their sense of group identity.

Ironically, the same trends that have produced a pan-Canadian nationalism have also produced competing nationalisms within Canada—for example, Quebec nationalism. Insofar as a group's territorial boundaries are not coextensive with Canada's, pan-Canadian nationalism is undermined. Quebec nationalists, for example, give priority to their identity as Québécois, a group bounded within the territory of the province of Quebec. Canadian nationalists, for their part, can be intolerant of new immigrants or those with a more international frame of reference. Nationalists have their own vision of what a society should be like and fear losing control of that vision.[60] This brings us back to the conflict perspective because it raises questions about who determines the content of the nationalism being advocated.

Both conflict and integration theories are valuable for understanding the evolution of Canadian nationalism and the forms it has taken. Industrial change and communication technologies have brought residents of the society closer together in recent years, creating a new environment that has promoted the sense of a national society. At the same time, Quebec nationalists and some First Nations have rejected a pan-Canadian form of nationalism as a coercive ideology of assimilation.

REFORMULATING AND RECONSTRUCTING THE NATIONAL IDENTITY

As a result of the conquest of the French by the English in 1759, persons of British descent thought they had a clear picture of what a Canadian nation would look like: a political entity affiliated with and bearing the imprint of the mother country, Britain. This view of Canada, which prevailed for a long time, is known as *anglo-conformity*. Other views of Canada's history were submerged, but by 1960, a *two-nation view* entered the mainstream of Canadian thought. This was the idea that Canada had not one founding nation but two, and what was needed was a new accommodation between English and French in the structures of Canadian society. By the 1990s, however, the two-nation view was being discredited by First Nations, who argued persuasively on the basis of their prior presence for a *three-nations view* of the Canadian national community.[61] Add to this the new-source non-European immigration into Canada and concepts like multiculturalism, and suddenly it is no longer clear what the core and essentials of Canadian nationality are.

The anglo-conformity view of nationalism is described as *hegemonic* because its values and ideals are dominant in the society and are represented as natural and inevitable. Counter-hegemonic ideas undermine this hegemony and seek to negotiate change. Québécois and Aboriginals, and more recently feminists and multiculturalists, have sought to develop new strategies of inclusion.[62]

The anglo-conformity view of Canadian society had a strong centralist vision, meaning it saw a strong role for the federal government. It implied assimilation of all other groups to the anglo-majority. After all these years, that objective has clearly not been attained among First Nations and Quebec francophones, who have their own concepts of self-determination. Even the two-nations view is under siege, as the Quebec independence movement demands statehood on behalf of Québécois as a territorially defined ethnic people. In fact, francophone Quebecers, seeking to prevent the incremental expansion of anglo-conformity, are motivated more by the need to make a positive affirmation of their own nationalist identity than by a rejection of Canada. As long as Québécois nationalism exists in competition with anglo-conformity pan-Canadian nationalism, these two visions of society will remain fundamentally incompatible.[63] It has been argued that the popularity of sovereignty in Quebec is at least in part a response to the rest of Canada's refusal to

The Search for a New Canadian Identity

If Québécois and Indigenous people have a sense of nationhood, does that leave the rest of Canada a *no-nation*? If Quebec can be described as *French Canada*, does that make the rest of Canada *English Canada*?

As Quebec has numerous traits that set it apart, it is often difficult to know how to refer to the remaining parts of Canada. Perhaps the most-used phrase is *Rest of Canada (ROC)*. The problem with referring to the rest of Canada as "English Canada" is that the expression seems to connote British nationality or loyalty to British institutions.

Resnick argues that in spite of the existence of other ethnic and linguistic minorities, what the ROC has in common is an overwhelming commitment to the use of the English language. Just as French is the anchor for the Québécois identity, so English is the glue that binds ROC Canadians together—for example, through political and educational institutions and the media. Resnick argues that since Meech Lake and Charlottetown, the Quebec question has provoked new dialogue in the ROC about what it means to be Canadian and what kind of society we really want. In other words, English Canadians are debating with new vigour their collective identity in a manner similar to that of Québécois and First Nations. And this is a good sign, because—despite the existence of divergent opinions—it brings English-speaking Canadians together to hammer out who they are as a collectivity.

Of course, the big question is how and whether these English, French, and Aboriginal conceptions of nationhood can come together in one political state.

Further Reading: Philip Resnick, *Thinking English Canada* (Toronto: Stoddart, 1994) and "English Canada: The Nation That Dares Not Speak Its Name," in Kenneth McRoberts, ed., *Beyond Quebec: Taking Stock Of Canada* (Montreal: McGill-Queen's University Press, 1995), 81–92.

recognize Quebec as a distinct society, for the essence of Quebec nationalism is to continue the struggle to exist collectively by obtaining recognition of that fact politically.[64] The fact is that anglophone Canadians have difficulty coming to terms with any notion of a "distinct society," whether it comes from Quebec or from Indigenous peoples.[65] Among both Quebec francophones and First Nations, an important paradigm-shift has taken place from "internal colony" to "nation" (in the case of Quebec, with a political structure; in that of First Nations, without one), but that shift is being met with considerable resistance by many other Canadians.[66] In that regard, it has been argued that the new face of Canadian nationalism in English Canada is less accommodating (e.g., impatient with Quebec and multiculturalism) and more homogenizing (e.g., promulgating a "One Canada" theme).[67]

As long as Canada exists as a political entity, there will always be some pressures towards a pan-Canadian nationalism. People who define themselves in terms of their Canadian nationality will always seek to persuade other residents to submerge their other identities or at least to include Canada in their chain of identities. Thus it is not surprising that some people want immigrants to change their behaviour and assimilate to the majority, nor that people who have attached their identity to symbols and values that once were dominant but are now on the wane react in a *status preservationist backlash*.[68]

According to the *post-modernist perspective,* contemporary society no longer has a central core and structure with which all can identify; society has effectively become *decentred* into multiple identities and communities. Gwyn argues that Canada is the world's first post-modern state because it is not only becoming decentred but also participates in a global economy and has a globally representative population.[69] Post-modernism suggests that Canadians hold little in common because we celebrate our differences rather than our similarities.[70] The reassessment of societal history by groups who resist the old, hegemonic (anglo) interpretation and point out the faulty or biased interpretations of the past is a typical post-modern process known as *deconstruction*.[71] The absence of a master narrative of history that would provide a single societal vision is compounded by a constant rethinking of the basic premises of the society. Much of the current conflict in Canadian society is a struggle over the shape, form, and substance of the Canadian nationality and identity, and *post-modernism* points out the fragility, plasticity, and impermanence of political states in that context.

THE DYNAMICS OF NATION-BUILDING

Much of this book has highlighted the difficulties Canadians face in forming a national society. Amidst all the centrifugal forces, none is perhaps more fundamental to the weakness of a singular national identity than the fact of the two solitudes, the French and English segments of the population. Building bridges between these two groups was a primary objective of the federal government in the '60s and '70s, but the evidence to date is that such efforts have had limited success and perhaps have even failed.[72]

However, both language groups have gone through a highly significant metamorphosis. Whereas nationality was at one time determined by ethnic characteristics, both language groups now manifest a utilitarian trend towards greater inclusiveness, building a *civic nationality* based on territory.[73] For example, the civic nationality of Quebec is being built by extending the concept of belonging, formerly based on French ethnic descent, to encompass all those in Quebec who share the French language, regardless of descent. In English Canada, this transformation occurred much earlier as non-British immigrants became part of the English-speaking community. In fact, it has become acceptable to use the word "anglophone" to speak of the unity of persons who, in spite of their ethnic differences, have found common ground in the English language. Thus, we can see that some nation-building is occurring in both language groups.

Differing Perspectives

Structural Functionalism

Societies are indeed diverse and complex entities. But in spite of the plurality of groups, perspectives, and individual differences, the national society provides the institutions and structures which all members of the society share, giving members a sense of collective belonging. Differences are not problems; they are assets, provided that all members of the society are conscious of the ties that bind them together in spite of these differences. Thus, two official languages should not be perceived as a problem but as an opportunity for unilingualists to become at least partially bilingual in order to build bridges between groups. In this way, societal harmony can be maintained. Building a strong sense of Canadian nationalism is the way to develop solidarity, loyalty, and commitment to the national fabric. In sum, the structures of society will ensure that unity is the ultimate goal.

Conflict

National unity is a very fragile thing in Canada because of intense social divisions, particularly related to language, region, and ethnicity. The society is fragmented into social units that are competitive more often than cross-cutting. Hostilities seem never to be far beneath the surface, and wax and wane as people are mobilized. What all of this reflects is repeated conflict over what Canadian society should be like. Those who have the power to define the contours of the society will attempt to repress dissent, and, using whatever methods possible, to spread their ideals as being in the best interests of the collectivity. What we are experiencing is conflict between the old anglo-conformity concept of Canadian society and new visions of Canadian society with a different place for Québécois and Indigenous groups. Individuals or groups with traditional power or who benefit from the status quo are particularly resistant to change.

Symbolic Interactionism

Societies are like individuals in that they seek to form their own identities and to differentiate themselves from other entities. A societal identity is also always in process and in a state of change. It depends on the creation of unique symbols, such as language, literary themes, heroes, documents, songs, and flags, with which members of the society can identify. It is created out of important events or characteristic activities that help societal members understand more clearly who they are. Through interaction, members of a society develop shared interpretations of the world around them and of their common collective life. The reformulation of the society's old symbols into new ones, as painful as that might be, is an evolutionary process that reflects the fact that Canadian society is redefining its collective identity.

It is frequently argued that the French–English duality is at the heart of the Canadian identity. How such dualism can produce a sense of unity within Canadian society continues to be a perplexing question. But while acknowledging its divisive nature, we cannot ignore the fact that there indeed are factors propelling all persons sharing the Canadian political entity and geographic territory towards a pan-Canadian civic nationality. This is not to suggest that countervailing forces are not as strong or stronger, but to point out that certain factors do contribute to a broader sense of nation-building. It is important that these be recognized and evaluated for their contribution to a sense of society and national identity. Five factors that promote nation-building will be discussed.

1. The Socialization Process

Nationality is at least partially related to place of birth. Barring other intervening factors, place of birth is usually the basis for determining citizenship. This correlation, however, does not imply that nationality is inborn. A national identity is acquired through social learning. The process of learning (through interaction) the expectations, attitudes, and behaviour demanded by a society is known as *socialization.*

It is through the basic institutions of a society (i.e., family, school, church, government, media) that one learns about, and develops attitudes towards, the society to which one belongs. Singing the national anthem at athletic events, reading about current events in the newspaper, celebrating Canada Day, paying income tax, or obtaining a passport are all activities that remind Canadians of their civic nationality. Many of these things are taken-for-granted aspects of daily life, but they implicitly reinforce membership in Canadian society. The Canadian problem is that the society not only must teach its younger members about their relationship to the societal unit, but it must also *resocialize* many of its immigrant members into identification with the national society.

Perhaps the most important socializing agent is the school system because of its key role in informing the young about the societal tradition.[74] It is here that students gain a sense of societal history and geography and an awareness of significant societal events. School assemblies cultivate patriotic fervour through the teaching of songs that reflect the societal heritage. The classroom provides a setting in which students become familiar with other aspects of their society's culture. In other words, the school system is expected to teach not only spelling and mathematics but all of the basics of good citizenship.

Two observations can be made about schools' role in inculcating nationalist sentiment. In English Canada, one of the historic problems schools faced was the lack of Canadian classroom materials. The use of British or American materials meant that it was more difficult to create an understanding of Canadian history and culture. Since the 1960s, however, enormous developments have occurred in the publication of Canadian materials, making it possible to provide students with a greater degree of societal awareness. Second, because education is a provincial rather than a federal matter, textbooks begin with an orientation to the national society through provincial eyes. Nowhere are the implications of this fact more noticeable than in Quebec, where language differences combine with Quebec nationalist views to produce a markedly different perception of Canadian society.

Lamy speaks of the differences in the educational experiences of English and French adolescents as "*socialization into discord.*"[75] French students acquired more positive feelings towards the provincial society, whereas anglophone students were more favourably oriented towards the national. One of the problems cited by the Royal Commission on

Bilingualism and Biculturalism was that the textbooks of each language presented different views of Canadian history.[76] French-language textbooks stressed the survival of French-Canadian society, placing special emphasis on the period prior to the English Conquest. Subsequent events, including Confederation itself, were presented from the point of view of a minority facing English domination. English-language textbooks, on the other hand, stressed the Conquest as a beginning rather than an ending, and glorified the historical significance of Confederation as the birth of a new strong single entity—Canadian society. The result of this different socialization was that when school children were asked to identify national heroes, francophones and anglophones each identified with prominent figures of their own language group, sharing few "reconciliation symbols."[77] Schools might thus be viewed as perpetuating a rift in Canadian society rather than promoting national unity. Since public-school texts are frequently written for and approved by provincial educational authorities, schoolchildren in Newfoundland or British Columbia also first learn about their national society through provincial eyes.

Schools clearly have a pivotal role in creating a knowledge base about the national society and in cultivating positive attitudes towards it. As school becomes an influence very early in a child's life, it can be assumed that perceptions of Canadian society established there will be formative.

RESEARCH CLIP 7.1	**Are Immigrants a Threat to the Institutional Fabric of Canadian Society?**

Given the fact that about 16% of the Canadian population is foreign-born, it is important to find out whether there is evidence that such a large population group is problematic for the society. Are the political values and attitudes of immigrants different from those of native-born Canadians?

A study of adults and children, conducted in three Canadian cities, measured attitudes to authority (e.g., government, Prime Minister, Supreme Court), images of Canada (e.g., fair–unfair, friendly–unfriendly, rich–poor), and attitudes towards issues (e.g., keeping Canada together, Native peoples, limiting immigration, gun control).

While there were some attitude differences between immigrants who had just arrived and those who have been in Canada for many years, few differences were found between native-born and foreign-born; immigrants seemed to quickly adopt the political perspectives of the native-born. The fear that immigrants may change Canadian political values or social institutions must therefore be discarded.

However, when parents and their children were compared, substantial intergenerational differences were found for both native-born and foreign-born (with the exception perhaps of recently arrived immigrants).

For Discussion:

Why are generational differences a more important factor in political views than country of birth?

Source: J.S. Frideres, "Edging into the Mainstream: A Comparison of Values and Attitudes of Recent Immigrants, Their Children, and Canadian-Born Adults," in W.W. Isajiw, ed., *Multiculturalism in North America and Europe* (Toronto: Canadian Scholars Press, 1997), 537-61.

2. The Political Process

A second factor in nation-building emanates from the political process, particularly from politicians and political parties. Many people join political parties, take positions on national issues, and recruit people to their point of view. Others are less directly involved in the political world but are made conscious of important political figures through the media. The media are continually soliciting politicians' reactions on virtually every issue that arises, whether that politician is part of the government or in opposition. Through their statements and the controversy they generate, citizens are drawn into the issues and made aware of their national implications. Thus, the political process in its myriad forms—from electoral battles for party leadership to the articulation of positions on issues of national consequence—reinforces the national context of the society, disagreements and different levels of participation notwithstanding. In sum, political activities serve as constant reminders of the contours of Canadian society.

The political process also produces political decisions, legislation, and policies representing visions of what Canadian society should be like or compromises between competing groups. Policies such as bilingualism and multiculturalism, or even minority-language or women's programs, represent attempts by the state to promote inclusiveness rather than fragmentation and create a unitary sense of society.[78] The fact that these policies may not always be widely supported should not blind us to the fact that they do have an effect. Most anglophones may not be bilingual, but their exposure to French words and phrases builds a tolerance and affinity for that language quite different from the American predilection to

---

Citizenship and the Naturalization Gap

There is evidence that adult immigrants are more likely to naturalize and to do so much faster in Canada than in the United States, in a phenomenon known as the *North American naturalization gap*. Bloemraad discovered that Canadian government support (through the federal departments of Citizenship and Multiculturalism) to ethnic associations helped establish linkages and institutional supports promoting the benefits of citizenship; such support was absent in the United States. It was not that immigrants to the United States never became citizens, but that they took longer to do so.

Another explanation for the gap might be related to the fact that since 1977, Canada, in a gesture symbolizing tolerance and multiculturalism, has explicitly allowed dual citizenship. The number of people reporting dual citizenship has been rising, although that number is small and decreases with length of residence in the country. While in some ways dual citizenship might seem to undermine nation-building, there is evidence that it may be a useful way to help promote integration and national attachment during an immigrant's early years in a country.

Source: Irene Bloemraad, "The North American Naturalization Gap: An Institutional Approach to Citizenship Acquisition in the United States and Canada," *International Migration Review* 36, 1 (2002): 193-228; and Irene Bloemraad, "Who Claims Dual Citizenship? The Limits of Postnationalism, the Possibilities of Transnationalism, and the Persistence of Traditional Citizenship," *International Migration Review* 38, 2 (2004): 389-427.

learn Spanish as a second language. Thus, decisions issuing from the political agenda, as controversial as they may be, become part of the nation-building process, prescribing a uniquely Canadian means of resolving Canadian societal problems.

Other government decisions may deliberately seek to promote and build national loyalties. For example, government-funded student-exchange programs may seek to build bridges among young citizens across the country. In 1996, the government declared February 15 "National Flag Day," with the slogan "Canada—Take It to Heart."[79] Government funds are also set aside for celebrations of "Canada's birthday" on July 1, and an entertainment extravaganza is usually televised from the nation's capital. In short, politicians take action intended to directly engender and support nation-building—though many analysts would say that, in the light of other realities, much of this is superficial control of the masses.

It is ironic that at the same time as the government pours money into nation-building, on the other hand—in the name of free-market principles and a less-costly public service— it has withdrawn from regulating and controlling many elements of society, making the creation of national unity more difficult.[80] Traditional means of nation-building—from the protection of culture to the support of key sector institutions (e.g., the Canadian Broadcasting Corporation)—are under threat, with no clear replacement for these traditional means of nation-building. In that sense, politicians are themselves responsible for the changed role of political processes in nation-building.

3. Economic Protectiveness

A third factor in nation-building pertains to the justification of economic decisions in terms of national well-being. We have already seen that nationalism can be manipulated by those with vested interests. S.D. Clark has pointed out that in Canada's early years, her "most ardent patriots" were her dignitaries—business leaders, bishops, ministers of the Crown, and military officers—whose well-being and superior positions were connected to the independent existence of Canada and to a strong Canadian society.[81] Earlier it was shown that business entrepreneurs may become strong economic nationalists because their livelihood depends on survival in the Canadian market. In general, economic nationalism tends to appear when business or labour groups are struggling for survival and feel they need protection.

In the wave of nationalism of the '60s and '70s, it was the expanded middle class or new petty bourgeoisie of salaried professionals (many of whom were working for the state) and budding professionals (still in university and concerned about employment opportunities) who were the most nationalistic.[82] This social class vehemently supported policies that protected and enhanced the national economy in areas related to technologies, research, management decisions, and corporate policies—i.e., in matters that specifically affected white-collar jobs.

Clearly, specific groups sometimes feel that when their own interests are threatened, the viability and well-being of the entire national society is at stake. Whether this is untrue, partially true, or completely correct may be open to debate, but insofar as such groups succeed in convincing the public and politicians, their arguments became part of the nation-building process when the action they urge is considered necessary to protect the national society.

Ironically, the tendency to protect the Canadian economy through nationalist thinking and action may now be at its lowest ebb in Canadian history. The economic elite, which for years spearheaded economic protectionism, has wholeheartedly embraced free trade and all of its implications. Primary producers, such as farmers, miners, and fishers, have always been oriented to international markets (although they sometimes ask the state to play a protective role). Labour unions fought free trade and invoked nationalist sentiment in the protection of Canadian jobs, but their influence has been muted by the globalization of capitalism. Thus, while economic protectiveness has been an important historic basis of nationalist sentiment in Canada, it is unclear how the new economic environment will change that factor in nation-building.

4. Institutional Linkages

Institutional linkages are the fourth factor facilitating national integration. Nationwide institutions (e.g., banks, railroads, churches, and various forms of communications) bind the society together by making people more conscious of the society's boundaries and of the aspects of the society that are held in common.[83] Not only do institutions such as the Royal Bank of Canada, CP Rail, the United Church of Canada, and the Southam newspaper chain have a high profile within the society as distinctly Canadian institutions, they also have a large number of employees, members, and clients—which means heightened consciousness of the ties binding Canadians together within a social and economic framework. The typical local–regional–national pattern of organizational structure—be it within corporations (sales meetings, seminars, transfers, etc.), professional organizations, leisure clubs, or amateur sports—makes members of the society increasingly aware of the national context in which their activities take place.

Perhaps no institution plays a more powerful role in forging national unity than the media. [84] While at the time of Confederation it was argued that the railroads would provide "the ties that bind," in the modern era it is broadcasting (and particularly the Canadian Broadcasting Corporation) that has this unique role. In spite of enormous American influences, radio and television continue to have a distinctive Canadian character, as evidenced by programming ranging from *Degrassi: The Next Generation* and *The Red Green Show* to *The Nature of Things* and Vision TV. The print media should also not be ignored; organizations like the Canadian Press gather stories from all parts of the society and disseminate them daily through newspapers. Nevertheless, radio and television are even more pervasive in their influence because they communicate not only news but entertainment—the society's culture in the form of music, drama, and documentaries. Also not to be overlooked are national advertising campaigns, which frequently refer to products in a national context. Note, as well, how television weather maps acquaint the audience with the geography and weather differentials of different parts of the country. Although, in all of these examples, the nationalist impetus is usually more implicit than explicit, they help frame a societal or national consciousness among members of the society.

5. Cultural Products

A fifth factor contributing to nation-building is the promotion of indigenous culture. This may be forms of *popular culture,* represented by Canadian television shows such as *Corner Gas, Royal Canadian Air Farce*, and *This Hour Has 22 Minutes* (note that all these shows are on CBC), or by Canadian entertainers such as Rick Mercer, Bryan Adams, Celine Dion, the Barenaked Ladies, or the Tragically Hip. An interesting but distinctive aspect of Canadian culture is what Acland has called the *"cult of the Canadian born"*—that is, the celebration of Canadians who have made it big elsewhere.[85] People such as

How Important Is Hockey in Promoting Societal Unity?

It is often argued that what all Canadians have in common is interest in the game of hockey. If there has been little to bring Canadians together and much to divide them, then perhaps hockey has provided the social glue that has united Canadians and helped to define the national identity. For example, the 1972 Canada–Russia hockey series (which Canada won) is often cited as a defining moment in national unity. As well, professional hockey has offered a vision of how young boys of humble background may become national heroes.

Hockey enthusiasts (especially Canadian NHL hockey owners) have emphasized hockey's role in the national psyche when seeking special financial considerations from the federal government. The Canadian government apparently accepted this logic when, in order to draw attention to the need for Canadian unity in the Quebec region, it bought advertising space on the side boards of the Montreal and Ottawa arenas.

But does hockey really play a role in uniting the society, or or is this notion mainly illusion or romanticism?

Two studies of the role of hockey in the formation of national identity point out that hockey became a national icon primarily as the result of media influences. Newspapers, magazines, radio, and most of all television created a national audience and a sense of pseudo-intimacy with the game's heroes. "Hockey Night in Canada," par-ticularly as a television show, created the imagery of a nation fixated on hockey every Saturday night.

Yet evidence suggests that hockey's vision of Canadian society was primarily white and male. How can a sport with such a select audience purport to play a pivotal role in societal unity? This question has become particularly relevant in recent years with the influx of non-European immigrants for whom hockey has not been part of a cultural tradition. Male dominance in hockey also does not square well with the increased prominence of women in public affairs. Furthermore, many of hockey's best players are now European rather than Canadian. Lastly, with the loss of Canadian NHL teams and the significant increase in American-based ones, hockey has become increasingly Americanized.

In spite of these facts, hockey does seem to play some role in making people feel Canadian and is at least one element in Canadians' self-understanding as a northern people. There may also be some kind of nostalgia at work. It is true that many Canadians have little or no interest in hockey; whether the sport will continue in the future to play a mythic role as an important part of societal unity is clearly uncertain.

Source: Based on Richard Gruneau and David Whitson, *Hockey Night in Canada: Sport, Identities and Cultural Politics* (Toronto: Garamond, 1993); and Neile Earle, "Hockey as Canadian Popular Culture: Team Canada 1972, Television and the Canadian Identity," *Journal of Canadian Studies* 30 (1995): 107-23.

Michael J. Fox, Avril Lavigne, or Shania Twain attained folk-hero status in Canada after having achieved acceptance and popularity elsewhere. Hockey has been described as a definitively Canadian vehicle of national unity;[86] the Grey Cup football event has also been an important national integrator. Popular culture can both directly and indirectly support nation-building.

The federal government has for many years supported cultural activity as a way to promote a Canadian identity. In addition to the Canadian Broadcasting Corporation there is the federally financed Canada Council, which supports artists and art organizations; the National Gallery, which promotes the work of Canadian artists; and the National Film Board, which produces documentaries on Canadian life.[87] The rationale has always been to harness the arts to the process of nation-building.

Indigenous culture is also promoted by the *intelligentsia*—the intellectuals (e.g., authors, journalists, professors, artists) who help to articulate the national identity.[88] Historians have a special role in formulating national feeling. In researching, writing, and interpreting a society's history, historians expound the pivotal events in Canadian history, contributing to greater awareness of the society's heritage. Writers portray the land and its people in novels and verse, developing romantic or thought-provoking images that enhance a sense of nationhood. Such literary figures are frequently celebrated and their work cited in the media; schools familiarize students with their writings. Sometimes these writers contribute to nationalist sentiment indirectly; sometimes they directly express nationalist fervour. In Canada, such persons include anglophones such as Northrop Frye, Stephen Leacock, Robertson Davies, Margaret Atwood, and Pierre Berton; and francophones such as Michel Brunet, Roch Carrier, Marie-Claire Blais, Fernand Dumont, Anne Hébert, Jacques Ferron, and Roger Lemelin, among others. Other examples of popular-culture products that reflect collective assumptions and values back to the society include The Royal Canadian Air Farce and even national news anchors such as Lloyd Robertson and Peter Mansbridge. Intellectuals and media commentators can also serve as critics of the society, and their work may stimulate widespread debate.

Two further observations should be made about the role of the intelligentsia. First, since literary culture is conveyed in a specific linguistic form, it is clear that each of the two language groups will have its own literature, which may (unless people are fully bilingual) reinforce the two solitudes. Second, since literary culture is such a critical vehicle of nationalist sentiment, many intellectuals vociferously propound cultural nationalism. *Cultural nationalism* is the advocacy and defence of all forms of Canadian culture. Cultural nationalists feel that indigenous forms of culture should be given priority, financial support, and special recognition, perhaps even to the extent of excluding or regulating foreign cultural products. Clearly, this perspective is controversial, but at its root is the belief that the intelligentsia and the artistic community provide an invaluable service in the articulation of the national identity.[89]

CONCLUSION

It would be an overstatement to say that the forces contributing to national unity and integration have subdued those promoting disintegration. The previous chapters have discussed many dilemmas, conflicts, contradictions, and forces of disunity which have siginificant implications for a national societal identity and for which no resolution appears readily attainable. For example, it is debatable whether a unitary societal identity can ever crystallize without a common culture, a common language, or a common sense of history. At the same time, however, modern societies are not static, homogeneous entities in which a sense of commonality necessarily supersedes individual preferences and/or local territorial identities.

One of the problems in talking about a national society is that we bring our notions of small-scale communities to discussions of national belonging. The sociologist Ferdinand Tonnies distinguished a *community* from a *society* by noting that social relationships are much more intense in a community, and much more distant, remote, and bureaucratic in a society.[90] When nations were smaller and comprised homogeneous ethnic groups or sub-groups, it might have been possible to talk about the typical face-to-face interactions that create a sense of community. Now, however, political states are frequently formed by welding together a multiplicity of ethnic groups into a national polity. The result has been the creation of societies in which feelings of unity are superficial and social bonding is weak. Because the members of even the smallest modern nation will never know most of their fellow citizens, contemporary national societies are best described as *"imagined communities."*[91] This term suggests a sense of society that begins in the mind, where the image of a level of common identity produces an ephemeral unity that may never correspond to the hard facts of social reality. It is left to institutions such as governments, corporations, and other large organizations to give this identity more tangible expression.

But it also must be said that the relationship between individual identity and collectivities is always one of negotiation and change rather than of permanence and fixity. The concept of *translational identity* acknowledges that we are always trying to relate, translate, adjust, and readjust our own interpretations of reality to those around us.[92] Our "ethnic" identity, our "linguistic" identity, our "regional" identity, and the "personal" identity that emerges from our own world view are in constant interaction with the identities of others. Thus identity is dynamic and in process, and individualistic as well as possessing its collective aspects. It has to do not just with what we inherit or what we are at any particular point but with how we change and adapt and negotiate with others around us. Similarly at the national level, identity is continuously reconstructed in relation to external and internal events and our perceptions of them and their meaning.[93]

With our unique framework for a national society, we should not expect Canada to ever be a single unified entity. In contrast to *ethnocentric nationalism*, which invests exclusive power in one national ideal and views differences and divisions in the society as defects, Canada has evinced a *polycentric nationalism*, characterized by a tolerance of contending ideals and identities, openness to others, and a freely self-critical spirit.[94] This has led some observers to see Canadian society as "a community of communities," where national homogeneity is rejected and decentralized community is encouraged.[95]

Ramsay Cook, a student of Canadian nationalism for many years, has argued that Canadian society is strongest when nationalism is muted.[96] And yet Raymond Breton maintains that with the recognition of Quebec as a distinct society and the continentalist pressures of free trade, too little effort has been given to specifying the nature and meaning of "Canadian" national society.[97] Is the state's role only to provide services to people organized into smaller sub-units?[98] Or is the state to embody and direct a collective identity, representing society members' united sentiments and commitment? Responses to this question will clearly vary because different levels of belonging structure the society.

It could be argued that insisting on a single national identity is old-fashioned and out of step with the times. Learning to live with more than one identity and accepting that condition in the identities of others may be a more important adaptive principle in the new millennium than ever before. The Canadian dilemma has been clearly stated by Charles Taylor, who notes that while Canada's Charter of Rights (1982) emphasized *individual rights* and equality, there are also pressures to accept *group rights,* such as those espoused by Québécois and Native peoples.[99] Fundamentally, the two objectives are irreconcilable, and this is at the root of the current impasse in Canadian society; anglophones prefer the emphasis on individual rights and francophones prefer the emphasis on collective rights. The challenge is to allow differences to be preserved at the same time that a larger social connectedness is sustained. This can only be accomplished if we recognize that people can hold multiple identities. Even people with a strong group identity (such as Québécois or Native people) can discover ways in which they are also Canadian. For example, the Québécois have created their own national identity partly by differentiating themselves from English Canadians.[100] This process has involved the use by both groups of stereotypes invented to establish group boundaries; however, this process is still a Canadian phenomenon in a Canadian context, in which mutual perceptions and definitions are constantly changing.

There are currently two major challenges to Canadian identity. One is Quebec nationalism; the question is what degree of distance will allow Quebec its sense of independence while bordered by the rest of Canada. Organizations with acronyms such as ROC (Rest of Canada) or CWOQ (Canada Without Quebec) struggle to redefine Canada, with or without Quebec, while acknowledging that sheer proximity and economic realities dictate that the relationship with Quebec will always be in negotiation.[101]

The second critical challenge to the Canadian identity arises from globalization; it has to do with the emergence of the *post-national state.*[102] From this perspective, national identities are becoming increasingly irrelevant as commonalities of history, language, and culture are replaced by common economic interests that supersede traditional political boundaries. The processes of capital accumulation dictate *flexible citizenship*—fluidity, opportunism, and

---

Identity Discourses

"You can't be a Quebecker unless you are only a Quebecker. If you feel Canadian, you don't really love Quebec"

　　—single national-identity discourse of Québécois *indépendantiste*

"You can't be a Canadian unless you are a Canadian first. You can be something else secondarily but must give your prior allegiance to Canada."

　　—dominant national-identity discourse of Canadian nationalist

"You can be Québécois and Canadian at the same time. Both identities as well as other identities can be held simultaneously."

　　—multiple-identities discourse of a post-modern Canadian

Question to consider
What might the discourses look like among other groups in Canada?

post-modern flexibility rather than sharp boundaries.[103] For example, one study found that there is indeed a high level of mutual trust between Canadians and Americans and that a significant number of North Americans are not resisting closer economic and political ties.[104] Yet as we have seen, the state is still an important global mechanism of identity.

Perhaps the most basic challenge, however, is the continuing tension between unitary and segmentalized conceptions of Canadian society. The dynamics of these opposing pressures make Canadian society volatile and unstable on the one hand, yet intriguing and vigorous on the other. It is because Canadians cannot take their society for granted that experimentation and the quest for new solutions and innovations continue, making this society an exciting place in which to live.

FURTHER EXPLORATION

1. Do you think the federal government should play a more active interventionist role in building and preserving a distinct Canadian identity? What could be done? What groups would disagree with your position and why?

2. Which view of Canadian society would you prefer—unitary or segmentalist? What are the advantages and disadvantages of each?

3. In the Canadian quest for greater independence, how important is it to remove all ties with the British monarchy?

4. List the factors that make Canadian society different from and similar to American society.

5. In what way is nationalism a good thing? In what way is it suspect? Can Quebec nationalism coexist with Canadian nationalism?

SELECTED READINGS

Earle, Robert L., and John D. Wirth, eds., *Identities in North America: The Search for Community.* Stanford: Stanford University Press, 1995.

Kaplan, William, ed. *Belonging: The Meaning and Future of Canadian Citizenship.* Montreal: McGill-Queen's University Press, 1993.

Keohane, Kieran. *Symptoms of Canada: An Essay on the Canadian Identity.* Toronto: University of Toronto Press, 1997.

McRoberts, Kenneth. *Misconceiving Canada: The Struggle for National Unity.* Toronto: Oxford University Press, 1997.

Roach, Kent. *September 11: Consequences for Canada.* Montreal: McGill-Queen's University Press, 2003.

Taras, David, Beverly Rasporich, and Eli Mandel, eds. *A Passion for Identity.* 4th ed. Scarborough: Nelson, 2001.

ENDNOTES

1 Keith Spicer, "Canada: Values in Search of a Vision," in Robert L. Earle and John D. Wirth, eds., *Identities in North America: The Search for Community* (Stanford: Stanford University Press, 1995), 13–28.

2 Randy William Widdis, "Borders, Borderlands and Canadian Identity: A Canadian Perspective," *International Journal of Canadian Studies* 15 (1997): 49–66.

3 Stanley Morse, "National Identity from a Social Psychological Perspective: A Study of University Students in Saskatchewan," *Canadian Review of Studies in Nationalism* 7 (1980): 299–312.

4 *A Future Together: Observations and Recommendations of the Task Force on Canadian Unity* (Ottawa: Minister of Supply and Services Canada, 1979).

5 In addition to the *Task Force on Canadian Unity*, see also Herschel Hardin, *A Nation Unaware* (Vancouver: J.J. Douglas, 1974), 12.

6 This distinction was initially made by Albert Breton and Raymond Breton in *Why Disunity? An Analysis of Linguistic and Regional Cleavages in Canada* (Montreal: Institute for Research on Public Policy, 1980), 58–59, and is developed further here.

7 John Conway, "An Adapted Organic Tradition," *Daedalus* 117 (1988): 388.

8 This is essentially the point of W.L. Morton, *The Canadian Identity* (Madison: University of Wisconsin Press, 1965), 111.

9 See Keith Banting and Richard Simeon, *And No One Cheered: Federalism, Democracy, and the Constitution Act* (Toronto: Methuen, 1983), chap. 1; and David Milne, *The New Canadian Constitution* (Toronto: James Lormier, 1982).

10 Keith Banting and Richard Simeon, eds., *Redesigning the State: The Politics of Constitutional Change in Industrial Nations* (Toronto: University of Toronto Press, 1985).

11 R. Kenneth Carty and W. Peter Ward, *Entering the Eighties: Canada in Crisis* (Toronto: Oxford University Press, 1980).

12 Leon Dion argues the point that a societal identity is a combination of fragments of tradition and contemporary changes. "The Mystery of Quebec," *Daedalus* 117 (1988): 307.

13 David Orchard, *The Fight for Canada: Four Centuries of Resistance to American Expansionism* (Toronto: Stoddart, 1991).

14 John Sloan Dickey, *Canada and the American Presence* (New York: New York University Press, 1975), 7.

15 International Travel, *Travel Between Canada and Other Countries*, Statistics Canada 2002, Catalogue 66–201.

16 Jeffrey Frank and Michel Durand, "Canadian Content in the Cultural Marketplace," *Canadian Social Trends*, Summer 1993, Statistics Canada Catalogue 11-008, 18–21; and Tom Gorman and Susan Crompton, "Canadian Television in Transition," *Canadian Social Trends*, Spring 1997, Statistics Canada Catalogue 11-008-XPE, 19–23. See also George Barnett and Thomas McPhail, "An Examination of the Relationship of United States Television and Canadian Identity," *International Journal of Intercultural Relations* 4 (1980): 219–32.

17 John Meisel, "Escaping Extinctions: Cultural Defense of an Undefended Border," in D.H. Flaherty and W.R. McKercher, eds., *Southern Exposure: Canadian Perspectives on the U.S.* (Toronto: McGraw-Hill Ryerson, 1986), 152–68. For a good discussion of broadcasting policy and nation-building, see Jean McNulty, "Technology and Nation-building in Canadian Broadcasting," in Rowland Lormir and Donald Wilson, eds., *Communication Canada: Issues in Broadcasting and New Technologies* (Toronto: Kagan and Woo, 1988), 176–98.

18 Richard Gwyn, *The 49th Paradox: Canada in North America* (Toronto: McClelland and Stewart, 1985), 11.

19 S.D. Clark notes that anti-Americanism is frequently the means whereby this societal differentiation occurs. "Canada and Her Great Neighbour," *Canadian Review of Sociology and Anthropology* 1 (1964): 193–201. See also Dallas Cullen, J.D. Jobson, and Rodney Schneck, "Anti-Americanism and Its Correlates," *Canadian Journal of Sociology* 3 (1978): 103–20.

20   Charles F. Doran and James P. Sewell, "Anti-Americanism in Canada," in Thomas P. Thornton, ed., *Anti-Americanism: Origins and Context, The Annals of the American Academy of Political and Social Science* 497 (1988): 119.

21   See David Bell and Lorne Tepperman, *The Roots of Disunity* (Toronto: McClelland and Stewart, 1979), 211–13.

22   Herschel Hardin refers to this phenomenon as American-ideology-in-Canada, in which Canadian objectives are coloured by American standards and patterns. *A Nation Unaware* (Vancouver: J.J. Douglas, 1974), 55.

23   Gordon Laxer, "Constitutional Crises and Continentalism: Twin Threats to Canada's Continued Existence," *Canadian Journal of Sociology* 17 (1992): 199–222.

24   Richard Collins, *Culture, Communications, and National Identity* (Toronto: University of Toronto Press, 1990), 329.

25   James Winter and Irvin Goldman, "Mass Media and Canadian Identity," in Benjamin D. Singer, ed., *Communications in Canadian Society* (Toronto: Nelson, 1995), chap. 9.

26   John N. McDougall, "North American Integration and Canadian Disunity," *Canadian Public Policy* 17 (1991): 397.

27   Pierre Berton, *Why We Act Like Canadians* (Toronto: McClelland and Stewart, 1982), 12.

28   Peter Brimelow claims that the notion of bilingualism binding the two language-groups together is a myth. *The Patriot Game* (Toronto: Key Porter, 1986), chap. 6.

29   Charles Castonguay, "The Fading Canadian Duality," in John Edwards, ed., *Language in Canada* (Cambridge, Cambridge University Press, 1998), 36–60.

30   Leon Dion, "The Mystery of Quebec," 286.

31   Robert F. Harney, "So Great a Heritage as Ours: Immigration and the Survival of the Canadian Polity," *Daedalus* 117 (1988): 51–97; and Neil Nevitte, "Nationalism, States and Nations," in Elliot J. Feldman and Neil Nevitte, eds., *The Future of North America: Canada, the United States, and Quebec Nationalism* (Cambridge: Center For International Affairs, 1979), 354.

32   Kenneth McRoberts, "After the Referendum: Canada With or Without Quebec," in his *Beyond Quebec: Taking Stock of Canada* (Montreal: McGill-Queen's University Press, 1995), 403–32; and Roger Gibbins, "Canada Without Quebec: Thinking Through the Unthinkable," in David Taras and Beverly Rasporich, eds., *A Passion for Identity*, 3rd ed. (Toronto: Nelson, 1997), 105–118.

33   James Overton discusses the neo-nationalism of regions opposing the centralization of power in "Towards a Critical Analysis of Neo-Nationalism in Newfoundland," in Robert J. Brym and R. James Sacouman, eds., *Underdevelopment and Social Movements in Atlantic Canada* (Toronto: New Hogtown Press, 1979), 219–49.

34   These ideas are an adaptation of a theme developed by Jeffrey Reitz, "Immigrants, Their Descendants, and the Cohesion of Canada," in Raymond Breton, Jeffrey G. Reitz, and Victor Valentine, eds., *Cultural Boundaries and the Cohesion of Canada* (Montreal: Institute for Research on Public Policy, 1980), 400–406.

35   Will Kymlicka, *Finding Our Way: Rethinking Ethnocultural Relations in Canada* (Toronto: Oxford, 1998), 171–72.

36   Janice Dickin and Elspeth Cameron, "Engendering Canadian Identity," in *A Passion for Identity*, 209–224.

37   Robin Matthews, *Canadian Identity: Major Forces Shaping the Life of a People* (Ottawa: Steel Rail, 1988), 5–6.

38   Augie Fleras and Jean Lock Kunz, *Media and Minorities* (Toronto: Thompson, 2001).

39   The stormy debate over the adoption of the Maple Leaf as the national flag is recorded in Blair Fraser, *The Search for Identity* (Toronto: Doubleday, 1967), chap. 23.

40 This discussion has benefited enormously from the work of Raymond Breton, "The Production and Allocation of Symbolic Resources: An Analysis of the Linguistic and Ethnocultural Fields in Canada," *Canadian Review of Sociology and Anthropology* 21 (1984): 123–44; and "Intergroup Competition in the Symbolic Construction of Canadian Society," in Peter S. Li, ed., *Race and Ethnic Relations in Canada*, 2nd ed. (Toronto: Oxford, 1999), 291–310.

41 Raymond Breton, *Why Meech Failed: Lessons for Canadian Constitution Making* (Toronto: C.D. Howe Institute, 1992).

42 Kieran Keohane, *Symptoms of Canada* (Toronto: University of Toronto Press, 1997), 28.

43 Roger Gibbins, *The New Face of Canadian Nationalism* (Kingston: Queen's University Institute of Intergovernmental Relations, Reflections Paper No. 14, 1995).

44 William Watson, *Globalization and the Meaning of Canadian Life* (Toronto: University of Toronto Press, 1998).

45 Craig Calhoun, "Nationalism and Civil Society," in his *Social Theory and the Politics of Identity* (Oxford: Blackwell, 1994), 304–35.

46 Jan Penrose, "Construction, De(con)struction and Reconstruction: The Impact of Globalization and Fragmentation on the Canadian Nation-State," *The International Journal of Canadian Studies* 16 (1997):15–49.

47 For example, see Mel Watkins, "Dene Nationalism," *Canadian Review of Studies of Nationalism* 8 (1981): 101–113.

48 This concept of nationalism is developed by W. Christian and C. Campbell, *Political Parties and Ideologies in Canada* (Toronto: McGraw-Hill Ryerson, 1974). See also Chapter 6 for a good study of Canadian nationalism in historical development.

49 Anthony D. Smith, *Nationalism in the Twentieth Century* (Oxford: Martin Robertson, 1979), 1–3.

50 Richard Collins, *Culture, Communication, and National Identity*, 106. An interesting discussion using the concept of "submerged nations" has been developed by Vatro Murvar, *Submerged Nations: An Invitation to Theory* (Milwaukee: University of Wisconsin—Sociology, 1982).

51 A.G. Bailey, *Culture and Nationality* (Toronto: McClelland and Stewart, 1972), chap. 9.

52 Silvia Brucan, "The Nation-State: Will it Keep Order or Wither Away?" *International Social Science Journal* 30 (1978): 9–30; and Jan Penrose, "Construction, De(con)struction, and Reconstruction" *International Journal of Canadian Studies* 16 (1997): 15–49.

53 Abraham Rotstein, "Is There an English-Canadian Nationalism?" *Journal of Canadian Studies* 13 (1978): 114.

54 Daniel Salée, "Quebec Sovereignty and the Challenge of Linguistic and Ethnocultural Minorities: Identity, Differences, and the Politics of *Ressentiment*," *Quebec Studies* 24 (1997): 6–23.

55 For a discussion on the CMA and nationalist sentiment as a long-standing phenomenon, see S.D. Clark, *The Canadian Manufacturers' Association: A Study in Collective Bargaining and Political Pressure* (Toronto: University of Toronto Press, 1939).

56 Patricia Marchak, "Nationalism and Regionalism in Canada," *Canadian Review of Studies in Nationalism* 7 (1980): 26. The explanation of nationalism developed here is actually built from modernization theories, which point to a new educated class and its expanding influence on the rest of the society.

57 Both general theories of nationalism discussed here are elaborated in greater detail in Anthony D. Smith, *Theories of Nationalism* (New York: Harper and Row, 1971). See also Howard Aster, "Nationalism and Communitarianism," in Wallace Gagne, ed., *Nationalism, Technology and the Future of Canada* (Toronto: Macmillan, 1976), 56–63.

58 Ernest Gellner, *Nations and Nationalism* (Oxford: Basil Blackwell, 1983), 140.

59 Roger Gibbins, *Prairie Politics and Society: Regionalism in Decline* (Scarborough: Butterworths, 1980).

60 Ramsay Cook, *Canada, Quebec, and the Uses of Nationalism* (Toronto: McClelland and Stewart, 1986), 9–10.

61 Alan C. Cairns, "The Fragmentation of Canadian Citizenship," in William Kaplan, ed., *Belonging: The Meaning and Future of Canadian Citizenship* (Montreal: McGill-Queen's University Press, 1993), 181–220.

62 Jo-anne Lee and Linda Cardinal, "Hegemonic Nationalism and the Politics of Feminism and Multiculturalism in Canada," in Veronic Strong-Boag, Sherrill Grace, Avigail Eisenberg, and Joan Anderson, eds., *Painting the Maple Leaf: Essays on Race, Gender, and the Construction of Canada* (Vancouver: UBC Press, 1998), 215–241. See also Keohane, *Symptoms of Canada*, 7. For an interesting comparison, see Jeffrey Lesser, *Negotiating National Identity: Immigrants, Minorities, and the Struggle for Ethnicity in Brazil* (Durham: Duke University Press, 1999), which shows how minorities from China, Japan, North Africa, and the Middle East are challenging the goal of making Brazil a European society.

63 Pierre Fournier, *A Meech Lake Post-Mortem: Is Quebec Sovereignty Inevitable?* (Montreal: McGill-Queen's University Press, 1991), 82.

64 Louis Balthazar, "The Faces of Quebec Nationalism," in Alain G. Gagnon, ed., *Quebec: State and Society*, 2nd ed. (Scarborough: Prentice Hall, 1993), 13.

65 Ken McRoberts, "English Canadian Perceptions of Quebec," in Gagnon, *Quebec: State and Society*, 2nd ed., 116–29.

66 Augie Fleras and Jean Leonard Elliott, *The Nations Within: Aboriginal–State Relations in Canada, the United States and New Zealand*, 227.

67 Roger Gibbins, *The New Face of Canadian Nationalism.*

68 Rick Ponting, "Racial Conflict: Turning the Heat Up," in Dan Glenday and Ann Duffy, eds., Canadian Society: *Understanding and Surviving in the 1990s* (Toronto: McClelland and Stewart, 1994), 102.

69 Richard Gwyn, *Nationalism Without Walls.*

70 Stacy Churchill, *Official Languages in Canada: Changing the Language Landscape* (Heritage Canada Catalogue no. Ch3-2-7/1998), 79.

71 Robert Fulford argues that this is a key characteristic of post-modernism. "A Post-Modern Dominion," in William Kaplan, ed., *Belonging: The Meaning and Future of Canadian Citizenship*, 104–119. The Canadian preoccupation with self-questioning is discussed in David V. J. Bell, *The Roots of Disunity: A Study of Canadian Political Culture,* rev. ed. (Toronto: Oxford, 1992), chap. 3.

72 Kenneth McRoberts, *Misconceiving Canada: The Struggle for National Unity* (Toronto: Oxford, 1997).

73 The distinction between civic and ethnic nationality is made by Raymond Breton, "From Ethnic to Civic Nationalism: English Canada and Quebec," *Ethnic and Racial Studies* 11(1988): 85–102.

74 Yvonne Hébert, "Citizenship Education: Towards a Pedagogy of Social Participation and Identity Formation," *Canadian Ethnic Studies* 29, 2 (1997): 16–33.

75 Paul G. Lamy, "Political Socialization of French and English Canadian Youth: Socialization into Discord," in Zureik and Pike, eds., *Socialization and Values in Canadian Society*, vol. 1., Political Socialization, 263–80.

76 Report of the Royal Commission on Bilingualism and Biculturalism, Book II: Education, 275.

77 Jean Pierre Richert, "The Impact of Ethnicity on the Perception of Heroes and Historical Symbols," *Canadian Review of Sociology and Anthropology* 11 (1974): 156–63.

78 Leslie Pal, *Interests of the State: The Politics of Language, Multiculturalism, and Feminism in Canada* (Montreal: McGill-Queen's University Press, 1997).

79 Katarzyna Rukszto, "National Encounters: Narrating Canada and the Plurality of Difference," *International Journal of Canadian Studies* 16 (1997): 150–162.

80 There are a number of very good discussions on this theme: Martin J. Morris and Nadine Changfoot, " The Solidarity Deficit: The Rise of Neo-liberalism and the Crisis of National Unity," *International Journal of Canadian Studies* 14 (1996):137–154; Stephen McBride and John Shields, *Dismantling a Nation*, 2nd ed. (Halifax: Fernwood, 1997); and John Herd Thompson, "Canada's Quest for Cultural Sovereignty: Protection, Promotion, and Popular Culture," in Stephen J. Randall and Herman W. Konrad, eds., *NAFTA in Transition* (Calgary: University of Calgary Press, 1995), 393–410.

81 S.D. Clark, "Canada and Her Great Neighbour," 195.

82 Philip Resnick, *The Land of Cain: Class and Nationalism in English Canada* (Vancouver: New Star, 1977), 147ff.

83 For an interesting discussion of factors promoting the integration of Canadian society, see Douglas Cole, "The Integration of Canada: An Overview," *Canadian Review of Studies in Nationalism* 7 (1980): 4–13.

84 Augie Fleras and Jean Lock Kunz, *Media and Minorities: Representing Diversity in a Multicultural Canada* (Toronto: Thompson, 2001); Mary Jane Miller, "Will English-Language Television Remain Distinctive? Probably." in *Beyond Quebec: Taking Stock of Canada*, 138–162; and David Taras, "The CBC and Canadian Television in the New Media Age," in *A Passion for Identity*, 265–279.

85 Charles Acland, "Cultural Survival: Sleeping with the Elephant," in Glenday and Duffy, *Canadian Society: Understanding and Surviving in the 1990's*, 234–35.

86 Richard Gruneau and David Whitson, *Hockey Night in Canada: Sport, Identities, and Cultural Politics* (Toronto: Garamond, 1993).

87 Joyce Zemans provides a good overview of these various cultural institutions and their relationship to nationhood objectives. "The Essential Role of National Cultural Institutions," in *Beyond Quebec: Taking Stock of Canada*, 182–201.

88 For a compendium of such contributions, see David Taras, Beverly Rasporich, and Eli Mandel, eds., *A Passion for Identity*, 2nd ed. (Scarborough: Nelson, 1993); for the role of the intelligentsia, see Anthony D. Smith, ed., *Nationalist Movements* (London: Macmillan, 1976), 21–24.

89 For a discussion of the relationship between Canadian literature and national identity, see Paul Cappon, ed., *In Our Own House: Social Perspectives on Canadian Literature* (Toronto: McClelland and Stewart, 1978). See also Government of Canada, *Report of the Federal Cultural Policy Review Committee* (Ottawa: Department of Communications, 1981).

90 Ferdinand Tonnies, *Fundamental Concepts of Sociology* (New York: American Books, 1940).

91 Benedict Anderson, *Imagined Communities: Reflections on the Origin and Spread of Nationalism* (London: Verso, 1983), 15.

92 Sherry Simon, "National Membership and Forms of Contemporary Belonging in Quebec," in André Lapierre, Patricia Smart, and Pierre Savard, eds., *Language, Culture and Values in Canada at the Dawn of the 21st Century* (Ottawa: Carleton University Press and International Council for Canadian Studies, 1996), 121–31.

93 Daniel Latouche cautions that anglo conceptions of Quebec must recognize that Quebec identity is not wooden and is changing in response to a changing North American environment. "Quebec in the Emerging North American Configuration," in Earle and Wirth, eds., *Identities in North America: The Search for Community*, 117–39.

94 See Anthony D. Smith, Theories of Nationalism, 158–59; and S.M. Crean, *Who's Afraid of Canadian Culture?* (Don Mills: General Publishing, 1976), 277–78.

95 Lloyd Axworthy, "The Federal System—An Uncertain Path," *Daedalus* 117 (1988): 141. Howard Aster uses the term "communitarian nationalism" to express the same idea: "Nationalism and Communitarianism," 66–67.

96 Ramsay Cook, *Canada and the French Canadian Question* (Toronto: Macmillan, 1966), 25. Cook argues that Canada's problem is too much, not too little, nationalism.

97 Raymond Breton, "The Concepts of 'Distinct Society' and 'Identity' in the Meech Lake Accord," in Katherine E. Swinton and Carol J. Rogerson, eds., *Competing Constitutional Visions* (Toronto: Carswell, 1988), 8–9.

98 Ramsay Cook, *The Maple Leaf Forever: Essays on Nationalism and Politics in Canada* (Toronto: Macmillan, 1971), 8.

99 Charles Taylor, "Shared and Divergent Values," in *Reconciling the Solitudes: Essays on Canadian Federalism and Nationalism* (Montreal: McGill-Queen's University Press, 1993), chap. 8; *Multiculturalism and the Politics of Recognition* (Princeton: Princeton University Press, 1992).

100 Daniel Latouche, "Quebec in the Emerging North American Configuration," 131.

101 For a variety of discussions on this issue, see Pierre Martin, "Association After Sovereignty? Canadian Views on Economic Association With a Sovereign Quebec," *Canadian Public Policy* 21 (1995): 53–71; Dean Usher, "The Interests of English Canada," *Canadian Public Policy* 21 (1995): 72–84; Scott Reid, *Canada Remapped: How the Partition of Quebec Will Reshape the Nation* (Vancouver: Pulp Press, 1992); and David J. Bercuson and Barry Cooper, *Deconfederation: Canada Without Quebec* (Toronto: Key Porter, 1991).

102 James Laxer, *Inventing Europe: The Rise of a New World Power* (Toronto: Lester, 1991), 304.

103 Aihwa Ong, *Flexible Citizenship: The Cultural Logistics of Transnationality* (Durham: Duke University Press, 1999).

104 Neil Nevitte, "Bringing Values Back In: Value Change and North American Integration," in Donald Barry, ed., *Toward a North American Community: Canada, the United States, and Mexico* (Boulder: Westview, 1995), 185–209.

WEBLINKS

www.pch.gc.ca

The home page of Canadian Heritage is a resource for the advancement of Canadian culture, heritage, and identity.

http://cbc.ca/sports/hockey

Visit the sports section of the CBC Web site to read about Canada's national sport, an integral part of our national identity. This page also features video clips from a longstanding Saturday-night Canadian tradition, *Hockey Night in Canada*.

www.canadians.org

The Council of Canadians is an independent, non-partisan citizens' interest group providing a critical and progressive voice on key national issues.

Index

315